D0999238

-4 OCT
DEPARTED
(1095)
HONG KONG

MINISTRY OF KOREA

IMMIGRATION DIVISION BANGKOK THAILAND
A
72
DEPARTED
-9 FEB 1997
SIGNED

DEPARTMENT OF IMMIGRATION
PERMITTED TO ENTER
AUSTRALIA,
on 24 APR 1996
For stay of 12 Months
SYDNEY AIRPORT 54

IMMIGRATION & ETHNIC AFFAIRS
.... Person
30 OCT 1999
DEPARTED
AUSTRALIA
SYDNEY 32

中华人民共和国
广东省公安厅

上陸許可
ADMITTED
15. FEB. 1996
4
Status: 4-1-
Duration: 90 days
NARITA(N)
Immigration Inspector

ADMITTED
21 OCT. 1998
Status:
Duration 4-1-16
Port: HANEDA
Signature

日本国
USED
Narita Air Port

T R A V E L E R ' S
HAWAII
C O M P A N I O N

№ 011278

THE UNITED STATES
OF AMERICA
NONIMMIGRANT VISA
ISSUED AT

U.S. IMMIGRATION
170 HHW 1710

JUL 2 0 2000

HONG KONG
(1038)
-7 JUN 1997
IMMIGRATION
OFFICER

The 2001–2002 Traveler's Companions
ARGENTINA • AUSTRALIA • BALI • CALIFORNIA • CANADA • CHILI • CHINA •
COSTA RICA • CUBA • EASTERN CANADA • ECUADOR • FLORIDA • HAWAII •
HONG KONG • INDIA • INDONESIA • IRELAND • JAPAN • KENYA •
MALAYSIA & SINGAPORE • MEDITERRANEAN FRANCE • MEXICO • NEPAL •
NEW ENGLAND • NEW ZEALAND • NORTHERN ITALY • PERU • PHILIPPINES •
PORTUGAL • RUSSIA • SOUTH AFRICA • SOUTHERN ENGLAND • SPAIN • THAILAND •
TURKEY • VENEZUELA • VIETNAM, LAOS AND CAMBODIA • WESTERN CANADA

Traveler's HAWAII Companion
First Published 1998
The Globe Pequot Press
246 Goose Lane, PO Box 480
Guilford, CT 06437 USA
www.globe-pequot.com

Distributed in the European Union by
World Leisure Marketing Ltd, Unit 11
Newmarket Court, Newmarket Drive,
Derby, DE24 8NW, United Kingdom
www.map-guides.com

ISBN: 0-7627-0608-2

Created, edited and produced by
Allan Amsel Publishing, 53, rue Beaudouin
27700 Les Andelys, France.
E-mail: allan.amsel@wanadoo.fr
Editor in Chief: Allan Amsel
Editor: Anne Trager
Original design concept: Hon Bing-wah
Picture editor and designer: David Henry

ACKNOWLEDGEMENTS
The authors would like to thank Susan Humphrey whose insights knowledge and researching
skills were invaluable. Many islanders gave of their time and knowledge with classic
Hawaiian generosity; special thanks are due to Gail Chew, Donovan Dela Cruz,
Donna Jung, Julie King, Darlene Morikawa, and Gigi Valley.

Printed by Samwha Printing Co. Ltd., Seoul, South Korea

TRAVELER'S
HAWAII
COMPANION

by Maribeth Mellin and Julia Clerk

Photographed by Nik Wheeler

The
Globe
Pequot
Press

GUILFORD
CONNECTICUT

Contents

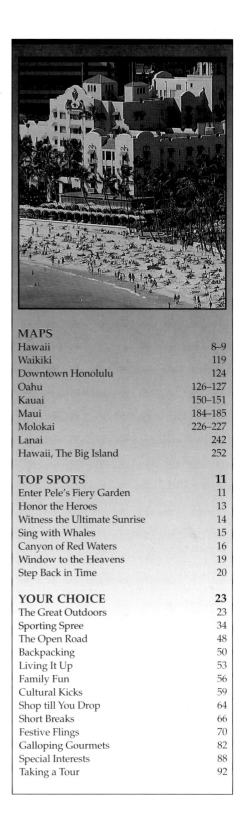

MAPS

Hawaii	8–9
Waikiki	119
Downtown Honolulu	124
Oahu	126–127
Kauai	150–151
Maui	184–185
Molokai	226–227
Lanai	242
Hawaii, The Big Island	252

TOP SPOTS	**11**
Enter Pele's Fiery Garden	11
Honor the Heroes	13
Witness the Ultimate Sunrise	14
Sing with Whales	15
Canyon of Red Waters	16
Window to the Heavens	19
Step Back in Time	20

YOUR CHOICE	**23**
The Great Outdoors	23
Sporting Spree	34
The Open Road	48
Backpacking	50
Living It Up	53
Family Fun	56
Cultural Kicks	59
Shop till You Drop	64
Short Breaks	66
Festive Flings	70
Galloping Gourmets	82
Special Interests	88
Taking a Tour	92

WELCOME TO HAWAII   97

HAWAII AND ITS PEOPLE   101
The Island Climate   102
The Polynesian Connection   103
Captain Cook and his Legacy   104
Kamehameha: Warrior King   105
The Missionary Influence   106
The End of a Dynasty   106
The Merry Monarch   107
The Fiftieth State   108
Hawaiian Culture   109
People of the Islands   112

OAHU   115
Background   117
General Information   118
Getting Around   118
What to See and Do   119
   Waikiki • Honolulu • Honolulu
   Environs • Downtown Honolulu •
   East Shore • North Shore • West Shore
Tours   131
Shopping   132
Sports   134
Where to Stay   135
   Waikiki • East Shore • North Shore •
   West Shore
Where to Eat   139
   Waikiki • Honolulu • East Shore •
   North Shore
Nightlife   143
How to Get There   144

KAUAI   147
Background   149
General Information   152
Getting Around   152
What to See and Do   152
   Lihue • South Shore • Waimea Canyon •
   The East Coast • The North Shore •
   Niihau
Tours   165
Shopping   165
Sports   166
Where to Stay   168
   Lihue • South Shore • Waimea Canyon •
   The East Coast • The North Shore
Where to Eat   174
   Lihue • South Shore • The East Coast •
   The North Shore
Nightlife   179
How to Get There   179

MAUI — 181

Background — 183
General Information — 184
What to See and Do — 184
    Kahului-Wailuku • Lahaina and the
    Northwest Coast • The Southwest Coast •
    Haleakala Crater and Upcountry Maui •
    Road to Hana and Hana
Tours — 194
Shopping — 197
Sports — 199
Where to Stay — 202
    Kahului and Wailuku • Lahaina and the
    Northwest Shore • The Southwest
    Coast • Upcountry • Road to Hana
    and Hana
Where to Eat — 213
    Kahului and Wailuku • Northwest
    Coast • The Southwest Coast •
    Upcountry • Road to Hana and Hana
Nightlife — 221
How to Get There — 221

MOLOKAI — 223

Background — 225
General Information — 225
Getting Around — 225
What to See and Do — 226
    Kaunakakai and Southeast Molokai •
    The East • The West • The Center
    and North • Kalaupapa Peninsula •
    The Mule Trail
Tours — 231
Shopping — 231
Sports — 232
Where to Stay — 233
    Expensive • Moderate • Inexpensive
Where to Eat — 235
    Expensive • Moderate • Inexpensive
How to Get There — 237

LANAI — 239

Background — 241
General Information — 242
What to See and Do — 242
Where to Stay and Eat — 244
    Very Expensive • Moderate •
    Inexpensive
How to Get There — 247

HAWAII: THE BIG ISLAND   249
General Information   250
Getting Around   250
What to See and Do   253
    Hilo • Eastern Hawaii • Volcanoes
    National Park • Western Hawaii •
    Coffee Country • Kona • Kohala Coast •
    North Kohala • Waimea and Mauna
    Kea • Honokaa • Waipio Valley •
    The Hamakua Coast
Tours   267
Shopping   269
Sports   270
Where to Stay   272
    Hilo and Environs • Volcanoes National
    Park and Environs • South Point •
    Kailua-Kona Area • Kailua-Kona •
    Kohala • North Kohala and Waimea •
    Hamakua Coast
Where to Eat   279
    Hilo • Volcano • South of Kona •
    Kailua-Kona • Kohala • North Kohala
    and Waimea • Hamakua Coast
Nightlife   286
How to Get There   287

TRAVELERS' TIPS   289
Getting There   291
    Mainland Carriers • International
    Carriers • Inter-island Carriers
Arriving and Leaving   291
    Visa and Travel Documents • Customs
Consulates   291
Tourist Information   292
Getting Around   292
    Car Rental • Other forms of
    Transportation
Accommodation   294
Eating Out   294
Basics   295
    Time • Money • Tipping • Taxes •
    Electricity • Weights and Measures
Communication and Media
    Telephones • Mail • Mass Media
Etiquette   296
Health   296
    Emergencies • Dangerous Animals •
    Tanning
Security   297
When to Go   298
What to Take   298
Language Basics   298
Web Sites   298

RECOMMENDED READING   299

QUICK REFERENCE A–Z GUIDE   300
to Places and Topics of Interest with
Listed Accommodation, Restaurants
and Useful Telephone Numbers

KAUAI

Princeville
Kilauea
56
56
Kapahi
Kapaa
550
580
Wailua
Waimea
583
50
Lihue
Kekaha
Kalaheo
Hanapepe
Poipu

Puuwai
NIIHAU

K a u a i   C h a n n e l

Sunset Beach
Waimea
Laie
83
Mokuleia
Haleiwa
KAENA
POINT
930
803
Wahiawa
OAHU
930
83
780
Waianae
750
Kaneohe
Kailua
Waimana
Ewa Beach
Pearl
Harbor
Waikiki
72
HONOLULU
K a i
C

TRAVELER'S
HAWAII
COMPANION

PACIFIC
OCEAN

N

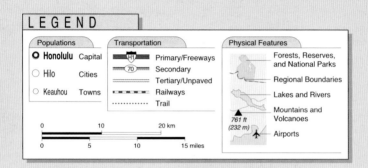

CANADA

UNITED STATES

PACIFIC
OCEAN

MEXICO

CUBA
BELIZE
HONDURAS
GUATEMALA
NICARAGUA
COSTA RICA

HAWAII

PACIFIC

OCEAN

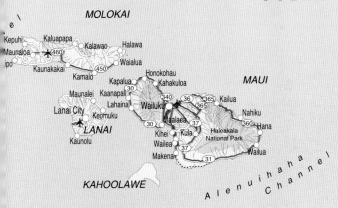

MOLOKAI

Kepuhi
Kaluapapa
Maunaloa ★ 460 Kalawao Halawa
ipo 450 Waialua
Kaunakakai Kamalo
Maunalei Kapalua Honokohau
Kaanapali 30 Kahakuloa
Lanai City Lahaina Wailuku 340 36 365 Kailua
Keomuku 365
LANAI Maalaea 37 Nahiku
Kaunolu Kihei Kula 360 Hana
Wailea Haleakala 37
Makena National Park Wailua
31

MAUI

KAHOOLAWE

Alenuihaha Channel

HAWAII, THE BIG ISLAND

Kapaau
Mahukona 270
270
Waipio Honokaa
Kawaihae 250 19
19 Waimea (Kamuela) Laupahoehoe
Puako 190 19
Kapalaaoa 200 Honomu
Kaupulehu Mauna Kea Onomea Onomea Bay
19 190 Puunanahulu 13,796 ft. 19
Keahole-Kona Airport ✈ (4,205 m)
19 Wailuku River ✈ Hilo Haena
Kailua-Kona 200 11
Holualoa Iwasaki Camp
Keauhou 11 Hawaii 130 Pahoa
Kealakekua Volcanoes Hawaii Volcanoes 137
Kealakekua Bay National Park National Park 11
Honaunau Kilauea Caldera 137 Opihikao
4,078 ft (1,247 m)
Hawaii Volcanoes
National Park
11 11

Hoopuloa

Ahualoa 11 Waiohinu Honuapo
Naalehu
Kailikkii

KA LAE
(SOUTH
POINT)

TOP SPOTS

Enter Pele's Fiery Garden

FIERY TENDRILS OF MOLTEN LAVA ETCH SHINY BLACK ROCK. Steam rises in a barren horizon. Some say Pele is angry. The goddess of fire and mother of all volcanoes lives in the spooky landscape of Hawaii Volcanoes National Park. It's hard to ignore her presence. She vents her outrage frequently; spuming, fuming, and tumbling rocks and molten lava into the sea. New landmasses form on the ocean floor and grow into islands. Pele gives, and Pele takes away.

Those who believe in Pele take her quite seriously. They leave bottles of gin (said to be her favorite spirit) by her lava flows and red ginger plumes atop sheer, sharp cliffs. People who live near the park talk about Pele like a short-tempered, crabby neighbor. "She doesn't like it when all

those planes fly through her hair," one waitress told me when I suggested taking a helicopter ride over the park.

She had a point. It's impossible to ignore the unseen forces that shoot fire and rock into the air and smother hillsides and towns in a deathly embrace. Call it Pele; call it science. Either way, the park is a powerful place. Silence surrounds the giant expanse of Kilauea Crater. A chill mist drifts through emerald fern forests and seeps through the walls of cavernous lava tubes. Few birds break the silence for fear of snapping a spell.

Writers, artists, spiritualists and geologists make regular pilgrimages to Volcanoes National Park, which sprawls over the southeastern craters and coast of the Big Island. Visitors ascend into a cool, moist zone, don sweatshirts and jeans, and cuddle in mountain cabins beside the fire. Lucky ones spend days and weeks exploring the park, hiking to smoldering craters, isolated houses and coastal campgrounds.

It helps to be alone if you want to sense Pele's invisible presence. I find it best to drive into the park and along Chain of Craters Road at dawn, when a gray fog shrouds the higher elevations. In the morning, the landscape changes subtly from hour to hour. Vast fields of smoky brown and gray rocks take on other-world forms, dropping into

OPPOSITE: Fresh lava from Kilauea tumbles into the ocean, creating clouds of steam — and new land on the Big Island. ABOVE: The art of Pele. New lava hardens in Volcanoes National Park.

nothingness as craters swallow the surface of the earth. The road runs level and flat as if at the top of the world, then drops toward the Pacific, which crashes against sheer black and red cliffs. At first, the air is chilly, then comfortable, then downright hot as shimmering rocks absorb sunlight.

By 10 AM the park is usually full of day-trippers larking about with little sense of Pele's presence. Those seeking a more spiritual experience should park at the Visitor's Center at the entrance to the park, watch the center's excellent film filled with scenes of eruption, then head down the Kilauea Iki Trail. The four-mile-long (six-and-a-half-kilometer) trail begins behind the Visitor's Center and winds through a forest of ferns before reaching the Kilauea Crater. Along the way, ohia trees rise firm and tall on cliff tops, shading duck-like nenes, the endangered state bird of Hawaii. As you approach the crater, the unmistakable stench of sulfur serves as a potent reminder that Pele never stops fuming.

The most exciting, rewarding and mystical experiences occur at night. As darkness falls, Chain of Craters Road becomes a dark and foreboding

challenge. Fog and moonlight alternate as the elevation diminishes; off in the distance ribbons of fire plunge to the ocean in hisses, sputters and fireworks only a god (or goddess) could create.

Unfortunately, there's no guarantee that you'll chance upon a spectacular lava show. Before you set a firm itinerary check the Hawaiian Volcano Observatory's web site at http://hvo .wr.usgs.gov. Though no human can possibly time Pele's wrath precisely, scientists contributing to the site offer cautious predictions; eruption update information is also available through the park's hotline at ((808) 967-7977. Travelers intent on watching the lava flow may want to keep their itineraries loose enough to allow for sudden changes. When news of an imminent dramatic eruption spreads, immediately book a flight to the Big Island and a room near the park.

You certainly won't be alone if Pele is behaving dramatically. Instead, you'll be among scores of worshippers overcome by the sheer majesty of the scene. Hike toward the flowing lava carefully, find a solitary spot, and let your imagination go. Picture Pele in all her massive, grand

fury blowing smoky plumes into the sky. Some artists see Pele's long, dark hair entwined with rivers of red lava coursing down the hillside toward the sea. As night gives way to dawn and the crowd dwindles, you can hear fire sizzling as the lava settles toward the ocean floor. The Goddess is at work once more.

Honor the Heroes

A RESPECTFUL, NOSTALGIC SILENCE SETTLES OVER BOATLOADS OF TOURISTS AS THEY APPROACH THE ARIZONA MEMORIAL. Orchid and plumeria blossoms bob beside a platform that seems to float atop sunken battleships. Visitors of all ages dab their eyes as they approach a stone wall inscribed with the names of fallen sailors and marines.

Oil bubbles from barely submerged steel-hulled ships to the water's surface around the stark white memorial building designed by German architect Alfred Preis. The setting evokes all the drama and emotion of December 7, 1941, the fateful, serene Sunday morning when Japanese bombers descended upon Pearl Harbor.

The attack signaled the United States'

entry into World War II. Among the vessels sunk with huge loss of life was the battleship, USS *Arizona*. The *Arizona* was never raised, and it serves as a watery grave for 1,177 Navy sailors and marines. The site where the great ship went down is a permanent memorial, not merely to those who perished that morning, but to all those lost in the senselessness of wars.

A visit to the memorial begins at the main building with a film of the events leading up to and including the attack on Pearl Harbor. Visitors wander through a museum that displays historic photographs, news clippings and memorabilia, and a gift shop packed with military books, posters and souvenirs. Behind the building, facing the water, is a large lawn edged with signs describing crippled and sunken ships still visible in the clear water and listing the names of those who died on those ships.

Visitors ride across the water from the center on a shuttle boat, which leaves every 15 minutes. At the memorial they

OPPOSITE: News of eruptions draw crowds to the shores of Volcano National Park. ABOVE: The USS *Bowfin*, a World War II submarine, attracts streams of visitors to Pearl Harbor, site of the infamous attack on the American fleet in World War II.

stare into the water, reflect upon the names on the stone wall and point to other battleships nearby.

Thousands of tourists and locals visit the Arizona Memorial most days of the year, yet crowds do not diminish its solemnity or importance. Some visitors are regulars who come back every time they visit Hawaii. Some come to pay homage to a deceased relative, others to renew memories. The memorial is crowded most days; arrive close to opening time to beat the tour buses.

Witness the Ultimate Sunrise

INSTEAD OF CLIMBING INTO THE SKY, THE SUN APPEARS AT THE TOP OF THE WORLD, flowing over the distant hulks of Mauna Kea and Mauna Loa on the Big Island. As the fireball tips its way over the faraway rims, the light seeps into the depths of Maui's Haleakala Crater, illuminating dense forests and the distant blue sea.

The name Haleakala means "House of the Sun," and the sunrises here are legendary. Over one million visitors come by each year; many arrive at dawn. Part of the attraction may well be the hardships

endured in experiencing this natural phenomenon. It can take up to four hours to reach the top of Haleakala, depending on the location of your hotel. Those determined to see the sunrise crawl from their beds shortly past midnight and bundle up in the warmest clothing they can find. They then drive through empty streets to the foot of the mountain and begin a two-hour ascent covering a mere 37 miles (60 km), but rising from sea level to over 10,000 ft (3,000 m) in altitude.

Transmissions balk at the steady incline as cars follow a dizzying series of switchbacks; first-timers driving up the mountain in the dark tend to get stressed. You may find it far more comfortable to board a tour van and sleep through the ride; Temptation Tours ((808) 877-8888 offers transportation to and from Mount Haleakala starting way before sunrise.

Far more exciting are Maui's legendary sunrise bike rides. Daring cyclists are picked up at their hotels long before dawn and given plenty of hot coffee before and after the van ride to the top. After sitting through the sunrise, they strap on helmets and kneepads, climb aboard sturdy mountain bikes, and begin their descent — testing the brakes all the while. Actually, the ride isn't as scary as it sounds. The cyclists stay in a group followed by a supply van and travel at a slow, easy pace, pulling into lookout points to allow cars to stream by. Once you've adjusted to your bike, you begin noticing the scenery. Birds chirp in the background, waterfalls splash over boulders, and your body gradually relaxes into a casual side-to-side swaying motion as you maneuver the road's many curves.

Maui Downhill ((808) 871-2155 was one of the first companies to offer a Haleakala two-wheel cruise, and they remain one of the best. Their guides are accustomed to soothing the nerves of fearful novices and taming the reckless urges of more daring types. The ride is easiest in the warm summer months; peddling in chill winter rains can be less pleasurable. Still, I've never heard anyone say they wish they hadn't biked down Haleakala. Few experiences offer

as many thrills packed into a few short hours. After all, how often do you get to drive up a steep slope under dark, starry skies, sit atop a mountain so high the sun rises beneath you, and soar with the wind back to the beach? Not a bad way to start the day.

Sing with Whales

A JOYOUS SOUND GREETS ALL WHO VENTURE ONTO OR INTO THE OCEAN IN DECEMBER.
A low moan rises into a high-pitched warble. Waves reverberate through saltwater, carrying the songs of mothers giving birth and babies at play. The humpback whales have returned to Hawaii.

Whale tales are an integral part of island history. Long before the Polynesians arrived, the humpbacks established their annual migration from Alaska's Arctic Ocean to the warm waters off Maui. From Kauai to the Big Island, residents of the islands and thousands of visitors line the shores or take launches and sailing craft out to sea for a glimpse of these fascinating mammals. Waterspouts flash in the air.

The whomp of tails hitting the water echoes across vast expanses of ocean. Occasionally, one of these huge creatures goes airborne, breaching the waters as it feeds. About 1,500 to 2,000 whales migrate to the islands each year. Some travel individually, others in pods. One winter day, whale watchers on the island of Oahu counted more than 700 whales in transit to Maui.

Marine scientists tag and track the whales in an effort to better understand their migratory movements. Researchers are particularly interested in determining the interisland movements of these mammals. The commonly held belief is that the whales approach the islands from the southwest end of the Big Island, then spend most of their time in the waters around Maui, Lanai and Molokai before cruising past Kauai on their way back to Alaska.

You're nearly guaranteed to see whales if you stay on Maui between December and April, even from your hotel room's lanai. The best places to spot

Palm trees on Maui's Makena Beach OPPOSITE and the mist-shrouded Na Pali cliffs at Kee Beach on Kauai both provide perfect backdrops for Hawaii's famed sunrises.

whales from while on land are Wailea Beach, the Maalaea shoreline by the Maui Ocean Center ((808) 270-7000, and the beaches off the Honoapiilani Highway. Drivers have a tendency to stop in the middle of the road when passengers spot spouting whales; pull off the road before grabbing for the binoculars. Your chances of getting close to the whales (but not so close as to disturb them) are far better on whale-watching boat tours. At the height of the season nearly every boat in the Maalaea and Lahaina harbors offers some sort of whale adventure; make reservations in advance for trips with Flexible Flyer ((808) 244-6655, Maui Classic Charters ((808) 879-8188, and Maui Princess ((808) 667-6165. You can also view the whales from rafts or kayaks off Maui with South Pacific Kayaks and Outfitters ((808) 875-4848 and Blue Water Rafting ((808) 879-7238. Anyone diving around Maui is likely to hear the whales singing and may even spot a humpback in the distance; contact Ed Robinson's Diving Adventures ((808) 879-3584 or any of the dive companies listed in the Maui chapter. And if your interest is truly peaked, visit Maui's Lahaina Whaling Museum ((808) 661-4775 and the Whalers Village Museum ((808) 661-5992 in Kaanapali. The Hawaii Maritime Center ((808) 536-6373 on Oahu also has an extensive display on whaling.

Maui is definitely the center for whale watching, but it's not like the whales disappear en route to the island. Whale-watching tours are possible from all the islands. Some of the best boat tours include *Navatek I* ((808) 848-6360 on Oahu, Captain Andy's Sailing Adventures ((808) 822-7833 on Kauai, Lanai EcoAdventure Service ((808) 565-7737 on Lanai, and Eco-Adventures ((808) 329-7116 on the Big Island.

You can get a whole different perspective from the air, especially if peering down through clear water. When booking a winter season helicopter or plane ride, ask about whale sightings. Some companies concentrate on flying over the ocean when the whales are around.

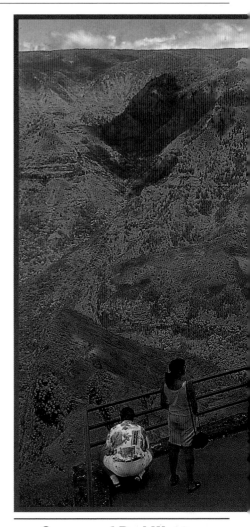

Canyon of Red Waters

AS MIGHTY AS ARIZONA'S GRAND CANYON MAY BE, FOR SHEER BEAUTY KAUAI'S WAIMEA CANYON IS HARD TO BEAT. On those days when the sun is high in the sky and racing clouds cast swift shadows, the canyon walls fleetingly change colors: pinks and oranges intermingle with the earthen tones already there. Somewhere high on Waialeale, already hidden in clouds, water is rushing off its steep shoulders, on the way to the ocean. The water, stained brown by vegetation, begins its surge to the ocean in the Alakai Swamp in Waialeale's crater. Closer to the ocean, the water turns redder and

redder as it mingles with the earth, giving Waimea its name, Reddish Water.

The high forests and valleys of Waimea are places of quiet beauty, laced with trails and isolated homesteads. Koa, ohia and eucalyptus trees grow alongside yellow ginger and other shrubs and vines. Maile vines, mokihana berries and ferns, so beloved by lei makers, add to the dazzling variety of the vegetation. Suspension bridges cross the Waimea Stream at several points. It is always a dramatic place where nature can turn suddenly quixotic, and the dreamlike quality can quickly be shattered by a flash flood up the mountain that turns the stream into a raging torrent, causing waters to rise sometimes as high as 20 ft (six meters).

Deep in the tropical foliage of the canyon, wild boars forage, while on the inner slopes of the canyon, mountain goats feed. Beautiful birds, many of them rare, inhabit the valley floor and the higher reaches of the Alakai Swamp.

Some of Kauai's best hikes (and there are many) lead through Waimea Canyon and the adjacent Kokee State Park in the high mountains above the canyon. Highly detailed maps of the trails are available at the Kokee Natural History Museum ((808) 335-9975 E-MAIL kokee@aloha.net in the park. Views of the canyon walls are best from the strenuous

The many hues of Kauai's Waimea Canyon leave visitors in awe.

Canyon Trail and the far easier Cliff Trail. The most spectacular hike in the park is along the Awaawapuhi Trail, which climbs high above the Na Pali Coast. Awaawapuhi is one of the most difficult trails in the park, and includes some slippery descents as you approach the Na Pali viewing points. Allow at least three hours each way, bring plenty of water, and carry a rain poncho, as you never know when a shower might muddy the trail. The Aakai Swamp Trail is a delight for birders and botanists, who tread cautiously and silently along a wooden boardwalk over the murky swamp while searching for rare birds and plants.

If you're interested in fully exploring the canyon and park, consider spending a few nights away from the beach. There are several campgrounds in the park; contact the Kauai State Parks Office ((808) 274-3445 for information and reservations. Some of the most popular overnight accommodations on the islands are located within the park, at the Kokee Lodge ((808) 335-6061. The lodge's classic mountain cabins are in heavy demand, for good reason. Nowhere else in Hawaii can you find such a dramatic escape from sun and sand. One night beside a campfire under a blanket of stars might well be your most cherished Hawaii memory. Plus, you can watch the sun rise and set in an unimaginable palette of colors on the walls of Waimea Canyon.

Window to the Heavens

AN EERIE SILENCE AND BARRENNESS PERVADES THE SUMMIT OF MAUNA KEA, RISING NOBLY OVER THE BIG ISLAND OF HAWAII.
A chain of white observatories stand in a straight line, silhouetted like domed sentinels in the clean, sharp air. The blues of the sky blend into shades of orange and pink, casting a spectrum of color onto quilted clouds that seem to gently lap at the barren rock faces. As late afternoon turns to twilight, the heavens respond in a final blaze of glory: the sun sinks into the billowy whiteness of the clouds, leaving behind a trail of color that washes the sky in a spray of purple and red.

Plenty of tourists travel to the top of Mauna Kea during daylight, timing their visits to coincide with sunset. But happiest are those who linger on into the night. Rising above 13,000 ft (4,000 m), Mauna Kea's cloud-free, dry atmosphere is the ideal astronomical observing site, as evidenced by the many telescopes on its summit. Astronomers say that the percentage of clear nights at Mauna Kea is among the highest in the world. The atmosphere's stability and the location of the summit far from city lights allow for detailed studies of the faintest galaxies that lie on the very edge of the universe.

Get the most out of your Mauna Kea experience by arriving in mid-afternoon. You need a four-wheel drive vehicle to get to Observatory Hill at the top of the peak, but a regular sedan can make it to the Onizuka Center for International Astronomy ((808) 961-2190 (for programs) or (808) 969-3218 (for weather), dedicated to the memory of the Big Island astronaut who perished in the space shuttle *Challenger* disaster in 1986. Onizuka, born in Keopu, Kona, was the first American of Japanese ancestry selected for the space shuttle program. Situated at a heady elevation of 9,190 ft (2,800 m), the facility that honors his memory includes a visitor center and exhibits on astronomy, geology, and

history. There are precious few tourist services on Mauna Kea, but the Visitor's Center at the Onizuka Center does have restrooms.

The summit is another six miles (nearly 10 km) up the mountain; the climb takes you from 9,000 to nearly 14,000 ft (2,800 to 4,270 m) above sea level. Altitude sickness is a definite concern; don't go hiking about if you feel lightheaded or have a headache, and always carry plenty of water.

Some visitors are disappointed by what they see atop Mauna Kea. To the uneducated eye it looks like a vast, bleak moonscape. The 11 observatories at the summit are closed to the public, and there's really not much else there. So why bother, you ask? Because Mauna Kea is otherworldly at night.

The Onizuka Center presents a stargazing program Thursday, Friday, Saturday, and Sunday nights, starting at 4:30 PM; call ahead to make sure it's happening when you plan to be there. Also call the weather hotline ((808)

OPPOSITE: Sugar cane fields once covered the hills of Hanapepe on Kauai. ABOVE: Taro sprouts from marshy gardens at Hanalei.

969-3218 before you go, since there's no sense in looking for stars in a cloudbank. Bring plenty of warm clothing, binoculars and telescopes if you have them, and snacks. Once the sun sets, the stars quickly begin to appear, so brightly they seem to illuminate the mountain. Visitors take turns peering through the center's telescope, as guides point out familiar planets and the Milky Way. Mauna Kea Summit Adventures ((808) 322-2366 offers six-hour sunset stargazing tours to the summit; the guides' expertise makes these trips far more enjoyable than visiting the summit on your own.

Step Back in Time

TRACES OF THE ANCIENT HAWAIIANS ARE VISIBLE ALL OVER THE ISLANDS, IN SIMPLE ROCK PILES AND MYSTERIOUS PETROGLYPHS. Some of the best examples of early drawings are found on the tiny island of Lanai. These precious landmarks were ignored for decades and even centuries as sugarcane fields, pineapple plantations and vacation resorts gobbled up the ancients' sacred lands. A few native Hawaiians passed down tales of their ancestors through storytelling, literally teaching legends to their young, and pointed out sacred territories. Today, thanks to an ever-growing resurgence of native pride and prominence, the archeology of Lanai is being uncovered and preserved.

Famous gods and goddesses are believed to have lived throughout the islands, though they initially shunned the small island of Lanai. According to legend, spirits ruled over Lanai long after the other islands were settled. No one dared spend the night among these malevolent spooks, who purportedly were quite fond of human flesh. A reckless and cagey prince banned from Maui was the island's first human inhabitant; he lasted thanks to the help of his guardian spirit, his *aumakua*. Once Prince Kaululaau proved man could survive on Lanai, the island became a haven for royal families.

Today, archeologists have uncovered more than 450 petroglyphs in Luahiwa, southeast of Lanai City. It's the largest collection found anywhere other than the Big Island. Stick figures representing humans, birds, turtles, and deer cover dusty boulders, and are most easily seen when the sun is not directly overhead.

Lanai also contains one of the best-preserved royal residences on the islands, at Kaunolu Bay. It's believed that King Kamehameha the Great used Lanai as his personal vacation retreat: his summer residence is now one of the most complete archaeological sites in Hawaii. Kaunolu Archeological Interpretive Park on Lanai's leeward coast is the site of ongoing excavations, as archaeologists from the

Bishop Museum continue to unearth partial structures. Thus far they've uncovered over 80 platforms believed to have held *hales* (houses), and over 30 stone shelters, along with Halulu Heiau, a place of worship. Petroglyphs believed to represent warriors decorate nearby boulders, some hiding burial caves.

Near the building believed to have been Kamehameha's home sits a flat surface rock covered with holes. The rock is somewhat akin to an early checkerboard, and was used for a game called *papamu*. Players used bits of coral as playing pieces, moving them about the rocks. Nearby, atop the cliffs, is Kahekili's Leap, where athletes and warriors practiced *lele kawa* (cliff jumping).

Since Lanai has few paved roads, you need a four-wheel-drive vehicle to visit these sites. You can easily drive on your own after renting a vehicle from Lanai City Service ((808) 565-7227 TOLL-FREE (800) 533-7808 FAX (808) 565-7087, or arrange a guided tour through the island's hotels. The concierges have brochures explaining the structures at the archeological sites.

Boulders appear as if dropped from the sky into artful sculptures at the Garden of the Gods on Lanai.

YOUR CHOICE

The Great Outdoors

Hawaii is a land of superlatives. Strung together, the islands form the Hawaiian archipelago, the longest in the world, stretching across 1,305 miles (2,100 km). Hawaii is the most remote inhabited island chain in the world, located in the Pacific some 2,400 miles (about 3,860 km) from Japan and California. The islands are actually the peaks and craters of volcanic mountains, some barren, some covered with rivers and rain forests. And all contain beaches that are among the best in the world.

Coral reefs and deep channels run around and between the islands, creating idyllic living conditions for tiny angel fish and monstrous humpback whales.

Snorkeling and diving are superb off every island; some spots are world famous. Molokini, a tiny islet off the coast of Maui formed by lava and volcanic rock, provides incomparable protection for sea life and awesome potential for divers. Its crescent-shaped shallow crater shelters two-inch-long (five-centimeter) pink and blue wrasse and delicate white anemones, while its underwater cliffs are a perfect haven for lobsters and eel. Molokini's 3,500-ft-high (1,067-m) sea cliffs are said to be the highest in the world, wrinkled into crevices and streaked with waterfalls.

It's nearly impossible to pick the best beach in Hawaii; the choice depends upon personal preferences. Do you prefer white, black, gold, or tan sand? Should your beach be backed by palm trees or pine forests? Are crowds of surfers and sexy sunbathers part of your dream, or would you rather have the sand to yourself? Oahu's Waikiki Beach is the obvious choice for man-made wonders and recreational opportunities, while its North Shore surf spots are among the most famous in the world. Hikers are extraordinarily blessed with trails beside the ocean, particularly at Kauai's Na Pali coast.

The superlatives continue above the water. Maui's Mount Haleakala is the largest dormant volcano crater in the world; snow-streaked Mauna Kea on the

OPPOSITE: Sunbathers find idyllic solitude on Kauai's Kee Beach. ABOVE: Pursuing a favorite island pastime, a surfer slashes through waves.

Big Island is the highest peak in the Pacific. Kilauea, also on the Big Island, is said to be the most active volcano in the world; it certainly has kept on spewing ash and dripping lava for what seems like an eternity (at least to the volcano's residents). On Kauai, the Waialeale Summit is considered the wettest spot on earth; its seven river valleys are impossibly green and moist, and dangerously slippery. An overabundance of rain clouds ensures constantly shifting weather patterns and the continual presence of rainbows in the moist air. It's possible to hike in this area, but you must go with a local guide.

Hawaii's exotic flora is among its most endearing attributes; the scent of tropical flowers is as pervasive as the sting of salt air. Silversword plants with their red flowers (that almost immediately turn silver) are found only on the Big Island and Maui. Over 1,400 species of bromeliads, with bizarre floral spikes and plumes, appear in gardens on all the islands, along with the ubiquitous plumeria trees that give the air its sweet scent. Red, white, and yellow ginger flowers, regal birds of paradise, and feathery heliconia appear like natural sculptures in the landscape. Mangoes, bananas, papayas, and breadfruit appear ripe and ready for picking along the roadside; taro fields spread like cornfields in agricultural valleys. Coffee plants cover terraced mountain slopes on Maui, Oahu, and the Big Island. Hundreds of orchid species bloom in nurseries on Lanai and Kauai.

A cynic could say the feral cat is Hawaii's most ubiquitous animal; several islands have active organizations working to combat this man-made plight. Dogs, pigs, and chickens are as abundant here as on the mainland, but Hawaii is one of the few places on earth to claim a total absence of snakes. The nene, Hawaii's state bird, is making a comeback from near extinction; nene crossing signs warn drivers to take special care when traveling at Haleakala, Mauna Kea, Kilauea, and Kauai. Bird watching is particularly fine on Maui, the Big Island, and Kauai.

Rainforests, volcanoes, river valleys and endless tropical beaches offer active travelers an overabundance of natural thrills. Many of Hawaii's most beautiful sights — Maui's Mount Haleakala, the Big Island's Volcanoes National Park, Kauai's Waimea Valley — are easily accessed by car. But they're also etched by miles of hiking trails leading to remote campgrounds.

For information on any of the state facilities contact the **Department of Land and Natural Resources** ((808) 587-0300 WEB SITE www.hawaii.gov.

OAHU

Oahu has a surprising number of remote areas of almost virginal beauty, and several trails present views that are equal to the more famous vistas on the neighboring islands. The most famous of all Hawaii's hikes is surely the trail to the top of **Diamond Head Crater**, 760 ft (230 m) above sea level. It's a relatively easy uphill walk; wear rubber-soled shoes and carry water. The views of Waikiki Beach and Honolulu are truly astounding.

Another easy family hike leads through **Sacred Falls State Park** on the windward side of the island. To get there, drive over the Pali on Highway 61, then take a left and proceed along Highway 83. Sacred Falls Trail (nearly four and a half miles or just over seven kilometers round trip) is clearly signposted. Almost from the instant you reach the trail, the waterfall comes into view, luring you onward like some mystic beacon. The trail crosses Kaluanua Stream and runs into a 1,600-ft (490-m) walled canyon. Guava and mountain apple trees grow in the valley. The Sacred Falls pool is often muddy, but it is cold and refreshing. Don't attempt this hike if it's raining; landslides are common, and people have died in sudden flash floods and slides. In fact, the trail was closed

The misty forests of Kokee State Park on Kauai are a paradise for hikers.

in 1999 after boulders tumbled from the hillsides into the pool. You can check on its status by calling the Department of Land and Natural Resources (see above).

The 2,013-ft (614-m) **Mount Tantalus**, in the southeast interior of the island, was named after the mythical Greek king. In this region a series of interconnecting footpaths run in a basic south-to-north direction, from the depths of the valley to the heights of the mountain. Two of the more popular elevated trails that branch off from Tantalus are the **Manoa Cliffs Trail** (six miles, or 10 km) and the **Puu Ohia** or **Ohia Tree Hill Trail** (four miles, or six and a half kilometers). Both appeal to the hardy walker. The Puu Ohia Trail, in particular, has a wonderful view of the Nuuanu Valley and Pali Highway areas.

For those who prefer a leisurely stroll, the valley trails are recommended. What these trails lack in panoramic splendor they more than make up for by the presence of unique flora. Among the scores of flowering plants look for Job's Tears, a type of branched grass with elongated and pointed leaves. This plant attains heights of up to six feet (two meters) and produces black, blue-gray and white pea-sized beans much in demand by lei makers.

Job's Tears can be found in profusion on the **Makiki Valley Trail**, which begins at the Tantalus Drive trailhead, heads eastward, descends into Makiki Valley, then passes the Nahuina Trail to the north. After a short distance, the Makiki Valley Trail crosses Kanealole Trail to the south. It is a place of pure enchantment and natural serenity. Cool springs bubble out of the ground and Job's Tears are everywhere. The trail winds its way through a heavily forested valley and around small gulches and tiny streams. Mountain apple trees tempt the hiker to pause and taste the delicious fruit. The trail eventually links up with other trails near the bottom of the hill. Also at the foot of the hill is the Makiki Environmental Education Center.

Aiea Loop Trail (4.8 miles or 7.7 km), in the Keaiwa Heiau State Recreation Area, is the site of an ancient healing

heiau (temple) around which grow many of the medicinal plants once used by the *heiau kahunas* (temple priests). This graded trail is a favorite with residents and offers an enjoyable experience for families. Passing through a forest of Norfolk pines and several varieties of eucalyptus, the trail offers a fascinating blend of nonnative greenery and some samples of traditional Hawaiian flora, such as ohia lehua, koa, and sandalwood. The Aiea Loop branches off sharply to the right after 1.6 miles (2.5 km) and then follows the ridge above North Halawa Stream before descending through a forest where many native trees are in evidence. At the three-mile (4.8-km) mark of the hike, be on the

lookout for the wreckage of a C-47 cargo plane that crashed on the ridge in 1943.

The **Wiliwilinui** and **Lanipo Trails** (three hours each way) are parallel walks to peaks in the Koolau range, from which there are great views of the windward side of Oahu. Wiliwilinui can be entered from Laukahi Street on Waialae-Iki Ridge, on the southeastern side of the island. It's a strenuous hike to an elevation of about 2,000 ft (610 m) overlooking Kapakahi Gulch to the west and Wailupe Gulch to the east. Despite the elevation, it is a fairly gentle ascent to the summit, but the trail can get muddy and caution is advised. Notable flora includes lavender, the Philippine orchid, and the multicolored lantana. Look

for interesting bird life on the trail, particularly the endemic elapaio, a gray bird that chirps a curious wolflike whistle, and the crimson apapane, which can often be found feeding on the nectar of ohia flowers. The road ends at 1,800 ft (550 m) and the trail continues to the summit where the views of Waimanalo in the east and Kualoa Point to the north are magnificent.

From the top of the Wiliwilinui Trail, Lanipo extends west along the crestline. Lanipo Trail provides one of the few vantage points from which to view **Kaau Crater**, an ash and lava cone formed within the last 150,000 years. Situated at

Haleakala Crater, a painter's palette of colors.

the base of the Koolau range, this crater, as is the case with so many Hawaiian landmarks, has an origin steeped in legend. It is said that the demigod Maui, wanting to join Kauai and Oahu, threw his hook hoping to catch the foundation of Kauai, and pulled a rock loose instead. The rock is said to have fallen at Kaena Point on the North Shore of Oahu while the hook landed in the Koolaus and created Kaau Crater.

The last stretch of the Lanipo Trail is more strenuous than Wiliwilinui, and great agility is required to traverse the precipitous ridge and thick brush. From the summit one can see all the way from Waimanalo to Kailua. If you're in good shape, try this one. It's worth it.

Nearly all of Oahu's campsites are controlled by a county, state or federal agency, and all require camping permits. Campsites at public beach parks extend from Haleiwa on the north shore to Bellows Beach on the windward coast. The **City and County of Honolulu** ((808) 523-4525 oversees 13 beach parks. Each has a different character. Campfires are not allowed, but cooking is permitted on grills. There are no public cabins on Oahu, but several under private jurisdiction. The **State of Hawaii Campgrounds** ((808) 587-0300 are similar to the city's. Reservations are taken 30 days in advance on Oahu, but a year in advance on the neighboring islands.

KAUAI

Half the battle to hiking in **Kokee State Park** (Waimea Canyon) is getting there. The park is roughly 38 miles (61 km) from Lihue. Your efforts, however, will be well rewarded when you reach the park headquarters on the edge of Waimea Canyon. There are 16 trails worth exploring in Kokee, each with a unique identity and splendid panoramic views ranging from the grandeur of Waimea Canyon to the rugged beauty of the Na Pali Coast and the lush vegetation of its rainforests. The area also contains facilities for picnicking, swimming and camping by permit (issued by the Hawaii State Division of Parks ((808) 984-8109).

The 3,657-ft-deep (1,115-m) Waimea Canyon has been blessed with vibrant forests set deep in tropical valleys. Several trails branch out from the canyon floor. Of these it is the strenuous **Canyon Trail** (1.7 miles or 2.7 km), ending at the Cliff Outlook, that presents Waimea Canyon at its best.

The **Berry Flat Trail** (one mile or 1.6 km) and the **Puu Ka Ohelo Trail** (530 yards or 500 m) are two forest trails highly recommended for the casual hiker. The trails wind through areas forested with Californian redwoods, Australian eucalyptus, native koa and Japanese sugi pines. The sweet smell of pine refreshes the spirit, making these two of the more enjoyable walks in the park.

Other relatively easy trails include the **Iliau Nature Loop** (530 yards or 500 m) and the **Cliff Trail** (200 yards or 180 m). The Nature Loop is akin to a walk through a botanical garden, offering a close-up view of several species of plants endemic to Hawaii, including the unusual iliau. The Cliff Trail gives a good view of Waimea Canyon.

Ditch Trail (3.5 miles or 5.6 km) and **Koaie Trail** (three miles or 4.8 km) are considerably more difficult to hike. The former covers some rather rough terrain, but has splendid views of Kohua Ridge and the waterfalls that run off it. Koaie Trail is somewhat easier and more popular. At the end of Koaie is a natural pool, ideal for a refreshing swim after this vigorous hike.

Other strenuous but beautiful trails include the **Kukui Trail Loop** (2.5 miles or four kilometers) with a view of a 2,000-ft (610-m) drop into the canyon, the **Alakai Swamp Trail** (3.4 miles or 5.5 km) and the very strenuous **Awaawapuhi Trail** (3.3 miles or 5.3 km) which climbs high above the Na Pali Coast.

Diehard hikers from all over the world long to conquer Kauai's Na Pali coastline on the **Kalalau Trail** (11 miles or 18 km) trail. Steep, slippery, and often treacherous, the trail was first etched along the cliffs by the ancient Hawaiians who populated the beautiful hanging

where ferns grow in wild profusion, are the three-tiered **Hanakapiai Falls**, cascading to the boulders below from a height of 2,950 ft (900 m) in a lacy sheet of water. The sun rarely touches this place of enchantment. Primitive, beautiful and serene, it refreshes the soul as much as the senses.

Kauai County ((808) 241-6660 has seven beach parks ranging from **Haena Beach Park** in the north to the **Lucy Wright Park** close to the ocean near Waimea. The three state parks ((808) 274-3445 where camping is permitted include **Na Pali Coast**, **Kokee State Park** and the **Polihale State Park**, 140 acres (56 hectares) overlooking Waimea Canyon. There are also privately owned cabins in Kokee State Park ((808) 335-6061.

MAUI

The grandeur of Maui's **Mount Haleakala** is best appreciated by walking its trails on an overnight hike. It's a journey that traverses rainbow-colored splatter cones and towering cliffs. This once-active volcano is also sanctuary to about 200 of the nene, or Hawaiian goose, and the wildly beautiful *ahinahina*, the Haleakala silversword. This member of the sunflower family is found nowhere else on the planet. The silversword blooms only once in a 5- to 20-year life cycle — and then it dies.

Hikers have several choices at Haleakala, but for the dedicated walker, the **Crater Loop Hike** (20 miles or just over 32 km) is a must. The trailhead is located 10,023 ft (3,055 m) above sea level at the visitor center. The initial section down the **Sliding Sands Trail** to the floor of the crater is a comfortable walk and gives hikers an opportunity to adjust to the elevation. In the early morning, views along this trail sweep across the entire expanse of the crater. The longer you spend on this trail, the more vivid the colors become. Red, ochre and shiny black sand merge with stones flecked with golden hues to form rivers of colors.

valleys of these regions. Even the hardiest hikers find it best to spend at least one night camping at Kalalau Beach at the end of the trail and return the next day. Permits are required for hiking and camping in this area and are issued by the **Kauai State Parks Office** ((808) 274-3445, 3060 Eiwa Street, Lihue, HI 96766. Only a limited number of permits are issued, so write in advance if you have your heart set on exploring this unspoiled wilderness.

You don't need a permit to hike the first two miles (just over three kilometers) of the trail to **Hanakapiai Beach** and waterfalls, which would give you a first hand experience of the famous hanging valleys of the Na Pali wilderness. At Hanakapiai Beach, an icy stream feeds into the ocean in an area dotted with caves. The trail into the valley, source of Hanakapiai Falls winds through mango groves and a forest of mountain apple, breadfruit and guava trees. It also circles a deep, clear pool where you'll want to take a dip to refresh yourself before tackling the last stretch to the falls.

Finally, deep in the valley (about a three-hour roundtrip hike from the trail),

Outrigger canoe racing is a major sport in the islands.

Another aptly named section of the trail is **Paint Pot**, the most colorful of the cinder cones in the crater. Here purples intermingle with rich grays and bright reds. The final climb to the rim of the crater at the Crater Road junction is a spectacular ascent on switchbacks that gain 1,400 ft (426 m) of elevation in 3.9 miles (6.3 km).

Day hikers can take the roundtrip **Halemauu Trail** (eight miles or 13 km) to the Holua cabin area down the Halemauu Trail in approximately six hours. Very fit hikers, without the encumbrance of heavy backpacks, can cross the crater via the **Sliding Sands-Halemauu Loop** in a day (eight to 10 hours).

Because the altitude on Haleakala's trails never dips below 6,000 ft (1,829 m), be prepared for cold nighttime temperatures and the chance of frost. Days are often sunny, dry and hot in the shadeless hollow of the crater, but afternoons get cold, foggy and wet when the clouds roll in.

It is necessary to check in at park headquarters located on the Haleakala Crater Road at the 7,030-ft (2,142-m) level. Backcountry permits are issued here, and cabins, if available, can be assigned.

For information contact **Haleakala National Park** ((808) 572-4400. Recorded park information can be heard at ((808) 572-7749. For other information and reservations write to Superintendent, Haleakala National Park, PO Box 369, Makawao, HI 96798. The National Park Service also runs the campgrounds at Haleakala. The **Home Grove** campsite is often cool, windy and rainy. Grills, potable water and chemical toilets are available. **Kipahula** can be warm, wet and breezy. No water is available here, so bring drinking water. Chemical toilets are provided. There are cabins at **Kapalaoa** (5.8 miles or 9.5 km), **Holua** (6.3 miles or 10.1 km) and **Paliku** (9.8 miles or 15.8 km), with tent sites also at the latter two areas. Paliku and Holua have limited non-potable water that must be treated before drinking.

No open fires are permitted. The 12-bunk cabins are so popular that they are awarded on a lottery system. Apply by writing up to 90 days in advance. Hikers who do get a cabin should arrive with appropriate equipment and supplies. The rangers have detailed park maps and updated information on trail conditions.

Maui County ((808) 243-7389 has three parks for camping — **Baldwin Beach Park**, near the ocean town of Paia, **Rainbow Park**, in the upcountry village of Haliimaile, and **Kanaha Beach Park**, near the airport.

The state has two sites — at **Waianapanapa**, near Hana (12 cabins, tent sites and ocean views) and a lone cabin at **Polipoli Springs** at an elevation of 6,200 ft (1,890 m). Since cabin requests greatly exceed the number available, a monthly lottery is held for reservations. Only one request per group is accepted. Call ((808) 984-8109.

MOLOKAI

Kamakou Mountain, at an elevation of 4,970 ft (1,515 m), is the highest point on Molokai. Native Hawaiian forest covers its slopes. Within the 2,774 acres (1,123 hectares) of the Nature Conservancy's **Kamakou Preserve** are numerous rare plants and animals. The wetter slopes of the mountain are heavily forested with ohia trees, huge tree ferns, orchids and silver lilies. In the drier areas, hardwoods, including small groves of sandalwood, thrive.

The trails of Kamakou Preserve, rich in historical sites and covering a wide variety of climates and terrain, fascinate hikers. The mountain is home to five endangered species of forest birds. The 'olomao (Molokai thrush) and kakawahie (Molokai creeper) live only on the island. The red i'iwi, green amakihi, and the crimson and black 'apapane are seen more frequently, as is the pueo or Hawaiian owl.

TOP: Swimming and snorkeling in the clear waters of Hanauma Bay, Oahu. BOTTOM: A fishy scenario at Sealife Park, Oahu.

YOUR CHOICE

The **Nature Conservancy of Hawaii**
((808) 553-5236 FAX (808) 553-9870 offers
guided hikes into the preserve. Hikers
are advised to seek the advice of the
Conservancy about trails and trail
conditions. For much of the year, the
forest is a very wet place.

To reach the entrance of the preserve,
go east on Forest Reserve Road to a point
where it leaves Highway 46, about half a
mile (one kilometer) south of the junction
of Highway 46 and Highway 47
(Kualapuu Road). A 45-minute drive will
bring you to the preserve's entrance at
the Waikolu Lookout, provided it hasn't
been raining. In wet weather, the road
may be impassable.

Molokai has three campsites for tent
campers. The two sites operated by the
county are at **One Alii Beach Park** and
Papohaku Beach Park ((808) 553-3204.
The parks have restroom facilities with
showers, drinking water and barbecue
pits. There's also tent camping at **Palaau
State Park**, which is run by the **Hawaii
State Division of Parks** ((808) 984-8109.

LANAI
The island abounds in hiking trails.
One of the favorites, a trail lined with
Norfolk pines and unique flora native
to New Zealand, is named after the
naturalist George Munro, which Munro
introduced to the island.

There is no potable water on the trails
of this dry island, so you must carry your
own. Many people treat the camp water
before drinking it.

Hulopoe Beach campground is owned
by the Lanai Company ((808) 565-3982,
PO Box 310, Lanai, HI 96763. Bordered by
a spectacular white-sand beach and arid
kiawe forest, the comfortable, camping
area provides clean restrooms, private
outdoor cold showers, and cooking areas.
It's necessary to make reservations well
in advance, since there are only three
shaded campsites. Stays are limited to
seven days.

BIG ISLAND
All the hikes in **Hawaii Volcanoes
National Park** offer dramatic contrasts.

Devastation Trail is the site of a violent
volcanic eruption that, in 1959, smothered
a once beautiful forest with cinder and
ash. All that remains are charred tree
trunks and lava rock. A boardwalk now
paves part of the trail to keep hikers
from walking on the cinder fall and
prevent damage to the slowly
returning vegetation.

The trails in Volcanoes National Park
range from easy to difficult. Among the
easier ones are **Sandalwood Trail**
(1,320 yards or 1.2 km), **Sulfur Bank Trail**
(600 yards or 550 m) and the **Thurston
Lava Tube Trail** (550 yards or 500 m), the
most exciting of the three. As lava flowed
through this area, the outer layers cooled
and solidified while the inner flow
remained molten and kept traveling,
eventually emptying itself and creating a
tube. Sulfur Bank and Sandalwood Trails
have trademarks of their own, though
not pleasant ones. Odors created by
sulfurous fumes, which escape through
steam vents in the craters, diffuse the air.
The pungent smell may cause nausea
or headaches if you stay in the area
too long.

Semi-difficult trails are more abundant
in the park. One such trail is **Crater Rim**

Trail, made all the more difficult by recent overflows of lava onto the path. The trail begins at Volcano House and loops around the Kilauea Military Camp and the Hawaii Volcano Observatory. On a clear day you might see Mauna Loa looming in the distance. The Crater Rim Trail passes through pretty woodlands alive with ohelo shrubs that produce bright red berries, believed to be favored by the volcano goddess Pele. The legend advises us that a quantity of the berries picked must be thrown into the crater as an offering. Other trails in the semi-difficult category include the **Halemaumau Trail** (3.2 miles or 5.1 km) which traverses the Kilauea Caldera, the **Kilauea Iki Trail** (two miles or 3.2 km) and the **Byron Ledge Trail** (2.5 miles or four kilometers).

While it is one of the more strenuous hikes in the park, the **Hilina Pali Trail** (6.4 miles or 10.3 km) rewards those who persist with superb views of the Big Island's southeast coast. The best time to walk this trail is in the afternoon — however, dusk comes quickly in these mountains, and one shouldn't be caught out here unequipped in the dark. It is almost 2,000 ft (610 m) down to Halape Trail Junction.

One of the best hikes in Hawaii Volcanoes National Park is along the **Mauna Loa Trail**, which begins at an elevation of 2,032 ft (619 m), at the end of Mauna Loa Road, and terminates at 13,250 ft (4,038 m), at the summit cabin. A minimum of three days is required to complete the round trip to the summit. Four days is strongly recommended.

The trail passes through nene (Hawaiian goose) country and an open ohia forest. Once above Red Hill at 10,035 ft (3,059 m) — where there's a cabin with eight bunks — the trail follows Mauna Loa's northeast ridge. Bring your own water for use on the trail. There is no charge to use the cabins, but hikers must register at park headquarters. At the summit cabin (12 bunks) an arrow points to water and ice in a lava crack. A word of caution: This is not a particularly dangerous

climb, but if you are burdened with a heavy backpack, it could be difficult. Remember too that the summit has a cold climate and weather conditions can change rapidly and without warning. Winter storms can last several days and the snowpack can be from six to nine feet (two to three meters) deep.

A second trail (6.1 miles or 9.8 km) — marked with yellow blazes — to the summit of Mauna Loa begins at an elevation of 11,000 ft (3,350 m) near the Mauna Loa Observatory. It will take you from six to eight hours to complete the hike because the terrain is steep. The round trip may take an entire day, so in order to return before dark, you must begin hiking by 10 AM. On this trail, the rapid climb from sea level could cause altitude sickness. Walk at a pace that allows for acclimatization.

There are a dozen county-operated beach parks on the Big Island that permit camping. A list of these sites may be obtained by calling the Department of Parks and Recreation ((808) 961-8311.

OPPOSITE: Protea grow to enormous sizes in the islands' cooler climes. ABOVE: Rare silversword is found only on the upper slopes of Haleakala on Maui.

The campgrounds range from the **Waipio Valley Lookout** to **White Sands Beach Park** near Kailua-Kona.

The state oversees cabins at **Mauna Kea**, **Kilauea** and **Kalopa**. Each cabin contains linen, cooking facilities and utensils. Two of the cabins are for hikers attempting to climb Mauna Loa and are available at no cost on a first-come, first-served basis: the **Red Hill Cabin** (eight bunks) at Puu Ulaula (10,035 ft or 3,058 m) and the **Mauna Loa Cabin** (12 bunks) at Mokuaweoweo Caldera rim 13,250 ft (4,038 m).

Ten housekeeping cabins are also available at **Namakani Paio**; each sleeps four. Reservations must be made at least a month in advance with the National Park Service ((808) 967-7311.

Sporting Spree

Naturally, ocean activities make up a big part of any Hawaiian holiday. The waters around the islands are perfect for surfing, swimming, windsurfing, scuba diving and snorkeling, canoe and kayak paddling, yacht racing, and fishing. But landlubbers enjoy equal perfection for favored sports, golf reaching a particular height on the varied landscapes of the islands.

SURFING
Surfing carnivals are held in Australia, southern California, South Africa and

South America, but there isn't a more exciting venue on earth than Oahu's north shore, where only the bravest and the most skilled dare to confront the mountainous waves of Waimea Bay and the famed Banzai Pipeline off Ehukai Beach.

If the variety of surf sites off the islands' shores have made Hawaii the surfing capital of the world, the immensity of its waves has made **Oahu** the mecca of surfing aficionados. In the summer, when most storms occur in the South Pacific, the island's south shore bears the brunt of wave activity, and as a result, beaches from Ala Moana to Makapuu and Sandy Beach draw the wave riders. The north shore, on the other hand, is like glass at this time of year, making it a favorite with snorkelers and windsurfers.

When the storms begin to brew, however, and swells are generated in the Gulf of Alaska and the Sea of Japan, snorkelers are nowhere to be seen; surf season is here again. The transformation off the north shore is remarkable.

Winter swells bring waves that average about six to eight feet (two to two and a half meters), and often reach monstrous proportions of up to 30 ft (nine meters).

For the professional surfer the north shore is the equivalent of the mountain climber's Himalayan range, and Sunset Beach, Ehukai Beach, Waimea Bay and the Haleiwa Alii are the Everest of his ambitions. These "arenas" are the finest in the island. Numerous competitions are held around the island; the most notable are the Triple Crown of Surfing in November and the recently initiated Eddie Aikau "Big Wave" meet.

If you are totally inexperienced but wish to try your hand at this sport, rest assured that there are a number of safe areas where you can experiment. Other beaches on Oahu that are fairly calm year-round and offer perfect introductory waves are Kuhio and Queen's Beaches in the Waikiki area. Boards are usually available for rent at these areas. If you want some instruction, look no further than the "beach boys" who ply their trade on Waikiki Beach.

Local surfing experts insist that these men provide the uninitiated with an excellent introduction to the sport. On the west coast, Tracks, across from the Hawaiian Electric power plant at Kahe, is a good bet for beginners. The more experienced surfers gravitate to Maile Point, which protrudes into the ocean like a peninsula. Here the waves can range from two to 15 ft (one half to four and a half meters).

Makaha, however, remains the premier surfing beach on the west side. As befits its reputation, international surfing contests have been held here since 1954. On days when the waves range from small to medium, boogie boarders join the surfing elite to bounce around in the notorious "Makaha backwash," the rush of water that races back down the steeply inclined beach and out to sea. On days when the north swells are in evidence, waves can reach heights of over 25 ft (eight meters).

OPPOSITE: Hikers on Haleakala gaze out over a swirling bank of clouds. ABOVE: Looking down into the House of the Sun.

Near the end of the highway is Keawaula Bay, more popularly known as Yokohama Bay, or Yokes. The waves in this bay break in very shallow water, creating a ride much like the Banzai Pipeline on the north shore.

Since all the islands possess popular surfing beaches, selection is a matter of personal taste and experience.

The Hanalei area on the north side is **Kauai's** answer to Oahu's north shore. In winter, the waves are definitely for experts only. Beginners might try the waves around Poipu Beach.

Maui boasts Honolua Bay and Maalaea on the west side of the island as its gift to the surfing world. The big surf on the Valley Isle is to be found at La Perouse Bay. Don't take a chance in these waters unless you know what you're doing. Beginners may wish to try areas near Kaanapali Beach in west Maui where boards can be rented.

The **Big Island's** main surfing challenge is in the Hilo area, where it can get extremely rough between September and March. If you're just starting out, most professionals recommend the Kailua-Kona side as one of the "mellowest" areas at which to catch a wave.

Extreme surfing, a blend of traditional surfing, windsurfing and water skiing, allows the most experienced big-wave riders to catch waves in excess of 30 ft (nine meters). Teams of surfers ride to the outer reefs on jet skis, then take turns getting towed into a wave that is much too large to catch under normal conditions.

The surfers ride boards with straps (similar to those found on windsurfing boards), which allow the riders to launch themselves into the air to do flips. It's mind boggling to see someone riding a 30- to 40-ft (9- to 12-m) wave and then polishing it off with a 360-degree loop.

Another surfing variation that has caught on fast in the islands is **kite sailing**, which is surfing with a parasail. Being attached to the sail allows surfers who have caught a wave to become airborne and remain so for quite a long time.

WINDSURFING

When talk turns to windsurfing, no matter where in the world, one of the most frequently discussed destinations is Hookipa on **Maui**. Renowned windsurfer Mike Waltze is credited with having discovered the site. It has since become the windsurfing capital of the world and has been the setting for championship events since 1981. Hookipa, however, is not the place for novices. Waves can often reach sets of 10 to 15 ft (three to four and a half meters), and it is an intimidating prospect trying to windsurf here unless you have all the skills. For the less experienced or for those who want more fun than thrills, try Kihei, Spreckelsville or Kanaha. If you want to rent windsurfing equipment, try the town of Paia, not far from Hookipa.

There are several good windsurfing spots on **Oahu**. Diamond Head and Lanikai Beach are favorites. And Maunalua Bay in east Oahu is gaining popularity. The lookout at Diamond Head is a spectacular viewing site. On a clear day, with the ocean alive with myriad colored sails, and tanned bodies soaring high off the lips of waves, it's a sight to behold.

SNORKELING AND DIVING

In and around Hawaii's emerald waters are some of the world's greatest diving sites. Tectonic activity and underwater eruptions over eons have created spectacular cathedral-like caverns, lava tubes, huge arches and towering pinnacles, all home to myriad forms of sea life.

While scuba diving here you may see everything from sea turtles to dolphins, manta rays and sharks. Try to catch the annual migration of the humpback whales, which lasts from December to April (see SING WITH WHALES, page 15 in TOP SPOTS).

Hawaii's waters contain a host of reef fish, one third of which are indigenous and come in a spectrum of colors and

Boogie boarders TOP enjoy the curls, while the shores of Oahu BOTTOM offer some of the world's most exciting surfing.

tongue-twisting names. For instance, the official state fish is the Humuhumunukunukuapua'a.

There are no seasonal restrictions. Diving and snorkeling sites are accessible throughout the year. For up-to-the-minute information on weather and sea conditions, check with the United States National Weather Service at WEB SITE www.weather.com/weather/us/states/hawaii.html.

Dive sites are found mainly on the south and west shores of **Oahu**. Several wrecks are viewable, including a 165-ft (50-m) minesweeper and a 196-ft (60-m) sunken barge. Four harbors around the island make for quick and easy access to most areas, and the major dive operations are located close to harbor launch sites.

No diver should leave Oahu without paying a visit to Hanauma Bay — formed naturally when the sea eroded the edge of an ancient volcano — enclosed by a large reef about 100 ft (30 m) offshore, creating the ideal diving location.

Also on the south shore of Oahu, in Maunalua Bay, is Turtle Canyon, accessible only by boat. At depths of nine to 40 ft (three to 12 m), the canyon, which derives its name from the green sea turtles which thrive in its waters, offers vistas of lava flow ridges and huge sandy faces.

For the more experienced diver, the sinister sounding Shark's Cove on the north shore offers depths of 15 to 45 ft (four and a half to 14 m), exploring a series of huge caverns in which light filters down through the roof creating a breathtaking stained-glass effect. This is without doubt the most popular cavern dive on the island. Dive here only in the summer.

Kauai's dive shops are found mainly in the Wailua and Poipu areas. There is a choice of four launch areas, all within 30 minutes of the major dive sites. Some of the island's most popular diving locations are to be found off the Na Pali Coast. For the snorkeler or diver there is

Oasis Reef. A feature of this boat dive is a lone pinnacle, surrounded by sand, which rises from a depth of 35 ft (11 m) to just below the water's surface. Divers should try the 65- to 80-ft (20- to 24-m) cavern dive to the quaintly named General Store, which in reality is two caverns nestled under a horseshoe-shaped ledge. This is also the site of a nineteenth-century shipwreck. In the Poipu area, the Sheraton Caverns dive shows off three huge lava tubes running parallel to each other. Turtles, lobsters and the occasional white-tip shark are frequently found here.

Divers should not miss the experience of scuba diving around the "Forbidden Island" of Niihau, to the west of Kauai. The waters around Niihau are notable for features including underwater caverns and amphitheater-like "rooms." Tuna, jacks, rays, barracuda, sharks and other large game fish are common here.

When on **Maui**, don't miss the marine preserve at Honolua Bay on the northern shore, where many tame fish and coral varieties can be found. This is a popular spot for introductory dives but is usually rough in the winter. There's also the splendid Five Caves site at Makena. Fifteen minutes off the west coast of Maui, the top of crescent-shaped Molokini Crater, another marine preserve, rises out of the ocean.

One of the more popular diving sites off the coast of **Molokai** is the eastern Mokuhookini Rock. This was a military bombing target during World War II, and numerous artifacts from that era can still be found there. There are many pinnacles and drop-offs with barracuda, gray reef sharks and ulua.

The **Lanai** coast is one of the best diving sites in the world. Some of the waters are so clear it is possible to dive at night with underwater flashlights. Be sure to visit the First and Second Cathedrals on the south shore. Here several pinnacles rise from 60 ft (18 m) to the surface with roomy caverns inhabited by moray eels, lobsters and shrimp. Menpachi Cave, with its 100-ft-long (30-m) lava tube, and Sharkfin Rock,

Colorful surfboards await renters on a Waikiki rack.

protruding out of the water like a shark's dorsal fin, are other favorite sites.

The waters off the western Kona Coast of the **Big Island** are generally calmer and clearer than around many other islands, as they are protected from the wind and rain by the mountains of Mauna Kea and Mauna Loa.

There is diving at Honaunau Bay and the Aquarium at Kealakekua, both state preserves. The Kona Cathedrals are a large room created by a lava-domed roof. Beams of light from the surface penetrate and create a church-like, stained glass effect. The Cathedrals teem with tropical fish, while manta rays and white-tip sharks are not uncommon. Fantasy Reef is a large, open cavern with a skylight and the largest collection of colorful "Christmas tree" coral in Hawaii. Snorkeling is possible both here and at the cathedrals.

The Chimney is another interesting site. Here, a white-sand canyon is bracketed by two lava walls that run to a height of 40 ft (12 m). The Chimney itself is actually a 40-ft-high (12-m) lava tube which can be entered at a depth of about 65 ft (20 m) and exited near the water's surface. Helmet shells are common and many red fish, including menpachi and aweoweo (bigeye), can be found under ledges.

For the more experienced diver, there is Plane Wreck Point, located just south of Keahole Point. A twin-engine Beechcraft lies broken in half on a bed of white sand at a depth of approximately 100 ft (30 m). The fuselage is penetrable and is now a playground for a variety of marine life.

Most Big Island dive operations are in the Kailua-Kona and Keauhou areas.

Submarines offer an alternative way of exploring the mysteries of the underwater world — without actually getting wet. Atlantis Submarines launched the world's largest submarine in Hawaiian waters in 1994. Operating off Waikiki, *Atlantis 2000* is 92 ft (28 m) long, displaces 150 tons and can carry 64 passengers. The *Atlantis 2000* tour includes a visit to a sunken World War II

oil tanker, which rests on the ocean floor and serves as a habitat for an incredible variety of fish. Maui is served by the Atlantis Submarines ((808) 973-9811 TOLL-FREE (800) 548-6262 WEB SITE WWW .goatlantis.com/hawaii, 665 Front Street, Lahaina, Maui or 75-5669 Alii Drive, Kona, Big Island.

CANOEING AND KAYAKING

Three major international ocean canoeing and kayaking races take place each year from the island of Molokai to Oahu. The resort at Kaluakoi is the perfect launch site on Molokai for these events, which attract contestants from the mainland

United States, Australia, South Africa and Japan. The **Bankoh Kayak Challenge** (May), once a traditional Hawaiian event, has developed into the world championship of ocean kayak racing and one of the toughest sporting events in the world. The race finishes in Oahu in the suburb of Hawaii Kai. **Na Wahine O Ke Kai** (September) is an outrigger canoe paddling event for six-women crews, and now regarded as the world championship of canoeing. Teams come to Kaluakoi from as far afield as Australia, New Zealand, Tahiti, Canada, and the mainland. The race covers 40 miles (65 km) of the Molokai Channel,

one of the roughest stretches of water in the Pacific. Crews contend with huge swells and riptides on their way to Kahanamoku Beach in front of the Hilton Hawaiian Village on Oahu. **Molokai Hoe** (October) is the men's version of the world outrigger canoe championship. The course and the hazards are the same as for the women's event, but it finishes at Fort DeRussy Beach, Waikiki. For more information contact ((808) 261-6615.

Ocean kayaking for the experienced kayaker is available through **Molokai**

Kauai's Waimea Canyon is often compared to the Grand Canyon.

Ranch and Fun Hogs ((808) 552-2791. You can kayak for pleasure in most Hawaiian waters, but experienced kayakers should explore Kauai's sea cliffs of Na Pali. This is a veritable wonderland of pretty coves, marvelous sea caves and grottoes. For a leisurely paddle, the Hanalei River provides an easy journey down a serene river past fields of taro and thickets of hau. For information, contact **Kayak Kauai Outbound (** (808) 826-9844 TOLL-FREE (800) 437-3507 FAX (808) 822-0577 WEB SITE ww.kayakkauai.com, Highway 560, one mile (one and a half kilometers) past Hanalei Bridge in Hanalei.

FISHING

The waters off the Kona Coast on the Big Island draw **big-game fishing** aficionados from around the world every year, in August, for the Hawaii International Billfish Tournament. Their quarry is that magnificent game fish, the Pacific blue marlin. This fish, with its distinctive swordlike snout, has tipped the scales at 1,000 lbs (450 kg), but typically they weigh between 300 and 400 lbs (135 and 180 kg). The fast, strong marlin makes a difficult catch. Its meat is moist, white and superb. Big game fishermen on Lanai go after *mahimahi*, yellowfin tuna, wahoo and the Pacific blue marlin. Fishing charters — shared or private — are available on all the islands. Check local tourist publications or the concierge at your hotel for information.

Spear fishing is popular with the islanders; the octopus or tako are favorite target. The locals bake or steam the octopus and use it for *poke*, a delicious salad.

Freshwater fishing is available on Kauai at Kokee State Park. For a modest fee you can get a 30-day freshwater fishing license from the Department of Land and Natural Resources, Division of Aquatic Resources (** (808) 241-3400, PO Box 1671, Lihue, HI 96766, or through most fishing supply stores.

GOLF

Some of Hawaii's golf courses are justifiably described as being out of this world. There are courses high on the slopes of volcanoes, in lava fields, on old plantation lands, in affluent residential districts. All have three things in common: they are well designed, well maintained and a joy to play.

While it is expensive to play most of these courses, there are many good golf packages. Tour operators or hotel representatives can provide information on these discounted golf vacations. Also, public courses are much cheaper, but they are heavily used by residents.

Oahu has more golf courses than any other Hawaiian island, and most of them are open to the public. One of the most popular facilities is **Ala Wai Golf Course (** (808) 296-2000, 404 Kapahulu Avenue, on the fringe of Waikiki and perhaps the most played-on course in the world. This par-70 course is flat and generally friendly, but it will test you on occasion, especially if you're not used to playing on dry, hard fairways.

The 6,350-yard, par-72 **Hawaii Kai Championship Course** and the neighboring 2,386-yard **Hawaii Kai Executive Course (** (808) 395-2358, 8902 Kalanianaole Highway, Honolulu, were designed by Robert Trent Jones. The latter course, a par-54, is for golfers who want to test their short game. Ocean winds and cleverly protected greens make these courses more challenging than they may appear. On the sunny Ewa Plain 40 minutes

out of Honolulu, the **Hawaii Prince Golf Club** ((808) 944-4567, 91-1200 Fort Weaver Road, incorporates three courses with 27 holes in total. Spread over 270 acres (109 hectares), this facility was designed by Arnold Palmer and Ed Seay and offers splendid views of the Waianae Mountain Range.

West Oahu rarely sees rain, so the greens can be fast at **Koolina Golf Club** ((808) 676-5300, 92-1220 Aliinui Drive, Kapolei. This is a gorgeous par-72 course with 6,867 yards. Koolina is part of the Ihilani resort. **Koolau Golf Course** ((808) 236-4653, 45-550 Kionaole Road, Kaneohe, in windward Oahu, is a challenge worth accepting. Tucked at the base of the fabulous Koolau Mountain Range, this 18-holer has 6,324 yards and tests the range and skills of the best. The spectacular views may take some of the pain away.

The **Sheraton Makaha Resort and Country Club** ((808) 695-9578, 84-627 Makaha Valley Road, Makaha, is recognized as one of the top five courses on the island. This course is long and flat, guarded by eight water hazards and 107 bunkers. Nestled in the beautiful Makaha Valley, the course is a par-72

with 7,077 yards. The oceanfront Turtle Bay Hilton and Country Club **Links at Kuilima** ((808) 293-8574, 7091 Kamehameha Highway, is located on the famous North Shore of Oahu where the spectacular high winter surf lures the world's greatest surfers. In fact the sound of the surf is ever present on this Arnold Palmer-designed course.

The 6,663-yard, par-72 **Waikele Golf Club** ((808) 676-9000, 94-200 Paioa Place, Waikele, is in west Oahu, near the shopping outlets of Waipahu and on the plains in what was once sugar country. **West Loch Golf Course** ((808) 296-2000, 91-1126 Okupe Street, Ewa Beach, adds a new twist to the driving range. Here, you don't drive the ball into a dust bowl or a patch of green — you drive it into a lake. The yard markers are buoys and the balls float. The finishing holes are especially tough. At approximately 6,480 yards, this 18-holer is par 72.

The Garden Isle of **Kauai** has a healthy crop of golf courses — many with fine views. The 6,353-yard, par-70

OPPOSITE: Snorkelers drift amid tropical fish above the coral at Tunnels Beach on Kauai. ABOVE: Hookipa on Maui ranks as world class for windsurfing aficionados.

Kiahuna Plantation Golf Course ((808) 742-9595, 2545 Kiahuna Plantation Drive, Koloa, is located at the resort of Poipu. This Robert Trent Jones Jr.-designed course is noted for its cleverly placed lava rocks. The most talked-about holes are the twelfth and sixteenth, both pins being set at opposite ends of a single oval-shaped green.

Two courses are laid out at the **Kauai Lagoons Golf Course** ((808) 241-6000 TOLL-FREE (800) 634-6400, 3351 Hoolaulea Way, Lihue. The 7,070-yard, par-72 Kiele Course combines the natural beauty of Hawaiian landscapes with dramatic views along cliffs that overlook the Pacific Ocean. The Lagoons Course — a par 72 with 6,942 yards — is a softer, gentler course, but it's still a tough one.

The centerpiece of Princeville Resort on Kauai's northern shores is its golf courses. A 27-hole, par-72 course with 10,345 yards, the **Makai Course** ((808) 826-3580 TOLL-FREE (800) 626-1105 E-MAIL info@princeville.com WEB SITE www .princeville.com, 4086 Lei O Papa Road, Princeville, is considered the most beautiful course in all Hawaii. Designed by Robert Trent Jones Jr., it has three nine-holers: Ocean, Lakes and Woods.

The par-three third hole on Ocean epitomizes all that is remarkable about this course. You have the illusion of driving your tee shot straight into deep blue waters. The 18-hole **Prince Course** ((808) 826-2727 is a par-72 course with 7,309 yards. While Makai is a "fun" course, Prince is for the serious. One of the most fascinating holes on this course is the par-three seventeenth, "the Pali." It's a relatively short hole, only 205 yards to the pin, but you have to clear both water and heavy foliage to get there.

Lovely but treacherous **Poipu Bay Resort Golf Course** ((808) 742-8711, 2250 Ainako Street, Poipu Beach, on the south shores, has rolling terrain and deceptive greens that will test the patience of the best golfer, and has been the home of the PGA Grand Slam of Golf since 1994.

Many consider the **Wailua Municipal Course** ((808) 241-6666, 3-5351 Kuhio Highway, Kapaa, to be the finest municipal course in the islands. Built oceanside, this 6,918-yard, par-72 course is full of doglegs, fast greens and large trees.

The first challenge of golfing in **Maui** is keeping your mind on the game. You can't ignore the views. **Kapalua Golf Club** ((808) 669-8044, 300 Kapalua Drive, Lahaina, has three gorgeous 18-holers: the Bay Course, the Village Course and the Plantation Course. The Bay Course, designed by Arnold Palmer, is the venue for the Kapalua International Championship, one of the premier events on the Hawaiian golf calendar. The long, wide fairways make this par-72 course of 6,600 yards popular with high-handicap players. The par-71 Village Course, with 6,632 yards, was also designed by Palmer and has an even more spectacular setting than the adjacent Bay Course. The 7,263-yard, par-73 Plantation Course is equally beautiful and the most expensive of the three.

About 40 minutes from the Kahului Airport are the two courses of the **Makena Resort Golf Club** ((808) 879-3344, 5415 Makena Alanui, Makena. The North Course was completed in 1981. It's a par 72 with 6,914 yards and has

great views on one side of the ocean the island of Lanai in the distance, and in the other direction, the imposing summit of Haleakala. The fairways are narrow and the fast greens are protected by 64 bunkers and four water hazards. The par-71 South Course was designed by Robert Trent Jones Jr., who used 64 traps and four ponds on this lava landscape to create a 7,017-yard masterpiece.

Maui's most famous, the **Kaanapali** ((808) 661-3691, 2290 Kaanapali Parkway, Lahaina, also has two 18-holers, both par 71. The North Course has rolling fairways with the 541-yard, par-five first hole and the 438-yard, par-four eighteenth hole creating challenges because of the water hazards. The South Course tests golfers' accuracy with an extremely difficult 537-yard, par-five eighth in close proximity to the sugar cane fields and exposed to strong winds.

On **Molokai**, Ted Robinson designed the **Kaluakoi Golf Resort** ((808) 552-2739, Maunaloa. The verdant fairways are fringed by a rocky shoreline on one side. Five holes are played along the coastline. Among the occasional hazards are wild deer, turkeys and pheasants. This is a par-72 course with 6,564 yards.

On **Lanai**, the **Experience at Koele** ((808) 565-4653 TOLL-FREE (800) 321-4666 E-MAIL reservations@lanai-resorts.com WEB SITE www.lanai-resorts.com, Lanai Avenue, Lanai City, was the first course designed by Australian Greg Norman with Ted Robinson. Nine of the holes meander through a mountain valley surrounded by pines. The seventeenth green sits on an island, leaving no room for error. Koele is a par-72 course with 7,014 yards. The Jack Nicklaus-designed 7,039-yard, par-72 **Challenge at Manele** ((808) 565-2222, One Manele Bay Road, Lanai City, is ranked among the top 100 courses in the United States. Golf addicts compare it to Pebble Beach. This course is built on several hundred acres of natural lava outcropping, among wild ilima and kiawe trees. The signature hole is the twelfth, a fine par three.

The **Big Island** of Hawaii is well known for its oasis-like courses spread over mounds of dark lava. Rated as one of the world's great courses, the

OPPOSITE: A golfer lines up a shot at Poipu on Kauai, where the fine views can distract even the most practiced players. ABOVE: Plantations of coconut palms line the eastern shores of Kauai.

YOUR CHOICE

Mauna Kea Resort Golf Course ((808) 882-5400, 62-100 Mauna Kea Beach Drive, Kamuela, is a Robert Trent Jones Sr. masterpiece. Throughout the 7,114 yards, undulating fairways, steep greens, uphill holes, doglegs and strategically placed bunkers — 20 in all — make this course both a golfer's dream and nightmare.

The magnificent Jack Nicklaus-designed **Hualalai Golf Club** ((808) 325-8480, Queen Kaahumanu Highway, Kailua-Kona, at historic Kaupulehu is home to the annual Senior PGA MasterCard Championship. Nicklaus designed this 7,117-yard, par-72 course taking advantage of the remarkable natural features of the landscape. Holes weave around lava formations and deep bunkers, play over ancient Hawaiian fishponds and skirt the shoreline. At the **Mauna Lani Resort, Francis I'i Brown Golf Course** ((808) 885-6655 WEB SITE www.manualani.com, 68-1310 Mauna Lani Drive, Kohala Coast, fairways are narrow, so accuracy is the key. The South Course is a par 72 with 6,938 yards; the North Course, a par 72 with 6,913 yards.

A Scotsman saw the potential of developing a course on the natural slope of Mauna Loa, in the shadow of the great volcano, creating a nine-hole course in 1922. In 1967, Jack Snyder broadened it to 18 holes. In 1983, Bill Hayashi added 30 bunkers and four ponds, making the **Volcano Golf and Country Club** ((808) 967-7331, Golf Course Road, Hawaii Volcanoes National Park, even more challenging. This par-72 course of 6,505 yards has many doglegs and fast greens. Because of the high altitude, the ball tends to fly.

Robert Trent Jones Jr. designed the **Waikoloa Beach Golf Club** ((808) 886-6060 TOLL-FREE (800) 552-1422, 1020 Keana Place, Waikoloa — recognized as one of the finest in the islands. Completed in 1982, it is built around the historic King's Highway, on the edge of which are fishponds and rock carvings. The greens on this 6,566-yard, par-70 course require technique.

MARATHONS AND ENDURANCE SPORTS

In 1973, 162 runners competed in the inaugural **Honolulu Marathon**. The field has steadily grown to over 30,000, making it the third largest marathon in the world and the second largest in the United States, behind the Boston Marathon. For all its international notoriety, the Honolulu Marathon — held every December — continues to be recognized as "the people's marathon," for it attracts not only professional, world-class athletes, but also weekend runners who join in for the pride of just finishing this grueling event. The 26-mile (42-km) course stretches from downtown Honolulu to Hawaii Kai in east Oahu and back. The organizers here like to declare: "New York has the crowds, Boston has the prestige, but Honolulu has it all!" For more information contact the Honolulu Marathon Association ((808) 734-7200 WEB SITE www.honolulumarathon.org, 3435 Waialae Avenue, Room 208, Honolulu, HI 96816.

The strength-sapping, spirit-breaking **Ironman Triathlon** — a combination of three existing long-distance races popular on the island of Oahu — was conceived in Hawaii by John Collins, a Navy man, and now enjoys a place in sporting history.

The Ironman Triathlon, held in October, is a combination of the Waikiki Rough Water Swim (two and a half miles or four kilometers), the Around-Oahu Bike Race (112 miles or 180 km) and the Honolulu Marathon (26 miles or 42 km). The combined event, now held at Kona on the Big Island, is recognized as the world championship and has become so popular that qualifying meets and lotteries have to be held to keep the numbers of participants down. For information contact ((808) 329-0063 WEB SITE www.ironmanlive.com.

Ala Wai, on the edge of Waikiki, is the most heavily used public golf course in the world.

The Open Road

Driving, preferably in a lipstick-red convertible, is essential to the Hawaiian experience. Nearly ever island has scenic routes begging to be explored. Fortunately, driving in Hawaii is absurdly easy. The universal speed limit seems to be 35 mph (60 km/h), and two-lane roads traverse most of the areas of interest to tourists.

Road signs are the biggest headache for travelers unaccustomed to the Hawaiian language. Many streets and highways are named for Hawaiian heroes, whose lengthy names consist of a string of vowels broken by few consonants. Newcomers have a hard time distinguishing between Kaumualii and Kamehameha at first glance, and the sight of nervous drivers trying to spell out overhead signs is quite common. Here's a tip — sound out each letter as you speak a name aloud.

Car rental agencies abound on most islands. Consider fly-and-drive packages when you book your trip; rates can be significantly lower. Drop-off charges are a consideration as well. Travelers with short itineraries may well want to fly into Hilo, rent a car and depart from Kona, for example. But the drop-off fee can easily cost the same as a full day's rental. There may also be a charge for additional drivers. The rental companies provide booklets with detailed maps of the most popular scenic routes, which are sufficient in most situations.

Don't bother with a car if you're staying in Honolulu or Waikiki, the most congested area on the islands. Instead, rent for a day or two during your stay while you explore the outer edges of Oahu. And you don't necessarily need wheels on the small islands of Lanai and Molokai. But you'll long for mobility everywhere else.

Oahu's most dramatic drive is also its shortest. It takes less than 30 minutes to climb the Pali Highway (61) from Honolulu to the Nuuanu Pali Lookout, a steep escarpment shrouded in cool mist. You need a full day to explore the North Shore, taking time to watch the surfers at the Banzai Pipeline and Sunset Beach. If you're staying around Waikiki, head east on the Kalamanaole Highway (72), which becomes the Kalanianaole Highway (also 72) and connects with the Kamehameha Highway (83) outside Kailua. By now, you should be thoroughly confused by the names. Fortunately, Kamehameha keeps its name along the east and north coasts to the town of Haleiwa and back south through the center of the island to Honolulu. En route Oahu proves itself to be for more than an urban island. The road passes by waterfalls, empty beaches, small communities, and mountains as green as on any of the islands.

Kauai is a driver's paradise, though those accustomed to high speeds may be greatly frustrated. The best route by far is inland from the coast to the rim of Waimea Canyon and Kokee State Park (see CANYON OF RED WATERS, page 16 in TOP SPOTS), but there are small circuits providing awesome views of rainforest and waterfalls throughout the navigable parts of the island. The Kuhio Highway running north from Kapaa passes through a slice of rural Hawaii before skirting Hanalei Bay. The drive from here out can be gorgeous or infuriating, depending on the traffic, which clogs the narrow streets of Hanalei town on sunny days. As Kuhio Highway reaches the its culmination at the Na Pali Coast,

the road narrows to one lane in places, and crosses one-lane bridges and small streams in others. Courtesy and patience go a long way in making this drive pleasurable. Forget deadlines and commitments — go with the flow, wave to passersby, and take time to enjoy the scenery.

The most lauded drive in all Hawaii is on **Maui**. Writers have devoted entire books to the Hana Highway (Highway 360) with its curves, switchbacks, and 56 one-lane bridges. There's something new to look at every minute, it seems, as you cruise past wild orchids, waterfalls, hillsides dripping with damp moss, and a chain of perfect beaches. At certain times of the year the air is filled with the scent of blossoms and ripened fruit from mango, guava, and banana orchards. Fruit stands and gardens pop up just frequently enough to make you want to stop at them all. Devote every minute of daylight to this 50-mile (80-km) drive and you'll still wish you had more time.

Cars pile up at nearly every section where the road's shoulders are wide enough for safety — and many places where nicks and dents seem inevitable.

Locals in pickup trucks either putter along even more slowly than ogling tourists or take on an attitude of benign tolerance towards everything except for the most egregious driver's errors. Do try to keep an eye on the road and those traveling around you. Sometimes the scenery is so overwhelming it blocks out all common sense.

The sheer spookiness of a predawn drive up Maui's Mount Haleakala makes a 3 AM wakeup call almost tolerable. The air grows chillier as you climb 10,023 ft (3,050 m) to the summit, and though you can hardly see where you're going, every sense knows you're high in the clouds. After sunlight breaks through, cruise down the mountain at a casual pace, stopping at some of Hawaii's prettiest villages along the way.

You don't have to worry about rush hour on **Molokai**, there isn't one. And those pesky stoplights? Forget it. They don't exist here. From the island's center, Highway 480 heads northeast, 470 north, 450 east and 460 west. That's about all you need to know. A drive to the arid

LEFT: Riders hit the trail on Molokai.
RIGHT: Father Damien's grave is a place of pilgrimage, on Molokai.

western side of the island, by far the most developed area of the island for tourists, won't take you very long, but don't hurry. Nobody drives fast on Molokai, because there is never anywhere to rush. Allow about a half day to fully enjoy a ride to Halawa Valley on the eastern end of the island. You'll pass St. Joseph's Church and the nearby Lady of Sorrows Church, which were both built by Father Damien de Veuster in the late 1800s. Along the way there is a string of fishponds and ancient heiau. This side of the island is lush, green and tropical, dotted with small, sandy beaches.

You need a four-wheel-drive vehicle to explore the back roads of **Lanai**, since the island has precious few paved roads. Be sure to get a map from Lanai's single rental company. Dirt roads quickly become hiking trails, and your sense of direction can be hampered by views of the ocean in every direction.

The **Big Island**'s name pretty much says it all. You definitely need wheels to see even a small portion of the island's mind-boggling topography. Tops on the list of scenic drives are those up Mauna Kea, down Chain of Craters Road in Volcanoes National Park, and through the coffee growing region west of Kona.

Backpacking

There is no getting around the fact that Hawaii is expensive. Food can take a big chunk out of your budget, if you are not careful. The best advice here is cook as much as you can for yourself and stay away from tourist sites. Try and find the most local-looking eating establishments possible and always look for the "plate specials" on menus as they are usually the best deal.

For accommodation, backpackers can take advantage of privately run youth hostels and the state's more than 30 government-run campsites. The hostels primarily offer dorm-style bed space. However, many also have a few private rooms at very reasonable rates. Unless otherwise noted, hostel accommodations include shared baths and communal kitchens. A few offer continental breakfasts. Most require you to bring your own towels and bed sheets. Guests are encouraged to book at least one month ahead to ensure that space is available.

Some of the campsites are free; others charge a nominal fee. All campsites require a permit, and stays are limited (for details see THE GREAT OUTDOORS, page 23).

OAHU
Hosteling International Honolulu
((808) 946-0591 FAX (808) 946-5904, 2323A Seaview Avenue, Honolulu, in the Manoa Valley, is convenient to hiking trails. Amenities include a television room, laundry facilities, activity bulletin board, and lockers/baggage storage. **Backpackers Vacation Inn and Plantation Village**
((808) 638-7838 FAX (808) 638-7515, 59-788 Kamehameha Highway, Haleiwa, is on Hawaii's North Shore, at Three Tables Beach.

Hosteling International Waikiki
((808) 926-8313 FAX (808) 922-3798,

2417 Prince Edward Street, Honolulu, is in Waikiki near the beach. Amenities include a communal television, laundry, activity bulletin board, and reading room. **Banana Bungalow Waikiki Beach** ((808) 924-5074 FAX (808) 924-4119, 2463 Kuhio Avenue, Honolulu, is centrally located in Waikiki, offering dorm and private rooms. It's a large outfit, with accommodation for 300 guests. Linen is provided at no cost and beds are made daily. All rooms have their own bathrooms, televisions and phones. There is a common room, laundry, grocery store, and an on-site Italian restaurant.

But the closest hostel to Waikiki Beach is the **Polynesian Hostel Beach Club** ((808) 922-1340 TOLL-FREE (877) 504-2924 FAX (808) 923-4146 E-MAIL reservation@hostelhawaii.com WEB SITE www.hostelhawaii.com, 2584 Lemon Road, Waikiki. They offer free coffee and tea, a nightly movie, a barbecue area, and safes as well as boogieboard, surfboard and snorkel gear. Discounts are given for web site bookings.

One block from Waikiki Beach is the **Waikiki Hostel and Hotel** ((808) 922-3993 FAX (808) 922-3993 E-MAIL Reservations@interclubwaikiki.com WEB SITE www.interclubwaikiki.com, 2426 Kuhio Avenue, Honolulu.

Aloha Inns—Piikoi Arms ((808) 596-2080 FAX (808) 593-8183 E-MAIL alohainns @aol.com WEB SITE www.alohainns.com, 111 Piikoi Street, Honolulu, is situated between Waikiki and downtown Honolulu and has modest apartments which operate rooming-house style with largely individually rented bedrooms. There is a coin-operated laundromat, as well as pay phones and vending machines.

KAUAI

YWCA Camp Sloggett ((808) 245-5959 FAX (808) 245-5961 E-MAIL kauaiyw @pixi.com WEB SITE www.pixi.com/ ~kauaiyw/, 3094 Elua Street, Lihue, is in Kokee State Park. It offers campsites, hostel accommodations and a lodge

Bikers ride through Parker Ranch on the Big Island.

(for groups of five or more). The lodge has a fireplace and kitchen.

Kahili Mountain Park Cabins ((808) 742-9921, Kahili Mountain Park, PO Box 298, Koloa, Kauai, off Highway 50 West, beyond mile marker seven, one mile (a kilometer and a half) inland on a dirt road, is operated by the Seventh-day Adventist Church. It offers cabinettes and cabins, some with private bathrooms and kitchens. Rates are based on double occupancy. Linen and kitchen supplies are provided.

MAUI

At the **Banana Beach Bungalow** TOLL-FREE (800) 846-7835, 310 North Market Street, Wailuku, Maui, amenities include a television room and the hostel organizes group outings. With separate men's and women's dormitories, **Maui North Shore Inn** ((808) 242-8999 TOLL-FREE (800) 647-6284 FAX (808) 244-5004 WEB SITE www .hostelhawaii.com/hostel-hawaii-maui.html, 2080 Vineyard Street, Wailuku, Maui, has laundry facilities, storage room for windsurfing equipment, a television room and a free safe for valuables.

MOLOKAI AND LANAI

On Molokai, the **Waialua Pavilion and Campground** ((808) 558-8150 FAX (808) 558-8520 E-MAIL vacate@aloha.net, HC-01 Box 780, Kaunakakai, offers the most

tranquil of settings right on the beach with kitchen and bathroom facilities. For information on other camping sites call the **Department of Homelands** ((808) 567-6104 or the **County of Maui** ((808) 553-3204.

On Lanai, camping is allowed in the backcountry and by Manele Bay; call ((808) 565-3982 for information and reservations.

BIG ISLAND

Arnott's Lodge and Hiking Adventures ((808) 969-7097 FAX (808) 961-9638 E-MAIL infor@arnottslodge.com WEB SITE www.arnottslodge.com, 98 Apapane Road, Hilo, has an all-you-can-eat barbecue Wednesday and Saturday, airport and town shuttle, hiking tours and laundry facilities. Also in Hilo is the **Wild Ginger Inn** ((808) 935-5556 TOLL-FREE (800) 882-1887 WEB SITE www .wildgingerinn.com, 100 Puueo Street, which offers Hawaiian-style shared or private accommodation with Internet access, satellite television, hiking trips, weekly barbecue, laundry and safety deposit boxes.

Pineapple Park ((808) 968-8170 TOLL-FREE (877) 865-2266 E-MAIL park@aloha.net WEB SITE www.pineapple-park.com, PO Box 5844, Hilo, located near Volcanoes National Park, is a bed-and-breakfast facility with a choice of bunks or private rooms. The hostel has barbecues, laundry, and a pool table, and offers tours and bike rentals. **Hostelling International, Holo Holo Inn** ((808) 967-7950 FAX (808) 967-8025 E-MAIL holoholo @interpac.net WEB SITE www.enable.org/ holoholo, 19-4036 Kalani Honua Road, PO Box 784, Volcano, is a mile (one and a half kilometers) from Volcanoes National Park. Ten beds are available here, and laundry facilities.

Hotel Honokaa Club ((808) 775-0678 TOLL-FREE (800) 808-0678 WEB SITE www .home1.gte.net/honokaac, PO Box 247, Honokaa, has been around since 1908 and offers hostel accommodation in dorms or private rooms. Hotel rooms include continental breakfast, with linen provided.

Living It Up

EXCEPTIONAL HOTELS

Every island in Hawaii has a few world-class hotels that capture the essence of the tropics. Several are one-of-a-kind pleasure palaces, unencumbered by brand names. On **Oahu**, the enduring standout is the gracious **Halekulani Hotel**, once a private residence at the edge of Waikiki. The hotel's cool white decor reflects a sense of refreshing simplicity that eases guests into submission. Many of the staff members have been serving the same clientele for over a dozen years, giving long-timers the sense of returning to a beloved

vacation home each time they enter the lobby, bow their heads to receive a ginger lei, and are escorted to their rooms. The restaurants are among the island's best, and though the grounds are private they sit beside Hawaii's most exciting stretch of sand.

The west side of Oahu is a land of raw beauty, where a rugged stretch of coastline has been transformed into an elegant oasis. Amid a larger compound of golf courses and private villas, the **J.W. Marriott Ihilani Resort and Spa** is a quick car ride away from Honolulu, yet boasts

The gardens of the Kauai Marriott OPPOSITE and the Hyatt Regency at Poipu ABOVE have regained their lush splendor after being battered by Hurricane Iniki in 1992.

all the trappings of a private island. The spa is arguably the finest on the islands, offering scrubs, wraps, massages, and beauty treatments that leave clients with a calm, healthy glow. On the east side, the **Kahala Mandarin Oriental** is a remake of a 1960s Hollywood hangout replete with tasteful antiques and a dolphin lagoon.

Oahu's landmark historic hotels — the **Sheraton Moana Surfrider** and the **Royal Hawaiian** — suffer from an overabundance of attention. They can hardly be called peaceful hideaways, given their location at the center of Waikiki. But a night in each is irresistible if you truly love Hawaii and have an active imagination. Both hotels were built in the early 1900s, when wealthy travelers arrived on steamships. The original buildings have a regal style, somewhat impaired by the crowds of tourists clad in shorts and loud shirts streaming through the lobbies. But when you're standing on a balcony as the strains of a slack-key guitar fade in the plumeria-scented air, the urge to don a ball gown or tuxedo is nearly overwhelming.

Kauai is beloved for its natural attributes, which only enhance the island's best resorts. A river runs through the **Hyatt Regency Kauai**, mimicking nature with man-made waterfalls and hidden ponds beside lap pools. It may seem silly to choose a hotel strictly for its swimming pool, but this one is a water-baby's dream, complete with a thrilling water slide. The rooms and restaurants are great as well, offering a sense of tropical ease. At the opposite end of the luxury spectrum is the opulent **Princeville Resort** on Kauai's North Shore. Set like a Greco-Roman mansion above Hanalei Bay, the hotel exudes excess. An abundance of black, white and pink marble gleams in the light of chandeliers; Italian antiques provide a precious touch. At yet another extreme, the **Waimea Plantation Cottages** sit beneath the road to Waimea Canyon on Kauai's more rustic south shore. Once part of a sugar cane plantation, the

property sits by the ocean yet feels like a country hideaway, with lots of rattan, Hawaiian quilts, and ceiling fans.

If ever an island were deliberately designed for romance, it would emulate **Maui**. In fact, lonely singles may want to stay away from the island's best hotels where it seems dozens of weddings take place every day. Brides and grooms gravitate to Wailea where they wed in tasteful surroundings at the subdued **Four Seasons Maui** and the Mediterranean-style **Kea Lani** — or go all out and book a gazebo at the overwhelming **Grand Wailea Resort and Spa**. Hotel connoisseurs either love or hate this ornate, overgrown palace. Spa devotees claim its one of the best.

Far more remote and serene, the **Heavenly Hana Inn** inspires those seeking a peaceful, natural retreat on the island's wild side. Golf is one of the main draws in the Kaanapali region, where the stately **Hyatt Regency**, **Marriott**, **Westin**, and **Sheraton** compete for upscale travelers with a bounty of luxurious amenities. The Hyatt Regency stands out for its oceanfront spa Moana and isolated hilltop setting near a forested ancient Hawaiian burial ground. The sacred sites are roped off, but there are tours with excellent guides who impart a healthy dose of respect for their ancestors.

On **Molokai**, the **Molokai Ranch Lodge** with its huge fireplace and pastoral views evokes the spirit of this unusual island. On **Lanai**, the **Lodge at Koele** is most of the most lauded hotels in Hawaii as much for its individuality as its excellence. The real charm of staying here is the feeling of being in an old-fashioned hunting lodge in a pine forest — an unusual occurrence in tropical Hawaii. The grounds are graced with a large pond, a greenhouse filled with orchids, and a magnificent golf course in the island's high country. The lodge's Great Hall, Library, Dining Room, and Tea Room all evoke the gentility of a royal European residence. Though less stunning, the **Manele Bay Hotel** is the perfect counterpoint to the Lodge, offering the beach side version of isolated luxury.

The **Big Island** is blessed with a surfeit of one-of-a-kind hotels that echo the best of Hawaii. Even those that carry brand names have a flavor all their own, as evidenced by the **Four Seasons Resort Hualalai**. New in 1996, the hotel rises unobtrusively from a field of black lava in an oasis of golf greens, swimming pools, and coconut groves. The staff is so friendly guests return time and again because they feel at home in this peaceful setting where tiki torches glow all night long outside private lanais. The subdued **Kona Village Resort** offers as setting as close to traditional Polynesian style as possible. The **Mauna Lani Bay Hotel and Bungalows** is set amid a nature preserve and Hawaiian fishponds at the edge of the beach and lagoons. In Hilo, the **Shipman House Bed and Breakfast** offers traditional Hawaiian hospitality in a historic house.

EXCEPTIONAL RESTAURANTS

Hawaii's chefs have created a cuisine and dining ambience that is unique to the islands. They combine Asian, French, Italian, and Hawaiian flavors and culinary techniques in an ever-changing

palette, spurred by competition and an eager, sophisticated audience. Yet Hawaii's fine restaurants are rarely formal; few require men to wear jackets and ties. But people do dress up in fine silk aloha shirts and slinky sundresses, and a sense of casual glamour prevails.

Oahu is blessed with an overabundance of excellent dining spots. One could eat lavishly every evening for a week. The Halekulani Hotel's **La Mer** is arguably the most elegant restaurant on all the islands; dinner is a multi-course affair lasting many hours. Another hotel restaurant, **Hoku's**, draws locals to the Mandarin Oriental, a favorite spot for celebrity sightings. George Mavrothalassitis, once La Mer's chef, now reigns over his own aptly named restaurant, **Chef Mavro**, where wine pairings enhance his signature seafood dishes. In the same neighborhood, the eponymous **Alan Wong's** continues to rival all contenders as the best and most exciting restaurant in Hawaii. Roy Yamaguchi, another brand-name chef with a loyal following,

OPPOSITE: Frothy fruit cocktails (with or without potent rum) are an essential part of the Hawaii experience. ABOVE: The Ritz Carlton Hotel at Kapalua.

directs the sometimes frenzied action at **Roy's**, where diners seem to feel the excitement brewing in the open kitchen. Chef Russell Siu holds forth at **3660 On the Rise**, a more subdued dining room.

Kauai's most famous chef, Jean-Marie Josselin, keeps right on cooking. His **A Pacific Café Kauai** is conveniently located in a shopping center midway between the north and south shores; easy access makes reservations essential. Like all Hawaii's famous chefs, Josselin prepares certain signature dishes that make ordering difficult for those of us who only stop by occasionally. Personally, I have to taste his *mahimahi* with a sesame-garlic crust every time I visit. Few places compare with his second location, the **Beach House**, for sunset dining. Locals would prefer tourists not know about **Casa di Amici** in Kilauea, where nouveau Italian dishes are served in a romantic garden.

Trendy **Maui** presents a challenge for creative chefs, who have to adapt to the whimsical attitudes of locals and frequent returnees. The current stars of the Lahaina dining scene are chef James McDonald's **Pacific 'O** and **I'O**, both offering innovative blends of fresh seafood and organic vegetables. At **Avalon**, Chef Mark Ellman spices up regional dishes with chilis and black been sauce. David Paul keeps the attention focused on his **Lahaina Grill** by changing his approach to lobster and lamb. At the **Plantation Inn** Chef Gerard Reversade sticks to expertly prepared escargots, foie gras, and rack of lamb. **Humuhumunuknukuapuaa** at the Grand Wailea Resort and Spa, is named after Hawaii's state fish — which fortunately does not appear on the menu. This is one place where you really feel like you're in Hawaii, thanks to its tropical ambience and Polynesian cuisine. At the **Haliimaile General Store**, Chef Beverly Gannon eschews the Asian influence of her peers and focuses on local cheeses, herbs, and shellfish in hearty helpings.

The **Formal Dining Room** at the Lodge at Koele on **Lanai** is one of the finest restaurants on the islands. Granted, the restaurant has the benefit of its surroundings in the handsome, exclusive Lodge. But the food is outstanding. Venison, lamb, and beef are prepared with unusual tropical fruit marinades — or simply and perfectly roasted or grilled for purists.

Hidden in the hills of the **Big Island** is the cozy restaurant at the **Kilauea Lodge**, where owner-chef Albert Jeyte delights in preparing local venison and rabbit. Down on the Kohala Coast, the **Canoe House** at the Mauna Lani Hotel offers *ahi* tempura and Kona lobster under the light of the moon, while **Roy's Waikoloa Bar and Grill** brings Roy Yamagichi's clever blends to the Big Island.

Family Fun

Hawaii is a kids' paradise: marine parks, the great volcano on the Big Island, horseback riding, helicopter excursions, and, of course, plenty of beach activities keep youngsters interested and happy and give families an ample choice of things to do together.

The island also excels in providing grown-ups and kids a break from each other, recognizing that big people and little ones don't always agree on what constitutes a fun time. Parents who want to take a break and play some golf or tour a museum can do so knowing that their children will be entertained and looked after. Almost every hotel in Hawaii, and certainly all the resorts, has excellent planned children's activities.

Children's programs offer everything from sports, kite flying and nature hikes to arts and crafts activities, such as lei making and coconut painting. There's also storytelling, an art at which the locals are quite accomplished. Children's activities are supervised by well-trained, accredited hotel staff. Most programs operate from 9 AM to 3 PM.

Oahu's Kahala Mandarin Oriental Hawaii offers the year-round "Keiki Club," while the Hilton Hawaiian Village boasts the "Rainbox Express": with a huge range of education and fun activities. On Kauai, check into the Kauai Marriott

Resort and Beach Club, the Hyatt Regency Resort and Spa, or, for a more modest alternative, the Holiday Inn SunSpree.

On Maui, the Ritz-Carlton Kapalua has a great kids' program, as does the Grand Wailea Resort and Spa which has the added benefit of an awesome pool area. For a more moderately priced establishment, try the Kahana Sunset, with its swimming beach, pool and large lawn area.

On Molokai, the number one recommendation would have to be the Molokai Ranch, due to the sheer range and standard of its activities.

The Big Island's elegant Kona Village Resort tenders custom-designed programs for tots to teenagers at no extra cost, while the Orchid and the Mauna Lani Bay in Kohala both offer kids' programs that include water sports, Hawaiian culture and other fun activities.

Beyond the hotels, there are numerous kid-friendly activities throughout Hawaii. All the islands are small enough for the whole family to experience a tremendous variety of scenery and activities in just

a few hours. For example, a tour of Maui's Upcountry can include a visit to the beach in Paia, the art galleries of Makawao, the Keiki (Children's) Petting Zoo in Kula, cowboy life at 'Ulupalakua Ranch and maybe even a horseback ride.

It may be a good idea to pack your sleeping bags, as there are several camping possibilities throughout the islands in national, state and county parks. Many parks also have cabins, but be sure to book these months in advance. For full details about camping in Hawaii, see THE GREAT OUTDOORS, page 23.

If you want someone else to plan your camping experience, several outfits will gladly oblige. On the Big Island, try Hawaii Pack and Paddle ((808) 328-8911 E-MAIL gokayak@kona.net WEB SITE www .hawaiipackandpaddle.com, 87-3187 Honu Moe Road, Captain Cook, which organizes trips combining kayaking, snorkeling and hiking.

A school of young boogie boarders makes a splash on Oahu, where calm waters in sheltered bays provide a safe place for family water sports.

Rural ranching is alive and well on the Big Island, with many opportunities to experience the *paniolo* (cowboy) lifestyle. The Hawaii Island Economic Board ((808) 966-5416 FAX (808) 966-6792 WEB SITE www .rodeohawaii.com, 200 Kanoelehua Avenue, suite 103, Hilo, publishes a free brochure on where you can meet today's *paniolos* as well as information on ranches, outfitters, activities, shops and more.

The new Maui Ocean Center offers up a 650,000 gallon (2.5-million-liter) ocean aquarium for the whole family

to gawk at, while the Lahaina-Kaanapali and Pacific Railroad (also known as the Sugar Cane Train) chugs from its depot just above Lahaina to Kaanapali and returns in about half an hour. And in the evening, take them to the Hyatt Regency Maui ((808) 661-1234, 200 Nohea Kai Drive, for the one-hour star search program with the world's first recreational computer-driven telescope.

One of Hawaii's top family-oriented activities is surely a tour with the Molokai Mule Ride ((808) 567-6088 TOLL-FREE (800) 567-7550 WEB SITE www.muleride.com, PO Box 200, Kualapuu 96757.

On Oahu, the kids will enjoy a trip to the state's only water theme park, Hawaiian Waters Adventure Park ((808) 945-3928 WEB SITE www .HawaiianWaters.com, 400 Farrington Highway, Kapolei. This park, which opened in 1999, is a half hour from Waikiki and offers up a full 25 acres (10 hectares) of rides and slides, including the Cliffhanger, which free-falls down six stories.

It may be a bit touristy, but the kids will still have fun and probably learn something about Hawaii's heritage at the Polynesian Cultural Center WEB SITE www.polynesia.com, 53-370 Kamehameha Highway, Laie, Oahu. Activities range from face painting to games played by Polynesian and Melanesian children.

Kids visiting the Kokee Natural History Museum ((808) 335-9975 E-MAIL kokee@ aloha.net, Kekaha, Kauai 96752, can ask for a copy of a treasure hunt map and quiz each other on the museum exhibits. During the summer months, the museum has "Wonder Walks" each Sunday which teach kids about the flora, fauna, history and legends of the island.

For the ultimate Hawaiian experience, how about enrolling the whole family in a surf school? Try Margo Oberg's School of Surfing ((808) 742-8019, Nuku Moi Surf Shop, Poipu, Kauai. A seven-time world champion, Margo guarantees that by the end of the lesson, you'll all be able to stand and catch a wave.

Cultural Kicks

For its size and remoteness, Hawaii has an extraordinary diversity of cultural and art exhibits at excellent museums on almost every island. From the ancient to the modern, there's something for everyone with an appreciation for beauty and learning.

OAHU

The **Bishop Museum and Planetarium** ((808) 847-3511, 1525 Bernice Street, Honolulu, has an international reputation as one of the world's finest museums on Hawaiian and Polynesian art, culture and history. On display are ancient Hawaiian feather cloaks, weapons, clothing, koa calabashes and jewelry. The first Sunday of every month is Family Sunday, a cultural celebration with Hawaiian entertainment, food, displays and demonstrations. From time to time the museum also has special interactive exhibitions.

The museum's departments include the Gressit Center for Research in Entomology; the Herbarium Pacificum, with 500,000 Pacific Basin plant specimens; and, as can be expected in this volcanic and tectonic setting, an important geology section. In addition, the Planetarium ((808) 847-8201 offers a variety of entertaining and educational programs. The Journey By Starlight program is presented daily at 11:30 AM, 1:30 PM and every Friday and Saturday evening at 7 PM. On the first Monday of each month at 7 PM the museum presents The Sky Tonight. Reservations are recommended for evening shows and can be made by calling during business hours. At the conclusion of all evening programs, the museum observatory is open to the public for exciting views of the universe.

The **Contemporary Museum** ((808) 526-1322, 2411 Makiki Heights Drive, Honolulu, has one of the loveliest settings of any of the islands' many fine museums. Formerly the private residence

of Alice Cooke Spalding, the museum sits in the midst of three and a half acres (one and a half hectares) of magnificent gardens, with superb views of the city and the ocean. Initially designed as a retreat in which to meditate and experience the harmony of nature, the gardens provide a natural setting for works of art and a quiet place for contemplation. The museum consists of five galleries as well as the Milton Cades Pavilion. Selections from the museum's permanent collection are shown in the exhibition schedule. Highlights of this collection are David Hockney's works inspired by the Ravel opera *L'Enfant et les Sortilèges* (The Child and the Bewitched). Free garden tours are offered by appointment. The museum also has a café and a gift shop.

Much of Hawaii's history is tied to the ocean. It has its roots in the great voyages of exploration by the early Polynesians, and has depended for generations on shipping. The **Hawaii Maritime Center** ((808) 536-6373, Pier 7,

OPPOSITE TOP: Kukui nut necklace adorns young dancer. BOTTOM: The sounds of the ukulele are the sounds of the islands. ABOVE: Hula dancer… all sensuous grace.

Honolulu Harbor, Honolulu, presents an exciting guided tour through all the different eras in Hawaii's maritime development. Fifty displays focus on a variety of themes — from the first Polynesians to land here in their canoes to the boisterous whalers who made Hawaii the center of the whaling industry, to the legends of surfing, and finally to the service provided by ocean liners since the 1930s. Among the major attractions are the *Falls of Clyde*, the last four-masted, fully rigged vessel in the world, and the Polynesian voyaging canoe, *Hokulea*, that retraced the steps of the original voyaging groups which discovered these islands centuries ago. An admission fee is charged.

Dedicated in 1927, the **Honolulu Academy of the Arts** ((808) 532-8701, 900 South Beretania Street, Honolulu, is noted for its fine collection of Asian and Pacific art as well as American and European masterpieces. Its regular program of exhibitions, films, concerts and educational and community activities make it the most comprehensive art center in the islands. An admission fee is charged.

One of the city's great attractions is also a place of tragedy. The **Arizona Memorial** ((808) 422-0561, 1 Arizona Memorial Drive, Pearl City, marks the watery grave of 1,102 officers and enlisted men who died in the Japanese attack on Pearl Harbor on December 7, 1941. The huge American battleship sank five minutes after being hit, entombing almost its entire crew. The white monument with its smooth, clean lines was designed by local architect Alfred Preis and is today a national shrine. From 8 AM to 3 PM, navy launches shuttle tourists from the shore to the memorial. Entrance to the site is about half a mile (just under one kilometer) east of Aloha Stadium on Highway 90. An admission fee is charged.

The **USS Bowfin Submarine Museum and Park** ((808) 423-1341, USS Arizona Memorial Visitor Center, Pearl Harbor, is adjacent to the USS Arizona Memorial Visitor Center at Pearl Harbor. The *Bowfin*

is a World War II submarine that was launched on December 7, 1942, and completed nine successful war patrols. Opened to the public in 1981, it was designated a National Historic Landmark by the Department of the Interior in 1986. Visitors to Bowfin Park are given a portable cassette player that narrates their tour as they explore this historic submarine, imagining life on board for the 80-man crew. In addition to the submarine tour, there is a 10,000-sq-ft (929-sq-m) museum whose exhibits include an impressive collection of submarine-related artifacts such as submarine weapon systems, original recruiting posters, photographs, paintings, and detailed submarine models, all illustrating the history of the United States Submarine Service. New exhibits include a Poseidon C-3 missile that allows visitors to examine the inner workings of a missile. It is the only one of its kind on public display. A mini-theater screens submarine-related videos. In Bowfin Park stands a public memorial honoring the 52 American submarines and the more than 3,500 submariners lost during World War II. The park is open daily from 8 AM to 5 PM and the last tour of the submarine begins at 4:30 PM. Children under the age of four are not permitted on the submarine for safety reasons, but are allowed to tour the museum and mini-theater at no charge. The fee for the submarine and museum tour is $8 for adults and $3 for children ages 4 to 12.

KAUAI

At the **Kauai Museum** ((808) 245-6931, 4428 Rice Street, Lihue, the culture and history of Kauai unfold in the museum's artistic, geological and ethnic displays, providing insights into the island's social and natural history. Kauai was once home to the most mysterious tribes from central Polynesia, the menehune, who inhabited Kauai and none of the other Hawaiian islands. The menehune legend is documented at the Kauai Museum, along with the arrival in 1778 of British Captain James Cook, which started an

era of irrevocable cultural and social change for the island. An admission fee is charged.

Grove Farm Homestead Museum ((808) 245-3202, 4050 Nawiliwili Road, Lihue, is the former house of George Wilcox, son of missionaries and founder of one of Kauai's largest sugar plantations. Touring this gracious residence and its 80-acre (32-hectare) garden recalls life on a nineteenth-century sugar plantation, and provides a reminder of how the birth of the sugar industry changed Kauai. An admission fee is charged.

MAUI
The **Alexander and Baldwin Sugar Museum** ((808) 871-8058, 3957 Hansen Road, in a former sugar superintendent's house, is a historic, award-winning museum exhibiting photographs, artifacts and a working model of sugar processing machinery. The museum is located next to Hawaii's largest sugar mill. The museum is open daily from mid-June to the end of August; an admission fee is charged.

The **Hale Kohola Whale Museum** ((808) 661-9918, Whalers Village, 2435 Kaanapali Parkway, Lahaina,

is devoted to the evolution of the humpback whale and features "touch and see" displays — computer terminals where visitors may punch up whale facts, a theater showing videos on whale migratory patterns, and impressive whale models, including a 16-ft (five-meter) model of the skeleton of a baby humpback.

The compact, quaint **Hana Cultural Center** ((808) 248-8622 WEB SITE www.planet-hawaii.com/hana, 4974 Uakea Road, Hana, concentrates on telling the story of the Hana Coast. Its displays include rare Hawaiian artifacts such as a 100-year-old fishing net, baskets, quilts, and shells as well as photographs and bottle collections. The latest addition to the museum complex is Kauhale O Hana, an authentic Hawaiian Living Complex complete with ethnobotanical gardens. There is no admission fee, but donations are accepted.

Hui Noeau Visual Arts Center ((808) 572-6560, 2841 Baldwin Avenue, Makawao, occupies the historic upcountry estate designed in 1917

A hula dancer communes with nature.

by internationally-acclaimed Hawaii architect C.W. Dickey for the Baldwin family, who made their money in sugar. The center is set amidst 12 acres (five hectares) of beautiful garden on the cool slopes of upcountry Maui. Along with art and craft classes, Hui Noeau provides visiting artists' workshops and outreach programs for the community and courses for teachers. Visitors to the center will often see a printmaker at work in the print studio, and several potters at their wheels in the open-air ceramics area.

Situated at the foot of dramatic Lao Valley overlooking Kahului Bay is the **Maui Arts and Cultural Center** ((808) 242-7469, Maui Central Plaza, PO Box 338, Kahului, Hawaii's first and finest comprehensive arts facility. The center's 12-acre (five-hectare) site in central Maui is the island's hub, a gathering place for a broad range of artistic and social events. The $56 million complex features two theaters, an outdoor amphitheater and a gallery. Also featured is an outdoor *pa hula*, a rock-faced mound dedicated to Hawaiian culture. Gracious arcades, classrooms, dance studios and a grassy courtyard are among the creative spaces where public and private events are held. Some of the entertainment industry's biggest stars have performed to sold-out audiences at the center. Cultural events such as the center's *Tales of Maui*, which chronicles the legend of the demigod Maui in chant and in hula, and the premiere of *Holo Mai Pele*, a hula epic performed in its entirety for the first time in 200 years, are also on the list of sold-out shows.

MOLOKAI

Guided and self-guided tours are available at the historic **R.W. Meyer Sugar Mill Museum and Cultural Center** ((808) 567-6436, PO Box 986, Kaunakakai, Molokai, which now serves as both a research center and a museum housing artifacts collected by the pioneering Meyer family. An admission fee is charged.

LANAI

Lanai's **Visiting Artist Program** ((808) 548-3700 TOLL-FREE (800) 321-4666 is one of the finest programs on culture and the arts in the islands. Introduced in 1993, the Visiting Artist Program brings nationally renowned writers, musicians, filmmakers, artists and chefs to the two resort hotels. Locals and visitors meet and mingle with the talent during performances, gourmet meals, and informal chats in the hotels' libraries and lounges.

BIG ISLAND

The **Lyman Mission House Memorial Museum** ((808) 935-5021 E-MAIL lymanwks @interpac.net, 276 Haili Street, Hilo, was built in 1839 for the first Christian missionaries in Hilo. In 1973 an adjacent museum was constructed to showcase rare Hawaiian artifacts. An admission fee is charged.

The **Parker Ranch Visitor Center and Museum** ((808) 885-7655, PO Box 458, Kamuela, documents the history of the Parker family and the largest individually owned ranch in the United States through displays, photographs, memorabilia and a 15-minute video. Tours are given at nearby Puupelu and a replica of Mana, the Parker family houses. An admission fee is charged.

LEFT: The Bishop Museum is internationally recognized as a leading museum on Polynesian art and culture. ABOVE: The Waimea Plantation Festival features children's activities.

Shop till You Drop

Hawaii is a haven for serious shoppers. There are enough malls on Oahu alone to send the fashion conscious into a spending frenzy. All the designer labels are represented in chic boutiques. But you might as well be in Miami or Vegas if you spend all your time at the malls. Hawaii's best shops on are the streets of small towns, along rural highways, and in museums and hotels.

The most popular purchase may well be a Hawaiian button-down shirt in a tropical pattern, called an **aloha shirt** on the islands. The majority of shirts seen on tourists are truly tacky — meant to be worn on vacation and shoved in a dark corner once home. Fragile antique shirts in the fabrics of the 1930s and 1940s are collector's items, and can set you back a few thousand dollars. The best investment is a new silk or rayon shirt in a vintage design. You can easily spend $80 on one of these soft, sensual works of art, but you'll wear it until it falls apart. The same can be said for sundresses, sarongs, and scarves. Avanti Fashion on Oahu has long been the leader in producing irresistible tropical clothing, and the line is sold in shops on other islands. Sig Zane Designs in Hilo on the Big Island takes Hawaiiana to a higher level with its aloha wear, bed coverings, and jewelry and household adornments.

Clothing, **furnishings**, **fabrics**, and **knick-knacks** from the days when the Matson Line's steamships brought wealthy tourists to Hawaii are all the rage among locals and visitors alike. You can't help but grin at the hula-girl lamps and salt shakers, pineapple-print tablecloths, and kitsch lampshades at shops specializing in Hawaiiana. Check out Yellowfish Trading Company and Bambulei if you're on Kauai.

Some of the finest collections of **Hawaiian folk art** are on display in museum shops. On Oahu, the Bishop Museum's gift store displays hand-stitched Hawaiian quilts, bone and woodcarvings, and shell leis, along with old Waikiki postcards and photo reproductions. The Kauai Museum features a gorgeous array of shell leis from Niihau, the last bastion of traditional Hawaiian life. Delicate Niihau leis made with tiny shells are extremely expensive; particularly intricate ones can cost $2,000.

As islanders become more and more immersed in Hawaiian traditions they are taking traditional folk arts and textiles in exciting directions. Native Books and Beautiful Things on Oahu features quilts, paintings, jewelry and clothing made by Hawaiian artists, as do several of the shops in the Aloha Tower Marketplace. The Maui Crafts Guild and the Hana Coast Gallery, both on Maui, specialize in the works of local folk artists. Wood carvers find unlimited inspiration in their surroundings, and have a fine selection of local woods — koa, monkey pod, mango — to shape into smooth bowls and whale sculptures. Some of the finest work is on view at Waipio Valley Artworks on the Big Island.

Hawaiian **heirloom jewelry** is based on jewelry favored during the monarchy period. Designers work in gold and silver, etching floral patterns and names onto pendants, bracelets, earrings and charms. Heirloom jewelry is expensive, but it is elegant and a reminder of Hawaii's royal past.

The other jewelry much prized by local residents is made from the beautiful Niihau shells — tiny seashells collected from the beaches of the equally tiny island of that sits off the coast of Kauai. Niihau shell jewelry is designed and made by the women of this island, most of which is off-limits to visitors.

There was a time when Hawaii produced some remarkable jewelry fashioned out of whalebone, known as scrimshaw. But since the whale became an endangered species, artisans, such as those on Molokai, have turned to carving on deer horn, which seems to be a good substitute. During the season, deer drop their antlers, and Molokai carvers go and collect them from around the kiawe groves. The horn is carved and made into pendants for both men and women.

Weekly **farmer's markets** are popular on most islands, and the variety of produce available is astounding. Get in the habit of stopping by these markets for snacks and souvenirs. The **Aloha Flea Market** at Aloha Stadium on Oahu is the ultimate shopping event. Sometimes as many as a thousand vendors hawk everything from eelskin wear to leather goods, seashells, baskets, flowers, clothing and exotic produce. Scan supermarket shelves for edible souvenirs including

OPPOSITE: Shells and coral make lovely necklaces and plant hangers. LEFT: Handpainted coconuts make playful and unique souvenirs. ABOVE: Brilliant blossoms spill out of a farmer's market stall.

Hawaiian coffee, macadamia nuts, and jams, relishes, and chutneys made with pineapples, papayas, mangoes, and bananas.

My favorite Hawaii souvenir is the **lei** — I always buy at least one just before I head home and hang it near my bed. One of the best flower markets on the islands edges the parking lot of the Honolulu airport. Tour guides pick up carnation and plumeria leis by the dozens as they head into the airport to meet their latest group; locals are more particular, choosing flowers and styles to suit the occasion. I tend toward the most fragrant flowers — tuberose, ginger, plumeria — so the scents of Hawaii linger long after I'm home. The single best place to learn about leis and tropical flowers is Maunakea Street in Oahu's Chinatown, where ladies string flowers all day long beside rows of refrigerated cases packed with blossoms. I also enjoy sending Hawaiian flowers to friends, choosing from sprays of orchid, spiky birds of paradise, and bizarre antherium and ginger plumes. Floral shops and nurseries are particularly abundant in the high country of Maui and the Big Island and all over Kauai, "the Garden Isle." Many are pros at shipping flowers anywhere in the world. Soaps, shampoos and lotions scented with the perfumes of flowers and tropical fruits provide pleasant memories as well.

Short Breaks

If you only have a few days in Hawaii, make the most of it by concentrating on one specific area — perhaps even one resort. Every island has hotels that provide instant immersion into Hawaiian sensations. Two islands — Lanai and Molokai — are perfect for short escapes, as *kamaains* (longtime residents) know. Those who live on sun-drenched beaches delight in spending a few nights at the Lodge at Koele on Lanai. City dwellers seek relief by camping on Molokai. Specific areas of the other islands offer a complete retreat in just a few days.

If you're determined to rush about and see all you can, the three-day itineraries below allow you to explore the islands without running yourself ragged.

OAHU

Three days on Oahu should let you see much of the island. On day one, drive over the Pali Highway to the Pali Lookout. Take in the great view of the

windward coast. Resume your journey down the Pali Highway to Kailua. Pick up something to eat in Kailua town, and proceed to beautiful Lanikai Beach. Early in the afternoon, set off along Highway 72 going south and drive through the town of Waimanalo and up the cliffs to Hanauma Bay. Spend the rest of the afternoon here — it's one of the finest marine sanctuaries in the world. End the day by dining on the terrace of Roy's Restaurant. The sunset, looking across the bay to Diamond Head, is fabulous.

Make day two of your Oahu stay a cultural one. Spend the morning at the Arizona Memorial, and then visit one of the Pacific's great museums, the Bishop Museum at 1525 Bernice Street. Drive to the waterfront for cocktails at Gordon Biersch Brewery and Restaurant in the Aloha Tower Marketplace.

Confine day three to visiting the North Shore. You may want to start very early. To get there quickly, drive the Kamehameha Highway through the interior to Haleiwa, and start your day in typical Hawaiian style with a shaved ice at the M. Matsumoto Store. Wander through Haleiwa's shops and the Surf Museum, then lunch on a juicy burger at Kua Aina Sandwich. Cruise east along the shoreline to Waimea Bay and watch the big rollers pound the shores. Head a little further down the coast to Sunset Beach and swim and watch the surfers attack the famous Banzai Pipeline. Spend the afternoon at the Polynesian Cultural Center. You can tour this fine cultural center at your leisure and dine and watch the evening Polynesian show here.

KAUAI

If you're going to Kauai and have only three days to spare, find accommodation at Poipu on the island's southern shores. It's roughly halfway between the spectacular north shore and its lovely beaches, and the grandeur of Kokee State Park and Waimea Canyon. If you have the spirit of adventure, join a boating

OPPOSITE: For artists the islands offer endless inspiration. ABOVE: The rolling range of the Big Island's Parker Ranch.

expedition to the magnificent sea cliffs and caves of the Na Pali Coast. This is an all-day event, available only in the summer. For a different dining experience, try Kilohana Plantation.

On day two travel along the southern shoreline (Highway 50, going west) and then catch Highway 55 to Highway 550 into the hills to Waimea Canyon and Kokee State Park. Spend the day in the park exploring the lush forests and the canyon from many different perspectives. Return to Poipu.

On the third day, plan a full-day trip to the northern shore via the eastern route (Highway 50 to 56). This will take you through the many little picturesque towns of Kauai all the way to the fabulous Princeville Resort, and then on to the Na Pali Coast State Park, where the road ends.

MAUI

Three days on Maui could be turned into an exciting adventure — depending of course on the time of the year. If you happen to be visiting any time between October and April, then you have an extraordinary range of choice. Book a hotel or condominium on Maui's south or west shore. Swim or snorkel in the ocean's clear waters in the morning, but make sure you spend the afternoon whale watching. This is the season when the humpbacks come into the channel between Maui and its neighboring islands to spend the winter months.

The next day, cruise upcountry Maui, checking out the coastal town of Paia en route. Check into Kula Lodge or Silver Cloud Upcountry Ranch (a bed and breakfast in the cool hills on the slope of Haleakala). Dine at Kula Lodge, or in one of the many fine restaurants in the cowboy town of Makawao. Rise early on the third day, about 4:30 AM, and drive to the summit of Haleakala to watch the sun rise over the great crater. It's an experience you won't forget. After coming down the mountain, spend the day at the beach in Kihei before setting off for the airport.

BIG ISLAND

Our number one destination for a short trip is the Big Island, including a visit to Hawaii Volcanoes National Park. Make your bookings for accommodation and car rental in advance. Plan to fly to Hilo and pick up a car there, and arrange to drop the car at Kona on the western side of the island. It will probably cost you more to do this, but it pays for itself in time saved and convenience.

Three days is sufficient to see the highlights of the Big Island. First, book lodgings at Kilauea Lodge or Volcano

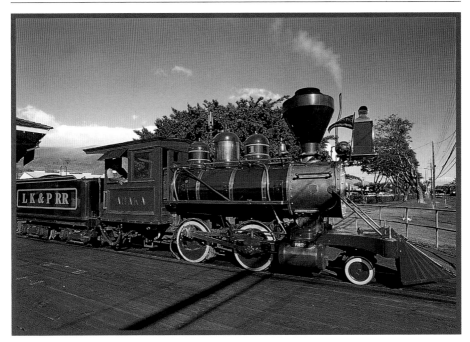

House in Volcanoes National Park; next, book accommodation in the town of Waimea (or Kamuela, as it is otherwise known). Finally, make a booking for accommodation on the Kona Coast at one of the resorts in the town of Kailua-Kona. Fly into Hilo in the morning and pick up your car. Drive to Volcanoes National Park (it's about 40 minutes from the airport). The park is huge. Tour it at your leisure for the entire day, then check in at your accommodation in the late evening. Dine at Kilauea Lodge.

The next morning, start early and take a leisurely drive to the black sand beach at Punaluu and watch the turtles at play. Retrace your steps and make your way back to Hilo. Have lunch there, explore Hilo town, and then proceed along the Hamakua Coast Road (Highway 19, going north). This is a beautiful drive. Take the scenic route, which is clearly marked. It leaves the main highway for several miles and wanders along backroads, hugging the coast, with dramatic views of forests and ocean. After getting back on the highway, your next diversion should be to Waipio Valley — The Valley of the King. Exit Highway 19 onto Highway 240 following it until it ends

at the Waipio Valley Lookout. Gradually make your way back to the Hamakua Coast Road and on to Waimea. There are several excellent restaurants in this small town.

On the third day, again, start early and head off along Highway 250 through rich pastureland and quaint towns to the Pololu Valley Lookout, near the northernmost tip of the island. From here you can look into one of those lovely, mysterious Hawaiian valleys. On the way back, catch Highway 270 and travel through the town of Kawaihae and then along the Kona Coast. Stop in and check out some of the superb resorts along this coast. Plan to have lunch at one of the hotels. If you have kids with you, the Hilton Waikoloa Village is fun. Take a dip in the hotel's huge pool or watch the dolphin show before your lunch break. Proceed to Kona International Airport, check in your rental car and catch the flight back.

OPPOSITE: Sugar machinery, dying relic of a once thriving industry. LEFT: An Atlantic bottlenose dolphin is given a birthday party at the annual Dolphin Days festivities. ABOVE: Maui's sugar train is now a tourist attraction.

Festive Flings

HULA FESTIVALS

The chant floats eerily over the hush of the enormous crater. It's an invocation to Pele, the deity of the volcano. Dancers lining the rim of Halemaumau at the Kilauea Caldera slip into motion. The chant resonates in the early morning air. Wisps of sulfur rise lazily from the crater floor. As quickly as it begins, the tribute to the fire goddess is over. One *halau* (school) leaves. Not long afterwards, another shows up. The ritual is repeated.

It's April on the east side of the **Big Island**, and these annual tributes to Pele signify the approach of the **Merrie Monarch Hula Festival** at the 5,000-seat Edith Kanakaole Tennis Stadium in Hilo. The woman who first conceived of such a festival, and remains its driving force, is Dottie Thompson. Her objective was simply this: "To gather the best hula dancers from all the islands, revive the arts and create a performance that is a rite, a celebration… and a statement about Hawaii and its people."

Thompson has succeeded beyond her wildest dreams. Her people have heeded the call, and they gather each year in the quaint capital of the island in an exuberant celebration that has made the Merrie Monarch — named in honor of King David Kalakaua — one of the world's great pageants. The week-long festival begins with performing arts celebrations, arts and craft shows and culminates in two nights of friendly but fierce competition among the *halau*. Highlights of the festival take place on its last two nights with the *kahiko* (ancient) and *awana* (modern) competitions. For more information call ((808) 935-9168.

Unlike the Merrie Monarch, the **Molokai Ka Hula Piko** is not a competition. It is purely a celebration of hula on the island that claims to be its birthplace. The Molokai Ka Hula Piko began in 1991 and has turned into a week-long event that takes place in May at Papohaku Beach Park at Kaluakoi.

It features art exhibits, craft fairs, lectures on Molokai's history, and Hawaiian story telling. It ends with a long day of music and dance featuring *halau* from around the state, as well as teams of dancers from other parts of the world, such as Japan. At the heart of all this activity is *kumu hula* John Kaimikaua, of Halau Hula 'O Kukunaokala, an imposing figure of a man. Like Thompson, he has become the inspiration for Ka Hula Piko. Visitors to this event are growing in numbers, and accommodation is becoming tight, so book both transportation and accommodation early. For information call ((808) 553-3876.

Every year, on the third Saturday in July, hula aficionados flock to Moanalua Gardens on Oahu to see the **Prince Lot Hula Festival** ((808) 839-5334. Each year has a different theme relating to the traditions of Moanalua. The Prince Lot Hula Festival is not a competition. Hula *halau* are invited to participate on the earthen mound stage, in the open air under stately trees — the perfect setting for an event of such cultural significance. The festival provides an opportunity for *kumu hula* throughout the islands to demonstrate their skills in *hula kahiko* and *hula awana*. The hula mound on which the dancers perform is named after Kamaipuupaa, a favorite female *kahuna* (priestess) in Lot's household.

The **Queen Liluokalani Keiki Hula Competition** ((808) 521-6905, named in honor of a much beloved monarch, attracts children, or *keikis*, aged 6 to 12. It is not uncommon for over 500 of these youngsters from over two dozen *halau* to perform at this festival.

CALENDAR OF EVENTS

JANUARY

Ka Molokai Makahiki ((808) 553-3673, Kaunakakai Baseball Park, Molokai, celebrates the Makahiki season, a time of peace and celebration of Hawaiian heritage. Festivities include traditional

Actors portraying the royal court march in the King Kamehameha Day parade.

Hawaiian games, Hawaiian craft, food, and entertainment from local music groups.

Hula Bowl TOLL-FREE (888) 716-4852, War Memorial Stadium, Wailuku, Maui, takes place on the third weekend of January and features an all-star game with America's top college football players.

The annual **Keiki Fun Run** ((808) 246-9090, in Kilohana in Lihue has a one-mile (one-and-a-half-kilometer) run for ages 6 to 10 and two miles (three kilometers) for ages 11 to 16.

Ala Wai Challenge ((808) 923-1802, Ala Wai Park in Waikiki, Oahu, is an all-day affair with events including ancient games (such as *oo ihe* — pear throwing at a target), an outrigger canoe race and a tug of war.

Whales Alive ((808) 874-8000, Four Season's Resort, Wailea, Maui, is an international forum where experts discuss whale watching excursions, entertainment, social functions and art exhibits.

Aloha State Square and Round Dance Festival ((808) 456-8465 WEB SITE www.inix.com/squaredancehawaii, is seven days of dancing and workshops

in Oahu with 500 dancers from the United States and elsewhere participating.

The world's best female bodyboarders compete at the **Extreme Bodyboard Series** ((808) 638-1149, Pipeline, North Shore, Oahu. This event includes open divisions in drop knee, air show and stand-up. Men compete at the same location in the **Pipeline Body Surfing Classic** ((808) 638-8825.

FEBRUARY

The annual running of the 134-mile (216-km) **Oahu Perimeter Relay** ((808) 486-2692 starts at Kapiolani Park, Oahu.

One of the largest Big Island attractions of the year is the start of the rodeo season, which traditionally begins at the **Waikoloa Stables** on what once was Parker Ranch land. The rodeo opens the Hawaii Rodeo Association's schedule of seven sanctioned events on the Big Island, Maui and Kauai. The **Great Waikoloa Rodeo** attracts the finest *paniolos* (cowboys) in the region, who compete in a program of events ranging from bull riding, steer undecorating and *poo wai u*, an event unique to Hawaiian rodeos in which *paniolos* display the technique they use to rope and tie cattle in the mountains.

The **Waimea Cherry Blossom Heritage Festival** ((808) 885-3633 takes place on the Big Island at historic Waimea Church Row Park. The festival celebrates Japan's Hanami, which is the viewing of the flowers during spring. It presents the history of the cherry trees, a tea ceremony, cherry pie and ice cream tasting, mochi-tsuki demonstration, bonsai, oriental arts and crafts, entertainment and distribution of cherry trees for planting in the Waimea area. On Kauai, the **Waimea Town Celebration** ((808) 338-9957 is a party and parade celebrating the Hawaiian and multi-ethnic history of the town where Captain Cook first set foot in Hawaii. Food booths, games, entertainment as well as foot, canoe and bike races make up the day and evening.

Whales are celebrated in Wailea during the annual **Whale Week of Maui** ((808) 879-8860. Events include a parade, regatta and a day of fun and celebration on Whale Day.

MARCH

March is kite-flying month. At the three-day **Annual Oahu Kite Festival** ((808) 735-9059, the public is invited to show off their kites at Kapiolani Park on Oahu; while at the **International Kite Festival** ((808) 735-9059, Sandy Beach, Oahu, the "battle of the kites" features some of the top kite flyers in the world. The **Hawaii Challenge International Sportkite Championship** ((808) 735-9059, Kapiolani Park in Honolulu, is the venue for the longest-running sport-kite competition in the world, attracting top kite pilots from all over the globe.

The **Kona International Brewer's Festival** ((808) 936-9005 is celebrated on the grounds of the King Kamehameha' Beach Hotel in Kona, Big Island, with tastings from microbrewers from around the world as well as other entertainment.

The celebration of the Pacific humpback whale continues during **Whalefest Week** on Maui ((808) 667-9175 in the old whaling ports of Lahaina and

Kaanapali with festivities, naturalist presentations and special activities for children. Also during this month, volunteers around Maui count the humpback whales spotted in one day during the **Great Whale Count** ((808) 879-8860, sponsored by the Pacific Whale Foundation. You can call to volunteer for this five-hour project.

The **Prince Kuhio Celebration** honors this member of the Hawaiian Royalty with dance, chant and ceremony at Kiowea Park, Kapuaiwa Coconut Grove, near the town of Kaunakakai in Molokai.

The **Honolulu Festival** ((808) 792-4600 features street performers, food booths, sumo, kite flying and traditional dancing as part of this annual event to celebrate Japanese culture. Events are held at various locations around Oahu.

In mid-March *paniolos* provide lots of action during the full range of rodeo events at the **Kona Stampede** ((808) 323-2388, at Honaunau Arena, Honaunau, Kona.

The art of the lei. OPPOSITE: A crown for gray tresses, and a festive wreath of blossoms for the family vehicle. ABOVE: Exquisite and rare Niihau shell necklace adorns an island woman.

The **Maui Marathon** ((808) 871-6441 is an annual run from Kahului to Whalers Village at Kaanapali with an international field of runners.

Celebrating the life of Kamehameha I's most favored wife, the **Queen Kaahumanu Festival** ((808) 877-3369, takes place at Kaahumanu Center, Kahului, Maui, with exhibits and entertainment with games and storytelling for children.

A fund-raiser for the Hawaii Maritime Center, the **Altres King Kalakaua Regatta** ((808) 591-4975 is held in Oahu and is a multi-divisional race for men and women of all ages in a variety of water sports — from boating to paddling and surfing. The race begins at Ala Moana Magic Island and finishes at Aloha Tower Marketplace.

The **East Maui Taro Festival** ((808) 248-8972 takes place at Hana Ball Park in Hana and celebrates this staple of the Hawaiian diet with exhibits, demonstrations, live music and hula.

APRIL

Wesak, or **Buddha Day**, is on the closest Sunday to April 8, and celebrates the birthday of Gautama Buddha. Ornate offerings of tropical flowers are placed at temple altars throughout Hawaii, with a flower festival pageant at Lahaina Jodo Mission, Lahaina, Maui ((808) 661-4304.

Kapalua Celebration of the Arts ((808) 669-6200 at the Ritz-Carlton Hotel

games and rides are side shows to the **Honolulu International Bed Race** ℂ (808) 696-6262 where local teams are matched against competitors from as far away as Australia pushing beds through the streets of Honolulu to raise money for local charities.

The **Kihei Sea Festival** ℂ (808) 874-9400 features ocean sports, music, food and crafts and activities at the Kamaole Beach, Kihei, Maui.

MAY

May 1 is celebrated as May Day in many parts of the world, but in Hawaii everyone dons a lei for **Lei Day**. Festivities abound throughout the state, including the **Brothers Cazimero Annual May Day Concert** ℂ (808) 597-1888, a tradition at the Waikiki Shell for more than two decades. It's a flower-filled evening of Hawaiian music and picnics. In Kauai, the **May Day Lei Contest** is held at the Kauai Museum.

Barrio Festival ℂ (808) 243-7855 is a celebration of Filipino food, dance and music which is held at the War Memorial in Wailuku, Maui.

The **Prince Albert Music Festival** ℂ (808) 826-9644 E-MAIL paf@getmail.net is an outstanding classical music festival held over four days at the Princeville Hotel on Kauai. The concert celebrates the life of Prince Albert Edward Kauaikeaouli Lei O Papa a Kamehameha (1858–1862). A statewide *keiki kane* hula competition for boys aged 6 to 12, and a Holoku Tea, featuring traditional formal wear and a Songs of Hawaii competition, enrich the festival.

During the **World Fire-Knife Dance Championships** ℂ (808) 293-3333, fire-knife dancers compete in performances of extraordinary bravery at the Polynesian Cultural Center on the North Shore of Oahu.

The **Big Island Bounty** ℂ (808) 845-9905 is a two-day event on the Big Island that aims to replenish the mind, body and spirit through culinary excellence and lifestyle enhancement seminars.

in Kapalua, Maui, celebrates the people, art and culture of Hawaii, with free workshops, demonstrations and entertainment.

Bankoh Ki-Ho Alu ℂ (808) 239-4336 features some of the islands' foremost slack key guitar talent. Capacity crowds pack the grounds of the King Kamehameha Kona Beach Hotel, Kona, Big Island.

Moikeha Hawaiian Sailing Canoe Race ℂ (808) 885-7420 is a one-of-a-kind sailing canoe race along the Kohala Coast, Big Island. The race starts in Kawaihae, with viewing possible all up the coast.

An international food fair, live entertainment, a children's carnival,

Preparing the roasted pig at a Big Island luau.

Oahu Oceanfest ((808) 521-4322 features an array of ocean-based competitions and entertainment (from surfing to swimming) at Waikiki and other Oahu beaches. Held in conjunction with this event is the Outrigger Waikiki Kings Race, an ocean iron-man race and the **Hawaiian International Ocean Challenge** ((808) 521-4322, which is held at Waikiki Beach and welcomes lifeguards from around the world to face-off against each other.

Hawaii's only qualifying race for the Ironman Triathlon, **Keauhou-Kona Triathlon** ((808) 329-0601 is staged in May on the Big Island's western shores.

JUNE

Many events in the month of June honor King Kamehameha the Great, a Big Island native son. **King Kamehameha Day**, June 11, is a state holiday with festivities on all islands. Big Island has its **King Kamehameha Day Celebration** ((808) 935-9338 at Malia Puka O Kalani Church in Hilo with a noontime reenactment of a historical event in the King's life. The statue of King Kamehameha, across the street from Iolani Palace in Honolulu, is draped in fresh-flower leis measuring 13 ft (four meters) in length for the **King Kamehameha Statue Decoration Ceremonies** ((808) 329-1603. Music and hula performances create an excellent photo opportunity. The **Annual Honolulu King Kamehameha Floral Parade** features floral floats, marching bands, colorful mounted units and a King's Court participating in a four-mile (six-and-a-half-kilometer) parade from downtown Honolulu to Kapiolani Park. Finally, the **Annual King Kamehameha Hula Competition** ((808) 586-0333 is held at the Neal S. Blaisdell Center Arena. More than 20 *halau* (schools) compete in both traditional and contemporary hula styles. For information on Molokai events call ((808) 553-3876, or ((808) 245-3971 for Kauai events.

The **Pan-Pacific Festival Matsuri in Hawaii Celebration** ((808) 923-0492, in Oahu, begins with a mini-parade that

includes a *mikoshi* (a ceremonial shrine) brought from Japan just for this event. Entertainment includes arts and crafts, karaoke and sporting events as well as food booths.

Bankoh Ki-Ho Alu ((808) 242-7469 is a celebration of Hawaiian slack key guitar playing in all its diversity. This annual event is staged at the Maui Arts and Cultural Center.

Dozens of guest chefs get together in June at the Hawaii Preparatory Academy in Kamuela, Big Island, for the **Annual Forage Field Day** ((808) 885-0018, to prepare an unmatched feast of grass-fed island meats from local ranches and farms.

JULY

The week of the July 4 offers the all-American sport of rodeo along with all the parades. Don't miss the July 4 annual **Parker Ranch Fourth of July Rodeo** ((808) 885-7311, at Paniolo Park on Parker Ranch rodeo grounds in Waimea, Big Island, or the **Makawao Rodeo** ((808) 573-0090, the largest rodeo of the year in Hawaii at Kaanaolo Ranch on Maui. Towards the end of the month, rodeo action moves to Kauai for the **Kauai's Hawaii Rodeo Association Plantation Days Rodeo** ((808) 742-6096 held at CJM Country Stables.

The **Annual Concert in the Sky** ((808) 245-5006, a July 4 celebration, is held in Lihue, Kauai, at Vidinha Stadium, beginning at 3 PM. The day features food, crafts and game booths, pony rides and petting zoo, and family games, such as a watermelon eating contest, a coconut toss and a wheelbarrow race, and concludes with a spectacular fireworks show which draws more than 10,000 people each year.

Three- and four-year-old turtles are released into the ocean after being reared in the Mauna Lani ponds on **Turtle Independence Day** at the Mauna Lani Bay Hotel and Bungalows ((808) 885-6622.

TOP: Rodeo on the Kona Coast. BOTTOM: A wrangler sports a belt attesting to his Caucasian, *haole*, ancestry.

On the Big Island, the **Ka Hula Lea Festival** ((808) 886-6789 is held at the Outrigger Waikoloa Beach, while the **International Barefoot Hula** ((808) 961-8706 is held in Hilo town.

The **Kilauea Marathon and Rim Runs** ((808) 735-8733 offers a choice of a marathon, a 10-mile (16-km) or a five-mile (eight-kilometer) run or a five-mile (eight-kilometer) walk around the volcanic craters of Volcanoes National Park.

Paradise Ride Hawaii ((808) 242-4900 is an annual pledge bicycle event in the fight against AIDS. Participants ride their bicycles across four islands in seven days.

Koloa Plantation Days are a celebration of sugar plantation life on Kauai, featuring the culture of many immigrants, with cane cutting contests, entertainment, sports, crafts, foods and a parade in colorful Koloa Town.

The **Pineapple Festival** ((808) 565-7600 features pineapple cooking contests, and offers arts, crafts and entertainment off the Hulopoe Beach in Lanai.

Join the birthday party for the Atlantic bottlenose dolphins at the **Annual Dolphin Days** ((808) 886-1234, Hilton Waikoloa Village on the Big Island. The three-day extravaganza features guest celebrities and a variety of activities.

The **Pro-Am Billfish Tournament** ((808) 254-3474, a hugely popular big-game fishing tournament, includes parties and daily weigh-ins at Kona Pier.

The **Hawaii International Billfish Tournament** ((808) 329-6155 in Kailua-Kona is the top billfishing tournament in the world, featuring teams from many countries, a parade, and weighing-in ceremonies at Kailua Pier.

Have a great time Tahitian style with the people of Kauai as they honor their Polynesian roots with the week-long **Kauai-Tahiti Fete**. Dancers from Tahiti, the Hawaiian islands and the mainland participate in intense competition in this event.

The **Maui Onion Festival** ((808) 875-0457, at Whalers Village, Kaanapali, celebrates Maui's famous agricultural product and gourmet ingredient.

Displays, music and entertainment highlight the event.

Moanikeala Keiki Auana Hula Competition ((808) 293-3333 showcases hula *halaus* from around the islands at the Polynesian Cultural Center in Laie, Oahu.

In early September, don't miss the **Parker Ranch Scholarship Rodeo**, Paniolo Park in Waimea.

Earth Maui Nature Summit ((808) 527-2582 is held at the Kapalua Resort, Maui and features a weeklong series of events, including nature side-trips, to raise consciousness for environmental issues.

The largest long-distance canoe racing event in the world, **Queen Liliuokalani Outrigger Canoe Race** ((808) 329-0833 draws teams from around the Pacific Basin to Kailua-Kona on the Big Island. A lantern parade of competitors is a side attraction.

A Taste of Lahaina & The Best of Island Music ((808) 667-9175 takes place over two days, outdoors at Lahaina Cannery Mall, Maui and offers the best of Maui County restaurants and Hawaii's Island music.

The annual **Oahu Aloha Festival** ((808) 885-8086 kicks off with opening ceremonies in Honolulu. Floral parades, Hawaiian Royal Balls, the Steel Guitar Festival, storytelling, horse racing, paniolo hat and lei contests, fishing tournaments and ukulele performances are featured statewide.

The **Mokihana Festival** ((808) 822-2166 is a week-long celebration of Hawaiian culture at Kekaha and other locations in Kauai. It features men's and women's hula and *hoolaulea*.

Top female paddling crews from around the world compete in the annual 40.8-mile (65.7-km) women's Molokai-to-Oahu world championship long-distance outrigger canoe race, **Na Wahine O Ke Kai**.

Run to the Sun ((808) 871-6441 is one of the world's toughest endurance runs — from the town of Paia, at sea level, to the 10,000-ft (3,000-m) summit of Haleakala.

OCTOBER

Intertribal Powwow ((808) 734-5171, at Thomas Square in downtown Honolulu, highlights a variety of aspects of Native American culture.

Aloha Festivals of Lanai ((808) 589-1771 TOLL-FREE (800) 852-7690 is a 10-day celebration with community parades, plus lots of other cultural programs, shows, and entertainment.

The **Annual Bankoh Molokai Men's Outrigger Canoe Race** ((808) 261-6615 is a grueling 41-mile (66-km) Molokai-to-Oahu six-person outrigger canoe championship. Nearly 100 nine-man teams of the best male outrigger canoe paddlers in the world compete for the title. The finish can be seen at Fort DeRussy Beach, Waikiki, in Oahu.

Hookipa Beach, Maui, is the site for the **Aloha Classic World Windsurfing Championships** ((808) 575-9151, the final event of the Pro World Tour, with an international field of competitors.

Halloween in Lahaina ((808) 667-9175, held on Front Street in Lahaina, Maui, is a Mardi Gras-like celebration with all the right ingredients — outlandish costumes, great food and good times.

Maui Triathlon ((808) 579-9502, Maui, features the international individual and team championships for the Ironman, Half Iron and Olympic Distance awards. And, of course, October is the month for the **Ironman Triathlon World Championships** WEB SITE www.ironmanlive.com, on the Big Island, when 1,500 men and women compete for a $250,000 purse and sheer glory over an arduous two-and-a-half-mile (four-kilometer) ocean swim, 112-mile (180-km) bike race and 26-mile (42-km) run, ending along Alii Drive.

NOVEMBER

Children from around the state come to Kailua-Kona to perform hula at the **Annual King Kalakaua Keiki Hula**

OPPOSITE: Feather leis can be highly prized works of art. ABOVE LEFT: Orchids bloom wild in the damp, hot climate of the islands. ABOVE RIGHT: Participants in a children's festival.

Festival, which offers plenty of fun mixed with serious competition.

At various locations around the Kona coast, taste the only coffee commercially grown in the United States at the **Annual Kona Coffee Festival** ((808) 326-7820. Parades, arts and crafts displays, ethnic foods and entertainment are all part of the festivities.

The **Hawaii International Film Festival** ((808) 528-3456 presents films, seminars and workshops in Oahu as part of one of the world's fastest growing movie festivals.

The **Taro Festival at Honokaa** ((808) 775-9987 takes place on the Big Island's northern coast, where taro was grown in giant river valleys in ancient times. This event celebrates a renewal of the culture of taro, the staple food of old Hawaii. Located in Honokaa, an historic town on the Hamakua Coast, it features displays, food, crafts and entertainment.

The annual **Winter Wine Escape** ((808) 880-3023, at the Hapuna Beach Prince Hotel, invites the public to meet top wine makers from around the world. Top chefs place the perfect wine with the best of Hawaiian regional cuisine.

The **Annual Triple Crown of Surfing Series** ((808) 638-7266 is a professional, big-wave surfing championship on Oahu's North Shore. The men's Pipe Masters signals the conclusion of the Surfing Professionals world tour, after which a men's and women's world champion and a Triple Crown champion are named.

DECEMBER
With more than 30,000 participants, the **Honolulu Marathon** ((808) 734-7200 WEB SITE www.honolulumarathon.org is one of the largest marathons in the world.

The **Pacific Handcrafters Guild's Annual Christmas Festival of Art and Fine Crafts** ((808) 637-1248 features the work of over 100 artists and craftspeople over this two-day festival at Thomas Square Park, Oahu. Local entertainment and food round out the festivities. **Na Mele O Maui** ((808) 661-3271 aims to

perpetuate Hawaiian culture through children's song contests, hula and arts and crafts.

Honolulu City Lights ((808) 527-5784 kicks off with a Christmas tree lighting ceremony at City Hall, which is followed by a parade with more than 20 vehicles and marching bands. Nightly choir performances are held through to January.

Waimea Lighted Christmas Parade ((808) 338-9957, in Waimea Town in Kauai, is led by the fire department's engines and winds its way through town before ending up at Hofgaard Park. This is a real community celebration that the kids love.

On New Year's Eve, hold onto your hat, because they do it up big in Hawaii. The merriment flows all over the islands. Firecrackers are illegal, but they go off everywhere. The Maui Arts and Cultural Center ((808) 242-7469 host **First Night Maui**, 12-hour, alcohol-free, family-style festivals to celebrate the New Year on Maui.

OPPOSITE: Native Hawaiians sport a variety of beautiful leis. ABOVE: Perpetuating the art of lei making.

Galloping Gourmets

In the past decade, Hawaii has become a center of the culinary arts. Chefs trained in France and mainland United States are busy creating a Hawaiian cuisine that transcends fusion and Pacific Rim. It combines an outstanding selection of fresh seafood, local beef and game with exotic vegetables, fruits, herbs, and spices in amazing concoctions. Sometimes these brave new dishes work; sometimes they rattle the taste buds. I for one have trouble with strawberries and kiwi topped with cracked pepper. But certain dishes surpass the imagination, often because of their simplicity.

Hawaii claims a dozen or more chefs with considerable fame and daring. Those who have imprinted their names on critics and discerning diners all seem to yearn for restaurants bearing their names. On Oahu, where all the great chefs eventually migrate, there are at least a half dozen restaurants bearing the names of their kitchen masters. The big names — Alan Wong, Roy Yamaguchi, George Mavrothalassitis — compete and cooperate, often displaying their signature dishes at a wealth of culinary festivals. New names enter the fray, usually after long stints in elegant hotel dining rooms, and the restaurant scene is never dull.

It is, however, quite expensive. A fine dinner in one of Hawaii's best restaurants costs as much (or more) than it would in Los Angeles or Manhattan. Even mediocre restaurants are mostly overpriced. If you're only in the islands occasionally and crave *ahi* tartare or curry-blackened Hawaiian swordfish, dining could well be your greatest expense. But oh, what delights. All the islands have extraordinary restaurants; enjoying the new Hawaii cuisine is as essential to understanding the islands as is a day at the beach.

You needn't break the bank to dine well in Hawaii, however. Due to large

Chinese, Japanese, Filipino, and Korean populations, the islands are filled with inexpensive Asian eateries, and most restaurants carry a few staples. Saiman, a noodle soup with chicken or pork, shows up even on breakfast menus; kim chee (Korean pickled cabbage) is sometimes served with sandwiches. Chicken long rice, a dish of transparent noodles boiled with shredded chicken, is a filling, inexpensive dinner.

Outside of this cornucopia of Asian foods, there exists a cuisine that is uniquely Hawaiian. Hawaiian cooking speaks a delicious blend that incorporates the subtleties of Asian cooking with the lusty dining preferences of the native Hawaiians. This marriage has produced the "mixed plate," an eating tradition not to be found anywhere else in the world. As the name implies, a mixed plate is little bit of this and a little bit of that — Japanese and Chinese and Korean and Hawaiian and anything else for that matter, served with scoops of rice at either a restaurant or a lunch wagon. The plate lunch typically includes an entrée such as curried beef or grilled *mahimahi* with two scoops of sticky white rice and macaroni salad.

Dining authentic Hawaiian style is something else again. The ultimate experience is the luau, an elaborate affair. It encompasses the traditions of a native feast with the relaxed ambience of the Hawaiian lifestyle. There are numerous luaus organized for tourists; most include a buffet of Hawaiian specialties. Essential to the meal is the *kalua* pig (baked in an *imu* or pit oven). The buffets also include *laulaus* (similar to tamales, with pork, rice and salted butterfish steamed in ti leaves), several seafood dishes, a bowl of *poi*, lots of white rice, and coconut cake. Tourist luaus usually include Hawaiian music and dance performances.

There are numerous commercial luaus on all the islands, and they do offer a quick (if somewhat phony) immersion into Hawaiian foods and culture. If you're visiting for a while, check the local paper for luaus being run for political or charitable causes and join the locals to sample regional dishes and watch students from hula schools perform before neighbors and friends.

Buying snacks and supplies at grocery stores and Farmer's Markets is one of the easiest ways to sample Hawaiian cuisine.

SNACKS

The name causes novices to grin as they place their order for their first *pu pu* platter. Even Hawaiians have to admit appetizers and snacks sound better when they're called *tapas* or hors d'œuvres. But *pu pus* they are, and kitchens come up with some amazing combos presented on enormous plates aside tropical drinks. A typical platter might include coconut-coated shrimp, deep-fried Maui onion rings, crab wontons, tempura veggies, and skewers of teriyaki chicken. The choice is limited only by the chef's imagination. Though these treats can be ordered as single appetizers, the platter is far more fun — if you're dining alone order it as your main meal.

OPPOSITE: A Japanese breakfast. BELOW: Pacific Rim cuisine graces tables throughout the islands.

Typical mainland snacks including potato chips, pretzels, nuts, and trail mix are readily available, as are taro chips (made from sliced taro root) and spicy oriental snack mixes with rice crackers and sesame sticks. Sushi is often eaten on the run, and one of the most popular snacks currently is the horrific Spam musubi, with a slice of canned Spam wrapped in white rice and seaweed.

Islanders know the best way to cool down on a hot day is by sipping and scooping into a paper cone of shave ice. It may be hard to believe that a pile of ice topped with sweet syrup could warrant considerable fame, but shave ice even has songs written in its honor. It's hard to get singer Loyal Garner's tribute to the sweet treat out of your mind as you suck on an icy confection striped with rainbow-colored coconut, pineapple, and mango syrup. Though the combo sounds strange, the best variety of shave ice includes a scoop of ice cream and sweet adzuki beans.

Malasadas, or Portuguese donuts, and *pao dolce*, Portuguese sweet bread, are sold in many bakeries.

FRUITS AND VEGETABLES

Pineapples were Hawaii's leading cash cow for decades. Though their position on the market has waned, sweet, juicy, fragrant pineapples are still synonymous with Hawaii. Pineapple slices appear atop pizzas and barbecued ribs, and the juice flavors marinades for chicken and fish. Pineapples are even sold at the airport for last-minute souvenirs — make sure you buy them sealed, as those from the market will be confiscated by Customs.

The coconut is equally ubiquitous, their tough brown balls hanging from trees all over the islands. The Polynesians brought the first coconut trees to Hawaii and used every part of them in daily life. Once the trees were established, the trunks formed the framework for homes and were hollowed out for bowls, plates, cups and spoons. The fiber from coconut husk was twined into rope, and the meat and milk were critical to sustenance.

When a child was born, a coconut tree was planted to provide him with fruit for his healthy life.

Coconut milk flavors many of the frou-frou drinks so popular at beach bars, adding calories and sweetness to piña coladas and their offspring, the strawberry flavored "lava flow." Coconut cake is a favorite dessert, as is *haupia*, a coconut custard. Coconut crusted shrimp makes regular appearances on *pu pu* platters. And of course, the scent of coconut oil permeates the air wherever a group of sunbathers congregates.

The subtly-sweet papaya was introduced to the islands by Captain James Cook. Mottled green and yellow on the outside, the papaya contains a rosy orange meat filled with the enzyme papain, used to aid digestion and tenderize meat. If your stomach is a bit queasy, eat a papaya or drink it as a juice or tea — you'll find it works wonders. Mangos are also exotic and delicious, though some people find both fruits a bit slimy. When mangos ripen in trees from Hana to Honolulu, their fragrance becomes almost overwhelming, especially when the fruit covers the ground and begins to ferment. Passionfruit, called *lilikoi*, is an acquired taste. The tiny lemon-shaped fruits are unattractive, and look quite odd when cut in half. The slick white, seedy pulp has an odd texture and slightly tart flavor. But *lilikoi* is transformed when used in sherbets, ice creams, juices, and jams, and its distinct flavor does inspire passion in its fans.

Huge Latin American and West Indian avocados thrive in the island climate, and are found in markets nearly year round. Guavas are so prevalent they're considered pests; no one will complain if you pick a few from a roadside tree. Over 70 species of bananas grow on the islands, though the demand is so high those in the market often come from Latin America. Breadfruit was a precious staple for the Polynesians and early Hawaiians, though it's rather bland and unappealing.

Macadamia nuts, introduced to the islands from Australia in the late 1800s, have become one of Hawaii's main agricultural exports — tourists certainly contribute to this factor by carting home boxes and cans of the fat-filled nuts either salted or covered with chocolate. Chefs chop and grind the nuts and use them in coatings for fish, shrimp, chicken, and in desserts from pies to ice cream.

Hawaii's most famous vegetable may well be the sweet Maui onion, grown in the Kula area of the island and used for onion rings and in salads. Locals claim Maui russet potatoes make the world's best potato chips. Baby lettuces and fresh herbs are all the rage in upscale restaurants, and farms large and small specialize in everything from endive to watercress. Then there's taro, the staple of Hawaii used to make purple *poi*. Those who love it wax eloquent over the texture, rated as one, two, or three-finger *poi* for the number of fingers it takes to scoop up a glob of the thick paste. *Poi* is said to be quite healthy and filled with nutritious carbohydrates; to the uninitiated it tastes like bland paste.

SEAFOOD

The waters off Hawaii nourish an astonishing array of fish; some experts say there are over 800 varieties swimming about. At least a dozen kinds are available throughout the year, and seafood lovers are in their element no matter where they dine. Fresh, raw, marinated, grilled, chopped, wrapped in seaweed — seafood appears in so many forms even those who say they hate fish are eventually wooed by a tasty morsel.

The Hawaiian names for fish are amusing and vastly confusing. Only here would there be a state fish called the humuhumunukunukuapua'a. Fortunately, it's easier to wrap your tongue around those found on menus. The most common offering is the mild-flavored *mahimahi*, called dorado in other areas. Yellowfin tuna, or *ahi*, is wonderful as sashimi (slices of raw fish); *au*, or broad-billed swordfish, is used for the

priciest and most flavorful grilled steaks. Other fish commonly found on menus include *ono* (flaky white wahoo), *onaga* (red snapper), *opakapaka* (the most common snapper found on menus), and *moi* (with moist, delicate white meat).

Skipjack tuna, called *aku*, is often used in *poki*, a popular dish of chopped, marinated raw fish mixed with seasoned seaweed. *Lomi lomi*, salted fish kneaded, chopped and mixed with tomatoes and green onions, is typically made from salmon. Both dishes can be tough and strong tasting or butter smooth and delicious, depending on where they're served. Don't set judgement upon them if you've only had a taste at a huge luau, as the quality of the ingredients may not be up to par.

The prevalence of fresh fish sends chefs into a creative frenzy; some go way overboard trying to come up with new preparations. Purists are happiest with a hefty portion of *au* or *ono*, simply grilled with butter or oil. *Mahimahi* and the snappers undergo dramatic transformations when coated with macadamia nut or sesame seed crusts, and every type of fish eventually submits to fruit-flavored sauces. The best chefs dip into the Asian palette for ginger, lemongrass, wasabi, and curries. And if you like sushi you'll be in heaven.

Shave ice, in dozens of flavors, is an island favorite.

MEAT AND POULTRY

The Polynesians took particular care with the pigs they brought on their first journey to the Hawaiian Islands, and pork has remained one of the staples of the Hawaiian diet. The *pièce de résistance* of any luau remains the *kalua* pig, a central feature in most celebrations.

The pit oven is what gives the pig roasting ritual its stamp of authenticity. The *imu* is a trench about 18 inches (45 cm) deep, dug into the ground to accommodate a pig that weighs about 90 lb (40 kg) dressed. A fire of hardwood logs is started in the pit, and about two dozen stones are placed on the fire. The pig, meanwhile, has been eviscerated, skinned and shaved of bristles. It is rubbed inside and out with rock salt and soy sauce and left to soak in a marinade until the stones are red hot. The pig is then laid on a square of chicken wire. Hot rocks are placed in the throat cavity and between the legs and body. The chicken wire is wrapped around the pig and the pig is placed in the pit. Fresh corn husks or banana leaves, sweet potatoes, bananas and fish wrapped in ti leaves are piled on top of the pig. The mound is covered with burlap bags and soaked with water to keep it sealed. Earth is then piled on the mound to prevent the steam from leaking. Four hours later, the earth is cleared away, and the pig is unwrapped. The aroma of roasted meat, fruit and ti leaves assails the senses. Pig done this style is succulent and totally Hawaiian. Pork is also featured in Hawaiian style barbecued ribs, which are usually sweeter than Texas and Louisiana style barbecue.

Though beef cattle are raised on the Big Island, most of the steaks and burgers served in restaurants are made from mainland beef. Chicken receives many of the same preparations as fish; duck is featured in many Chinese restaurants. Venison, partridge, and other game show up on menus during hunting season, particularly on Lanai.

BEVERAGES

Hawaii just wouldn't be the same without fancy drinks topped with paper umbrellas and chunks of fruit. It's impossible to get through a vacation on the islands without sampling at least one even if you're a teetotaler, since most drink menus offer a few nonalcoholic choices. Most of the fancy, frou-frou drinks are made with rum, a favorite libation on the islands since the days of the whalers. Hawaii's signature drink is the mai tai, as common as the margarita in Mexico. Master mixologists create sublime mai tais with light and dark rum, curaçao, and orange, lemon and almond flavorings. The perfect mai tai is both deceptively sweet and sour, packing a mellow punch. Too often, however, these and other popular drinks are made with overly sweet prepackaged mixes. Beware of those served by the pitcher at buffets and luaus — you're better off with a bottle of island-brewed beer. Microbreweries are gaining in popularity, and bars throughout the islands typically have a few on tap. Dark European beers are harder to find. Wines from California, Chili, France, and Australia are readily available and often frightfully expensive.

Kona coffee, grown on the Big Island, is rich, robust and slightly sweet. It is considered one of the world's finest coffees, and scandals break out every few years when coffee beans from other countries are added under a Kona-labeled blend. It is an arabica variety that rivals similar gourmet arabica coffees such as Jamaican Blue Mountain.

King Kamehameha's Spanish interpreter, Don Francisco de Paula y Marin, is credited with having brought a coffee tree into Honolulu in 1813. But it was Samuel Ruggles, a missionary, who in 1828 first took cuttings from trees planted on Oahu and planted them in Kona's rich, volcanic soil.

The Kona coffee industry has had its ups and downs in the last century and a half. But it has survived thanks to the endurance of native Hawaiians and Asian laborers — Chinese, Japanese and Filipinos — who first came to work the sugar cane fields of the Big Island and then stayed to become coffee farmers. Coffee generally blooms from March to May, when trees are covered with white blossoms that coffee farmers call "Kona Snow." These blossoms turn in to green beans, and ultimately a dark cherry red when they are harvested from September to January.

Kona coffee is sold in souvenir shops, though it is less expensive in supermarkets. The Hawaii Department of Agriculture grades all Kona coffees. Kona Extra Fancy, for example, passes the most stringent tests, followed by Kona Fancy, Kona No. 1, Kona Prime, Kona No. 1 Peaberry and Kona Peaberry Prime. Coffee growers are now planting and harvesting beans on other islands as well; watch for local labels.

OPPOSITE: Maui's Old Lahaina luau is one of the most popular parties on the islands. ABOVE: Workers harvest pineapple, a fruit once closely identified with the islands. The pineapple industry is now all but gone.

Special Interests

HEALING THE HAWAIIAN WAY

The resurgence of interest in Hawaiian culture and the arts has also spawned a revival in spirituality and the traditional healing methods of the islands. People from across the globe now come in search of relief, and from Kauai to the Big Island native Hawaiian healers are willing to support, nurture and share their abilities.

A typical restorative session might include a steam bath and a body scrub with sea salt, aloe and red clay, for which the western side of Kauai is famous. This may be followed by *lomi-lomi* massage, used by ancient Polynesians to soothe pain and relax or limber up stiff muscles. This form of massage is often accompanied by chanting.

The **Association of Healing Arts Practitioners** ((808) 823-8088 TOLL-FREE (800) 599-5488 FAX (808) 823-8088 E-MAIL heal-hi@aloha.net WEB SITE www.lauhala.com/ahap, PO Box 160, Kapaa, Kauai, is a good source for information on health and healing subjects. Dozens of practitioners offer reiki, meditation, acupuncture, herbal and nutritional therapy, hypnotherapy, yoga, tai chi, chiropractic medicine, psychotherapy, sound therapy, astrology, psychic counseling and more.

Helping Hands ((808) 822-1715 E-MAIL helping@pixi.com, 4-1579 Kuhio Highway, Suite 210, Kapaa, offers courses in guided imagery, meditation, yoga, and qi gong — a classical Chinese method of gentle invigorating movement. Helping Hands also offers massage therapy combined with spiritual healing.

A three-day program, designed to revitalize, relax and reenergize body and spirit is available on the Big Island from **Hawaii Adventure Spa** ((808) 324-1717 FAX (808) 324-1182 E-MAIL vbright@kona.net WEB SITE www.hawaiiearth.com. Run by well-known wellness experts Valerie Bright B.P.E. and Karen

Chandler M.S., the package comprises three adventure components (hiking, diving, kayaking and the like), three tai chi or yoga sessions and three meditation sessions. Luxury accommodation is provided at the Orchid at Mauna Lani.

Pacific Adventures travel services ((808) 324-1338 WEB SITE www.pacific-adventures.com, 78-6031 Alii Drive #107A, Kailua-Kona, offers a program in Continuing Medical Education arranged by the Five Mountain Medical Community, located in and around the town of Waimea, Big Island. Designed for medical professionals and interested lay people, this course promises an opportunity to refresh and expand

understanding of health issues, combining the power of traditional Western medicine with complementary healing approaches like acupuncture and massage.

Some of the finest spas in the Pacific region are in these islands. It could be argued that the entire Kohala region on the Big Island is itself a natural spa with its warm and cool, dry and wet microclimates, freshwater pools and warm salt sea. Hawaiian traditions like *lomi-lomi* massage and a variety of health and fitness approaches reflect the multiculturalism of the island. The **Kohala Spa** at the Hilton Waikoloa Village ((808) 886-1234 WEB SITE www.waikoloavillage.hilton.com,

425 Waikoloa Beach Drive, for instance, offers total relaxation. This tranquil yet invigorating environment offers seaweed body masques, aromatherapy, tai chi classes and *lomi-lomi*.

Spa Without Walls, the Orchid at Mauna Lani ((808) 885-2000 WEB SITE www.orchid-maunalani.com, One North Kaniku Drive, and **Mauna Lani Spa** at the Mauna Lani Bay Hotel and Bungalows ((808) 885-6622 WEB SITE www.maunalani.com, 68-1400 Mauna Lani Drive, are two other respected health vacation destinations on the Big Island.

Formal botanical gardens are surrounded by wild forests on the garden isle of Kauai.

Other hotels on other islands also have fine spas, including the **Spa Grande** at the Grand Wailea Resort and Spa ((808) 875-1234 FAX (808) 874-2411 E-MAIL info@grandwilea.com WEB SITE www .grandwailea.com, 3850 Wailea Alanui, Wailea, Maui, and the spa at the **J.W. Marriott Ihilani Resort and Spa** ((808) 679-0079 TOLL-FREE (800) 626-4446 FAX (808) 679-0295 WEB SITE www .ihilani.com, 92-1001 Olani Street in Koolina.

GARDENS OF SPLENDOR

Hawaii is a treasure house of extraordinary tropical plant life. Native and introduced flora flourish in the perfect climactic conditions nurtured by an abundance of rain and sun. Within the islands are five major ecosystems. This diversity can be seen in Hawaii's botanical gardens.

Pacific Adventures ((808) 324-1338 WEB SITE www.pacific-adventures.com, 78-6031 Alii Drive #107A, Kailua-Kona, 96740, offers stays at the Waipio Garden Eco Retreat. The Waipio Garden is a pristine botanical garden with over 400 species of plants, flowers and trees. A short walk away is Nenewe Falls with several swimming pools and a secluded black sand beach. Optional tours of Waipio Valley are provided by Earth Voice Hawaii, a nonprofit organization with a mission to teach love and care of the land.

Beyond this program, there are numerous botanical gardens throughout the islands, which enthusiasts should not miss.

The 252-acre (101-hectare) **Lawai Garden** in the Lawai Valley and the 100-acre (40-hectare) **Allerton Garden** ((808) 742-2623 are on Kauai's south shore. Lawai specializes in native Hawaiian plants, palms, heliconia and erythrina. It is the headquarters of the National Tropical Botanical Garden. Allerton Gardens next door is a masterwork of landscape design that marries dramatic topography with the sights and sounds of water and the color and texture of foliage.

Black lava flows form a dramatic backdrop to the plant life at **Kahanu Garden** ((808) 248-8912, on the Hana Coast of Maui. The 122 acres (49 hectares) include ethnobotanical collections and the Piilanihale Heiau.

The **Waimea Arboretum and Botanical Garden** ((808) 638-8511 is situated in historic Waimea Valley on Oahu in a 1,800-acre (720-hectare) nature park. Waimea Falls is part of this park system. The arboretum and botanical garden concentrate on rare and endangered tropical and subtropical plants. Unique plant collections include those of the Hawaiian, Mariana, Mascarene and Ogasawara islands. There are also exceptional plants in other regional floral collections.

The **Harold L. Lyon Arboretum Honolulu** ((808) 988-7378, deep in lush Manoa Valley, is an active research facility and academic resource for the University of Hawaii as well as an enchanting tropical public garden. Its 194 acres (78 hectares) hold one of the most important collections of tropical plants and one of the two largest palm collections in any botanical garden. It has also established the United States' largest and most successful program for the propagation of endangered plants by tissue culture.

The **Amy B.H. Greenwell Ethnobotanical Garden** ((808) 323-

3318, Kailua-Kona on the Big Island, is a small yet fascinating garden on the slopes above Kealakekua Bay. On display are Hawaiian plants and Polynesian crops set in ancient agricultural stonework. Visitors learn about traditional Hawaiian farming techniques and the diverse use of natural and cultivated plants in Hawaiian agriculture — known as the Kona Field System.

The gorgeous **Hawaii Tropical Botanical Garden** ((808) 964-5233 FAX (808) 964-1338 WEB SITE WWW .htbg.com, in Onomea Bay on Big Island, is set in a valley that opens out onto the ocean. Streams and waterfalls flow through a tropical rainforest easily navigated along meandering trails. Over 2,000 species of tropical plants from many parts of the world are featured. Visitors may also see the garden's collection of Japanese koi and tropical birds such as the African lessor flamingo and colorful giant macaw.

OPPOSITE: Thick, velvety moss covers tree roots in Oahu's Manoa Valley. ABOVE: Crowds of tourists cluster under dripping fronds at the Fern Grotto on Kauai

SPORTING TRIPS

Diving enthusiasts can contact **Eco-Adventures** ((808) 329-7116 FAX (808) 329-7091 WEB SITE www.eco-adventure.com, King Kamehameha Kona Beach Hotel on the Big Island, for information on six- and seven-night diving and dive certification packages which include accommodation and car rental.

Hawaii Pack and Paddle ((808) 328 8911 E-MAIL gokayak@kona.net WEB SITE www.hawaiipackandpaddle.com, 87-3187 Honu Moe Road, Captain Cook, Big Island, offers multi-day hiking and backpacking expeditions, guided kayak tours and multisport trips.

A number of travel agents can arrange special sports-oriented holidays in Hawaii. For example, **Aloha Destinations** ((808) 893-0388 FAX (808) 893-0138 WEB SITE www.alohadestinations.com, on Maui, offers surf and windsurfing holidays, golf vacations and more. They also put together gay and lesbian travel packages.

WEDDINGS IN PARADISE

Many of the large hotels offer wedding packages that include all arrangements, from the ceremony itself to the honeymoon. Alternatively, there are a host of wedding planners who can arrange anything from a simple beach ceremony to an elaborate church affair. Other imaginative ceremonies include arriving by helicopter for a private ceremony on the volcanic slopes of Mount Haleakala or tying the knot on a private yacht at sunset. On Oahu, try **Aloha Beautiful Hawaii Weddings** ((808) 734-5088 FAX (808) 739-5322, 3762 Sierra Drive on Kauai, **Weddings on the Beach** ((800) 625-2824 WEB SITE www.hawaiian.net/~judyn/weddings, PO Box 1377, Koloa, or **Bali Hai Weddings** ((800) 776-4813 WEB SITE www.hshawaii.com/kvp/bal, PO Box 1723, Kapaa. The Hawaii Visitors and Convention Bureau's WEB SITE www.gohawaii.com has a whole section dedicated to providing more information on celebrating weddings and honeymoons on the islands.

Taking a Tour

There are many ways to see the islands. Some areas are best viewed from the ocean, while other parts are remote and impossible to reach other than by helicopter or small plane. In these flights you will be transported into secret valleys laced with waterfalls, or over lava flows rushing to the ocean. But however you may want to see the islands, you can be assured that there are all manner of operators and tour variations to choose from.

SEA ADVENTURES

On Oahu, some of the best tours are provided by *Navatek I* ((808) 848-6360 TOLL-FREE (800) 852-4183 WEB SITE www.royalhawaiiancruises.com. The company has developed a patented technology that ensures stability in the roughest of waters, to provide guests with the smoothest of rides. Cruises are conducted throughout the day, with on-board naturalists providing educational insights into the trips.

For something a little more strenuous, sailboarding and kayaking trips from Kailua Beach are offered by **Kailua**

Sailboard and Kayak Company ℂ (808) 262-2555, while a day of sports fishing on one of the myriad boats moored at Kewalo basin off Ala Moana Boulevard, can be arranged through **Hawaii Charter Skippers Association ℂ** (808) 594-9100.

For adventures under the sea off Oahu's North Shore, try a scuba trip from **Haleiwa Surf Center ℂ** (808) 637-5051, 66-167 Haliewa Road.

The Na Pali Coast on Kauai is the perfect venue for an ocean tour. The grandeur of the sea cliffs and the magnificent sea caves will leave you in awe. **Captain Andy's Sailing Adventure's ℂ** (808) 822-7833, Kikiaola Small Boat Harbor, Waimea, offers snorkeling and sunset cruises aboard their 55-ft (17-m) catamaran or the kayaks of **Outfitters Kauai ℂ** (808) 742-9667 TOLL-FREE (888) 742-9887 WEB SITE www.outfitterskauai.com, can take you past hanging valleys, under plunging waterfalls and into lava tubes or sea caves on full day and overnight trips. For a voyage of discovery of Kauai's marine life, a well-respected company for snorkeling and scuba is **Snorkel Bob's ℂ** (808) 823-9433 in Kapaa and ℂ (808) 742-2206 at Poipu Beach.

From mid-December to mid-May, whale watching is Maui's top visitor activity. There are numerous whale-watch cruises available out of ports from Kihei to Lahaina: try **Trilogy ℂ** (808) 879-8811 TOLL-FREE (800) 628-4800 WEB SITE www.sailtrilogy.com, or for a smaller vessel, **Hawaii Ocean Rafting ℂ** (808) 667-2191 TOLL-FREE (888) 677-7238 WEB SITE www.maui.net/~ocnraftn. Outside of whale-watching season, most outfits provide other types of sea tours, such as snorkeling or dolphin-spotting trips.

Maui also offers an amazing variety of sports fishing trips, try **Luckey Strike Charters ℂ** (808) 661-4606 WEB SITE www.luckeystrike.com.

There is certainly no shortage of choice for whale-watching tours off the Big Island. Indeed, if you are fortunate enough to vacation on the Kona-Kohala Coast at any of the great resorts during the winter season, you are almost certain to see these giant mammals swooping and diving and thumping the waters with their tails. One of the great viewing sites is the footpath along the Mauna Lani golf course.

Horseback riders canter beside the rustic cottages at the Hotel Hana on Maui.

Other types of ocean tours on the Big Island include open cockpit kayak trips from **Ocean Safaris** ((808) 326-4699 TOLL-FREE (800) 326-4699 FAX (808) 322-3653 E-MAIL kayakhi@gte.net, and glass bottom boat cruises from **Kailua Bay Charter Co**. ((808) 324-1749 E-MAIL kbcc@gte.net WEB SITE www.home1.gte.net/kbcc.

If you want to enjoy the marine life, but don't relish the idea of suiting up, try a tour on **Atlantis Submarines** ((808) 973-9811 TOLL-FREE (800) 548-6262 WEB SITE www.goatlantis.com/hawaii. This outfit will take you on an underwater safari to a depth of over 100 ft (30 m) through coral gardens populated by thousands of tropical fish. Atlantis operates out of Oahu from the Hilton Hawaiian Village, Slip 18 in Lahaina Harbor on Maui, and the Kailua Kona Pier on the Big Island. Semi-submersible options from Maui include **SeaView Adventures** ((808) 661-5550 and **Reefdancer** ((808) 667-2133.

And if you are lucky to be around during a full moon, when the whales are very active, it's a sight you'll never forget.

For a closer look at these magnificent creatures, any of the following tour operators are recommended: **Body Glove** ((808) 326-7122 TOLL-FREE (800) 551-8911 WEB SITE www.bodyglovehawaii.com, **Captain Zodiac** ((808) 329-3199 FAX (808) 329-7590 E-MAIL seakona@interpac.net, **Fairwind** ((808) 322-2788 WEB SITE www.fair-wind.com, and **Eco-Adventures** ((808) 329-7116 TOLL-FREE (800) 949-3483 FAX (808) 329-7091 E-MAIL ecodive@kona.net WEB SITE www.eco-adventure.com. The latter outfit also acts as a booking agent for a number of smaller tour operators, and so can offer many options.

AIR ADVENTURES

For islands such as Molokai and Kauai, where much of the land is inaccessible by car, a helicopter ride gives you the opportunity of seeing some of the most spectacular waterfalls, pristine beaches, otherworldly craters and verdant valleys imaginable. Based in Kauai are **Island Helicopters** ((808) 245-6258 and **Ohana Helicopters** ((808) 245-3996. **Blue Hawaiian Helicopters** ((808) 961-5600 TOLL-FREE (800) 745-2583 WEB SITE www.bluehawaiian.com has been in operation for many years, flying out of both Hilo and Kona airports on the Big Island and Kahului Heliport on Maui, and has been used in the filming of such films as *Jurassic Park* and *George of the Jungle*.

Fixed-wing tours are generally less expensive than helicopter tours due to lower operating costs. The best ones are offered in Molokai by **Paragon Air** TOLL-FREE (800) 428-1231 and in Hilo and Kona on Big Island by **Island Hoppers** ((808) 969-2000 TOLL-FREE (800) 538-7590 FAX (808) 331-2079 E-MAIL info@fly-hawaii.com WEB SITE www.fly-hawaii.com.

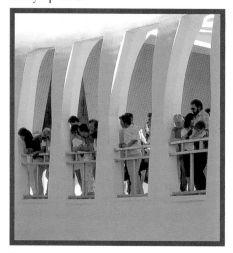

GENERAL TOURS

There are a range of tour operators offering Hawaiian vacations. Your travel agent is the best source of information on these. **Pleasant Holidays** TOLL-FREE (800) 242-9244 WEB SITE www.pleasantholidays .com, Westlake Village, California, packages a range of Hawaii vacations from the mainland, including their new "Discover Oahu," which promises to allow you to experience the Oahu beyond Waikiki. **Sunquest** TOLL-FREE (800) 357-2400 WEB SITE www .sunquest.org, Simi Valley, California, has five charter flights per week from Los Angeles to Hawaii and offers seven-night packages as well as specialized itineraries. During peak season, Sunquest offers six nonstop flights each week from LAX to Honolulu, Maui, Kauai and Kona. Many airlines also offer air and hotel packages, including **Northwest's World Vacations** TOLL-FREE (800) 800-1504 and **American Airlines Vacations** TOLL-FREE (800) 321-2121. **American Express** TOLL-FREE (800) 952-8687 offers packages from the mainland as well as having tour and activity desks in Oahu, Maui and the Big Island.

American Hawaii Cruises TOLL-FREE (800) 944-8020 WEB SITE www.cruisehawaii .com, makes stops on Kauai, Oahu, Maui and Hawaii during their seven-night, five-port cruise aboard the SS *Independence*.

You can scarcely go to a tourist site in Hawaii without seeing a vehicle from **Roberts Hawaii Tours** ((808) 539-9400 TOLL FREE (800) 831-5541. Based in Honolulu, they offer a range of tours on many islands. **Activity Warehouse** TOLL-FREE (800) 923-4004 (Maui, Big Island and Oahu) or (800) 688-0580 (Kauai) WEB SITE www.travelhawaii.com has over 500 adventure activities to choose from as well as accommodation and car packages.

OPPOSITE: An ancient sailing vessel, the *Falls of Clyde* is a major tourist attraction on Honolulu Harbor. LEFT: The Arizona Memorial attracts streams of visitors to Pearl Harbor, site of the infamous attack on the American fleet in World War II. ABOVE: The splendid Maritime Museum.

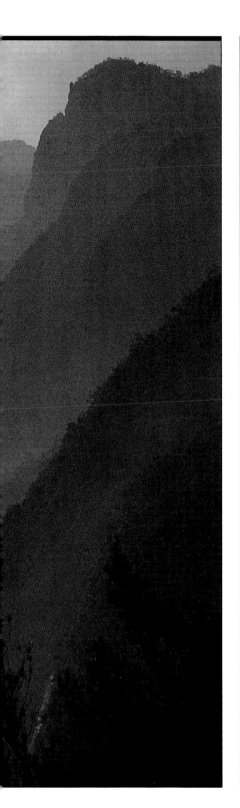

Welcome
to Hawaii

"NO OTHER LAND COULD SO LONGINGLY AND BESEECHINGLY HAUNT MY SLEEPING AND WAKING, through half a lifetime, as that one has done," Mark Twain wrote of Hawaii; "Other things leave me, but [Hawaii] abides."

Hawaii continues to haunt the dreams of modern-day visitors — more than seven million a year from every corner of the globe — who flock to the islands for endless sun, sand and tropical seas. In many respects, America's fiftieth state is the epitome of paradise, the essence of everything we expect from a tropical island vacation: black-sand beaches washed by pearly surf, coconut palms swaying in a gentle breeze, molten lava spewing from lofty volcanoes, dolphins frolicking in turquoise lagoons, and a native culture that is at once powerful and sublime.

The islands have given birth to myriad tropical cliches — hula girls in grass skirts, wall-to-wall bodies at Waikiki, and Elvis seducing bikini-clad beauties with his ukulele. But for every hackneyed image there's a flip side of the Hawaiian experience that is manifestly divine. Watching a sacred ceremony at Mookini Heiau temple on the Kohala Coast, where Hawaiians have venerated their gods for more than 15 centuries. Gleaming the Banzai Pipeline or hanging ten off the crest of a monster wave at Waimea Bay. Galloping across the Big Island backcountry on a sturdy *paniolo* pony. Or something as simple as finding a beachside café with fresh kona and a guy strumming a slide guitar.

One of Hawaii's greatest strengths is her geographical diversity. From the thunderous volcanic peaks of the Big Island to the fragile coral atolls of the Midway Group, no other tropical island chain can lay claim to such a medley of natural wonders. Hawaii Volcanoes and Haleakala national parks flaunt stark desert landscapes that wouldn't look out of place on the moon. At the opposite end of the spectrum, the lush Na Pali Coast is one of the earth's wettest places, a verdant mantel of waterfalls, rivers and jungle-shrouded cliffs that plunge straight down into the sea.

Urban Hawaii is personified by Honolulu, the bustling capital city where a third of the state's 1.2 million people squeeze into high-rise condos and posh garden plots between Diamond Head and Pearl Harbor. Honolulu brandishes several personalities: university town, military bastion, retirement hub, sports Mecca, convention center and after-dark playground. Contrast that to the wooden bungalows and sandy lanes of isolated hamlets like Waipio on the Big Island or Kualapuu on Molokai where life continues at a wonderfully languid pace.

Perhaps Jack London summed up the allure of Hawaii better than any other writer: "In what other land save this one is the

commonest form of greeting not 'Good day,' or 'How d'ye do,' but 'Love'? That greeting is *Aloha* — love, I love you, my love to you…"

Hawaii does have a way of dwelling in your heart, a romance with earth, wind and fire that never seems to end.

OPPOSITE: Wild surf pounds Oahu's North Shore.
ABOVE: Signs of life in a desolate field of hardened lava on the Big Island.

Hawaii and Its People

FORGED BY FIRE, BLESSED BY RAIN AND SUN, and carved by wind, the Hawaiian islands are among nature's most beautiful creations, encircled by leis of beaches set amidst the bluest of oceans.

The eight main Hawaiian islands — Maui, Kauai, Oahu, Molokai, Niihau, Kahoolawe, Lanai and Hawaii (also called the Big Island) — rose from the depths of the ocean to form one segment of a long chain of volcanoes which once extended all the way to Siberia. The northern part of the Hawaiian chain is composed of a series of sunken volcanic peaks known as the Emperor Sea Mounts. The northwestern Hawaiian islands, the central section of the chain, is a national wildlife refuge.

Over the past 80 million years, the Pacific Plate, one of the earth's 12 solid-rock tectonic plates, has been moving across a stationary "hot spot," or magma well, resulting in the formation of the Hawaiian chain. As the plate pushes towards the northwest at four inches (10 cm) a year, molten lava pushes through the earth's crust to form new volcanoes, magma piles up, lava hardens and new islands slowly make their way above the ocean's surface. Even as you read this, such an island is taking shape near the Big Island.

The islands lie 2,390 miles (3,846 km) west of California, 3,850 miles (6,196 km) east of Japan, and 2,400 miles (3,862 km) north of the Marquesas Islands, home of the first seafaring Polynesian adventurers who discovered the Hawaiian islands. Famed for their volcanoes, mysterious valleys, beautiful beaches and warm Pacific Ocean waters, the islands boast other records. Snow fields lie fewer than 62 miles (100 km) from desert, and some of the driest areas on earth stand on the fringe of green forests. Rising 33,476 ft (10,203 m) from its base on the ocean floor, snowcapped Mauna Kea on the Big Island is the world's highest island mountain. Mauna Loa, whose summit reaches an altitude of 13,677 ft (4,169 m) is a perfect shield volcano occupying 10,000 cubic miles (41,680 cubic km), the largest volcanic mass in the world. Mount Waialeale on Kauai, with an annual rainfall of more than 450 in (1,143 cm) ranks among the wettest locations on earth. The Big Island claims the world's most active volcanic crater, Kilauea, on the

east side of Mauna Loa volcano. The Alenuihaha Channel between Hawaii and Maui drops to a depth of 6,300 ft (1,920 m), one of the deepest areas of the Pacific Ocean. And the islands have probably the balmiest, most beautiful weather in the world — right in the midst of hurricane tracks.

THE ISLAND CLIMATE

Hawaii's tropical weather, more than any other factor, draws millions of visitors to the state each year.

Why are the islands so blessed? Much has to do with their alignment: a diagonal pattern from northwest to southeast across the path of prevailing winds known as the northeast trades. A high pressure area in the northern Pacific interacts with the powerful subtropical jet stream, creating cooling trade winds which blow at a constant 15 to 25 mph (25 to 40 km/h). Without the trades, Hawaii would stew in its own humidity, with summer temperatures ranging from 80°F (27°C) to above 90°F (32°C).

Standing right in the path of the trade winds are Hawaii's lofty peaks. When the winds strike these volcanic mountains, they cool and condense to create precipitation. These rain belts are usually found at elevations of 1,970 to 2,950 ft (600 to 900 m), with the higher summits of Haleakala on Maui and both Mauna Kea and Kilauea on the Big Island left dry. Another result of trade winds and high peaks is dramatically variable weather over short distances.

Some islanders refer to the local seasons not as fall, winter, spring and summer, but as the "season of the winter storms" (November to March) and the "season of the tropical storms" (April to November).

The winter storms bring cool, wet weather fairly consistently to Hawaii. The trade wind

This makes Hawaii an almost ideal holiday destination, and by virtue of its colorful history and culture, truly unique — one of America's most fascinating states.

THE POLYNESIAN CONNECTION

Historical evidence suggests that Hawaii's earliest inhabitants came from the Marquesas chain in what is now French Polynesia. Perhaps the first immigrants undertook these long and hazardous voyages because of tribal wars or overcrowding in their

patterns are interrupted in high pressure belts and the storms sweep in from the southeast to the leeward side and are referred to as Kona (Hawaiian for leeward) Winds. During this period, influenced by areas of intense depression across the northern Pacific, surf runs high on the islands' northern shores, drawing many of the world's best surfers.

There are limited interruptions to the trade wind patterns during the season of tropical storms. Beaches on the southern side of the islands are affected by storms in the southern hemisphere, and surf often runs high in these areas.

Despite storms and wind, there is no bad time of the year to visit the islands; rarely does poor weather ruin a vacation.

original homeland. Whatever the reason, the ancient mariners who reached Hawaii around AD 300 braved the elements in sturdy double-hulled canoes, navigating by the sun, stars, ocean swells, currents, and the migratory patterns of birds and marine life. It's not known how many voyages they undertook or how many lives were lost at sea before they sighted the lovely new land of wind and fire. What is known is that it would take several hundred years for the next Polynesian migrants, from Tahiti, to arrive in the Hawaiian isles.

OPPOSITE: Painted escarpment LEFT of Haleakala Crater, Maui. Carved icons RIGHT at Puuhonua O Honaunua — The City of Refuge — Kealakekua Bay, Big Island. ABOVE: Sparse signs of life on Devastation Trail, Hawaii Volcanoes National Park.

It was the Tahitians who most likely called the Big Island "Hawai'i," a name later adopted for the entire chain. Polynesians, like explorers throughout history, christened many of their discoveries with names derived from their homeland. So the name Hawaii was nothing new. It appears (with dialectical differences) as "Savai'i" in Samoa; "Ra'iatea" in the Society Islands; and "Havai'i" in Tahiti. In the ancient legends of the New Zealand Maoris, the homeland of their ancestors was called "Hawaiki."

60,000 people could be counted in the archipelago just 80 years later.

Cook continued his voyage in search of a northwest passage linking the Atlantic to the Pacific Ocean, but he returned to Hawaiian waters in November of that same year. After cruising off the islands for two months, his ships finally dropped anchor in Kealakekua Bay on the western, or Kona, side of the Big Island, at the height of an annual religious celebration honoring the deified ancestor Lono Ikamakahiki. A huge crowd greeted the British explorers and

CAPTAIN COOK AND HIS LEGACY

Westerners were unaware of the existence of these islands until English explorer Captain James Cook sighted Oahu and landed on Kauai in January of 1778. He named the archipelago the Sandwich Islands after John Montague, the Fourth Earl of Sandwich and First Lord of the Admiralty.

Sailors from Cook's command, which consisted of the British ships HMS *Resolution* and *Discovery*, initiated trade with the natives at Waimea, Kauai. Tragically, European diseases, including syphilis and gonorrhea, took their toll on the islanders. Historians note that from a population of about 300,000 at the time of Cook's visit, only

Cook was honored and lavished with gifts. In fact, the natives at first thought that Cook was the legendary Lono, who had sailed from Hawaii several generations earlier, promising to return.

On February 4, 1779, Cook set sail again, only to run into a fierce storm that would change the course of history. The British ships were forced back to the safety of Kealakekua Bay, but the mood this time was anything but festive. A brooding hostility prevailed among the natives due to several incidents with British sailors during their previous visit. The ruling chief, Kalaniopuu, after seeing so many of his female subjects seduced by the sailors, had imposed a *kapu* or ban on women boarding the ships. But the sailors were not to be denied and came ashore for the women, respecting neither the *kapu* nor the high chiefs. They also had no qualms about tearing down religious structures for firewood. Before their previous departure, Cook and his men had also seriously depleted the district's food supply to provision their ships, and this had not been forgotten by the natives.

As antagonism between the foreigners and the Hawaiians grew, the ships and the sailors found themselves subjected to petty thievery. Matters came to a head when the cutter from the *Discovery* was stolen and a high chief killed in the process of recovering it. Cook blocked the bay and went ashore with a party of marines to take Chief Kalaniopuu hostage, and in so doing broke the *kapu* forbidding the touching of a high chief by any but his own close relatives or retainers.

A scuffle broke out between the landing party and the Hawaiians, and the marines were attacked by a large number of armed warriors. Using stones and clubs, they set upon the British, killing five of them including Cook himself, who died in the blood-stained waters of Kealakekua Bay.

KAMEHAMEHA: WARRIOR KING

Upon the death of Kalaniopuu, somewhere around 1780, his son Kiwalao was declared paramount chief. But several other chiefs, dissatisfied with the manner in which Kiwalao was redistributing land, convinced his nephew Kamehameha to wrest control of the island from his cousin.

For more than five years thereafter, the islands were gripped by tribal warfare. By 1796, Kamehameha had defeated his rival chiefs on Hawaii, Maui, and Oahu. The turning point of the campaign occurred at Nuuanu Valley in 1795, where Oahu chief Kalanikupule and his allies attempted to make a stand. Kamehameha drove the defending forces up the Nuuanu Pali and many of the Oahu troops were driven over the cliffs by Kamehameha's warriors. Kamehameha's victory also secured sovereignty over the islands of Molokai and Lanai.

Kamehameha planned at least two expeditions to conquer Kauai and its satellite island, Niihau, and to this day Kauai's people will tell you he was repulsed and sent back to Oahu. Others say he never reached Kauai because storms swamped much of his fleet.

Not until 1810 did Kaumualii, paramount chief of Kauai and Niihau, come to Oahu at the invitation of Kamehameha. It was agreed that Kaumualii would remain ruler of those islands, but be tributary to Kamehameha, until "the black tapa cloth [death] covered Kaumualii." When he died, his islands became part of Kamehameha's kingdom.

Kamehameha strengthened his hold on the islands via the skillful application of the ancient feudal *kapu* system, by which a chief holds absolute power over his subjects, including over matters of life and death. Kamehameha gained a reputation as a wise, just and peaceful ruler. At his side during this period was his favorite wife, Kaahumanu. Kamehameha remained ever faithful to the ancient gods, never forsaking the religion of his forefathers even in the face of pressure and influence from the ever-increasing presence of Western civilization in Hawaii. But all of that was about to change.

OPPOSITE: A painting depicts Kamehameha the Great surrounded by his chiefs. ABOVE: Coat of arms guards the Iolani Palace gate in Honolulu.

THE MISSIONARY INFLUENCE

When the great king died in 1819, Kaahumanu declared herself Queen Regent and ruled the land with her foster son, Liholiho (Kamehameha II). Kaahumanu's influence on the history of the islands was considerable. Supported by Kamehameha II, she set about eliminating the *kapu* system by the simple act of having Hawaiians of different castes dine together, forbidden under the old laws. Destruction of sacred temples and idols followed. Kaahumanu also came under the influence of American missionaries and spearheaded the drive to spread the gospel throughout the islands. This era marked the beginning of Hawaii's first period of modernization.

In 1823, Kamehameha II and his wife Queen Kamamalu embarked on a long voyage to Britain at the invitation of King George III. It proved to be tragic. After being royally entertained in London, Kamehameha II and his queen contracted measles and died. Their bodies were brought back to Hawaii.

Kamehameha's 10-year-old brother Kauikeaouli (Kamehameha III) succeeded him as king, but for the greater part of his 30-year reign, it was Kaahumanu who wielded the greatest influence on the people of the islands. In a development of considerable significance, Kaahumanu converted to Christianity, and many other Hawaiian leaders followed suit. The void that had been created by the banning of the *kapu* laws and a disavowing of the ancient gods was being filled by a new religion that swept the islands.

THE END OF A DYNASTY

Under the rule of Kamehameha III and Queen Kaahumanu, a new form of government took shape, and the capital of the nation was moved from Lahaina on Maui to Honolulu on Oahu. Kamehameha III earned a permanent place in Hawaiian history by bringing about a constitution and enacting new laws. When he died in 1854, leaving no legitimate heir, he was deeply mourned by his people. His nephew and foster son, Alexander Liholiho (Kamehameha IV), assumed leadership at the height of an economic boom launched by the whaling industry, during which Lahaina and Honolulu had become major whaling ports.

Kamehameha IV's nine-year reign was one of mixed fortunes for the people of the islands. The whaling industry soon declined with the indiscriminate hunting of whales and fuel other than whale oil appearing on the market. Dreaded leprosy, brought to the islands, it is said, by Chinese immigrants, spread like wildfire. Kamehameha IV died of an asthma attack in 1863 and was succeeded by his elder brother Lot (Kamehameha V). Kamehameha V ran the islands with dictatorial authority. He did away with the old constitution, which he felt had placed too much power in the hands of the white business community, and had a new constitution drawn up. He also established a bureau of immigration, which in turn began encouraging laborers to come to the islands to assist the burgeoning sugar industry. Because Kamehameha V never married, his death signaled the end of the Kamehameha dynasty.

THE MERRY MONARCH

And so commenced a new dynasty under an elected king or *alii* (nobleman). Prince William Kanaina, a descendant of a half brother of Kamehameha I, took the royal name Lunalilo. He had many noble traits and could have become a fair and just ruler, but he was partial to drink, a habit allegedly induced by a broken romance, and he died 13 months into his reign.

Lunalilo was loved by the islanders and was known as the Citizen King. He requested that he be buried with his subjects, entombed on the grounds of Kawaiahao Church in Honolulu, becoming the only monarch of modern times not buried at Mauna Ala (the royal mausoleum) in Oahu's Nuuanu Valley.

The man who Lunalilo defeated in the royal election—Colonel David Kalakaua—succeeded him. Kalakaua set about developing a British-style monarchy and, in the process, established royal standards regarding the spending of taxpayers' money. He had extravagant tastes, but he also had a vision of the world rare in his time. Kalakaua

was a man of great intelligence and charm, and while he built a reputation as the "Merry Monarch" he also achieved several diplomatic triumphs. For instance, he was the first monarch from a foreign state to visit Washington, and while there, he negotiated a reciprocal treaty with the United States, enabling Hawaii to sell its sugar cheaper by eliminating a tariff.

In 1881, Kalakaua embarked on a world tour, the first monarch of any nation to do so. His first stop was Japan, where he was feted by Emperor Mutsuhito. Kalakaua and

his entourage went on to China, then Europe. In London he was received by Queen Victoria and the Prince of Wales. Inspired by the pomp and pageantry of the British court, Kalakaua decided to have a coronation in Hawaii. It was a lavish and colorful affair.

The political scandals that followed the coronation weakened Kalakaua's grip on the island nation. At the center of the trouble was the acquisition of much of Hawaii's prime land by a group of *haole* (white) businessmen, the root of a land ownership dispute that continues to simmer even today.

OPPOSITE: Carved icon guards Kamakahonu Heiau (temple) on the Big Island. ABOVE: Beloved Queen Liliuokalani is immortalized in this statue on the grounds of the state capitol.

Kalakaua was keenly aware of the common ancestry of the Polynesian race, and visited Samoa as a first step to establishing a United Kingdom of Oceania. He was hampered, however, by bad advisors at home, chiefly those in the American sugar community, as well as by the efforts of colonial powers such as Germany and Britain who were determined to see that his dream never come true. Kalakaua died in San Francisco in 1891, a man whose visions were far ahead of his time and far beyond the means of his small, young kingdom.

THE FIFTIETH STATE

Kalakaua's sister, Liliuokalani, brought to the throne a passion for the rights of native Hawaiians and a determination to diminish the power of the white minority in the government. The task proved too great for her. Powerful business forces marshaled against her, and with the assistance of sailors and marines from a visiting United States naval ship, staged a coup in 1893. The rebel leaders established a provisional government under the leadership of pineapple baron Sanford B. Dole, and forced the queen to abdicate.

The islands were soon engulfed by an era of great bitterness and political maneuvering. While President Grover Cleveland sought to reinstate Queen Liliuokalani, Dole and his supporters declared Hawaii a republic, with Dole as president. Liliuokalani was placed under house arrest after she supported a counter-coup.

In 1898, with the backing of newly elected United States president William McKinley, Hawaii became an American possession through the signing of the Joint Resolution of Annexation — an act that left native Hawaiians bitter and former President Cleveland "ashamed." Two years later, Hawaii became a United States territory through the Organic Act.

In 1941, Hawaii survived the bloody Japanese attack on Pearl Harbor. Following Japan's surrender in 1945, there were moves to have Hawaii accepted into the union. This finally came about in 1959 when Hawaii — once a kingdom, then a republic, and finally an American territory — became the fiftieth American State. Only the tiny island of Niihau, populated then, as it is now, by people of Hawaiian ancestry, rejected statehood.

In the same year, the first commercial passenger jet touched down at Honolulu International Airport, opening Hawaii as a cultural, economic and political pathway between East and West. Modern Hawaii was born.

The post-statehood years were marked by the political leadership of Governor John Burns (1962–1973) and a booming economy. Burns was followed by his lieutenant governor, George Ariyoshi, who stood at the state's helm through 1986.

On a national level, Hawaii's most notable modern leaders have been a pair of immigrant sons elected to the United States Senate: Japanese-American (and World War II hero) Daniel Inouye and Chinese-American Hiram Fong. Another local hero is Ellison Onizuka, Hawaii's first astronaut, who died when the space shuttle Challenger exploded in 1986.

The 1990s saw increased calls for sovereignty by native Hawaiians disenchanted with United States rule over the islands. Among their major complaints were, and still are, inferior health care (native people have the highest rates of diabetes, hypertension and respiratory illness in the United States), lack of economic opportunities, and a state education system that fails to emphasize traditional language and culture.

The independence movement gained valuable momentum 1993 during a statewide centennial commemoration to mark Queen Liliuokalani's overthrow. Governor John Waihee decreed that the Stars and Stripes not be flown over Hawaiian state office buildings during the five-day event, and the Hawaiian state flag was flown at half-mast on Capitol Hill in Washington DC during the same period. Later that year, the United States government ended more than a century of official silence on the overthrow of the Hawaiian monarchy when President Bill Clinton signed a resolution apologizing for American complicity in the 1893 coup.

A year later, a pro-independence group called the Ohana Council declared independence from the United States during a rally on the grounds of Iolani Palace in Honolulu.

Among provisions of the declaration were a return of all "land, natural wealth, resources, minerals and waters" to the native Hawaiian people and an immediate withdrawal of all United States military forces based on the islands. Although largely symbolic, the act served to galvanize many of the 300 different groups lobbying for native rights and land claims.

Another victory for self-determination advocates was the 1994 handover of tiny Kahoolawe Island from the United States Navy to the state government, after an 18-

year political and legal battle with native groups. The island is being held in trust as a possible site for a future sovereign Hawaiian nation, but must undergo a 20-year, $400-million cleanup after decades as a Navy bombing and gunnery range.

Another symbolic step toward independence came in 1996 when native Hawaiians voted overwhelming (73%) to form a committee to explore the formation of a native government. Delegates subsequently elected to this committee staged their first formal meeting in the summer of 1999, when the Native Hawaiian Convention convened in the Hawaii state capitol building. In the wake of the gathering, a United States government official visiting Honolulu declared that there

was very little likelihood of Hawaii ever gaining independence from the rest of the nation because two-thirds of the 50 states would have to vote to amend the United States Constitution to allow secession.

Not to be daunted, Hawaiians are continuing their campaign for more self-determination. "We are a free people and can't let go of that vision," says Mahealani Kamauu, a leading advocate of the native cause. "Our challenge is to make others, both Hawaiian and foreign, see that that vision makes sense."

HAWAIIAN CULTURE

To appreciate Hawaii, not merely for its physical beauty but for its traditions and historic past, one must probe the mysteries of its culture, which were almost forgotten but are now being revived. The culture of ancient Hawaii was once deeply entwined with religion. Life was lived according to sacred laws, or *kapu*, and religion, with its pantheon of gods, pervaded every aspect of life.

Religion was based on gods major and minor. Kane was revered as a god of creation, light and fresh water. He was the ancestor of chiefs and commoners alike. Kanaloa was god of the sea and constant companion of Kane. Together, they created Hawaii's freshwater springs. Ku was associated with the rising sun, masculine virility and war. Lono was said to be the last of the four great gods to arrive from Kahiki, one of the Hawaiians' ancient homelands. He was the god of agriculture, clouds, winds and fertility.

The Polynesian goddess Hina held equal stature with these four major gods. She and her mate Ku were said to have come to Hawaii before either Kane or Kanaloa. Hina was associated with the sunset and possessed female attributes complementing the ones of Ku. Together these two had the whole world as their realm along with all generations of mankind born and unborn.

Of all the gods and demigods in the Hawaiian pantheon, perhaps the most feared and most revered is Pele, goddess of fire. Pele is believed to be an *'aumakua* or ancestor who lives on as a guardian spirit. Many modern

For over three decades, the hula was banned by Christian missionaries. Now it is in the midst of a revival.

Hawaiians still pay tribute to her and believe in her powers.

There were many gods of different forms — fish, birds, animals and humans — and demigods with supernatural powers who performed feats of strength and endurance. Among the most famous folk heroes was Maui, sometimes nicknamed the Trickster. He is credited with fishing up whole islands, slowing down the sun by snaring it, discovering fire, and other wondrous things.

The *kapu* system of laws followed by the early Hawaiians had a fixed purpose in daily

life. It was repressive and often appeared illogical, but was designed for environmental, economic and ecological reasons. Its main purpose was the love and preservation of the land and the sea. In this system, ruling chiefs held the power of life and death over all their subjects. Human sacrifice was common.

The simple act of going fishing, as essential to the Hawaiians today as it was to their ancestors, was ruled by *kapu*. A fisherman had to know which fish were under *kapu*, or forbidden. He had to know which fish were personifications of his *'aumakua* or family guardian spirit; such fish could never be eaten. And he had to ask the gods for permission to fish, reading their answer in the

weather and waves. A portion of his first catch had to be released to appease the god of the sea. On reaching the shore, he was required to leave part of his catch at the *ku'ula* or local fishing shrine. Once home he had to know which types of fish the female members of his family were allowed to eat and which ones were strictly for males.

This scenario was enacted, to one degree or another, in every aspect of daily life, from the manufacturing of tools and weapons to the hewing of a canoe, from the planting of crops to the building of a house. Restrictive as it may seem, it was a system perfected over nearly 10 centuries prior to the arrival of Westerners.

The *kapu* system ensured the protection of natural resources. When it was eventually abolished, the people overfished the sea and depleted the forests of sandalwood, used to barter for Western tools, weapons, and cloth from Western sea captains. This trade signaled the end of the manufacture of local goods, and the ancient crafts began to disappear. Gardens and farms were neglected as people moved from their ancestral homes to be nearer the centers of commerce and trade. Indeed, neglect of the land or *'aina*, perhaps more than anything else, almost destroyed the Hawaiian race.

Traditionally, each island was ruled by an aristocratic class of warrior-nobles called *alii*. Each *alii* could trace his lineage back dozens of generations through one or more lines to the godlike parents of the Polynesian race. These founders, Wakea the sky father and Papa the earth mother, existed at the very beginning of life on earth.

The sovereign lord of each island was the *alii nui* (great chief). Generally this chief was the senior male of the island's ruling family. District chiefs, called *alii 'ai moku* or literally "chiefs who eat the land," were appointed by the *alii nui*. When an *alii* died or was overthrown, the ruling family settled upon a successor, who appointed district chiefs. As a general rule, the common people, *maka'ainana*, were not affected by changes in rulers. As long as their taxes were paid in the form of produce from land or sea and/or craft work (mats, bowls, tapa cloth, etc.), they and their descendants were permitted to stay where they were.

The *maka'ainana* were also expected to answer the call to arms in times of war, and acquired their land by proving loyalty to their chief. In 1848, Kamehameha III listened to white advisors and made it possible for anyone to purchase land. One-third of the land was to be held by the king; one-third of the land was set aside for the chiefs and awarded on an individual basis. These lands could be sold. The last third was set aside to be applied for and awarded to the *maka'ainana*. To be awarded the land, one had to show cause based on living and working on the plot or

Hawaiian didn't know that by selling his land he was forever barring himself and his family from returning to the land he and his ancestors had lived on for so long. Family unity was eroded, ancestral roots lost, and the culture all but wiped out.

After nearly 200 years of erosion, Hawaiian culture is in the midst of a renaissance. Spurring this movement are many young college-educated Hawaiians who identify with their roots. Balancing this cultural equation are a small number of *kupuna* (grandparents or older relatives) who, having

kuleana in question for some length of time. Each applicant was interviewed individually with corroborating witnesses. Once he was awarded land, the individual was free to do what he wished with his property.

Undoubtedly the king enacted this law with the welfare of his people in mind and with the intent of bringing Hawaii in line with modern Western culture. Instead, this act, coming along with the overthrow of the monarchy, and before Hawaiians learned the western concept of land ownership, is regarded by native Hawaiians as one of the lowest points in Hawaiian history.

Title to property was practically given away to foreigners who were "crazy" enough to pay a few dollars for it. The average

retained knowledge of Hawaiian culture passed down from their *kupuna*, have joined forces with the younger generation to lead this resurgence. Hawaiians in ever-increasing numbers are immersing themselves in the movement to relearn the old ways. Featherwork, wood carving and lei (garland) making in the ancient style are some of the traditional arts making a comeback. Interest in the Hawaiian language has never been higher. But none of these skills has matched the passion for the hula that the renaissance has brought about.

Today, just as in the times of the ancients, the hula student goes through rigorous and

Three faces of modern Hawaii reflect its diversity.

careful training of mind and body. Students learn about Hawaiian language and culture as they practice the movements of the dance. They also learn the names and stories of the ancient chiefs and heroes of the Hawaiian people. Pele, the fire goddess, and her sister, Hi'iaka, are prominent in the legends learned through chants and dances.

Le-Ann Stender Durant, a hula dancer and teacher, has written about her passion for the dance. "To share the hula is to share being Hawaiian; and to be proud to be Hawaiian," she writes. "We have just begun to discover where this pride will take us. To love the hula is to love life in our Islands."

PEOPLE OF THE ISLANDS

Nations around the world pay lip service to racial harmony, but few have achieved it on the grand scale that Hawaii has. It is the strength of the state. Ask a resident of the islands what his ethnic background is, and you may have to leaf through a geography book to understand the answer. Try this for size: "Chinese, Japanese, Portuguese, Irish, and of course, a little bit of Hawaiian." You'll hear that last line often: Many Hawaiians are proud of the Polynesian blood flowing through their veins.

The largest racial group in the islands today is Caucasian, or *haole*. They include descendants of the missionaries from New England who arrived in the mid-1800s and forever changed the traditional Hawaiian lifestyle. The Portuguese arrived in 1878 from the Azores and Madeira islands, after an arduous sea voyage. They brought their families with them, intending to stay. Portuguese contributions to the Hawaiian lifestyle include the ukulele and wonderful Portuguese food, including *malasada* (a light doughnut), Portuguese bean soup, and spicy sausage. But there is little architectural evidence of the Portuguese presence such as you find in Macao, 40 miles (65 km) from Hong Kong, or Melaka in Malaysia.

Around 1830, Spanish-Mexican cowboys were imported from California to work and train native cowboys. They came to be known as *paniolo* (from the Hawaiian pronunciation of "español," Spanish). Next came the Puerto Ricans in 1900. The sugar and pineapple plantations also imported labor from Italy, Russia, Spain, Austria and Germany, but few stayed long enough to make an impact on the demography of the state.

Though Caucasians make up the largest racial group of the population, the impact of Asian immigration is most evident in Hawaii today. Japanese-Americans probably wield the greatest influence in the islands, particularly in politics. But they paid for this right with blood, sweat and tears. Thanks to their stoicism, patience and hard work, and that of other migrant Asian labor, the sugar and pineapple industries prospered. Japanese Hawaiians now hold many important political positions on the islands, and Japanese tourism is essential to the local economy.

The Chinese arrived as early as 1802, and a large wave of immigrants settled on the islands just as the American missionaries were arriving. They worked hard, saved their money and married Hawaiians. Through the generations they have totally integrated, yet have managed, perhaps more than other ethnic groups, to preserve their language, their religion, and their culture. Their festivals, such as Chinese New Year, are observances in which all residents of Hawaii seem to participate. As the Chinese community grew in affluence and influence, many left the Chinatown region to take up residence on the loftier slopes in the better residential districts of Honolulu. Yet old habits die hard, and when the urge for dim sum, snake soup, salted eggs, salted fish or herb tea grips the soul, even the wealthy succumb to the temptation and gravitate to the narrow back streets of Chinatown.

The majority of Filipinos in Hawaii today are *Ilocanos*, from Ilocos Norte. Many of the earliest Filipino immigrants had macho reputations as "hell raisers," brought about, it is said, by a shortage of women. Fights over women were common, most settled with knives rather than fists. But the reputation they established in the old days as good labor-union organizers prevails. The Filipinos have made a niche for themselves in the islands, contributing to business, politics, and music.

The first party of 100 Koreans arrived in Hawaii in 1903. They were hired by the

Hawaiian Sugar Planters' Association. By 1905, their numbers had risen to more than 7,000. It was in Honolulu that Korean patriot Syngman Rhee fostered his revolutionary plans. Following Japan's defeat in World War II, he became the Republic of Korea's first president. Deposed by a military coup in 1960, Rhee lived in exile in Hawaii until his death five years later. The Korean community continues to thrive in Hawaii. They are a strong, passionate people. Korean restaurateurs and businesspeople often hold prominent positions in local communities.

Hawaiian Samoans playing in National Football League teams on the mainland and in colleges throughout the country.

The latest wave of immigrants has come from the war-torn nations of Southeast Asia — Vietnam, Cambodia, Laos and Thailand. They have brought with them their religious beliefs, customs and cuisine. All are integrating into the Hawaiian lifestyle and making their own contributions to it.

Given the abundance of immigrants and the subsequent interracial marriages and relationships, there are few native Hawai-

Since Samoans are Polynesians, it was relatively easy for the first big group of Samoans, who arrived in 1952, to adapt to the lifestyle here, even though the pace was faster than they were used to in American Samoa. There were, however, some cultural differences. Many of the continuing wave of Samoans coming to the islands are Mormons and gravitate to Laie on the North Shore of Oahu, site of the Mormon Temple and the Polynesian Cultural Center, run by Mormons.

While some members of the Samoan community find it hard to get jobs in a tight job market, this is not true for Samoan athletes, who have made names for themselves in professional football. There are several

ians left on the Islands. Niihau, a small privately owned island, has the largest concentration of Hawaiians still speaking the native tongue and following traditional customs. Molokai also is home to a strong community of Hawaiians, as is Oahu. As a group, Hawaiians are accumulating political and social strength. Non-Hawaiians are recognizing the value of the indigenous culture, and it sometimes seems everyone is racing to claim Hawaiian heritage and a loyalty to ancient traditions. Music, dance, arts, crafts, and cuisine all reflect indigenous roots, and the beliefs of early Hawaiians are gaining respect. The spirit of aloha lives on.

Entries in the Miss Chinatown pageant and their escorts parade down a rainy Honolulu avenue.

Oahu

WAIKIKI BEACH. DIAMOND HEAD. PEARL HARBOR. Most travelers think they've covered Oahu once they've seen these three landmarks. But Hawaii's most populous, cosmopolitan island offers far more than clichés. Oahu has misty, forested mountains, waterfalls, sacred sites, and miles of isolated windswept beaches. There is much to see beyond Waikiki.

Oahu means "The Gathering Place" in Hawaiian; these days it's more like a melting pot. Over 850,000 people live on the second-largest island in the chain. Islanders claim Chinese, Japanese, Filipino, European, Mexican, and Puerto Rican ancestry. Native Hawaiians gather on Oahu to assert their rights and join in celebrations. Ethnic strongholds such as Chinatown have blurred boundaries; for the most part Oahu encapsulates Hawaii's racial harmony.

All things Hawaiian are available on Oahu. Restaurants and markets carry a dazzling array of ingredients from all over the world. Restaurants specialize in traditional Asian and Hawaiian cuisine, or offer inspired blends of Pacific Rim flavors and European techniques. Theaters and clubs present revered slack-key guitarists and upcoming artists who have created a new Hawaiian sound. Museum exhibits trace Hawaiian history and culture; galleries and shops display the latest fine art and folk art trends.

And those who thrive on blatant excess are happy on Oahu. They're not intimidated by the crowds at Waikiki or the congested traffic around Honolulu. Island residents and visitors alike are constantly surprised by Oahu's options.

BACKGROUND

Sacred temples and petroglyphs from the seventeenth and eighteenth centuries are scattered all over Oahu, bearing witness to the island's enduring prominence. Mighty wars were waged here as several island kings battled for sovereignty over all the Hawaiian islands. King Kamehameha I claimed victory in 1795 by driving Oahu's warriors up and over a cliff at Nuuanu Pali, still one of the most dramatic places on the island. Kamehameha's descendents ruled the islands from Maui for nearly a century, while

interlopers made Honolulu the islands' commercial center. Honolulu Harbor was a natural haven for whalers and traders, and ships laden with supplies from Europe, America and Asia arrived regularly. Honolulu became the capital of the islands in 1845, and the royalty moved into Iolani Palace in 1882.

As the Hawaiians were centralizing their power, foreign businessmen and plantation owners were solidifying theirs by buying large portions of land and controlling commerce. In 1893 American marines joined these foreign leaders to overthrow the na-

tive monarchy, and Queen Liliuokalani was held captive in Iolani Palace for nine months. Hawaii became a possession of the United States in 1898, and Oahu's Ewa Plain soon disappeared under agricultural fields. The United States military set up bases on the island and took control of Pearl Harbor.

Tourists started arriving on steamships in the early 1900s; in 1926 the Aloha Tower rose over Honolulu Harbor as a beacon for foreigners. Luxury steamships carried wealthy adventurers from Europe and the United States to Honolulu, where they were greeted with fanfare and pampered in elegant

OPPOSITE: Reclining at dusk at water's edge in Waikiki. ABOVE: "The Pink Lady," Royal Hawaiian Hotel, is a Waikiki landmark.

hotels including Waikiki's Moana Hotel (now the Sheraton Moana Surfrider). When Japanese bombers blasted Pearl Harbor in 1941, Hawaii became an international focal point. The islands were a United States territory by then, and Honolulu was far more American than Hawaiian. Nearly two decades after it bore the brunt of the Japanese invasion, in 1959, Hawaii became the fiftieth United States state.

Today, Honolulu reigns as the state capital and the island's business hub. About five million tourists visit Oahu each year, and

and using these. Free papers and brochures are available at news racks all around Waikiki and Honolulu and at the airport.

GETTING AROUND

If you're sticking to the Waikiki and Honolulu areas, you really don't need a car. In fact, given the dreadful rush-hour traffic, you're best off without one. Some of the larger shopping malls, including Ala Moana, have free shuttles to many hotels. Check with the concierge or tour desk. The **Waikiki Trolley**

residents of neighboring islands stop by frequently to shop, attend cultural events and get a taste of big city life.

GENERAL INFORMATION

The **Hawaii Visitors and Convention Bureau** ((808) 923-1811, at 2270 Kalakaua Avenue, Waikiki, distributes information on all the islands. The **Oahu Visitor's Association** ((808) 524-0722 TOLL-FREE (800) 624-8678, 1001 Bishop Street, Pauahi Tower, Suite 47, Honolulu, has piles of information on the island's attractions. Several tourist publications are filled with details on attractions and savings coupons — travelers trying to stick to a budget can save a bundle by clipping

((808) 596-2199 TOLL-FREE (800) 824-8804, at 1050 Ala Moana Boulevard, has three lines. The red line covers the main tourist attractions; the yellow line reaches most dining and shopping areas; and the blue line travels along the coast to Hanauma Bay. Full day and multi-day passes are available. **TheBus** ((808) 848-5555, Oahu's public bus system, is convenient and inexpensive. Call the number above for routes and schedules. Rental cars come in handy for touring the islands (see GETTING AROUND, page 292 in TRAVELERS' TIPS for numbers). Drivers should do their best to stay off the highways between 4 AM and 8:30 AM and between 3:30 PM and 6 PM, when rush hour traffic turns major thoroughfares into parking lots.

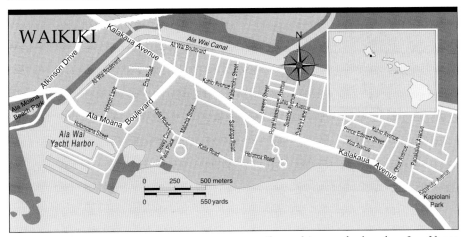

WHAT TO SEE AND DO

WAIKIKI

Just two miles (three kilometers) long and less than half a mile (one kilometer) wide, Waikiki is Oahu's number-one attraction, a place no self-respecting tourist can possibly ignore. It's the home of surfers famous and unknown, the genesis of Hawaii's tourism history, and possibly the most maligned beach in the world. Granted, Waikiki is incredibly crowded and filled with all the tacky, wacky accoutrements of a tourist trap. But it's one of my favorite places in Hawaii.

Waikiki was once mostly swamp. Then it made a natural transition to agriculture and rice paddies; taro patches and duck ponds flourished. Hawaiian royalty considered it their playground. Even then, Waikiki was much more than a beach. Today, it's a giant hotel-restaurant-shopping mall crammed between the ocean and the Ala Wai Canal just a few blocks inland. Two parks flanking the beach provide a green escape from the crowds. **Ala Moana Park** marks the beginning of Waikiki on the west. A long sidewalk runs along the sand from the Hilton Hawaiian Village past picnic tables shaded by palms and pines. From this point on, the bustle and liveliness of the area can be a bit confusing, with a jumble of narrow streets and alleyways between the beach and **Kalakaua Avenue**, a one-way street running southeast towards Diamond Head. Enormous shopping plazas and the entryways to some of Waikiki's most famous hotels give the ave-

nue the ambience of a low-key Las Vegas Strip. Tiki torches rather than neon signs point the way to restaurants, and the cement jungle is cooled by ocean breezes. Fortunately, you can stroll back and forth between the street and sand when the pace of commerce becomes too overwhelming.

Kalakaua's most tasteful monument is the **Sheraton Moana Surfrider Hotel** (see WHERE TO STAY, page 135). Named the Moana when it opened in 1901 amid much fanfare, the hotel leaves one longing for the gracious era of steamships and ball gowns. Oliver Traphagen, a well-known Minnesota architect of that period, designed the mansion using only fine woods — oak, mahogany or maple. Guests danced above the beach on the roof garden with sweeping views of Diamond Head. The hotel's first guests were said to be a group of Shriners who paid $1.50 per night for their rooms. Celebrities followed in quick succession. Among the long list of those who have stayed at the Moana were a Prince of Wales, the late Lord Louis Mountbatten, Amelia Earhart and Alice Roosevelt Longworth. The walls in the hotel's Historical Room are filled with photos from the 1920s and 1930s, when the hotel loaned modest wool bathing suits to its guests. Wander through the public spaces and the grounds, where cocktails are served under a banyan tree planted in 1885.

Just past the hotel, a small clump of stones sits on the sand, surrounded by a wire fence.

The Waikiki skyline and beach, a prime attraction on Oahu.

These are the **Wizard Stones**, said to have healing powers. A statue of the famed surfer and goodwill ambassador **Duke Kahanamoku** stands facing the street in front of the busiest part of Waikiki Beach. Surfers by the score paddle towards Waikiki's famed waves (which are hardly significant compared with those off Oahu's North Shore). Surfboard rentals and lessons are available from several stands on the beach. **Aloha Beach Services** ((808) 922-3111, 2365 Kalakaua Avenue, offers one the beach's greatest thrills — outrigger rides over the waves.

are any concerts scheduled. Beside the Shell an audience of locals and tourists cram the bleachers for the free **Kodak Hula Show** ((808) 627-3379, a Waikiki tradition. Dancers perform at 10 AM on Tuesday, Wednesday, and Thursday. Near the Diamond Head end of the park, the **Waikiki War Memorial Natatorium** appears close to collapsing after years of neglect. Said to be the largest pool in the United States, the memorial was built to commemorate those who lost their lives in World War II. Every so often there are rumors of the memorial's imminent destruction,

Next to this busy stretch of sand is **Kuhio Beach**, where a retaining wall built to keep the sand from eroding creates a shallow saltwater pool. **Kapiolani Park** runs east from the beach with a broad sidewalk separating the sand from lawns and picnic groves. In the park, the **Waikiki Aquarium** ((808) 923-9741, 2777 Kalakaua Avenue, sits beside the water; check out the coral reef tank. Giraffes eye the traffic from the **Honolulu Zoo** ((808) 971-7171, at 151 Kapahulu Avenue, a pleasant spot for a stroll. Admission is charged; the zoo is open daily. The **Waikiki Shell** in Kapiolani Park is a local gem, beloved for being the most romantic outdoor concert venue on the island. The Hawaii Symphony plays here frequently; ask at your hotel if there

followed by protests, but thus far the money has not appeared for its restoration.

HONOLULU

Honolulu is the financial, political and cultural capital of the Hawaiian islands. Sleek office and condo towers lining downtown streets create a contemporary skyline above historic palaces and museums. The dominant feature of the city's business district is **Iolani Palace** ((808) 522-0822, at 364 South King Street. The palace was the last bastion of Hawaiian sovereignty and was the home of King David Kalakaua and his wife Queen Kapiolani. Kalakaua was clearly impressed by the pomp and pageantry surrounding

European royalty, and the palace he built in 1882, at a cost of about $360,000, reflects his obsession. Though hardly comparable to most European palaces, the Iolani is an impressive structure surrounded by lawns and banyan trees. A magnificent gold and black statue of warrior-king Kamehameha sits outside the main gates of the palace on King Street. The statue is wreathed in long orchid and ti leaf leis on King Kamehameha Day (June 11).

Visitors must join a guided tour to climb the white marble staircase to the gray Italianate Renaissance palace and to walk

on his own head. The Friends conduct tours of the palace. Reservations are required.

The nearby **Kawaiahao Church** ((808) 538-6267, 957 Punchbowl Street at King Street, was built from 14,000 blocks of coral cut from Hawaii's reefs. Missionaries and Hawaiians worked together to design and construct the church, which opened in 1842. Converted Hawaiian royalty and the elite worshipped at the solid bastion of missionary success. In 1874, a little chapel on the grounds of the church became the final resting place of King Lunalilo, a beloved monarch who asked to

through its gilded throne room. Several rooms in the building have been restored under the guidance of the nonprofit Friends of the Iolani Palace, and visitors are led through by volunteers who expound on the building's history. The king enhanced the palace's grandeur by having the island's first telephones installed in the royal bedrooms. Royalty inhabited the palace for little more than a decade; Kalakaua's sister, Queen Liliuokalani, was imprisoned here during the revolution that led to the overthrow of the monarchy.

In the palace grounds is the copper-domed Coronation Bandstand, where King David Kalakaua and his queen were crowned. Indeed, history records that Kalakaua, like Napoleon, placed the crown

be buried with the people rather than at the Royal Mausoleum in Nuuanu.

Immediately behind Kawaiahao Church is the **Mission Houses Museum** ((808) 531-0481, at the corner of Kawaiahao and King Streets. The compound includes a prefab frame house brought by the missionaries from New England and built in 1821. Two coral block houses are also presented. Closed Sunday and Monday; admission is charged.

Architects and city planners were determined to do Hawaii proud when they designed the **State Capitol** ((808) 586-2211 at

OPPOSITE LEFT: Waikiki's Kalakaua Avenue. RIGHT: Night shopping at the International Marketplace. ABOVE: Sunbathers find room to spread their towels on uncrowded beaches beyond Waikiki.

510 Beretania Street. Two towers represent volcanoes, and the structure is surrounded by a reflecting pool representing the sea. The building opened in 1969, but had to be closed in 1990 for expensive renovations. It's back in use now, and visitors can wander past murals and artifacts and check out the view from the fifth floor. In front of the capitol, across Beretania Street, is the nine-foot-high (three-meter) War Memorial and eternal flame dedicated to the men and women who fought for the United States in World War II. On a cool, quiet spot on the Richard Street

Downtown's historic sites are a few blocks from the waterfront, home to the **Hawaii Maritime Center** ((808) 536-6373 at Pier 7. An 1,800-lb (nearly 820-kg) blue marlin hangs above the front door, while the interior is filled with intriguing exhibits. Even those with little interest in fishing and boating are fascinated by the early surfboards and surfing photos and the memorabilia from the Matson Line ocean liners that brought tourists to the islands starting in the 1930s. One can't help but marvel at the difference between these elegant ships

side of the capitol grounds is a more recently dedicated memorial to those who fell in the Korean and Vietnam wars. To the left and across the street is **Washington Place** ((808) 587-0790, at South Beretania Street, the official residence of the governor of Hawaii, built by an American sea captain named John Dominis, whose son married Princess Liliuokalani, future queen of Hawaii.

The **Honolulu Academy of the Arts** ((808) 532-8701, 900 South Beretania Street, is Hawaii's premier fine arts museum. The extensive collection of Asian art, along with prehistoric Hawaiian art and paintings by European and American artists, is displayed in a series of buildings amid gardens and lily ponds. Admission is charged.

and the first canoes the Polynesians used to reach Hawaii. The boisterous whalers who made Hawaii the center of the whaling industry are well represented with recordings of sea shanties, a large display of carvings and memorabilia, and a mammoth skeleton of a Pacific humpback whale hanging in the center of the museum. Three vessels float beside the museum. The *Falls of Clyde*, a four-masted, fully rigged iron built in Scotland in 1878, has been totally restored as a National Historic Landmark. The amazing *Hokulea* is a 60-foot (18-m) Polynesian sailing canoe used to recreate the voyages of early Polynesians, who relied on celestial navigation to set their course. In 1999, the *Hokulea* set sail to Rapa Nui (Easter Island) on an impressive voyage that received daily media coverage. Admission is charged.

Nearby is Honolulu's enduring beacon, the 10-story **Aloha Tower** at 1 Aloha Tower Drive. Built in 1926 at the edge of the harbor as the highest structure in Honolulu, the tower has four clocks facing in the cardinal directions and serves as a landmark for wandering tourists. You can ride the elevator to the viewing deck and gaze in any direction; hours (which vary by season) are posted by the elevator. The tower anchors **Aloha Tower Marketplace (** (808) 528-5700,

designed to bring more dining and shopping options to the waterfront. Shops and galleries display gorgeous furnishings and tropical *objets d'art*; restaurants run the gamut from a microbrewery to a cutting-edge sidewalk café.

The massive Honolulu Iron Works, which once filled the waterfront with a constant clatter, have been tamed and redesigned into **Restaurant Row (** (808) 538-1441 at 500 Ala Moana Boulevard. Within walking distance of downtown Honolulu, Restaurant Row attracts the lunchtime crowd and is particularly lively on Friday and Saturday nights. The complex has seven five-story buildings set amidst nine acres (three and a half hectares) of landscaped gardens. Outdoor seat-

ing at some of the restaurants gives a sense of place — inside, you can hardly tell you're in Hawaii. Nearby, sport-fishing boats dock at **Kewalo Basin** at Ala Moana Boulevard and Ward Avenue (see SPORTS, page 134).

Head northwest along prosperous King Street, and suddenly modern Honolulu is transformed and the air is thick with the language, sounds and smells of Hong Kong. **Chinatown**, bordered by River, Bethel, Merchant and Beretania streets, was created by early immigrants who came to work on the sugar fields; a few achieved astounding wealth. But there's nothing ostentatious about these crowded streets, where chickens hang from rafters in open-air stalls and octopus and eels slither in tanks. The **Maunakea Marketplace (** (808) 524-3409, at 1120 Maunakea Street, is stocked with Asian groceries and fast-food stands. Flower shops line Maunakea Street; check out the refrigerated cases filled with all types of leis. Try to resist the scent of ginger and plumeria, then give in and purchase leis for your whole party. River Street between Beretania and King Streets is lined with authentic Asian

OPPOSITE: Iolani Palace, America's only royal residence. ABOVE: This statue of King Kamehameha in Honolulu in one of many on the islands. RIGHT: The Bishop Museum, custodian of Hawaii's cultural history.

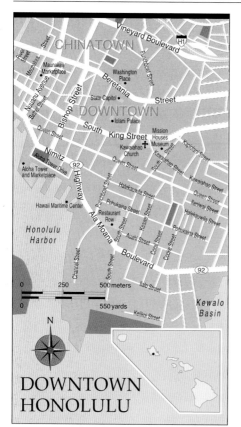

CHINATOWN

Vineyard Boulevard

DOWNTOWN

Honolulu
Harbor

DOWNTOWN
HONOLULU

N

0   250   500 meters

0   550 yards

Kewalo
Basin

Hawaii's prime attraction is located far from downtown and Waikiki at Pearl Harbor. Each year some 1.5 million people visit the **Arizona Memorial** ((808) 422-0561, 1 Arizona Memorial Drive in Pearl City (see HONOR THE HEROES, page 13 in TOP SPOTS). Tour buses fill the parking lots, and you can easily wait in line for two hours before passing through the entry and receiving a numbered ticket. Visitors browse through a museum and bookshop while waiting for their numbers to be called, then file into a theater for a short talk and film. Launches then carry visitors across the water to the white monument designed by local architect Alfred Preis. The monument spans the midsection of the sunken *Arizona*, which sank five minutes after being hit, entombing almost its entire crew. At the far end of the memorial, a marble wall is etched with the names of the 1,177 officers and enlisted men who died on the ship during the Japanese attack on Pearl Harbor on December 7, 1941. The memorial is open daily. Entrance to the site is about half a mile (just under one kilometer) east of Aloha Stadium. Admission is free, though donations are requested.

The **USS Bowfin Submarine Museum and Park** ((808) 423-1341 E-MAIL bowfin@ aloha.net is adjacent to the USS Arizona Memorial Visitor Center at Pearl Harbor. The *Bowfin* is a World War II submarine that was launched on December 7, 1942, and completed nine successful war patrols. Opened to the public in 1981, it was designated a National Historic Landmark by the Department of the Interior in 1986.

Visitors to Bowfin Park are given a portable cassette player that narrates their tour as they explore this historic submarine, imagining life on board for the 80-man crew. In addition to the submarine tour, there is a 10,000-sq-ft (929-sq-m) museum whose exhibits include an impressive collection of submarine-related artifacts such as submarine weapon systems, photographs, paintings, original recruiting posters, and detailed submarine models, all illustrating the history of the United States Submarine Service. New exhibits include a Poseidon C-3 missile that allows visitors to examine the inner workings of a missile. It is the only one of its kind to be on public

eateries offering superb dim sum and other Chinese specialties along with Vietnamese and Thai dishes. If you're on a strict budget and don't mind noise and crowds, you'd be wise to eat here often.

HONOLULU ENVIRONS

A must-see for anyone fascinated by Hawaiian cultures and history, the **Bishop Museum** ((808) 847-3511 WEB SITE www.Bishop.hawaii .org, at 1525 Bernice Street, is a short ride from downtown and is served by bus no. 2. Founded in 1889 by Charles R. Bishop in memory of his wife, Princess Bernice Pauahi, the museum began as a repository for the royal possessions of this last direct descendant of King Kamehameha the Great. It has since achieved international recognition as a center for Polynesian archaeology, ethnology and history. The **Herbarium Pacificum** with 500,000 Pacific Basin plant specimens has the largest and most comprehensive assemblage of vascular plants in the world.

display. A mini-theater screens submarine-related videos.

In Bowfin Park stands a public memorial honoring the 52 American submarines and the more than 3,500 submariners lost during World War II. The park is open daily from 8 AM to 5 PM and the last tour of the submarine begins at 4:30 PM. There is an admission fee. Children under the age of four are not permitted on the submarine for safety reasons, but are allowed to tour the museum and mini-theater at no charge.

The newest attraction and monument to the United States Navy is the **Battleship Missouri Memorial** ((808) 973-2494 at the Arizona Memorial Visitor Center in Pearl Harbor. Mighty Mo, one of America's most celebrated warships, stands in ironic juxtaposition to the *Arizona*. On the Missouri's deck, the Japanese signed a document sealing their surrender to the United States in 1945. The ship was decommissioned in 1991, and after years of debate over its future it was moved to Pearl Harbor in 1999. Visitors are allowed to wander the bridge and view staterooms on their own or with a guide. Admission is charged; the memorial is open daily.

Stark and serene, the **National Memorial Center of the Pacific** ((808) 544-1434 north of Waikiki at 2177 Puowaina Drive (off the Pali Highway) fills Punchbowl Crater, called Puowaina, or "Hill of Sacrifice" in Hawaiian. The ashen crater (now covered with perfect emerald-green lawns) is the final resting place of 35,000 American men and women who gave their lives in wars in the Pacific, from World War II through Korea and Vietnam. Simple white stones mark the graves of many of those killed on December 7, 1941, along with famed war correspondent Ernie Pyle and thousands of regular Joes. The Memorial Building houses a chapel and a gallery of maps of the Pacific conflicts of World War II and Korea, and it includes the series of stairways bordered by massive marble walls called the "Courts of the Missing." Leading up to Lady Columbia, a 30-ft (nine-meter) statue symbolizing all grieving mothers, are marble slabs inscribed with the names of more than 26,280 servicemen missing in action during World War II and the wars in and Vietnam

Korea. From the rim of Punchbowl Crater, visitors get one of the great panoramic views of the city, from Diamond Head all the way to the Waianae Mountains.

Continue up the Pali Highway to **Queen Emma's Summer Palace and Museum** ((808) 595-3167, 2913 Pali Highway, once home of Kamehameha IV and his wife Emma. The palace stands amid huge shade trees and remains a quiet, cool retreat from city life. It is open daily and there are tours of the premises. The **Royal Mausoleum** ((808) 536-7602, at 2261 Nuuanu Avenue, is

one of the most important burial sites in Hawaii, where Kings Kamehameha II, III, IV, Kalakaua and Queen Liliuokalani are interred. About three blocks down Nuuanu Avenue is **Foster Botanical Gardens** ((808) 533-3214, at 180 North Vineyard Boulevard. Trees planted in the mid-1800s shade the 14-acre (five-and-a half-hectare) garden, home to rare and endangered tropical plants.

The **Contemporary Museum** ((808) 526-1322, 2411 Makiki Heights Drive, has oriental gardens spread over three acres (just over one hectare) in a quiet suburban neighborhood, providing a peaceful setting for the museum's collection of modern art. Hawaiian artists are featured in the exhibits and the museum's lecture and workshop series. Admission is charged.

The Pali Highway climbs the Koolau Mountains to one of the greatest views on the island of Oahu. Strangely enough, the damp, chilly, 985-ft (300-m) **Nuuanu Pali Lookout** also commemorates those who have

The Arizona Memorial, Pearl Harbor.

fallen in battle. It was here, in 1795, that the warriors of Kamehameha routed the Oahu army, driving it to the cliffs. Defeated warriors who were unable to escape down the steep trails were driven over the cliffs. The lookout gets plenty of rain, and the landscape is dominated by forested cliffs chiseled by wind and water. The vista extends down mountains to the windward side of the island. Bring binoculars and a sweater — the wind can feel freezing, especially on sunburned skin.

EAST SHORE

Oahu's east, or windward, coast is filled with fascinating diversions, from gorgeous beaches to spooky rock formations and several tourist attractions. A tour of the coast begins at **Diamond Head** on Diamond Head Road. Hardy walkers should climb the volcanic crater — it's only 761 ft (just over 230 m) high, yet has a breathtaking view of Waikiki. The ocean below the lookout is a favorite with surfers and wave jumpers, and the myriad colored sails racing over the shallow waters are striking. The island's wealthy seclude themselves in huge mansions on opulent estates in the shadow of the volcano at **Kahala**, where celebrities hide out at the Mandarin Oriental Hotel (see WHERE TO STAY, page 137).

The Kalanianaole Highway skirts much of the coastline with turnoffs to the most popular sights. Watch out for confused drivers distracted by the turnoff to **Hanauma Bay**, everyone's favorite natural aquarium. The wide bay framed by volcanic cliffs is an underwater reserve filled with tropical fish. The water is shallow and clear, and the fish have no fear of humans. The parking lot here fills up quickly, and sunbathers lie shoulder-to-shoulder on the sand. Try to arrive by 9 AM. There is a fee to park and another fee for the shuttle that carries beach-goers down the steep road to the beach.

Exiting Hanauma Bay, Kalanianaole Highway continues downhill with towering, sculptured cliffs on the left and more sparkling views of the ocean on the right. At the first scenic lookout you'll get a view of the **Halona Blowhole** geyser where ocean water surges through a lava tube into the tidal basin.

Thrill seekers have attempted to ride this rush of water and some have perished. The undertow here can be deadly. **Sandy Beach** and **Makapuu** farther up the coast are gorgeous beaches with ferocious surf.

The cliffs above Makapuu are a favorite launching point for hang-gliders. On days when the winds are brisk and clouds are but a memory, the sight of these daring pilots suspended beneath colorful sails will take your breath away. In the shadows of the cliffs is **Sea Life Park ((808) 259-7933, 41-202 Kalanianaole Highway in Makapuu

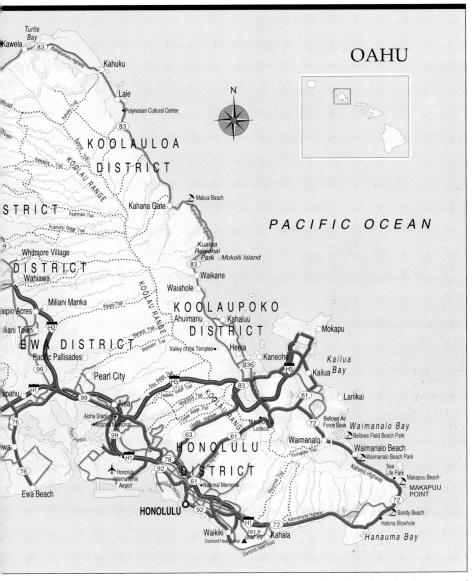

Point. This unique ocean-side setting is home to penguins, turtles, dolphins, sea lions and sharks. The park's imposing 300,000-gallon (1,140,000-liter) reef tank holds a marvelous cross section of the ocean's creatures. Guests can pay an additional fee to participate in the Swim with Dolphins program; make reservations far in advance of your visit. The drive along the highway gets increasingly beautiful as the road passes through Waimanalo. On the left is an area referred to as the **Hawaiian Homelands** and reserved for those of Hawaiian descent. On the right

is a stretch of perfect beach, the start of Waimanalo Bay.

Bellows Air Forces Base, a major military installation, occupies a large area of the shoreline on the right. Before you reach the main entrance of the base, however, there is a gate leading to **Bellows Field Beach Park**, one of the loveliest beaches on the island. Tall pines stretch to the edge of white sand, which explain the local name for the beach, "Sherwood Forest." This combination of tree-lined beach and clear blue waters is characteristic of this stretch of the coast, where Kalanianaole

Highway winds through the suburban towns of Kailua and Kaneohe. If you weren't looking for **Kailua**, the chances are you'd probably drive right through it. But despite its modest manner, this windward community has a great deal to offer. To begin with, Kailua is where people escape the bustle of the city — it's a wonderful alternative to Waikiki. **Kailua Bay** — a five-mile (eight-kilometer) stretch of white-sand beach that curves tantalizingly from Lanikai all the way to Mokapuu Point — is a fine beach for watersports enthusiasts, who cart surfboards,

replica of the 900-year-old Buddhist temple in Uji, Japan. An enormous three-ton bronze bell dominates the entrance to the temple. The centerpiece of the temple is a sitting Buddha, almost nine feet (three meters) high. Thousands of carp create a moving tableau of color in a huge pond, and peacocks roam the temple grounds. The temple is a place of rare serenity, and is beautifully situated with the majestic Koolau Mountains as a backdrop.

Leaving the temple, Kahekili Highway soon becomes Kamehameha Highway (often

kayaks, and sailboards to the shaded sand. Wind conditions here are so good that Kailua Bay is considered one of the world's premier windsurfing sites. It is here that world champion Robbie Naish cut his teeth in the sport he helped popularize. Kailua is green and clean, and the air, whether it is blowing off the rugged *palis* (cliffs) or coming in off the ocean, is fresh and invigorating. Also in the area is the **Heeia State Park** and 88 acres (35 hectares) of fishponds meticulously developed by ancient Hawaiians.

After driving through Kailua, follow signs to Kahekili Highway. Set deep in the **Valley of the Temples Memorial Park** is the **Byodo-In Temple (** (808) 239-5570, 47-200 Kahekili Highway. Built in 1968, it is a

written as Kam Hwy). The road hugs a magnificent coast with towering *palis* on the left, in whose shadows lie horse and cattle ranches. **Kualoa Ranch (** (808) 237-8515 TOLL-FREE (800) 231-7321, at 49-560 Kamehameha Highway, is a 4,000-acre (1,600-hectare) working ranch that doubles as a high-priced amusement park. Diversions include horseback riding, kayaking, canoeing, helicopter rides, and tours of movie sets where parts of *Jurassic Park*, *Godzilla*, and *Fantasy Island* were filmed. Though the setting is lovely, the park is often crowded with tour groups.

Across from the ranch is **Kualoa Regional Park**. There's not much of a beach here, but the waters are great for swimming and snorkeling. The currents, however, can be tricky, so be careful. According to legend, Mokolii, the little offshore island, is the lopped-off tail of a dragon. Most residents refer to this island as Chinaman's Hat.

A bit farther on is the East Shore's largest attraction, the **Polynesian Cultural Center** ((808) 293-3333, 55-370 Kamehameha Highway. The center is composed of several villages representing the main Polynesian cultures. Students from the Pacific Islands, in native garments, demonstrate arts and crafts techniques employed in their island homes. The Pageant of the Long Canoes, held in the afternoon, is a popular attraction with visitors, as is the fine evening performance of singing and dancing by the students, most of whom pay for their education by working at the center. The center is run by the nearby Mormon Church: alcohol, tobacco, and caffeine are not allowed on the grounds. Tickets to the Polynesian Cultural Center and its variety shows are not cheap, but most visitors enjoy the experience. The center offers a variety of packages, some including transportation. The center is closed on Sunday.

NORTH SHORE

Kamehameha Highway continues toward the North Shore and Hawaii's most famous surfing beaches. Surfers from all over the world make pilgrimages to these famed shores, and tales of the killer (literally) waves abound. Waves sometimes reach up to 30 ft (nine meters) in some areas, and only the most proficient surfers dare challenge such awesome surf. The best spot to watch the surfers in action is at **Sunset**, **Ehukai** and **Waimea** beaches. At the **Banzai Pipeline** near Sunset, surfers ride the tube inside great curling waves; those who have dared ride it say it feels like they're being shot out of a cannon.

Passing Sunset Beach, the seemingly endless white sand is interrupted by the tide pools of the **Pupukea Marine Life Conserve**. The pools are fun places to lie in, paddle around in or observe marine life. Around the outer fringes of the rocks, the coral formations and fauna in the clean, clear waters make Pupukea among the favorite scuba diving and snorkeling sites on these northern shores.

Pupukea Drive, across the street from the conserve's parking lot, leads to an exceptional *heiau* (temple). **Puu O Mahuka** (Hill of Escape) is on the National Register of Historic Landmarks and is one of the finest examples of an ancient culture's place of worship. Archaeologists haven't pieced together the puzzle lying in the stones, but they have been able to ascertain that human sacrifices took place here. The terraced *heiau* is dominated by what looks like an altar at the far left of the ruins. Follow the walk around this end of the *heiau* and you will find yourself gaz-

ing out over an unforgettable landscape — the **Waimea Stream** on the left, cane fields stretching out to the distant horizon above it, and immediately below you to the right, **Waimea Bay Beach Park**. Only the greatest surfers challenge the mountainous winter waves that pound these shores; more timid swimmers find calm water in the summer.

Waimea Valley Adventure Park ((808) 638-8511 at 59-864 Kamehameha Highway, also known as Waimea Falls Park, is tucked in an idyllic settling along the Waimea Stream. Visitors are immersed in educa-

OPPOSITE: Endangered Hawaiian monk seals find refuge on the rocks around Honolulu's harbor. ABOVE: A bridge leads to the serene Byodo-In Temple.

tional experiences from the moment they park beside an ancient shrine. Botanical gardens with clearly labeled trees and flowering plants are spread throughout the 1,800-acre (nearly 730-hectare) park; amusements include kayaking, horseback riding, mountain biking, and demonstrations of Hawaiian games and hula techniques. The 45-ft-high (13-m) waterfall isn't as spectacular as those on other islands, but cliff divers make it seem more impressive. If you're looking for entertainment for the whole family, this is your place.

A narrow bridge leads the way to **Haleiwa**, a charming small town that is the antithesis of Waikiki. As you stand on the shores of Haleiwa Beach, neighbors pass the time of day, delivery workers driving their routes stop by to check out the surf, and authentic *Baywatch* babes pose for the cameras. Yes, Haleiwa has hit the big time as a stage set for the popular television show, which moved filming from Los Angeles to Oahu in 1999. But neither Hollywood nor the hippies who took over the town in the 1960s and 1970s have changed the spirit of this community of farmers, fishermen, and entrepreneurs.

M. Matsumoto Store ((808) 637-4827, 66-087 Kamehameha Highway at the entrance

to town, serves up the most famous shave ice on Oahu from a cluttered general store. A stop here is essential to the Haleiwa experience. Browse through the tailor-made aloha shirts and *muumuus* at **H. Miura Store** ((808) 637-4845, 66-057 Kamehameha Highway, before hitting the fancier shops at the Haleiwa Shopping Center at 66-250 Kamehameha Highway. The center's biggest attraction is the **North Shore Surf and Cultural Museum** ((808) 637-8888, with its fascinating selection of surfing memorabilia including early boards, surf posters and album covers from the 1960s and early black and white photos. It's a hangout for local surfers, which may explain the locked doors and "Gone Surfing" signs. Another sign by the door reads "Open most afternoons."

Exiting Haleiwa at its western extremity, the road forks to the right at Thompson's Corner, taking the traveler to **Mokuleia**, a small town in the midst of cane fields. Be sure to stop by the roadside **Open Air Gallery** ((808) 637-3442, 68-639 Farrington Highway, where sculptor Don Rohrbach carves gorgeous humpback whales in koa and monkey pod wood. The carvings are in heavy demand; Rohrbach says he's two years behind on commissioned work — perhaps because of his sideline job as a glider pilot at **Dillingham Airfield** ((808) 256-0438 on Highway 930 in Mokuleia. Sailplanes and gliders streak through the sky over the airport's west end, while parachutists float to the east.

On your way back to Honolulu, Highway 99 runs through miles of pineapple fields. Stop at the **Dole Plantation** ((808) 621-8408 at 64-1550 near Wahiawa. The plantation's **Pineapple Garden Maze** was officially cited as the world's largest maze in the 1998 *Guinness Book of World Records*, and the souvenir shop displays a staggering array of pineapple-themed souvenirs.

Coming off the highway on your left is the town of Wahiawa, which attracts more native Hawaiians than it does tourists because of two historic sites. In north Wahiawa are the **Wahiawa Birthing Stones**, where the wives of chiefs came to give birth on the curved surfaces of the stones. The **Healing Stones**, in a building at 108 California Street, are said to have great powers of healing. Believers come bearing ritual offerings of ti leaves and flowers, convinced the stones can cure them of their pain. The H2 from Wahiawa connects with the H1 and will take you back to Honolulu past the towns of Pearl City and Aiea.

WEST SHORE

There is an exterior toughness to the largely undeveloped Waianae Coast. Its south end, closest to Honolulu, is an industrial region

460 ft (140 m) deep and 100 ft (30 m) high. Legend has it that this was the home of Kamahoalii, half-human, half-shark, who feasted on passersby. Another mile down the road is **Makua Beach**, where much of James Michener's epic, *Hawaii*, was filmed.

Keawaula Beach (Yokohama Bay) is another beach favored by board surfers, body surfers and fishermen. Beyond this bay is **Kaena Point**, the extreme northwestern tip of the island and the end of the highway. To proceed any farther you need a four-wheel-drive vehicle.

that gives way to the upscale developments in Koolina around the **J. W. Marriott Ihilani Resort** (see WHERE TO STAY, page 138). Nearby, a purported sacred area where Queen Kaahumanu bathed and performed rituals has been transformed into the tropical backdrop for the **Paradise Cove Luau** (see NIGHTLIFE, page 144).

Because of its prime fishing waters, the Waianae Coast was once the center of island life. Waianae has some marvelous surfing beaches, particularly at **Makaha Beach Park**, where international surfing contests are still held.

Three miles north of Makaha is the **Cave of Kane** (Kaneana), also known as Makua Cave. The cave is enormous, in some places

TOURS

Several tour companies offer a myriad of trips around Oahu, from the Arizona Memorial to the surfing beaches on the North Shore. Some cover an amazing array of sights in a half or full day, while others concentrate on one attraction.

You can arrange tours on your own by calling the numbers below, or through a concierge or tour desk at your hotel. Many companies advertise discounts in tourist publications. Among the longstanding, reputable companies are **Discovering Hidden Hawaii** ((808) 946-0432 and **E Noa Tours** ((808) 591-

Dolphins and seals are among the popular attractions at Sealife Park, on Oahu's eastern shore.

2561 WEBSITE www.enoa.com. **Oahu Nature Tours** ((808) 924-2473 offers sunrise hikes up Diamond Head, bird watching in the Koolau Mountains and other adventure fare. Oahu's archaeological sites, long overshadowed by modern diversions, are featured in guided walks with **Mauka Makai Excursions** ((808) 593-3525 TOLL-FREE (877) 326-6248. Snorkeling trips to Hanauma Bay including transportation and gear are provided by **Tommy's Tours** ((808) 373-5060.

It's an essential part of the island experience to spend time on the water, viewing the

mountains, beaches, and palatial homes from a boat. The *Navatek I* ((808) 848-6360 TOLL-FREE (800) 852-4183 WEB SITE www.royalhawaiiancruises.com, berthed at Pier 7 near the Maritime Museum, provides the most comfortable and enjoyable ride. Looking somewhat like a spaceship, the vessel skims smoothly across the water barely rippling in the surf. The *Navatek's* lunch tour includes a bountiful spread with everything from *ahi poke* to *kalua* pork, to *poi*. Entertainers sing traditional Hawaiian tunes and teach hula and lei-making classes as the ship glides along the Kahala Coast and Waikiki. Sightseeing and dinner cruises are also offered on the multideck *Star of Honolulu* ((808) 983-7827, which docks at the Aloha Tower Marketplace,

1 Aloha Tower Drive. Underwater adventures are available on **Atlantis Submarines** ((808) 973-9811 TOLL-FREE (800) 548-6262 WEB SITE www.goatlantis.com/hawaii, departing from the dock at the Hilton Hawaiian Village.

SHOPPING

Shopping is one of Waikiki's main attractions, and a pleasurable alternative to languid sun worship. Many shops remain open until 9 PM, and some until 11 PM. The big shopping malls cater as much to tourists as locals. The enormous **Ala Moana Shopping Center** ((808) 955-9517, 1450 Ala Moana Boulevard, is situated near Ala Wai Yacht Harbor at the gateway to Waikiki. Spread over 34 acres (14 hectares), it is like a mini city, attracting over 54 million people each year. Palm Boulevard is the most elegant section, housing high-end names like Chanel and Cartier. A Neiman Marcus opened in the mall in 1999, much to the delight of professionals needing fashionable work clothes. The **Royal Hawaiian Shopping Center** ((808) 922-0588, 2233 Kalakaua Avenue, consumes several full blocks in Waikiki. Retailers include Louis Vuitton, Chanel, and Versace. The Waikiki Trolley has a ticket stand here. Somehow, developers managed to find space to build the ultramodern **King Kalakaua Plaza** ((808) 955-2878, 2080 Kalakaua Avenue, with Niketown, Banana Republic, and trendy chain restaurants. **International Market Place** (no phone), 2301 Kalakaua Avenue, is a bustling bazaar of Asian and Polynesian shops, stalls, bars and restaurants that appeals to budget shoppers — just the place for that Hawaii souvenir. There is not much here that can't be bargained for if you stick to your guns. In fact, if you don't haggle you'll probably be paying too much. The **Rainbow Bazaar**, Hilton Hawaiian Village, 2005 Kalia Road, is worth strolling through to admire the mixture of Chinese, Japanese and Polynesian architecture. It also has more than the usual number of shops specializing in Asian antiques and jewelry crafts. The **Ali'i Plaza** adds upmarket boutiques (Benneton, Esprit and Georgio Armani) to the Hilton Hawaiian Village.

ABOVE: Visitors enjoy a canal cruise at the Polynesian Cultural Center. RIGHT: Schools of snorkelers frolic with friendly tropical fish at Hanauma Bay.

Dining is as important as shopping at **Ward Center**((808) 591-8411, 1200 Ala Moana Boulevard. The nearby **Ward Warehouse** ((808) 591-8411, 1050 Ala Moana Boulevard, is filled with one-of-a-kind shops including **Native Books and Beautiful Things** ((808) 596-8885, featuring quilts, paintings, jewelry and clothing made by Hawaiian artists. **Nohea Gallery** ((808) 596-0074, also at the warehouse, features the works of island painters, sculptors, glass artists, and woodcarvers.

The **Aloha Tower Marketplace** ((808) 528-5700 on the Honolulu waterfront at 1 Aloha Tower Drive presents a pretty façade to the tour boat and cruise ship piers beside the historic Aloha Tower. The rambling Mediterranean-style center contains an ever-changing array of shops, fast-food stalls, and restaurants. Take time to browse through the shops featuring Hawaiian-style furnishings, handmade ukuleles, and local art.

Diehard bargain hunters are in their element at the **Aloha Stadium Swap Meet** ((808) 486-1529 in the Aloha Stadium. The swap meet is open all day on Wednesday, Saturday, and Sunday; it's the perfect place to mingle with the locals while shopping for souvenirs.

It's inevitable. You'll eventually visit at least one branch of Hawaii's most famous souvenir shop; you might as well visit the largest **Hilo Hattie** ((808) 537-2926 at 680 Nimitz Highway. Many of the tourist shuttles stop here, and passengers typically re-board with armloads of Hawaiian shirts, hats and macadamia nuts. Aloha furniture, fabrics, shirts and kitsch souvenirs from the 1940s are all the rage these days. One of the best places to find authentic 1940s shirts (some costing well over $1,000) is **Bailey's Antiques** ((808) 734-7628, 517 Kapahulu Avenue. **Avanti** ((808) 924-1668, at 2229 Kuhio Avenue, is the islands' most famous purveyor of shirts and dresses in vintage designs and fabric patterns. Unlike the clothing found at souvenir shops, these duds are made to feel as silky as the originals and to last as long as the shirts in antique shops. Avanti has several locations on Oahu, and shops throughout the islands carry the line. Meanwhile, surfers pay homage to the masters at **Russ. K Makaha** ((808) 951-7877,

1695 Kapiolani Boulevard, a surf shop run by some of Hawaii's champions.

SPORTS

Anyone with a sense of balance can ride the waves (or so surfers say); at times it seems there are more surfers than landlubbers on Oahu. The waves on the North Shore hit their awesome peak in the winter months, when pros from all over the world flock to Sunset Beach and the Banzai Pipeline. Experienced surfers also hang out at Waimea Bay and Kualoa Beach; beginners are best off at Waikiki. **Surfing** lessons are given at the Hans Hedemann Surf School ((808) 924-7778, at 2947 Kalakaua Avenue. On the North Shore, surfboard rentals and lessons are available at Haleiwa Surf Center ((808) 637-5051, 66-167 Haleiwa Road. The center also runs **scuba diving** trips to caves and reefs, as does Surf and Sea ((808) 637-9887, at 62-595 Kamehameha Highway. **Sailboarding** and **kayaking** are excellent at Kailua Beach; gear and lessons are available from Kailua Sailboard and Kayak Company ((808) 262-2555, 130 Kailua Road. Aloha Beach Services ((808) 922-3111, 2365 Kalakaua Avenue, offers one the beach's greatest thrills — **outrigger rides** over the waves. For those who can't resist a day of **sport fishing** while in Hawaii, most fishing boats dock at Kewalo Basin off Ala Moana Boulevard; stop by for a look at the catch of the day. If you want to set up a fishing trip, talk with the staff at the dozens of stands beside the fishing boats, or contact the Hawaii Charter Skippers Association ((808) 594-9100.

Glider rides above the coastline are irresistible if you like flying without the aid of an engine. For the thrill of a lifetime, contact Skysurfing Glider Rides ((808) 256-0438 at Dillingham Field on Farrington Highway. Also exciting are **seaplane rides** with Island Seaplane Service ((808) 836-6273 at 85 Lagoon Drive and the ever-popular **helicopter tours** with Magnum Helicopters ((808) 833-1133, at 110 Kapahulu Place, and Rainbow Pacific Helicopters ((808) 834-1111, 110A Kapahulu Place, all located near the airport.

Horseback riding in the Koolau Mountains is available through Correa Trails

Hawaii ((808) 259-9005, 41-050 Kalanianaole Highway, and at Kualoa Ranch and Waimea Valley Adventure Park (see WHAT TO SEE AND DO, page 129). Oahu also offers several hiking opportunities; see THE GREAT OUTDOORS, page 23 in YOUR CHOICE for details.

Oahu is also a prime **golf** destination, with more courses than any of the other islands. Details can be found under SPORTING SPREE, page 42 in YOUR CHOICE.

WHERE TO STAY

Oahu offers the widest range of accommodations on the islands, from secluded, luxurious resorts to crowded chain hotels to lowly beach cabins. The majority of the hotels are clustered around Waikiki; those with ocean views are in greatest demand. The less crowded parts of the island have fewer to choose from. Advance reservations are strongly advised for all neighborhoods and price ranges, since the hotels are sometimes filled with large convention and tour groups. Waikiki offers a better selection of hotels than Honolulu.

WAIKIKI

Very Expensive

The **Halekulani Hotel** ((808) 923-2311 TOLL-FREE (800) 367-2343 FAX (808) 926-8004 WEB SITE www.halekulani.com, 2199 Kalia Road, located on Gray's Beach, was built in 1917 as a private residence and converted into what many believe is today the finest hotel on the island. Plush and elegant, the Halekulani spoils guests from the moment they are escorted to their rooms. The best of the 465 rooms have direct views of Diamond Head, even from the extra-large bathtubs. The white on white decor is soothing and refreshing and fresh orchid sprays provide a splash of color. Room service breakfast on the terrace comes with toast made fresh at your table. The hotel's fame is largely due to its excellent service; many of the staff members have worked there for a dozen years or more, and they remember their guests' names and preferences. At sunset, the Halekulani's "House without a Key" has the best view in Waikiki, while the gourmet restaurant La Mer is considered the best on the island (see WHERE

TO EAT, page 139). Though the Halekulani sits just steps from all the Waikiki action, it is a private haven beloved by celebrities. Opened in late 1999, **W Honolulu** ((808) 922-1928 TOLL-FREE (877) 946-8357 FAX (808) 526-2017, 2895 Kalakaua Avenue, is actually the former Colony Surf Hotel, recently transformed into a trendy boutique inn. The 48 lavish suites are filled with classy amenities, from CD players and Aveda toiletries to cushy beds covered with silky-soft 250-count sheets and goose-down comforters.

Expensive

Those who truly love Waikiki can't resist spending at least one night at the **Sheraton Moana Surfrider** ((808) 922-3111 TOLL-FREE (800) 782-9488 FAX (808) 923-0308 WEB SITE www.sheraton-hawaii.com, 2365 Kalakaua Avenue. Despite undergoing a major overhaul in 1989, the gray plantation-style inn is still the classy "First Lady of Waikiki." The original building is on the National Register of Historic Places and evokes an instant sense of a more gracious era. Guests survey the hoi polloi on the street from wicker rockers on the front porch; lookie loos wander through the hotel's grand columns and are reminded of its gentile past. From the striking windows that frame the ocean, to the sweeping Banyan Verandah, guests are never far away from nostalgic comfort. The hotel has 791 rooms, including 44 suites, three restaurants, two cocktail lounges, a two-tiered outdoor verandah and an oceanfront beach bar.

The **Royal Hawaiian** ((808) 923-7311 TOLL-FREE (800) 325-3589 FAX (808) 924-7098 WEB SITE www.royal-hawaiian.com, 2259 Kalakaua Avenue, a sumptuous hotel built in 1927, and the *grande dame* of Hawaiian hotels certainly deserves its native nickname, "The Pink Lady." Its Spanish Moorish-style architecture, coral-pink stucco and French provincial decor make it one of Waikiki's most charming attractions. The Royal Hawaiian has 527 rooms and 49 suites, a lovely tropical garden, the Surf Room restaurant (expensive), and a beachfront bar.

A complete resort complex with fabulous pools and a great beach, the **Hilton Hawaiian Village** ((808) 949-4321 TOLL-FREE (800) 445-8667 FAX (808) 947-7898 WEB SITE www

.hilton.com/hawaii/hawaiianvillage/ index.html, 2005 Kalia Road is surprisingly compact. Its Rainbow Tower covered with a tiled rainbow mural serves as a beacon whether you're finding your way back on the street or sailing home from a sunset cruise. There are over 2,000 rooms in five towers; best are those near the ocean in the Alii Tower or looking out to Diamond Head from atop the Rainbow Tower. The shopping plaza is one of the most pleasant for browsing in Waikiki, with boutique and souvenir shops interspersed with restaurants. The grounds

include several koi ponds, waterfalls, and tropical gardens. The Friday night Hawaiian music and hula and fireworks show is a must-see.

Though not on the beach, the **Hawaii Prince Hotel ℂ** (808) 956-1111 TOLL-FREE (800) 321-6248 FAX (808) 946-0811 WEB SITE www .princehawaii.com, 100 Holomoana Street, is a top-notch choice. Located at the gateway to Waikiki overlooking the Ala Wai Yacht Harbor, it compensates for its lack of real gardens by making the most of great design elements in its 33-story rose-colored, Italian marble and glass edifice. The fifth floor is a luxury terrace that includes a pool, sundeck and terraces for sunset viewing and drinks.

Two towers rise across the street from the center of Waikiki Beach at the 1,230-room **Hyatt Regency Waikiki ℂ** (808) 923-1234 FAX (808) 923-7839 E-MAIL info@hyattwaikiki .com WEB SITE www.hyatt.com, 2424 Kalakaua Avenue. The views are astounding from the upper floors, some of which are included in the Regency Club, with special amenities including free continental breakfast and a concierge desk. The rooms are undersized though, and sometimes oddly shaped, and the hotel can be overwhelming with its squawking macaws and live bands in the atrium lobby. But there are enough restaurants and shops to keep everyone happy. Japanese tourists and those who love precise service and a wealth of business amenities frequent the **Ilikai/Hotel Nikko ℂ** (808) 949-3811 TOLL-FREE (800) 245-4524 FAX (808) 947-4523 WEB SITE www.ililaihotel.com, 1777 Ala Moana Boulevard. The hotel overlooks the Ala Wai Yacht Harbor (though some of the 800 rooms have ocean views).

Moderate

Happy are those who discover the **Waikiki Parc Hotel ℂ** (808) 921-7272 TOLL-FREE (800) 422-0450 FAX (808) 923-1336 WEB SITE www .waikikiparc.com, tucked down a small side street at 2233 Helumoa Road. Sister hotel to the Halekulani, the Parc is an understated gem with 289 subdued blue and gray rooms. It's not on the beach, but has a rooftop swimming pool; some rooms have ocean view terraces. The restaurant is excellent and the staff courteous and accommodating. One of the best bargains in the heart of the tourist zone is the **Waikiki Beachcomber Hotel ℂ** (808) 922-4646 TOLL-FREE (800) 622-4646 FAX (808) 926-9973, 2300 Kalakaua Avenue. The 500 rooms were completely renovated in 1999 with Berber carpets, new beds and furnishings. The hotel is entertainment central, home to both Don Ho and John Hirokawa's Magic of Polynesia Show. The **Hawaiian Regent Hotel ℂ** (808) 922-6611 TOLL-FREE (800) 367-5370 FAX (808) 921-5255 E-MAIL info@hawaiianregent.com WEB SITE www.hawaiianregent.com/, 2552 Kalakaua Avenue, is directly across from the beach and designed around a pleasant courtyard decorated with fountains and waterways.

Outrigger Hotels is a name familiar to those seeking dependable, reasonably priced accommodations. The chain has over 20 hotels and condominium complexes on Oahu. The flagship hotel of the group is the 530-room **Outrigger Waikiki on the Beach** ((808) 923-0711 TOLL-FREE (800) 688-7444 FAX (808) 921-9749 WEB SITE www.outrigger .com, at 2335 Kalakaua Avenue. Also on the beach is the **Outrigger Reef** ((808) 923-3111 TOLL-FREE (800) 688-7444 FAX (808) 924-4957 WEB SITE www.outrigger.com, 2169 Kalia Road. **Aston Hotels** TOLL-FREE (800) 922-7866

WEB SITE www.aston-hotels.com is a smaller chain with several Oahu properties including the **Waikiki Joy Hotel** ((808) 923-4402 TOLL-FREE (800) 655-6055 FAX (808) 924-0433, 320 Lewers Street. With only 93 rooms, the hotel has the feel of a boutique inn, with friendly service and free continental breakfast served in the lobby each morning.

Inexpensive

It can be hard to find a room for under $100 a night in Waikiki, but there are a few. Some of the best rates are available in off-season packages that include air fare or car rental. **Outrigger** often runs such specials at the **Outrigger Surf** ((808) 922-5777 TOLL-FREE (800) 688-7444 FAX (808) 921-3677 WEB SITE

www.outrigger.com, 2280 Kuhio Street. Many of the 251 rooms have kitchenettes (a boon to those on a budget). Aston has several budget-priced hotels in Waikiki including the newly renovated **Coral Reef Hotel** ((808) 922-1262 FAX (808) 922-8785, 2299 Kuhio Avenue.

EAST SHORE

There are few hotels along the east shore; most visitors stay in condos and vacations homes. **Pat's Kailua Beach Properties** ((808) 261-1653 FAX (808) 261-0893 WEB SITE www .10kvacationrentals.com/pats, 204 South Kalaheo Road, represents several properties in the area. Small studio apartments are in the moderate range; beachfront houses are expensive to very expensive, but can be well worth the price if you're traveling with a group.

Expensive

The **Kahala Mandarin Oriental** ((808) 739-8888 TOLL-FREE (800) 367-2525 FAX (808) 739-8859 WEB SITE www.mandarin-oriental.com, 5000 Kahala Avenue, first opened as the Kahala Hilton in 1964. It quickly became a hideaway for Hollywood celebrities, a place where John Wayne, Frank Sinatra, and Liza Minelli lounged at the pool with their cronies. A $75-million restoration by the Hong Kong-based Mandarin Group in the 1990s enhanced the resort's reputation, and its 371 rooms and suites are among the loveliest on the island, designed with turn-of-the-century motifs, mahogany furniture, and teak parquet flooring over which are scattered Tibetan rugs. Wall coverings and rich fabrics accent the rooms.

The hotel's private lagoon has a fine collection of marine animals, including sea turtles, tropical fish and dolphins. The landscaped gardens are replete with waterfalls. At night, beams of light dance on the ocean waves, creating an atmosphere of perfect harmony that adds to the dining pleasure of those patronizing Hoku's ((808) 739-8777, the Kahala Mandarin Oriental's award-winning oceanfront restaurant (see WHERE TO EAT, page 143). The hotel also has an open-

OPPOSITE: Bountiful foliage at the lovely Waimea Falls Park. ABOVE: Pineapple harvests will soon be a thing of the past in Hawaii.

air restaurant, the beachfront Plumeria Beach Café (moderate), which serves a variety of buffets for breakfast, lunch and dinner.

Inexpensive
Schrader's Windward Marine Resort ((808) 239-5711 TOLL-FREE (800) 735-5711 FAX (808) 239-6658 WEB SITE www.hawaiiscene.com/schrader, 47-039 Lihikai Drive, doesn't quite live up to its name. The property is more like a motel, with 20 units in attached cottages. Families are particularly happy here, since sand and water can do little to harm the furnishings. Most cottages have kitchenettes with refrigerators and microwaves; the room rate includes continental breakfast. The highest priced rooms have lanais with views of Kaneohe Bay.

NORTH SHORE

Expensive
There's only one large hotel on the North Shore, the **Turtle Bay Hilton Golf and Tennis Resort** ((808) 293-8811 TOLL-FREE (800) 221-2424 FAX (808) 293-9147, 57-091 Kamehameha Highway. On 808 acres (327 hectares) with a golf course and a number of cottages as well as the main hotel, the property could be idyllic. Maintenance is obviously a problem, though, and the buildings are weather-beaten and crumbling in spots. The hotel has been through several sales; one hopes a new owner will give it some much-needed loving care. But despite its drawbacks, Turtle Bay is one of my favorite spots on Oahu. It has an air of seclusion, and guests become quick friends while watching the sunset by the pool bar. The best rooms are in the bungalows along the water's edge, and many guests settle in for a week or more, cooking meals in their kitchens. The Links golf course was designed by Arnold Palmer.

Moderate
Beach Homes North Shore ((808) 637-3507 TOLL-FREE (800) 982-8602 FAX (808) 637-8881 WEB SITE www.teamrealestate.com, at Team Real Estate, 66-134 Kamehameha Highway, Haleiwa, offers private home and condo rentals on the North Shore; surfers and escapists find this their best option for staying close to the waves.

Inexpensive
The 14 rooms at the **Backpackers Vacation Inn** ((808) 638-7838 FAX (808) 638-7515 WEB SITE//backpackers-hawaii.com, 59-788 Kamehameha Highway are quite basic, but weekly and seasonal rentals are available, and the place fills up quickly in winter.

Surfers more concerned with price than comfort fill the cottages at **Ke Iki Hale** ((808) 638-8229 TOLL-FREE (800) 377-4030 FAX (808) 638-8229, 59-579 Ke Iki Road. The units are battered by winds and the salt air, and the furnishings are rather worn, but they're close to both Waimea Bay and the Banzai Pipeline. Kitchen and laundry facilities are available, but there are no phones or televisions in the units.

WEST SHORE

Very Expensive
Blissfully secluded, the **J.W. Marriott Ihilani Resort and Spa** ((808) 679-0079 TOLL-FREE (800) 626-4446 FAX (808) 679-0295 WEB SITE www.ihilani.com, 92-1001 Olani Street in Koolina, is the ideal spot for a completely luxurious escape. The understated, spacious rooms are filled with special touches from deep soaking tubs to soft cotton robes and slippers. The intriguing telephone system with controls for the lights, air conditioning, fans, and messages thrills those entranced by clever gadgets. The hotel's dark blue pool is a stunner, but most guests gravitate toward the lounge chairs on the lawn facing a perfect cove. Like a saltwater lap pool, the cove's waters are calm and clear, perfect for lap swimming and snorkeling.

The Ihilani's Spa is housed in its own three-story building with a rooftop lap pool and tennis courts, a full fitness center, and separate-sex spa areas with whirlpool tubs, saunas, and steam rooms. Spa treatments include a muscle-soothing *lomi-lomi* massage and seaweed body mask. The spa has its own restaurant, and spa dishes are also served in the hotel's restaurants. The hotel's Naupaka Terrace serves breakfast, lunch and dinner, blending fresh local ingredients with the flavors of Southeast Asia. Ushio-Tei is a specialty Japanese restaurant serving sushi and other authentic Japanese cuisine, and Azul is the signature dinner restaurant.

The 18-hole Ted Robinson championship golf course is nearby at the Koolina Golf Club.

WHERE TO EAT

Oahu has a restaurant for nearly every taste, and is the testing ground for Hawaii's best chefs. You can easily dine at an excellent, innovative, expensive restaurant every night for a week and not check out all the big names. At the same time, the island has a wealth of moderate eateries serving all manner of cuisine, from pizza to dim sum. Every theme-oriented chain worth international fame seems to have a branch in or near Waikiki — sometimes the lines for souvenirs are longer than those for food at Hard Rock and Planet Hollywood. Speaking of queues — if you really want to dine by the beach, make reservations. You'll still have to wait at some of the most popular places, pacing about some shopping plaza with a pager in hand. Most of the hotels have several restaurants; those mentioned here are exceptional.

WAIKIKI

Very Expensive
The most elegant restaurant in all Waikiki is the Halekulani Hotel's **La Mer** ((808) 923-2311, 2199 Kalia Road. Men don jackets (but no ties) and women wear their fanciest dresses to this ocean-side dining room with views of far away Diamond Head. French and Hawaiian influences are blended by chef Yves Garnier into sublime foie gras, bouillabaisse topped with puff pastry, and kuma (goatfish) in a rosemary salt crust. A cheese platter and incomparable three-chocolate mousse or crème brûlée follow the entrées. Don't look at the prices — check out the starry sky instead, and settle in for a memorable evening.

Expensive
Also at the Halekulani, **Orchids** ((808) 923-2311, 2199 Kalia Road, is less glamorous but memorable. The Sunday brunch is heaven for those who love fresh raw and marinated seafood, as is the nightly seafood buffet available as an appetizer or full meal. Paella fans are thrilled with this kitchen's preparation. **Nick's Fishmarket** ((808) 955-6333, Waikiki Gateway Hotel, 2070 Kalakaua Avenue, isn't

as flashy as the big-name hot spots, but it endures as one of the finest restaurants in Waikiki. The waiters are courtly without being obsequious, and the seafood is dependably fresh and delicious. This is the place to splurge on Maine lobster by candlelight.

Bali by the Sea ((808) 949-4321 at the Hilton Hawaiian Village, 2005 Kalia Road, is elegant without being overwhelming. Starters include asparagus soup with smoked salmon garnish, and macadamia nuts are used in crusts on *opakapaka* and lamb. A pianist at the white grand piano at the entrance provides

the perfect accompaniment to a sublime meal. Also in the Hilton is **Golden Dragon** ((808) 949-4321, where chef Steve Chang oversees preparation of the flashy signature dish Imperial Beggar's Chicken (call 24 hours in advance to order). The chicken is wrapped in lotus leaves and baked in a clay dish. The Imperial Peking Duck is equally impressive and also requires an advance order. There's a touch of showbiz in this place — from the golden horses at the entrance to the tea lady who also tells fortunes.

If you would like a complete evening under one roof and are prepared to pay the rather high price, the **Hanohano Room** ((808)

Catamarans, yachts, cruise ships, and outrigger canoes all find shelter at Honolulu Harbor.

922-4422 in the Sheraton Waikiki Hotel at 2255 Kalakaua Avenue, is the place to go. It has the best early evening view of Waikiki on the Diamond Head side and a gorgeous sunset view on the downtown side. The food is excellent and a pianist performs nightly.

At the Hyatt Regency's **Furasato Japanese Restaurant** ((808) 955-6333, 22424 Kalakaua Avenue, the style is authentically Japanese with most of the seating on tatami mats, though there are small areas set aside for those who wish to be seated Western style. **Chez Michel** ((808) 955-7866, 444 Hobron Lane, is an excellent French restaurant on a quiet side street away from the beach. Try the veal chops or the salmon Wellington in Normandy sauce.

Moderate
A great find worth visiting several times is the **Parc Café** at the Waikiki Parc Hotel ((808) 921-7272, 2233 Helumoa Road. The Parc's buffets are legendary for fresh food and elaborate presentations. The Asian, seafood, and Hawaiian spreads are outstanding, as is the Sunday brunch. Indecisive diners can tackle two cuisines at **Ciao Mein** in the Hyatt Regency ((808) 923-2426, 2424 Kalakaua Avenue. This is a good place to dine with a group and share several dishes, juxtaposing spicy Sichuan eggplant and classic antipasti.

Singha Thai Cuisine ((808) 941-2898, 1910 Ala Moana Boulevard, is one of the best Thai restaurants at the beach. Royal Thai dancers perform on a small stage as diners savor Thai dishes with a Hawaiian accent, including the catch of the day in chili and black bean sauce, shrimp curry puff pastry morsels, *ahi* tempura, and squid salad.

It seems every tourist in Waikiki feels the need to have at least one meal at **Duke's Canoe Club** ((808) 922-2268, 2335 Kalakaua Avenue. It's a fun spot with surfboards all over the place and a rowdy crowd. But the food is far from exceptional. Stick with the salad bar, burgers and pork ribs.

Inexpensive
The cheapest meal in Waikiki is a plate lunch on the beach. The standard plate lunch includes an entrée such as grilled fish, shoyu chicken, or beef curry with rice and salad; these days some places offer green salads as

well. There are several stands on the sand serving plate lunches. **Eggs 'n Things** ((808) 949-0820, 1911 Kalakaua Avenue serves great omelets, pancakes and crepes throughout the day. The **Wailana Coffee House** ((808) 955-1764, 1860 Ala Moana Boulevard, is a longstanding, somewhat rundown 24-hour coffee shop with dependable sandwiches, soups, and egg dishes. Though it's part of a chain, **Sizzler** ((808) 973-5685, 1945 Kalakaua Avenue, is a good choice for its soup and salad bar. If you're really craving a steak but are on a strict budget, this is your place.

HONOLULU

Expensive
Hawaii's big-name chefs are so confident they name restaurants after themselves and lay claim to signature dishes. George Mavrothalassitis, aka Chef Mavro, joined the crowd in 1998 with his classy, sleek **Chef Mavro** ((808) 944-4714, in an understated building at 1969 South King Street. Mavro had his own restaurants in France more than a decade ago, but made his name in Hawaii at the Halekulani Hotel and Four Seasons Maui Resort. He's thrown tremendous imagination into his menu, offering wine pairing menus that allow dining partners to have Pinot Noir with their roasted squab and Pinot Blanc with Mavro's most famous dish — *onaga* (Hawaiian snapper) baked in a salt crust with an ogo (seaweed) infusion. His *ahi* tartare is also sublime, and you won't be able to leave a crumb of the *lilikoi malasadas* (Portuguese doughnuts) with coconut-pineapple ice cream.

One of Hawaii's most lauded chefs presides over **Alan Wong's** ((808) 949-2526, 1857 South King Street, Fifth Floor, just a stone's throw away from Mavro's. Wong's opened in 1995, after the chef had been classically trained in French and European cuisine and gained fame at several fine restaurants. One of the dozen or so chefs who set the standard for regional cuisine in the 1980s, Wong continues to delight — you can't miss with Kona lobster and *opakapaka* with ginger onion sauce. Many consider Wong to be the best chef in the islands. His restaurant has won innumerable awards, and he often makes guest appearances at food and wine festivals.

Roy's ☎ (808) 396-7697, 6600 Kalanianaole Highway, is the flagship restaurant of chef Roy Yamaguchi, who has several other restaurants in Hawaii and on the mainland. Fusing the flavors of East and West, Yamaguchi has created a menu whose magic is in the sauces — a subtle combination of Hawaiian fruit, nuts and vegetables, exotic spices of Asia, and smooth California wines. Roy's open kitchen allows diners to watch the chef in action; the one drawback is the excessive noise level. Chef Russell Siu holds forth at **3660 On the Rise** ☎ (808) 737-1177,

international and as hearty as the man himself. At the Diamond Head restaurant, start with the baked shiitake mushrooms stuffed with crabmeat and water chestnuts or his unusual fried *poke* (marinated seafood); and for an entrée, have Chef Sam's Kona cuisine combo — macadamia nut breast of chicken with jumping barbecue shrimp. Breakfast, Lunch and Crab, a spacious 380-seat restaurant lined with miniature aquariums is wildly popular. Several types of crab from Florida, Maine and Hawaii are featured, and the place fills up quickly. Book well in advance.

an intimate dining room at 3660 Waialae Avenue. Here, Hawaiian *opakapaka* is steamed in jasmine tea and served with coriander butter sauce and the desserts are justifiably famous. Locals trying to escape hordes of tourists favor the quiet space.

Chef Sam Choy is a larger-than-life figure who owns and operates two highly successful restaurants on Oahu — **Sam Choy's Diamond Head** ☎ (808) 732-8645, 449 Kapahulu Avenue, and the latest in his chain, **Sam Choy's Breakfast, Lunch and Crab** ☎ (808) 545-7979, 580 North Nimitz Highway. Choy grew up sampling the food of his Hawaiian-German mother and working at his father's restaurant, Sam's Place, in Laie on the North Shore. Choy's dishes are as

Chai Caowasaree, who made his name with Waikiki's Singha Thai Cuisine restaurant, has his own eponymous restaurant, **Chai's Island Bistro** ☎ (808) 585-0011, at Aloha Tower Marketplace. Unlike other places of its caliber, Chai's is open for lunch, making it a fine place for relaxing after a morning of sightseeing downtown. Relying on his Thai background, the chef serves *mahimahi* with red curry sauce; his macadamia-crusted tiger prawns are an inspiration.

Typical of the generation of Chinese who are helping to revitalize Chinatown is Glenn Chu, who owns and operates **Indigo** ☎ (808) 521-2900, 1121 Nuuanu Avenue, one of

Jagged palisades form a rugged backdrop to the expanse of Waimanalo's palm-fringed beach.

several excellent nontraditional Chinatown restaurants. Indigo is in a charming old building that once housed several shops. The courtyard is fascinating — reminiscent of a garden in a traditional Chinese village — with its huge iron gate leading nowhere, open lanai, and rattan blinds. On the menu, you'll find delectable dishes such as goat cheese wontons with fruit sauce, Thai beef salad with chili lime vinaigrette, and chicken curry with bananas.

Duc's Bistro ((808) 531-6325, 1188 Maunakea Street, is an elegant little restaurant that

specializes in French-Continental food with a hint of Vietnamese. For starters, gravlox — that wonderful Scandinavian dish of raw salmon with dill and aquavit served with mustard-dill dressing; or aromatic beef *la lot* — minced beef tenderloin wrapped in la lot leaf, broiled and served with pineapple anchovy sauce. There are a variety of salads, but duck salad *beaulieu* — sautéed breast of duck with raspberry vinaigrette — is especially good. For your main course, try *steak au poivre flambé au VSOP* (black angus New York steak sautéed with pink, green and black peppercorns).

Moderate

The **Aloha Tower Marketplace** at 1 Aloha Drive at the downtown waterfront, has several good restaurants. **Don Ho's Island Grill** ((808) 528-0807 is a fun spot overlooking the water. Every imaginable frou-frou drink is served in the Tiny Bubbles Bar, while the kitchen does a fine job with roasted chicken and pork, stir-fry veggies, and fresh fish. Pizzas are served on miniature surfboards.

The **Big Island Steak House** ((808) 537-4446 is a dependable place for a filling meat-and-potatoes meal. For drinks there's **Gordon Biersch Brewery Restaurant** ((808) 599-4877 serving Pacific Rim food and freshly brewed lager beer. There's also live music here Wednesday through Saturday.

Keo's Thai Cuisine ((808) 737-8240, 625 Kapahulu Avenue, was Honolulu's first Thai restaurant and has remained one of the very best. The restaurant is regularly named in local fine dining polls and continues to attract visiting celebrities to its orchid-filled rooms. In Chinatown, **A Taste of Saigon** ((808) 947-8885, 2334 South King Street, serves traditional Vietnamese food with distinctive Western overtones. The food and service are excellent and the price is right.

In a city filled with many good Chinese restaurants, the landmark, must-visit restaurant is **Wo Fat** ((808) 533-6393, 115 North Hotel Street. Established in 1882, this huge, ornately decorated space is filled with locals celebrating birthdays and other special events. The Cantonese menu is dazzling: it's best to go with someone who knows what they're ordering.

Inexpensive

L&L Drive Inn ((808) 951-8333, 2320 South King Street, has takeout stands all over Hawaii offering inexpensive traditional Hawaiian food. **Ono Hawaiian Food** ((808) 737-2275, 726 Kapahulu Avenue, serves excellent lomi salmon, chicken long rice, and other dishes tourists usually only sample at luaus. Vegetarians feast on curry veggie burgers and healthy salads at **Mocha Java Café** ((808) 591-9023, in the Ward Center, 1200 Ala Moana Boulevard.

Vegetarians are delighted to find **Andy's Sandwiches and Smoothies** ((808) 988-6161, 2904 East Manoa Road. Originally a juice stand, Andy's now serves hearty sandwiches loaded with avocado, cheese, sprouts, fresh tuna or whatever combo you care to create from the healthy selections. Be sure to try the mango smoothies, fresh fruit plates and muffins. The lunch-platter specials at **Sushi King** ((808) 947-2836, 2700 South King Street, are large enough for two light eaters. The platters include teriyaki or tempura, a California roll, soup and rice; other combos pair sashimi with sushi, and you actually get a good-sized portion of raw fish rather than the typical stingy layout of a few paper thin slices. The lunch specials become early-bird specials at dinner, served until 6:30 PM.

EAST SHORE

Very Expensive

Executive Chef Wayne Hirabayashi changes the menu frequently at the Mandarin Oriental Hotel's **Hoku's** ((808) 739-8777 at 500 Kahala Avenue. The restaurant is as popular with the hotel's wealthy neighbors as with guests, and Chef Hirabayashi keeps their curiosity and taste buds piqued with such offerings as locally farmed escargot sautéed with fern shoots, truffle-crusted scallops, and an unusual rack of lamb with breadfruit and coconut milk.

Moderate

The **Swiss Inn** ((808) 377-5447, 5730 Kalanianaole Highway, about a 15-minute drive from Waikiki, has been a fixture in this neighborhood for many years. It is run by the husband and wife team of Jeanie and Martin Wyss and is a family-style restaurant in every sense of the word. It serves excellent Weiner schnitzel, chopped veal, and trout caprice. Martin is the chef and Jeanie acts as hostess throughout the evening. Dining here is rather like being guests in a friend's house.

Homesick mainlanders cheer when they find **Brent's Bestaurant** ((808) 262-8588, 629-A Kailua Road. The deli counter is packed with bagels, pastrami, lox, dill pickles and other New York favorites. The menu ranges from blintzes to shrimp-topped salads; there's something to please every palate.

NORTH SHORE

Moderate

Jameson's by the Sea ((808) 637-4336, 62-540 Kamehameha Highway at Haleiwa, is a favorite spot to sip mai tais while watching the sunset. The downstairs dining area is casual and crowded with regulars stopping by for salads and sandwiches. The upstairs room is more formal; the menu features steaks and fresh seafood. More casual is **Haleiwa Joe's** ((808) 637-8005, 66-011 Kame-

hameha Highway, at the edge of the marina. Try the spinach and salmon salad, the prime rib (which runs out quickly), the sticky ribs with ginger and hoison sauce, or the seared and spicy black and blue *ahi*. The portions are enormous — share an entrée and save room for Key lime pie for dessert.

Inexpensive

Thanks to the abundance of surfers and budget travelers, low-key Haleiwa has some of the best inexpensive restaurants on Oahu. Locals and tourists all over the island praise the juicy burgers and fries at **Kua Aina Sandwich** ((808) 637-6027, 66-214 Kamehameha Highway. A few tables and a long counter fill the tiny café's interiors; most diners choose to sit at tables on the front porch. **Cholo's** ((808) 637-3059, 66-250 Kamehameha Highway in the North Shore Marketplace, offers a change of pace, with shrimp tacos, chicken fajitas and other Mexican specialties served amid Mexican folk art. The masks, frames, painted wood animals and paintings on the walls are all for sale. Pastries, sandwiches, egg dishes and all manner of coffee drinks make the **Coffee Gallery** ((808) 637-5355, 66-250 Kamehameha Highway in the North Shore Marketplace, a popular spot.

Walk beyond shelves stacked with brown rice, granola, and nutritional supplements to reach the aptly named **Paradise Found Café** ((808) 637-4540, 66-443 Kamehameha Highway, in the back room at Celestial Natural Foods. The menu wanders the globe from all-American veggie burgers, to Middle Eastern tabouleh, to Italian pastas covered with marinara sauce. Hearty soups and chili warm those who've spent entirely too much time in the cold water, while thick fruit smoothies hit the spot on a hot day. Stop in the store for trail mix and strips of candied papaya — the perfect beach snack.

NIGHTLIFE

Waikiki and Honolulu have a proliferation of nightclubs, discotheques, music clubs, and stage shows that appeal to both the sophisticated and the college crowd. With clubs perpetually opening, closing and reopening,

Testing the waters at a secluded inlet.

it is difficult to keep track of what's hot and what's not, but there is always plenty to choose from. Nearly all the hotels have lounges and bars with live music; check the *Honolulu Advertiser*'s Friday TGIF ("Thank God it's Friday") section for club listings.

The best way to end the day is by sipping a mai tai or piña colada to the sounds of Hawaiian guitar and the surf. The Halekulani Hotel's **House without a Key** ((808) 923-2311, 2199 Kalia Road, may well be the most romantic spot of all, thanks to the talents of Kanoelehua Miller (and the superiority of the Mai tais). A former Miss Hawaii, Miller sways her hips and extends her graceful arms in a welcoming embrace as she dances under a century-old kiawe tree in the torchlight. Crowds pack the **Banyan Court** ((808) 922-3111 at the Sheraton Moana Surfrider, 2365 Kalakaua Avenue, for its gracious ambience, historical fame, and excellent musicians. The **Mai Tai Bar** ((808) 923-7311 at the "Pink Lady" Royal Hawaiian Hotel, 2255 Kalakaua Avenue, is tucked away in a corner of the hotel's courtyard, literally a step away from the beach.

A rowdy crowd celebrates the end of the day at **Duke's Canoe Club** ((808) 922-2268 by the sand at 2335 Kalakaua Avenue, the quintessential overpacked surf bar where microbrews are the preferred libation. **The Row** ((808) 528-2345, in Restaurant Row at 500 Ala Moana Boulevard, is a popular after-work spot, as is the **Ocean Club** ((808) 526-9888. **Gordon Biersch** ((808) 599-4877, in the Aloha Tower Marketplace at 1 Aloha Tower Drive, has plenty of tables on a deck by the waterfront and great beers on tap. The **Hard Rock Café** ((808) 955-7383, 1837 Kapiolani Boulevard, is as popular as ever. It's a good place to eat, and if you like classic rock, it's a good place to roll.

Memphis has Elvis. Vegas has Sinatra. Hawaii has **Don Ho**, who performs weekly at the Waikiki Beachcomber Hotel ((808) 931-3009, 2300 Kalakaua Avenue. Ho has been signing Tiny Bubbles and other corny Hawaiian songs since the mid-1960s; his show draws an eclectic crowd, from octogenarians in matching floral shirts to 20-somethings experiencing the 1970s.

Another longtime act that never fails to amuse is the **Society of Seven**. This colorful show band, whose original members were prominent Filipino musicians playing the Asian circuit, has been a fixture at the **Outrigger Waikiki** ((808) 923-4450, 2335 Kalakaua Avenue, since moving to Hawaii from Hong Kong in 1970. With its mix of zany humor and musical talent, the band blends contemporary music with show tunes and comedy skits. **Magic of Polynesia** ((808) 971-4321 at the Waikiki Beachcomber features magician John Hirokawa, who uses illusions to illustrate Hawaiian legends.

Wave Waikiki ((808) 941-0424, 1877 Kalakaua Avenue, remains the most popular of all Waikiki dance establishments among the alternative music crowd. A separate cigar lounge and a blend of music that ranges from jazz to disco attract a sophisticated set to **Mystique** ((808) 533-0061, 500 Ala Moana Boulevard. A younger, livelier crowd prefers the adjacent **Ocean Club** ((808) 526-9888 also at 500 Ala Moana Boulevard. **Scruples Beach Club** ((808) 923-9530 in the Waikiki Marketplace, 2310 Kuhio Avenue is a casual dance club where the disc jockeys play Top 40 and alternative music. The most popular gay disco is **Hula's Bar and Lei Stand** ((808) 923-0669, 134 Kapahulu Avenue.

The largest and most enjoyable luau on the island is the **Paradise Cove Luau** ((808) 842-5911 held at Paradise Cove in Koolina. Transportation is available to the 12-acre (nearly five-hectare) show grounds, where guests play Hawaiian games, learn how to make leis, pose for photos with a monkey on a leash and take part in a hula and music show. The dinner, served either buffet style or at your table depending on your price of admission, includes *kalua* pig, teriyaki chicken, rice, and coconut cake. **Germaine's Luau** ((808) 949-6626, also in Koolina, has a similar setup.

HOW TO GET THERE

Honolulu's International airport is a hub of the Pacific, receiving flights from the Far East and the West. Inter-island flights arrive at a separate terminal, connected to the main airport by a shuttle.

Hanauma Bay, where snorkelers and fish swim in perfect harmony.

Kauai

EVERYONE WHO VISITS HAWAII HAS A FAVORITE ISLAND. For many, it's Kauai, long the inspiration of poets and artists. Impossibly green and lush, the island is shaped and replenished by the waters that run off the towering rock faces of Mount Waialeale, from whose crater once poured the great lava flows that built the island. Waterfalls glisten far above the coastline, tucked into the velvety folds of jagged peaks. Rainbows shimmer between streams and the sea; rivers tumble through hidden canyons.

Born nearly 10 million years ago, Kauai is the oldest island in the chain. A volcanic eruption some 14,800 ft (4,500 m) in the depths of the Pacific Ocean began the process, with lava piling on lava and, over millions of years, creating the island. Geologists estimate that most of the surface portion of Kauai is 5.6 million years old. Its basic shape, almost round, is said to have been formed by the initial eruption. At the center of all the activity was the volcano that came to be named Mount Waialeale (Rippling Waters). Waialeale is the largest shield volcano in the islands. It has a volume of about 1,000 cubic miles (4,200 cubic km) and a diameter at the top of 10 to 12 miles (16 to 19 km).

The volcano is silent now, but the mountain remains the source of the island's natural irrigation system — a system that, for millions of years, has carved the magnificent canyons and valleys, fed the lush rainforests and watered the plains, giving the island its unique topography. Waialeale's crater, the Alakai Swamp, is some 30 sq miles (78 sq km) of seeping bog and mud almost always shrouded in mist and pelted by rain — a treacherous place where sunlight is scarce and where moss and ferns flourish and trees grow only to knee height. But the swamp is a botanist's Aladdin's Cave and a fascinating, endless source of discovery. Alakai Swamp is also the source of seven rivers and innumerable waterfalls that have gouged spectacular canyons, sharpened knife-edged cliffs, and fed the valleys and the plains. Indeed, Kauai is the only inhabited island in the chain with navigable rivers.

Waialeale's peaks rise to 5,243 ft (1,598 m), just the right height to draw the rain clouds like a mantle. The resulting yearly rainfall of 450 inches (1,143 cm) makes Waialeale among the wettest places on earth. Add rich volcanic soil, mix in some sunshine and you have the ideal conditions for a vast tropical garden — which has earned Kauai its sobriquet "The Garden Isle."

The combination of sun, rain and fertile soil causes hillsides to come alive with wild bougainvillea in flaming reds, purples, oranges, pinks and whites, encourages water lilies to open in bursts of rich burgundy and mauve, and turns the grass in the grazing meadows an iridescent green. It was this abundance of rain and sunshine that attracted planters to create the islands' first sugar cane plantation at Koloa in 1835. This plantation, in south Kauai, spawned an industry that created a financial boom for Kauai. Evidence of former plantations can be seen throughout the island, from Kilauea to Kohala. You can still see cane fields burning in the fall, but sugar no long rules the economy.

Tourism has become one of Kauai's leading industries, yet the island is not overrun with large chain hotels and resorts. Nature is its most important attraction, and the island's residents fiercely protect their version of paradise. Kauai was the one island King Kamehameha the Great never conquered by force (instead, he signed a treaty to bring the island under his control). To this day, the island retains a strong independent streak.

BACKGROUND

Kauai's early history is as turbulent as that of any of the other islands in the chain. Armed combat often occurred between the chiefs and the *alii*. The vanquished were shown little mercy. Enemy warriors not slain in battle were sacrificed to the gods at the *heiaus*. Even women and children were not spared.

In the midst of such turmoil, a chief named Kaumualii — born to the hereditary ruling chieftess of Kauai, Kamakahelei, and Kaeo and the high chief of Maui and King of Kauai — rose to be king of Kauai. Kamakahelei is said to have given birth to Kaumualii at the Birthstones in Wahiawa on the island of Oahu, where royalty traditionally came to give birth. Kaumualii, who was also the

Dappled waters and palms of Haena Point on Kauai's lovely northern shores.

grandson of the great Maui warrior-king Kekaulike, was only 16 when he became king, but even at that age believed that because of his royal blood he was a superior being to Kamehameha and refused to heed his call for a united Hawaii.

In the spring of 1796, Kamehameha decided to end the impasse once and for all, and assembled an enormous fleet of 1,500 canoes and an army of warriors totaling 10,000. This impressive armada set sail at midnight from the beaches of Waianae, Oahu. Halfway across the Kaieie Waho Channel that divides Kauai from Oahu, a sudden storm swamped the canoes. To prevent his entire fleet from being destroyed, Kamehameha gave the order to return to Oahu.

It was almost eight years before Kamehameha tried to conquer Kauai again. This time his forces included 7,000 warriors and about 50 Europeans armed with muskets. He also had some heavy artillery cannons, swivel guns and mortars, as well as several armed schooners to support his fleet of canoes. Just as he was about to launch his attack from eastern Oahu, Kamehameha's forces were struck by what scholars now believe was typhoid fever. Among the hundreds of warriors who died were many loyal and powerful chiefs.

Kamehameha did not give up hope of bringing Kauai into his kingdom, but he decided to resort to diplomacy in order to do so. Finally, in 1810, he and Kaumualii met in Oahu, and it seemed as though the islands would enter a period of genuine peace. But when Kaumualii was told of a plot to poison him, he returned in haste to Kauai.

When Kamehameha died, his son Liholiho (Kamehameha II) succeeded him. In 1821 Liholiho set sail for Wailua from Honolulu, ostensibly to inspect the gathering of sandalwood. En route he ordered the vessel to change course and headed for Kauai, where he met Kaumualii. The two kings made declarations of peace and then embarked on a 45-day tour of the island of Kauai. On a Sunday in September, they met once more in Waimea Harbor, where Kaumualii joined Liholiho on his yacht, the *Pride of Hawaii*. That night, Liholiho gave orders for the vessel to set sail for Oahu, and in so doing, kidnapped the Kauai king.

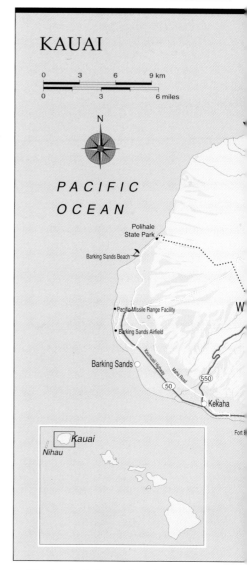

The brain behind this deception was Kamehameha's widow, the imperious Kaahumanu. Four days after landing on Oahu, Kaahumanu forced Kaumualii to become her husband; then, a short time later, she married Kaumualii's son, Kealiiahonui. After her conversion to Christianity, Kaahumanu released Kealiiahonui from his forced marriage.

In 1824 Kaumualii fell ill and died suddenly, and Kauai was plunged into mourning. His death divided the kingdom of Kauai between those loyal to Liholiho and those who still wished for the independent days

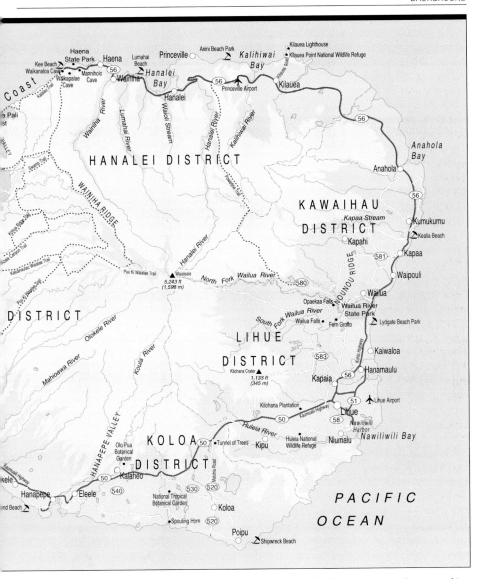

of Kaumualii. A rebellion, led by Kaumualii's son, George Kaumualii, and supported by Deborah Kapule, the late king's favorite wife, ended in a disastrous rout for the rebels after troops under Governor Hoapili of Maui were brought in.

In the aftermath of this defeat, the island was looted and the chiefs deported to Oahu, Maui and Hawaii.

History records that the nobles of Kauai always worked in the best interests of the people, who loved and honored them. This unity may still characterize the people of Kauai more than it does the people of the other islands. That pride and sense of independence survive even today, and stand the people in good stead in times of crisis. Evidence of the character of the people of this island has been seen in the wake of two devastating storms — one in 1982, the other 10 years later. Hurricane Iwa in 1982 brought the island to its knees. Then, in September 1992, Hurricane Iniki struck the island an almost lethal blow. It was the strongest storm to strike Hawaii in a century. The hurricane's eye, 15 miles (25 km) in diameter, leveled almost everything in its path. Wind, waves and rain battered the island, leaving houses and hotels in ruins. The hurricane caused an estimated $1 billion in structural damage and left Kauai's tourism industry in shambles.

Fortunately, ferns and palms grow quickly in Kauai's fertile climate, and Iniki's damage has been largely erased by nature's benevolence. Nearly all the hotels destroyed by the winds and rains have reopened, and Kauai's revival continues to gather momentum. Loyal, tenacious islanders rebuilt their businesses and newcomers are constantly investing in Kauai's future. "Iniki slowed us down," a waitress whose family outlasted the hurricane told me. "In at lot of ways it was a good thing." The Garden Isle merits being protected from rampant development and preserved as a monument to Hawaii's natural state.

GENERAL INFORMATION

The **Kauai Visitors Bureau** ((808) 245-3971 FAX (808) 246-9235 is at 3016 Umi Street, Suite 207, Lihue. For a free **Kauai Vacation Planner**, call TOLL-FREE (800) 262-1400, or visit their WEB SITE at www.kauaivisitorsbureau.org.

GETTING AROUND

A car is essential if you plan on doing a lot of exploring on the island. The major rental agencies have offices in Lihue. **Kauai Bus** ((808) 241-6410, the island's public bus system, runs along most major roads around the island. Buses run Monday through Saturday, except holidays, and the fare is $1, with seniors, students and the disabled paying half fare. The drivers will not allow you to bring a backpack larger than 9"x14"x22" onto the bus. Also forbidden are boogie boards, surfboards and bicycles. Taxi service is available on Kauai. A ride from the airport to the northern resort area of Princeville will cost approximately $60.

WHAT TO SEE AND DO

One could easily spend several vacations exploring the many sides of Kauai. Lihue, on the southeast shore, is home to the airport, full-scale resorts and many tour companies. The South Shore, dominated by the

golf courses, hotels, and hideaways around Poipu, runs along craggy beaches and bays northwest to Kekaha. A road rises inland to Waimea Canyon and Kokee State Park in the highlands. Northeast of Lihue, the coastal road edges along the East Shore's coconut groves, popular beaches and rural towns. As the road curves along the island's north coast, Kauai's raw, rugged terrain carves sheer cliffs at Princeville and culminates at the dramatic Na Pali Coast. Each section of the island offers endless possibilities for hikers, kayakers, snorkelers, and relaxed types content with driving by cascading waterfalls and misty canyons.

Lying just 15 miles (24 km) off Kauai, the tiny island of Niihau pays precious little attention to outsiders. Tourism to Niihau is virtually nonexistent, except for day trips via helicopter. Still, its history and culture play important roles in Hawaii's sovereignty movement. Niihau is a curiosity worth exploring.

LIHUE

Visitors to Kauai arrive at the Lihue airport. But Lihue is far more than a gateway to Kauai. It's the island's business and government seat and largest neighborhood. The resort area is anchored by the Marriott resort (See WHERE TO STAY, page 168), the harbor, and **Kalapaki Beach**, one of the island's best stretches of soft sand and calm water. The biggest attraction in town is the **Kauai Museum** ((808) 245-6931, 4428 Rice Street. There is an admission fee charged to tour the exhibits on the island's history, and the museum is closed on Sundays. The gift shop alone is worth touring.

Sprawling over 80 acres (32 hectares), **Grove Farm Homestead Museum** ((808) 245-3202, 4050 Nawiliwili Road, is a fine example of Hawaii's sugar plantation homesteads. George N. Wilcox founded the plantation in 1864; his home is filled with antiques and several outbuildings hold artifacts from plantation days. The museum is open only on request; reserve a tour. More accessible is **Kilohana Plantation** ((808) 245-5608, 3-2087 Kaumualii Highway, the old plantation mansion of Gaylord P. Wilcox, nephew of George Wilcox. Set amidst 1,704 acres (690 hectares) of cane fields, Kilohana in its heyday attracted political and religious leaders, businessmen, and intellectuals; who gathered to socialize and discuss the events of the day. The magnificent open horseshoe-shaped lanai has been converted into a restaurant, appropriately named **Gaylord's** (see WHERE TO EAT, page 174). Most of the smaller rooms on the ground floor, with the exception of what were once the main living room and dining room, are now used for retail shops, as are a few restored guest cottages. A great variety of items are offered; from island crafts and fine jewelry to Niihau shell

point is the rugged Na Pali Coast, accessible only by boat.

On leaving Kilohana Plantation, continue along Kaumualii Highway (Highway 50), then turn left on Route 520 and you will find yourself traveling through the beautiful **Tunnel of Trees** on the road to Koloa, and the picturesque complex of **Old Koloa Town**. This was Hawaii's original plantation town and also served as the mercantile and retail center for the south side of the island. Within its three acres (just over one hectare), in a setting of monkeypod trees and neat court-

necklaces and scrimshaw, high fashion, and fine art. Visitors to Kilohana can tour the plantation in a 106-year-old horse-drawn carriage shipped from Fairbanks, Alaska. Also on the plantation grounds is **Wings Over Hawaii** ((808) 245-8838, a fascinating commercial butterfly farm.

SOUTH SHORE

Kauai's South Shore encompasses the former plantation town of Koloa, the resorts of Poipu, the sugar towns of Hanapepe and Waimea, and the 15-mile (24-km) white-sand beach at Kekaha. Further along this stretch of coast is Polihale and Barking Sands, site of the Pacific Missile Range Facility. Beyond this

yards, is a collection of restored old buildings housing a variety of shops, services and restaurants. At night, a carnival atmosphere grips the town. Driving down the darkened highway, the fairy lights of Old Koloa Town — first seen through the trees — are a welcome sight to the traveler.

The fertile lowlands of south Kauai were an agricultural base for the earliest Polynesian settlers. It was at Koloa that the first plantation in Hawaii was started in 1835. Sugar brought a new prosperity to Hawaii with Koloa and Lihue plantations setting the pace. Today, the industry has fallen on hard times, and many plantations and mills have

An antique outrigger canoe adorns the lobby of a luxury resort.

been forced to close. But the enterprise of the sugar barons left a legacy that the people of Kauai continue to build on. Descendants of the Japanese and Filipinos who came to work the plantations now make up the largest percentage of the population, and their skills are dispersed in new industries, chiefly tourism. Towns have been turned into tourist attractions, and plantation houses are now quaint and colorful lodgings, museums, restaurants and specialty galleries.

Poipu, not far beyond Koloa, is Kauai's resort playground. The wonderful beach led to the construction of hotels and resorts boasting every luxury the pampered tourist could ever wish for. The last hurricane to strike Kauai, the 1992 Hurricane Iniki, was especially severe in this area, however many of the resorts have been remodeled and restored, and the area has returned to its former beauty. The south shores offer the best swimming, surfing and windsurfing waters in Kauai. Poipu is the best area for beginning surfers, and the most spectacular windsurfing site is **Shipwreck Beach**. All varieties of water sports from snorkeling to sport fishing are available here.

If you get as far as Shipwreck Beach, then you should make the extra effort to walk or drive over to **Mahaulepu**, east of the golf course. This rugged coastline differs from almost everything else on the southeastern shores of this island. The limestone cliffs here stand out dramatically against the blue waters. The pounding of huge ocean rollers has caused deep chasms in the cliffs. You can walk for miles on the trails above the bluffs and during winter watch whales spouting in the waters below. You can also join a trail ride at the nearby stables, or rent a mountain bike and explore the coastal trails and the cane haul roads.

A favorite Poipu attraction is **Spouting Horn** geyser at the end of Lawai Road. This jet of water springs from an ancient lava tube, emitting a sigh as it shoots out. According to legend, the sound you hear is that of a lizard trapped in the tube. There's a full-scale bazaar in this most unlikely of spots, where you can purchase a wide variety of interesting souvenirs from an equally interesting group of vendors. Across from the Spouting Horn is **Allerton Garden** of the National Tropical

Botanical Garden ((808) 742-2623, Lawai Road, Poipu. Once a vacation home of Queen Emma, wife of Kamehameha IV, the Allerton was transformed into one of the most beautiful botanical gardens in the state by Chicago cattleman Robert Allerton and his son John Gregg Allerton. Guided tours of the extraordinary 100-acre (40-hectare) preserve are offered by reservation only; a fee is charged and children under five years of age are not permitted.

On Kaumualii Highway, going west again, keep an eye out for **Olu Pua Botanical Garden and Plantation** ((808) 332-8182, just past the town of Kalaheo on the mountain side of the road. Olu Pua's name means "floral serenity." Once the manager's estate for the Kauai Pineapple Plantation, it has been converted into a botanical showplace for an outstanding collection of tropical plants, fruits and trees gathered from around the world. Wander through the Jungle (shaded paths among exotic foliage and flowering plants), Hibiscus Garden, Kau Kau Garden (edible plants), Front Lawn (with flowering shade trees), and the Palm Garden. Olu Pua is open on Monday, Wednesday and Friday, with guided tours scheduled at various times during the day; a fee is charged for the tour.

The charming towns of the Waimea Coast, with names such as Eleele, Hanapepe and Kekaha, could have been torn from the pages of an Old West chronicle. The dominant color of the landscape in this scenic region is red — red clay and red dust. On the drive to Hanapepe (Crushed Bay), a pattern begins to emerge. Waving green cane fields start to form a mosaic with the rich red earth for which Hanapepe is so famous. Stop at the **Hanapepe Canyon Lookout** to gaze over a once prosperous valley. Old taro terraces are still discernible beneath the undergrowth. It was in this exotic, seemingly wild valley that Steven Spielberg filmed portions of his blockbuster film *Jurassic Park*. Directly opposite the lookout is the site of the final Kauai revolt against Kamehameha by Kaumualii's son George, which was put down by the governor of Maui.

Spouting Horn TOP, on the southern coast near Poipu, is a geyser which shoots water out of an ancient lava tube. A placid pool BOTTOM at the National Tropical Botanical Garden (, Poipu.

Hanapepe, situated on the banks of the Hanapepe River, is one of the prettier plantation towns on the island. Although residents like to refer to it as "the biggest little town in Kauai," Hanapepe has obviously seen better days, and there is a sense of decay about the town. But artists love it for that very reason. It remains charming and true to what it was in days gone by. Natural and unspoiled, it's a reminder of a more leisurely paced era. Many artists have taken up residence in the storefronts on the town's main street, helping to keep the town alive after the demise of the sugar industry.

It is easy to understand why those artistically inclined love Hanapepe. For all its rundown appearance, the town is awash in color. Pastel and brown tones of the old wooden buildings reflect in the waters of the river; bougainvillea explodes in vibrant colors amidst the red earth on the hillsides — all this against a backdrop of vivid blue ocean and cloud-enclosed mountains.

Lolokai Lele Road will take you to **Salt Pond Beach**. The crescent-shaped beach, protected by a reef, is a safe swimming area year round. A small lagoon created by rocks is a perfect bathing pool for kids. The tide pools are also worth exploring, and sunsets seen from Salt Pond are superior. This lovely beach gets its name from the salt pans that exist in this area. Salt is still harvested by descendants of ancient salt makers who worked these pans as far back as the 1700s. Salt makers mix the salt with the red earth (*'alaea*) and sell this red salt, which is highly prized. Permission from the salt makers is required to enter the pan area; ask those working there.

The town of **Waimea** has a special place in Hawaiian history and folklore. It was here that British explorer Captain James Cook first set foot on Hawaiian soil in January, 1778. Mistaken for the Hawaiian god Lono and treated with great respect, Cook remained on Kauai for less than two weeks. He was to return the following year only to meet his death. Every February the townspeople of Waimea stage a carnival commemorating the Cook expedition's historic visit to the island and this town. There are mule and horse races, mountain bike and foot races, carnival rides and lots of great food.

Just outside Waimea town is the old **Russian Fort Elizabeth State Historical Park** on the ocean side of Highway 50. The fort was built by a charismatic Russian doctor named George Scheffer, who was sent to the islands to establish a colony. Scheffer sailed to the Big Island in November 1815 and gained the confidence of Kamehameha through his medical skills. Later he came to Kauai and established an excellent rapport with Kaumualii. So strong was this relationship that eventually the two men — Hawaiian and Russian — plotted the conquest of Oahu, Molokai,

Lanai and Maui. Part of the plan called for Scheffer to build a fort on every Hawaiian island, to be under the command of a Russian. But at this point Scheffer overplayed his hand. The Russians began construction of a blockhouse on Oahu and raised the Russian flag — much to the ire of the Americans, who informed Kamehameha. The Hawaiian monarch ordered the blockhouse attacked and the Russians were driven from it. This isolated Scheffer, who was on Kauai at the time. Scheffer's days were numbered, and he left Kauai in 1817 for Macao before eventually migrating to Brazil. Most of the fort at Waimea was completed by late 1816. It was an impressive structure with 17-ft-thick (five-meter) walls rising to heights of 20 ft (six meters).

Little remains of the fort except for some of its star-shaped foundations.

Waimea Stream meanders through the town on its way to the ocean. Running parallel to the river is Menehune Road. *Menehune* are the legendary "little people" of the island, a kind of Hawaiian leprechaun, who according to Hawaiian legend did most of their work at night. Though shy forest dwellers, the *menehune* were also said to be master builders capable of creating complicated irrigation systems in a single night. Nearby Menehune Ditch, or *Kiki A Ola*, is pointed to as evidence of their work. It is an unusual construction said to have been built by the little people for High Chief Ola of Waimea, who paid them in shrimp. Many Hawaiians believe the *menehune* were no fairytale, but were among the original settlers here. The *menehune* supposedly had a great love for the fragrant mokihana berry (which only grows on Kauai), and thrived on a diet of sweet potatoes, squash and taro leaves. The densely jungled valley of Honopu on the Na Pali Coast is thought to have been the last home of the *menehune* and is still referred to as the "Valley of the Lost Tribe." Some people insist the *menehune* exist to this day deep in the forests of the island.

The last town on this stretch of coast is **Kekaha**, home of a still prospering sugar plantation. The grounds surrounding the humble plantation houses are alive with flowers. The people of Kekaha stage major festivals here several times a year.

If you are looking for adventure, keep going past Kekaha along Kaumualii Highway to the **Pacific Missile Range Facility** at Barking Sands. The beach here is generally opened to the public, but you will be required to show your license and auto insurance card to get past the guard gate. **Major's Bay Beach** is rarely crowded, the waves are great, and the sunsets are fabulous.

The remote **Polihale State Park** lies at the end of the road. The going is rough, but it's worth the effort. Polihale Beach is the longest beach in all the Hawaiian Islands. It's a dramatic, lonely place where the wind sighs across vast open stretches of sand and huge waves crash onto the shoreline. Use extreme caution when wading and swimming here; the waves are powerful and the undertow

can be lethal. At the base of the Na Pali Range in the Polihale State Park lies the Polihale *heiau*, where ancient Hawaiians believed that the spirits of the dead departed the island.

WAIMEA CANYON

The interior of the island is a network of rivers feeding sugar plantations and ranches. Most of the land is private, much of it inaccessible by motor vehicle. One of the best ways to see the island is by helicopter (See TOURS, page 165). But you can get a sense of the inland's majesty by driving along Waimea Canyon to Kokee State Park. Your ascent along Kokee Road leads to a spectacular panorama: Waimea Canyon — "the Grand Canyon of the Pacific" — one mile (1.61 km) wide, 14.5 miles (23.3 km) long and 2,750 ft (833 m) deep. The canyon was created by a fault in the earth's crust and has been eroding for centuries. It's a vast canvas in shades of brown, red, ochre, and green with an occasional splash of purple.

Eight miles (13 km) from the canyon lookout, in a huge green meadow deep in the 4,345 acres (1,758 hectares) of **Kokee State Park** are **Kokee Lodge** and the **Kokee Natural History Museum** ((808) 335-9975 E-MAIL kokee@aloha.net, between the 15 and 16 mile markers on Kokee Road. Here, at an elevation of 3,600 ft (1,100 m), the air is cool and invigorating.

Soon after the park at Kokee was officially established in 1952, construction began on four rental cabins (see WHERE TO STAY, page 171), a natural history museum and a small grocery store, built mostly from surplus salvaged from the United States Army. The country store eventually became Kokee Lodge, which now consists of a restaurant serving breakfast and lunch, a cocktail lounge, a general store and a gift shop.

The Kokee Natural History Museum is quaint and informative and is devoted to the flora, fauna and natural history of the area. It also has an interesting collection of shells and Hawaiian artifacts and a riveting exhibit on hurricanes. It's open daily from 10 AM to 4 PM; guided hikes can be arranged by appointment for a small fee.

Terraced gardens contrast with the jagged mountains in Kauai's rugged interior wilderness.

Kokee State Park has freshwater fishing streams and a network of 45 miles (72 km) of hiking trails (see THE GREAT OUTDOORS, page 23). Hunting is permitted in certain areas. Hunters can go after wild boar, feral goats, blacktail deer and numerous game birds during certain times of the year. The only rainbow trout season in the state opens each August in Kokee. There's also a plum season in summer when the succulent wild methley plum is ripe for the picking.

For information about hunting and fishing, contact the Hawaii State Department of Land and Natural Resources ℓ (808) 274-3344, PO Box 1671, Lihue, HI 96766.

A few miles further into the park will take you to **Kalalau Lookout**, elevation 4,120 ft (1,256 m) and a glimpse into one of the more mysterious valleys on the island. The lookout and the valley are often shrouded in mist. The magnificent valley slopes like a massive green carpet toward the ocean and is bounded on three sides by cliffs, which once isolated and protected the Hawaiians who first settled here. For more than 1,000 years, native Hawaiians lived an idyllic existence here, cultivating the fertile land for their taro crops. With the coming of the Caucasians, new centers of civilization were established at places such as Lihue, and the country people gradually drifted away until the valley was deserted.

In the mid-1950s Bernard Wheatley stood at the lookout gazing into Kalalau. This physician from the Virgin Islands had lost his young wife and child in a tragic car accident. Wheatley walked the 10 hard miles (16 km) into the valley carrying his lunch in a paper bag, and settled in a cave beneath the cliff near the beach. He remained there for 23 days before falling ill, and was picked up by a passing fishing boat and taken to hospital. When he recovered, he hiked back to Kalalau and set up residence in his cave.

Wheatley asked nothing of anyone, only to be left in peace. He ate the fruit in the valley, showered in the waterfalls, swam at the beach and reveled in the glorious sunsets and the magnificent night skies. When he needed food, he walked to Kilauea for supplies. For more than 10 years he lived here, writing poetry and philosophy, coming to be known as the Hermit of Kalalau. Visitors were al-

ways welcome and invited to stay in a guest cave near his own. One day he disappeared and hasn't been seen since. He wrote:

"There is more here than just quietness. There is big peace. There is music in the wind and the surf. I like sundown best and the moonlight on the ripples in the sand. I like to sit in my cave and watch Venus in the night sky."

His words capture the essence of Kauai.

THE EAST COAST

A journey tracing the eastern seaboard takes you along the Kuhio Highway (Highway 56), past Wailua and Wailua Bay, Waipouli, Kapaa, Anahola and Anahola Bay. This area, known as the **Coconut Coast**, is more commercial than the southern or northern shores.

Many of Kauai's timeshare and moderately priced resorts lie amid thousands of coconut palms planted more than a century past. Hurricane Iniki blew through this unprotected area with mighty force; some of the landmark hotels have yet to reopen.

North of Lihue on your way up the coast, Maalo Road (Highway 583) leads to **Wailua Falls**, an 80-ft (24-m) cascade that drops into a pool once regarded as the private playground of the nobility. The falls were featured in the television series *Fantasy Island*. Ancient Hawaiians dived from the top of the falls to prove their courage; more recent divers attempting the same feat often lose their lives. Be careful when walking along the trail at the top of the falls — human sacrifice is no way to end a vacation.

Off Highway 56 and just before you reach the little town of Wailua, you'll come across **Lydgate Beach Park**, one of the most popular beaches on the island. Kids love this spot not only for swimming, but for the great playground designed by the children of Kauai and built by residents.

The town of **Wailua** is situated at the mouth of the Wailua River. The source of the river is the Mount Waialeale watershed, which feeds all seven of the island's rivers. Going upstream from the ocean, the river splits; the north fork going far inland to the base of the mountain range, the south fork past the famed **Fern Grotto** and **Opaekaa Falls**.

Waimea Canyon is a place of spectacular natural beauty.

At the edge of Wailua River State Park on Kuhio Highway are the two boat companies allowed to take visitors to the Fern Grotto. **Waialeale Boat Tours** ((808) 822-4908 and **Smith's Motor Boats** ((808) 821-6892 both use large boats carrying up to 150 passengers to ply the river throughout the day. Fern Grotto is one of the most photographed and publicized caves in the world. This huge subterranean amphitheater with its emerald glow and cascading ferns has been the scene for numerous weddings, many attended by hundreds of strangers on tours. If you're a water and nature freak, as I am, go ahead and take the tour despite its tourist trappings. The ferns are gorgeous, especially when dappled with sunlight. Opaekaa Falls is accessible by car from Highway 580 (off the Kuhio Highway). As the highway continues north, the Nounou Ridge etches the **Sleeping Giant** rock formation against the horizon. Don't try to spot it as you're driving. Instead, pull to the side of the road and look south toward Wailua and follow the curve of the giant's head. According to legend, the early islanders lit fires behind the giant's outline at night, thinking his size would intimidate warriors approaching from the sea.

Waipouli, just north of the giant, is tourism central, with rows of timeshare and condo complexes. Shops and restaurants cater to the tourists and locals in nearby **Kapaa**, which tries hard to hold on to its individuality while accommodating chain stores and takeout stands. The town center (away from the mini malls along the Kuhio Highway) is lined with small family-owned businesses, from Hawaiian diners to produce stands.

The farther you get from Lihue, the greener and more rural the countryside becomes. Beyond Kapaa, **Kealia Beach** is a favorite with the locals. Kapaa Stream exits near this beach and can create strong currents, so be careful. Farther north, the water is calmer. Surfers love this spot, and the beach is a great place to watch the action.

A dirt road leads from the highway to **Donkey Beach**, but since private vehicles are not permitted here, the only way to reach this beach favored by nudists is on foot. This is an undeveloped stretch of coast that is quite beautiful. From Donkey Beach you can see the migration of the whales each winter. Still further north is **Anahola Bay**. It is a wide sweeping bay, with a reef-enclosed bassin at the south end that is perfectly safe for swimming.

THE NORTH SHORE

From Kilauea, the north shore tour carries you through the superb Princeville Resort and Hanalei, with its gorgeous bay, all the way to where the road ends at Kee Beach. Ahead is the Na Pali Coast.

A few hundred yards past the 23-mile marker on Kuhio Highway, a sign directs the traveler to Kilauea Lighthouse, the northernmost point in the Hawaiian Islands. Kolo Road leads off the highway into the peaceful town of **Kilauea**, once the center of a large sugar plantation.

When the large sugar plantation upon which the economy of Kilauea depended was shut down, the people rallied. Supported by the International Longshore Workers' Union to which most of the townspeople belonged, the residents and the plantation owners put together a deal enabling most of the workers to buy their houses. A new job training program was started, and the people did the rest.

Kilauea prospers today. Several buildings from the late 1800s now house Kauai's finest arts and crafts store, Kong Lung (see SHOPPING, page 165), which began as a general store in 1892. Lawns surround small stone houses and churches in the village center, home to the excellent Kilauea Bakery and several small markets and shops. The **Christ Memorial Church** with its English stained glass windows and hand-carved altar is worth a look as you stroll about the quiet streets.

Kilauea Road leads past residential neighborhoods to **Kilauea Point National Wildlife Refuge** and **Kilauea Lighthouse**. The lighthouse, built in 1913, stands stark and lonely on the lip of a high cliff. It once housed the largest lens of its kind in the world. When an automated light was installed in 1967, the old lighthouse became obsolete and was taken over by the United States Fish and Wildlife Service, which also oversees the

Wailua Falls tumble into deep clear pools.

sanctuary surrounding the lighthouse. The refuge consists of 31 acres (12.5 hectares) of cliffs and headlands rising 200 ft (60 m) above the surf. It is home to red-footed boobies, shearwaters, frigatebirds, red-tailed and white-tailed tropicbirds, Laysan albatrosses, and brown boobies. The sanctuary is open daily from 10 AM to 4 PM, except national holidays; there is an entrance fee.

From Kilauea, continue your journey on Kuhio Highway and turn right on **Kalihiwai Road**. Guava trees line this byway, their heady scent filling the air. The fruit is delicious when ripe and there's plenty of it. When you can drive no further, you'll find yourself facing **Kalihiwai Bay** and one of the loveliest beaches on the island. This great swimming beach with its fine white sand and warm clear waters may be one of Kauai's best kept secrets. Stately ironwood trees line the arc of the beach, and dunes fringe the point where the Kalihiwai River empties into the ocean.

If you take the second Kalihiwai Road you'll end up at **Anini Beach Park**. The waters here are considered among the safest on the island for swimming since a reef 200 yards (182 m) offshore provides perfect protection. Novice windsurfers love it here because the winds are constant and the bottom is shallow. Underwater experiences offer an astonishing variety of marine life in and around the reef. As for the beach itself, beachcombers praise the variety of seashells that wash up on the sandy shores.

Kuhio Highway leads through the **Kalihiwai Tree Tunnel**, a glorious canopy of green all but destroyed by the winds of Hurricane Iwa and battered again by Iniki, but slowly regaining its resplendence. From the scenic lookout shortly after exiting the tunnel, you'll see the valley and the waterfalls that feed the Kalihiwai River.

The road now drifts inland, though the ocean is never far away. On the left is **Princeville Airport**, where private planes ferrying the rich and famous to homes in the area. The 11,000 acres (4,450 hectares) that make up the Princeville region were once a ranch owned by one of the most charismatic westerners to serve the Hawaiian kings. Robert Wyllie served three kings and represented the islands in their dealings with foreign powers. Princeville is named after the son of King Kamehameha IV and Queen Emma, Prince Albert Edward Kauikeaouli, who captured the heart of Wyllie while on a visit to the ranch as a two-year-old. Two years later the little prince was dead, a victim of a terrible fever. Kamehameha IV died a year later, many said from a broken heart. Princeville is now one of Hawaii's largest private developments, with acres of golf courses and lawns framed by villas, condos, and hotels. The main road into the compound leads to the Princeville Hotel, which sits atop steep cliffs facing one of the most gorgeous views on Kauai. From atop the cliffs you can look across Hanalei Bay to the green spires of Bali Hai. The bay, once a busy harbor for whalers and traders, is today used mostly as a harbor for pleasure boats and tour boats that ferry tourists to the diving sites and on water tours of the Na Pali Coast. At sunset, the view from Princeville tops anything one can imagine.

Small, funky **Hanalei**, at the edge of the bay is the antithesis of Princeville's haughty ambience. Cozy restaurants do a thriving business, as do shops and stores that supply campers, hikers, fishermen, hunters and aquatic sportsmen. Surf shops, art galleries, clothing stores and markets fill the town's older buildings and new mini malls. To those who moved here a decade or more ago, Hanalei seems downright cluttered. Bumper-to-bumper traffic is common on sunny days, when a stream of cars heads to and from the North Shore's best beaches.

Before proceeding along the highway, make a point of exploring the town's inner roads leading to the beach. **Black Pot** and **Pine Trees Beach Park** are both lovely.

From here north Kuhio Highway has but two lanes with a few one-lane bridges. None of the famous beaches along the road are marked; if you see a bunch of cars parked by the side of the road, you can be sure there's a path leading to a spectacular natural playground. The eight miles (13 km) from Hanalei to the beginning of the Na Pali Coast remain a primal landscape of volcanic rock festooned with rain-drenched forests. White-sand beaches, featured in classic movies such as *South Pacific*, *King Kong*, and more recently, *The Thornbirds*, and *Jurassic Park*, line the edges of these forests.

Leaving Hanalei, the highway crosses the Waioli Stream. Note the plum trees that grow profusely on the north shore. The road continues around the edges of Hanalei Bay in the direction of **Kee Beach**. It is quiet in this rural area, so the buzz, hum and traffic of **Lumahai Beach** come as a bit of a surprise. To reach Lumahai, take the small trail that begins at the second stone wall beside the road. And beware; Lumahai's beautiful waters are also treacherous. It is easy to be dazzled by the combination of lava rock, blue waters, white sand fringed by hala trees, and

being the birthplace of hula, but with no written record, it is impossible to substantiate this claim.

Haena, which is down the road from Wainiha, was struck by two devastating tidal waves in April 1946 and March 1957. Long ago, the mountains above Haena were the domain of the ancient kings of Kauai. From this vantage point, lookouts were stationed to watch for and warn people of the approach of raiders from the other islands. Haena attracts music and film stars seeking anonymity.

forget the danger lying offshore. Lumahai's currents have a habit of turning nasty. In the winter months, waves 20 to 30 ft high (six to nine meters) pound these shores. Even on a calm summer's day, and even if you are a good surfer or swimmer, approach Lumahai with caution; people have perished here.

The next little community down the road is **Wainiha**, with its pretty valley on the left and the bay on the right. Although some people fish in the bay, few dare to swim here as it serves as a nursery for young tiger sharks and hammerheads. The parents stay further out, but locals decided long ago that discretion was the better part of valor. Wainiha means "fierce water." Wainiha, incidentally, is one of many secluded sites to lay claim to

Shortly after passing a geodesic house, the road on the right leads to **Tunnels**, one of the most popular beaches on the island. Tunnels gets its name from the numerous small holes and caves in the lava rock below the waterline carved by centuries of battering by ocean swells. Tunnels also is the breeding ground for a dazzling array of fish, making its waters a paradise for snorkelers.

As you proceed towards the Na Pali Coast, your journey takes you past three caves, which legend says were dug by the fire goddess Pele in her desperate quest for fire. She eventually gave up in frustration and went looking elsewhere, finally locating that

Tour boats pass by Opaekaa Falls as they cruise to Fern Grotto.

source of energy on the Big Island. The first cave you'll come to is **Manniholo Cave**, which extends almost 76 yards (70 m) into the base of the mountain. The white sand here was deposited there by the 1957 tidal wave. Water drips from sections of the cave's roof, but it is generally dry inside.

You drive the final two miles (three kilometers) to the end of the road in the shadows of the imposing mountain known as **Bali Hai**, immortalized as Bali Hai Island in the film *South Pacific*. A rushing stream fills a dark, cold pool on the edge of the highway near

Haena Beach Park. A dip in this pool on a hot and humid day will bring the color back to your cheeks in a hurry. The wet caves just past this point are within walking distance of each other. The first, **Waikapale**, has two large rooms tucked away in the recesses of the mountain. One of these caverns extends almost 98 yards (90 m) into the base of the mountain. The entrance to **Waikanaloa Cave** is off the road and up a gradient. An equally steep gradient takes you down to the water's edge. If you decide to explore the wet caves, bring a flashlight.

Finally you arrive at **Kee Beach**, entrance to the famed **Na Pali Coast**. The beach itself looks like the Hawaii of dreams, with miles of white sand backed by mountains that seem

to drip in a green mist. East of the beach, an 11-mile-long (nearly 18-km) trail leads into a wild vision of towering cliffs, spooky caves, and breathtaking coves. Hiking the steep, slippery, narrow trail is an arduous and risky task that should not be tackled by casual walkers. You can feel the majesty of Na Pali by walking just a short way up the trail, or by viewing it from a helicopter or boat.

NIIHAU

Often called The Forbidden Island, tiny Niihau is considered the last bastion of Hawaiian culture. The 72-sq-mile (186-sq-km) island lies just 17 miles (27 km) off the western end of Kauai, yet it remains virtually untouched by modern conveniences. It has no paved roads, no motor vehicles and no electricity except for some independently owned generators. Inhabitants of the island get about on horseback or bicycle, and shun alcohol, tobacco, and firearms. The main language is Hawaiian, and traditions long ignored on the other islands are a part of everyday life. The 200 or so inhabitants have little contact with the outside world, except during medical emergencies when the island's single helicopter transports patients to modern facilities. Though some islanders have moved to more worldly lands and most islanders have relatives living on Kauai, the majority seems to prefer the simple life.

Niihau has been owned by the same *haole* (white) family since 1864, when Eliza McHutcheon Sinclair, a Scottish sea captain's widow, purchased it for $10,000 from King Kamehameha V. Her descendants, the Robinson family, have controlled the island ever since. Most islanders work for the Robinson's cattle and sheep ranch, an unlikely sight on this barren land of volcanic rock. A plateau of scrub grass and a few shallow lakes relieve the landscape and feed the animals, while humans must rely on rainwater and a few streams for fresh water. Most islanders live in the village of **Puuwai**, which consists of tiny wooden houses, a church and a school. Bougainvillea splashes the village with color.

The waters around Niihau abound with dolphins, green turtles and Hawaiian monk seals. The beaches are strewn with delicate and valuable Niihau shells used to make extremely expensive leis and jewelry. *Kahelelani* shells resemble brown and pink grains of rice; *momi* are small, lustrous snail shells. Of the two types, the fine-grained *kahelelani* is more highly prized. A long necklace of this variety can sell for as much as $2,000 — provided the maker of the necklace is willing to part with it.

Tourists may now visit the island with **Niihau Helicopters** ((808) 335-3500. The flights over the island cost $250 per person and are only scheduled when four passengers have paid their fare. The 'copters land for a short while on an uninhabited part of the island, where tourists can search for shells. A few islanders occasionally meet the helicopters, but outsiders are not allowed into the village.

TOURS

Since much of Kauai is inaccessible by car, it's the perfect place to experience a **helicopter ride**. Some of us can't resist booking a chopper several times to see the many moods of Kauai. At times, the highlands are shrouded in a mystical mist; at others, rainbows shimmer beside waterfalls. The best rides skirt the Na Pali Coast, skim over the edge of Waimea Canyon, then soar over Waialeale Crater, an incredibly lush pocket of waterfalls tucked in the high forest at Mount Waialeale, among the wettest spots on earth. Most companies depart from an airfield near Lihue airport and offer 60 or 90-minute rides. One of the oldest companies is **Island Helicopters** ((808) 245-6258, and it also offers videos of the ride. **Jack Harter** ((808) 245-3774, 4500 Ahukini Road in Lihue, was one of the earliest pilots offering these tours on the island. I've had great experiences with **Ohana Helicopters** ((808) 245-3996, 3416 Rice Street in Lihue.

Seeing the island from the water is nearly as exciting, especially in the summer season (May to October) when tour boats cruise along the Na Pali Coast. **Captain Andy's Sailing Adventures** ((808) 822-7833, Kikiaola Small Boat Harbor, Waimea, offer snorkeling and sunset cruises in a 55-ft (17-m) catamaran along the South Shore, and tours from Port Allan to Na Pali in summer.

Also on the South Shore, **Bluewater Sailing** ((808) 828-1142 offers snorkel cruises on a 42-ft (13-m) sailboat departing from Port Allan. On The North Shore, **Captain Sundown's Catamaran** ((808) 826-5585, Hanalei Beach, uses a catamaran for its tours, and takes snorkeling trips off Na Pali in the summer. On land, **Kauai Backroads** ((808) 245-8809 in Lihue takes adventurers on a four-wheel drive to hidden spots on the island.

SHOPPING

Kauai's low-key attitude is reflected in its shopping outlets. Though an alarming proliferation of mini malls continues to spread in the resort areas, some of the finest shops and galleries are found off the beaten track. On the North Shore **Kong Lung** ((808) 828-1822, Kilauea Road on the way to the lighthouse, is deservedly famous for its seemingly never-ending displays of Asian art and furnishings, Hawaiian crafts, local art, and gorgeous silk aloha shirts. Displays fill a 1940s stone building that was once part of the Kilauea Plantation; it's nearly impossible to leave here without a few purchases in hand. Just before you reach Hanalei on Highway 560, **Ola's** ((808) 826-6937 tempts shoppers with driftwood furnishings, original art, and a wealth of crafts. **Yellowfish Trading Company** ((808) 826-1227, on Kuhio Highway in the Hanalei Center, delights those enamored with the 1950s, with Hawaiian memorabilia from hula-girl salt and pepper shakers to bolts of vintage cloth in classic Hawaiian patterns. Owner Gritt Benton is a collector's collector; her eye for kitsch is superb and her displays make you long for a hula-girl lamp or a complete set of curved rattan couches and chairs. Also in the center, **Tropical Tantrum** ((808) 826-6944 has batik silk dresses and shirts that rival the colors of more standard aloha wear. One of my favorite finds is **Bambulei** ((808) 823-8641 off the Kuhio highway in Wailua. This small house buried in vegetation is packed with wonderful handmade dresses and vintage and new Hawaiian knick-knacks.

Kauai Village, a shopping center off Kuhio Highway in Kapaa, is home to the **Kauai**

A Niihau weaver sports a Polynesian frond hat.

Heritage Center of Hawaiian Culture and the Arts ((808) 821-2070. Along with its displays, the center sells some of the finest woodcarvings, feather leis, Niihau-shell leis and jewelry found anywhere in the islands. Similar art works are also sold at the **Kauai Museum** ((808) 245-6931, 4428 Rice Street in Lihue. The **Kokee Museum** ((808) 335-9975 in Kokee State Park is the best place to find books on Hawaii's natural side, along with nature-themed cards and gifts.

SPORTS

Kauai is an endless playground for sports enthusiasts of all types. Even amateurs get into the action, paddling down peaceful rivers, snorkeling in tranquil coves, body surfing on gentle waves. Much of the action takes place on the water, with the greatest thrills coming from **kayaking** along the sea caves and grottoes along the Na Pali Coast. An adventure best left to the pros, the trip is alternately peaceful and heart-pounding, depending on surf conditions. Full day and overnight trips along the coast are available in the summer months through Kayak Kauai Outbound ((808) 826-9844 TOLL-FREE (800) 437-3507 FAX (808) 822-0577 WEB SITE www .kayakkauai.com, Highway 560 in Hanalei, and Outfitters Kauai ((808) 742-9667 TOLL-FREE (888) 742-9887 WEB SITE www.outfitters kauai.com, 2827A Poipu Road in Poipu. Calmer tours include easy paddling in Hanalei Bay or along the South Shore. For a leisurely paddle, the Hanalei River trip is recommended. This is an easy journey down a serene river past fields of taro and thickets of hau. You don't have to take much with you except sunscreen and some light refreshments. Naturalists will enjoy a trip up the Huleia River into the Huleia National Wildlife Refuge, offered by Island Adventures ((808) 245-9662 at Nawiliwili Harbor in Lihue. Several shops offer kayak rentals; good bargains can be found at Rental Warehouse ((808) 822-4000, 788 Kuhio Highway in Kapaa. Paradise Outdoor Adventures ((808) 822-0016 TOLL-FREE (800) 662-6287 WEB SITE www.kayakers.com offers kayak lessons.

Though the waves aren't as spectacular as at Oahu's North Shore, Kauai has a few good **surfing** spots. Beginners are best off at Poipu Beach, where the surf is usually gentle, while the pros head for Hanalei Bay. Margo Oberg's School of Surfing ((808) 742-8019 on Hoone Road at Poipu Beach Park is one of the best places in Hawaii to learn how to ride the waves. Margo is a world surfing champion; her tips benefit all levels of surfers. Surfboards are available for rent at the Rental Warehouse (see above) and Hanalei Surf Company ((808) 826-9000, 5-5161 Kuhio Highway in Hanalei.

The gentle waters off the south shore of Kauai offer a spectacular and diverse variety of marine life, perfect for a **scuba diving** or **snorkeling** adventure. In the Poipu area, the most famous area is Caverns, off the Sheraton beach, where three huge lava tubes run parallel to each other. Turtles and lobsters are frequently found here, with an occasional spotting of a white-tip shark. Fathom Five Adventures ((808) 742-6991, 3450 Poipu Road in Koloa, rents gear. Beginner snorkelers and divers find calm waters and plenty of fish off Lydgate Beach Park in Wailua, while those with some experience are thrilled with the action at Tunnels off Highway 560 in Haena on the North Shore. Kee Beach, at the end of Highway 560, has an idyllic setting and an abundance of marine life. Snorkel and dive gear are available for rent at Snorkel Bob's ((808) 823-9433, 4-734 Kuhio Highway in Kapaa, and ((808) 742-2206 at Poipu Beach.

The best dive sites are accessible only by boat; **dive trips** are available through Bubbles Below Scuba Charters ((808) 822-3483, 6251 Hauaala Road, Kapaa. In the summer, the company offers trips to the "Forbidden Island" of Niihau, which is only about 17 miles (27 km) to the west of Kauai. This area offers near-virgin diving sites, featuring huge underwater caverns and amphitheater-like "rooms." If larger marine life is what you're after then look no further than Niihau waters, where tuna, jacks, rays, barracuda, sharks and other large game fish are common. Note, however, that your boat must anchor offshore, as no outsiders are allowed on the cultural preserve of Niihau or on the nearby island of Lehua, a seabird sanctuary. Summer is also best for dive trips off the North Shore and the Na Pali Coast. When not being pounded by winter surf, the area has intriguing lava tubes and caverns and calm bays filled with tropical fish.

One of the greatest thrills on land is a **bike ride** from the famed Waimea Canyon all the way down to the coast—a distance of about 12 miles (19 km). Outfitters Kauai (see above) organizes this early morning adventure which begins with blueberry muffins and a cup of hot coffee and a view of a spectacular sunrise over the canyon. Then it's a downhill rush on smooth roads to the coast. If you do this trip in the afternoon you will be treated to soft drinks and cookies and a sunset over

It takes the average hiker six to eight hours to traverse the 11 miles (nearly 18 km) to Kalalau Beach at the end of the trail. To obtain a permit contact the Kauai State Parks Office ((808) 274-3445, 3060 Eiwa Street, Lihue, HI 96766. See THE GREAT OUTDOORS, page 23 in YOUR CHOICE for more on hiking.

The Garden Isle has a healthy crop of **golf courses** — many with fine views. The 6,353-yard, par-70 Kiahuna Plantation Golf Course ((808) 742-9595, 2545 Kiahuna Plantation Drive, is at the Poipu resort. This Robert Trent Jones Jr.-designed course — noted for its

the isle of Niihau. On both cruises you'll have opportunities to stop and take stock of one of the most beautiful stretches of country on the planet. You'll be regaled with narrative on the history, culture, legends and folklore of Kauai.

Locals lace up their **hiking** boots on a regular basis to hit the many trails on the island. Among the best hiking areas are Waimea Canyon and Kokee State Park, both with marked trails. But the most exciting hike on the island is along the Kalalau Trail through Na Pali Coast State Park. Winding through the wild, remote coast, the trail is open to hikers and campers, though you must have a permit if you plan to go more than two miles (three kilometers) into the park.

cleverly placed lava rocks — is one of the finest in the state. The most talked-about holes are the twelfth and sixteenth, both pins being set at opposite ends of a single oval-shaped green. If you love to golf, don't leave Kauai without playing this course. It's an experience to be treasured.

Two courses are laid out at the Kauai Lagoons Golf Course ((808) 241-6000, 3351 Hoolaulea Way in Lihue. The 7,070-yard, par-72 Kiele Course combines the natural beauty of Hawaiian landscapes with dramatic views along cliffs that overlook the Pacific Ocean. The Lagoons Course —

Kokee State Park's cool misty rains and rugged trails offer a worthwhile contrast to Kauai's sunny white-sand beaches.

a par 72 with 6,942 yards — is a softer, gentler course than Kiele, but it's still a tough one. All the holes — with the exception of the first and the eighteenth—are named after animals. The par-four fourth, the par-three fifth, and the par-five sixth, are named, dauntingly, the Ox, the Eagle, and the Gorilla. The Ox may be the most difficult par-four on the course. The tee shot has to carry a deep bunker on the left to a bowl-shaped green set between two mounds.

The Princeville Resort on Kauai's northern shores has been rated as one of the best resorts in the world. The centerpiece of this first-class resort is its two golf courses, Makai and Prince. A 27-hole, par-72 course with 10,345 yards, the Makai Course ((808) 826-3580 is considered the most beautiful course in all Hawaii. Designed by Robert Trent Jones Jr., it has three nine-holers: Ocean, Lakes and Woods. The par-three third hole on Ocean epitomizes all that is remarkable about this course. You have the illusion of driving your tee shot straight into deep blue waters. Jones did such a great job with the Makai course, he was invited back to design the Princeville Resort's Prince Course ((808) 826-2727. This is an 18-hole, par-72 course with 7,309 yards. While Makai is a "fun" course, Prince is for the serious. The course covers 390 acres (65 hectares) of forest and orchard, flowering trees and shrubs. One of the most fascinating holes on this course is the par-three seventeenth, "the Pali." It's a relatively short hole, but you have to clear both water and heavy foliage to do get there. The tenth, or "Burma Road," is no easier. The green is over a jungle bisected by a stream and ringed with bunkers.

Lovely but treacherous Poipu Bay Resort Golf Course ((808) 742-8711, 2250 Ainako Street, Poipu Beach, on the south shores of Kauai, has rolling terrain and deceptive greens that will test the patience of the best golfer. If these obstacles don't challenge you, then the wind, always a factor on this course, will. You'll have to navigate a succession of bunkers, mounds and doglegs to get to the eighteenth. A fun time is guaranteed at this 6,959-yard, par-72 course. Many consider the Wailua Municipal Course ((808) 241-6666, 3-5351 Kuhio Highway, Kapaa, to be the finest municipal course in the islands at 6,918 yards and par-72. Built alongside the ocean, it is full of doglegs, fast greens and large trees. Clubs are available for rent at Rental Warehouse (see above).

WHERE TO STAY

The biggest factor in choosing a Kauai hotel is its location. If you're intent on exploring the island, consider dividing your stay between the south and north shores so you don't spend entire days driving about. Each region has at least one luxurious hotel, but casual accommodations are more the norm here, and room rates are a bit lower than on Maui or Oahu. Kauai is filled with vacation homes and condos, many available to tourists. For information contact **Garden Isle Vacation Rentals** ((808) 822-4871 TOLL-FREE (800) 801-0378 FAX (808) 822-7984 WEB SITE www.kauai properties.com, 4-928 Kuhio Highway, Kapaa, HI 96746, or **Kauai Vacation Rentals** ((808) 245-8841 TOLL-FREE (800) 367-5025 FAX (808) 246-1161 WEB SITE KauaiVacation Rentals.com, 3-3311 Kuhio Highway, Lihue, HI 96766. **Bed-and-Breakfast Kauai** ((808) 822-1177 TOLL-FREE (800) 733-1632 FAX (808) 822-2723 WEB SITE www.bandb-hawaii.com, PO Box 449, Kapaa, HI 96746, has a good selection of moderate and inexpensive accommodations.

LIHUE

Expensive

The most convenient hotel for travelers without cars is the **Kauai Marriott Resort and Beach Club** ((808) 245-5050 TOLL-FREE (800) 220-2925 FAX (808) 245-5049, 3610 Rice Street, Kalapaki Beach. This full-scale resort, the largest on the island, is just a few minutes from the airport on the edge of Kalapaki Beach and Nawiliwili Harbor. Before Iniki, this resort property was a lavish Westin, complete with dolphin pools and extravagant statuary. Marriott has taken a more subdued approach to the design, using a series of waterfalls, fountains and pools to enhance the natural setting. Sea birds migrate to 40 acres (16 hectares) of freshwater tropical lagoons around the buildings and the 36-hole Jack Nicklaus golf course, adding a natural touch to this oasis on the edge of Kauai's biggest town. There are shops and restaurants along Nawiliwili Harbor, if the hotel's tennis courts, pools, health club, cafés, and boutiques don't offer enough diversions.

Moderate

Kaha lani means "heavenly place," and the **Aston Kaha Lani** ((808) 822-9331 TOLL-FREE (800) 922-7866, 4460 Nehe Road, certainly has a paradisiacal setting. The spacious one-, two- and three-bedroom suites with fully equipped kitchens are spread out amid lush

free) far in advance of their stays, appreciating the low rates and friendly staff. The rooms have microwaves, refrigerators, coffee-makers; some have ocean views and air conditioning. The inn is a short walk from Kalapaki Beach, shops and restaurants. Rock bottom rates make the **Tip Top Motel** ((808) 245-2333 FAX (808) 246-8988 E-MAIL tiptop @aloha.net, 3173 Akahi Street, a great find. It's a classic low-rise motel with simple furnishings and a large parking lot; the adjacent coffee shop is pure Hawaiian, filled with downtown workers at lunch.

landscaping facing miles of white beach. Amenities include pool and tennis courts. The **Outrigger Kauai Beach** ((808) 245-1955 TOLL-FREE (800) 688-7444 FAX (808) 246-9085, 4331 Kauai Beach Drive, Lihue, is one of the best of the chain's offerings. Rooms have all the right amenities — mini refrigerators, coffeemakers, and family-friendly furnishings. The beach is perfect to look at, though high winds can make swimming unsafe.

Inexpensive

The family-owned and operated **Garden Island Inn** ((808) 245-7227 TOLL-FREE (800) 648-0154, 3445 Wilcox Road, Kalapaki Beach, is near the Kauai Marriott. Returning guests often lay claim to the 21 rooms (all smoke

SOUTH SHORE

Very Expensive

One of Hawaii's finest hotels, the **Hyatt Regency Kauai Resort and Spa** ((808) 742-1234 TOLL-FREE (800) 554-9288 FAX (808) 742-6229, 1571 Poipu Road, Koloa, is the most luxurious resort on the island. The main focus is a five-acre (two-hectare) waterway of lagoons and pools separated into dozens of private lounging areas. The lagoon flows from a small adults-only pool at the top of a sloping hill past waterfalls and grottos to the main pool near the beach. At the center is a 150-ft (46-m) water slide that's addictive;

Hikers face extreme challenges and unparalleled beauty along the Na Pali coast.

adults race kids up the wooden stairway to the top of the slide just to beat the line for the ride back down. Recluses sunbathe in privacy on small platforms tucked amid boulders and shrubs, while more convivial types join in volleyball games at the main pool. Kayakers and swimmers float through a large saltwater pool beside Keoneloa Bay (nicknamed Shipwreck for a sampan that was wrecked on the beach east of Poipu). The waves here are better suited to experienced boogie boarders and body surfers than casual swimmers.

The resort's 600 rooms, all with private balconies or terraces, are sumptuous enough for honeymooners, yet manage to offer comfort to kids as well. Hawaiian paintings and artifacts are displayed throughout the property, and the shops and galleries are among the finest on the island. Several restaurants provide plenty of variety, and a golf course, tennis courts and the superb 25,000-sq-ft (2,300-sq-m) spa with its own 83-ft (25-m) lap pool provide further diversions. A program of guest activities called "Discover Kauai" is conducted under the auspices of the Kauai Historical Society and Na Hula Kaohikukapulani, one of the island's most respected hula *halaus*. Incorporating the traditional Hawaiian "talk story" form, guests are taken on conducted tours of the property's numerous archaeology sites. They are introduced to the lore and legends of the island, including the hula and the history of the Koloa region. A dunes walk at Keoneloa Bay features an explanation of native plants and sea life. Best of all, guests are greeted with orchid leis, a tradition that has fallen out of favor at many hotels.

Expensive

The full-scale **Sheraton Kauai Resort** ((808) 742-1661 TOLL-FREE (800) 782-9488 FAX (808) 923-2023 WEB SITE www.sheraton-kauai.com, 2440 Hoonani Road, Koloa, is a good choice for families seeking diversions for all ages. The 413 rooms and suites face gardens or the sea and have refrigerators and coffeemakers. The property includes a gym, three pools (one with kids' play equipment), activities center, and golf. The setting is idyllic, the ocean perfect for swimming, and the ambience friendly. Many of

Kauai's nicest rooms are in small properties, including the **Gloria's Spouting Horn Bed and Breakfast** (/FAX (808) 742-6995, 4464 Lawai Beach Road, Koloa. Tucked between the road and the beach near Spouting Horn Park, the inn's three rooms enhance romance with their oceanfront lanais, cushy beds, willow furnishings, and deep bathtubs. All have VCRs, refrigerators, microwaves and all the accoutrements for instant housekeeping. The day begins with an elegant breakfast and ends with sunset cocktails, and the communal cookie jar is always full.

Condo and house rentals are particularly abundant on this side of the island; some of the best are handled by **Grantham Resorts** ((808) 742-2000 TOLL-FREE (800) 325-5701 FAX (808) 742-9093 WEB SITE www.grantham-resorts.com, PO Box 983, Koloa. Some of the condos fall into the inexpensive category, and there are some spectacular houses in the selection. Another good non-hotel choice is the **Poipu Kai Suite Paradise** ((808) 742-1234 TOLL-FREE (800) 367-8020 FAX (808) 742-9121 WEB SITE www.poipu-kai-resort.com, 1941 Poipu Road, Koloa. The properties are completely furnished vacation houses, most within walking distance of beaches, golf courses and shopping facilities. The low-rise condominiums set amidst gardens of ginger, bird of paradise, banana trees and tall palms are built in clusters, each with its own pool. The resort has nine tennis courts (free to Poipu Kai guests) and a resident tennis professional. **Colony Poipu Kai Resort** ((808) 742-6464 TOLL-FREE (800) 777-1700 FAX (808) 742-7865, 1941 Poipu Road, Koloa, has one-, two- and three-bedroom condominiums with lanai and ocean or garden views. Amenities include six pools, nine tennis courts and a resident tennis professional. **Coastline Cottages** ((808) 742-9688 FAX (808) 742-7620, PO Box 1214, Koloa, has plantation-style bungalows on a secluded beach, nestled between the sea and a sugar cane field in a romantic, tropical setting.

Moderate

As usual, Outrigger has a decent moderately priced property at the **Kiahuna Plantation Resort** ((808) 742-6411 TOLL-FREE (800) 688-

7444 FAX (808) 742-1698, 2253 Poipu Road, Koloa, with furnished one- and two-bedroom condominiums spread about 35 acres (14 hectares) of tropical gardens. Several condos have beachfront terraces; the pool and tennis courts are across the street.

WAIMEA CANYON

Moderate

An unusual option for those interested in Hawaiian culture, the **Waimea Plantation Cottages** ((808) 338-1625 TOLL-FREE (800)

whale watching, sailing at sunset, and biking. Cottages come in several sizes, from the one-bedroom, one-bathroom variety to the five-bedroom, four-bath cottage that accommodates up to nine people, all the way up to the six-bedroom, three-bath cottage that can sleep up to 12.

Inexpensive

Locals and other islanders are enamored with the mountain escape offered at **Kokee Lodge** ((808) 335-6061, PO Box 819, Waimea. A dozen simple wood cabins vary

922-7866 FAX (808) 338-2338 WEB SITE WWW .aston-hotels.com, 9400 Kaumualii Highway, Waimea, is an extraordinary hideaway far removed from the other tourist activities on the island. Set amidst a 27-acre (11-hectare) coconut plantation on the ocean's edge, these former sugar workers' cottages were built in the early 1900s by owners of the then-flourishing Waimea Sugar Mill Company. Extensively renovated, the rooms have ceiling fans and period furniture of mahogany, rattan and wicker, plus all the modern comforts. Amenities include a swimming pool and tennis courts, as well as facilities for more sedate sports, such as croquet and horseshoe pitching. Available activities include

in size from one large room sleeping three, to two-bedroom cabins that will accommodate seven. They are furnished with stoves, hot showers, refrigerators, eating and cooking utensils, linen, towels and blankets. Wood for the wood stoves is available for purchase. The cabins are within the state park; the options for hiking are endless. Fortunately, stays are limited to five days; it's easy to imagine checking in for months. The park's museum and restaurant are within easy walking distance. Make your reservations far in advance of your visit; these cabins are in great demand.

Lava outcroppings battered by strong surf enhance the beauty of Lumahai Beach, where novices are better off strolling than swimming.

THE EAST COAST

Moderate

New in 1999, the **Holiday Inn SunSpree Resort** ((808) 823-6000 TOLL-FREE (888) 825-5111 FAX (808) 823-6666 WEB SITE www .holidayinn-kauai.com, 3-5960 Kuhio Highway, Kapaa, was once the Kauai Resort. Completely remodeled, the hotel is a family-friendly escape beside popular Lydgate Beach Park. The pool is small and the beach a bit of a hike away from the rooms, but the 216 units have all the amenities to keep families happy, from ironing boards to refrigerators. Children under 19 stay in their parents' rooms for free. Ideally designed with families in mind, the **Kauai Coconut Beach Resort** ((808) 822-3455 TOLL-FREE (800) 222-5642 FAX (808) 494-3960 WEB SITE www.kcb.com, PO Box 830, Kapaa, sprawls beside Waipouli Beach and has 311 large, airy guestrooms with lanais. The property extends over 10 acres (four hectares), allowing plenty of room for gardens, pools, tennis courts, and shuffleboard. Children 11 and under eat at the restaurants for free when with an adult. The nightly luau is said to be the best on the island.

Behind the Coconut Marketplace, the **Islander on the Beach** ((808) 822-7417 TOLL-FREE (800) 822-7417 FAX (808) 688-7444, 484 Kuhio Highway, Kapaa, is a Hawaiian plantation resort set in six acres (two and a half hectares) of tropical garden on perfect beach. Some suites have full kitchens. In the same neighborhood, **Lae Nani** ((808) 822-4938 TOLL-FREE (800) 367-7052 FAX (808) 822-1022 WEB SITE www.outrigger.com, 410 Papaloa Road, Kapaa, is a condominium complex now managed by Outrigger. The property is near the Coconut Marketplace and is on a quiet stretch of beach with a swimming area protected from the waves by lava rocks. All 82 one- and two-bedroom condos have full kitchens, lanais, and daily housekeeping service.

Inexpensive

It's nearly impossible to find a room on the beach for less than $100 a night in Hawaii. But the **Hotel Coral Reef** ((808) 822-4481 TOLL-FREE (800) 843-4659 FAX (808) 822-7705 WEB SITE www.hshawaii.com/kvp/coral/index.html, 1516 Kuhio Highway, Kapaa,

manages to offer just that. Some of the 24 units face the ocean and have two rooms; others are simpler, but have televisions and refrigerators. You can actually stay here without a car, since there are several good shops and restaurants within walking distance.

THE NORTH SHORE

Very Expensive

Unabashedly ostentatious, the **Princeville Resort** ((808) 826-9644 TOLL-FREE (800) 826-4400 FAX (808) 826-1166 WEB SITE www .princeville.com, 5520 Ka Haku Road, overlooks the wide expanse of Hanalei Bay from atop a grass-covered cliff. Though the frothy marble statues and fountain at the entryway seem a bit over the top, the hotel actually does

a good job of framing breathtaking views of the bay backed by sheer green pinnacles. Pastel Italian marble, fireplaces, overstuffed couches and chairs, and seventeenth- and eighteenth-century antiques grace the lobby. In the library, a grand piano poses beside a wall of windows facing spectacular sunset views (the outdoor bar tables here are filled at least an hour before the sky changes color). A marble staircase leads down from the lobby to two gourmet restaurants, while a series of hallways and elevators descend from the entryway to the 252 rooms. All facing the water view, the rooms and suites are suitably luxurious, with soft carpeting, pale furnishings and tasteful art and floral arrangements. Naturally, a spa, golf course, tennis courts, and beach club all offer top-notch services.

The **Kilauea Lakeside Estate** ((808) 379-7842 TOLL-FREE (800) 488-3336 FAX (808) 826-1188 WEB SITE www.kauailakeside.com, PO Box 607, Hanalei, is a gated retreat on a three-acre (just over one-hectare) peninsula. A private 20-acre (eight-hectare) freshwater lake affords over 1,000 ft (300 m) of frontage, and a secluded white-sand beach is nestled in a cove. Forty varieties of fruit trees dot the property. The lake offers water sports including boating, kayaking and fishing. Children love the treehouse overlooking the lake, and the rock-filled freshwater stream meandering through a rainforest. The house has three bedrooms, three baths and soaring cathedral

While surfers paddle off Brennecke's sandy beach, anglers climb atop cliffs and cast off for the catch of the day.

ceilings with windows that open onto magnificent views of the property.

Expensive

Also within the Princeville compound, the **Hanalei Bay Resort** ((808) 826-6522 TOLL-FREE (800) 827-4427 FAX (808) 826-9893, 5380 Honoiki Road, Princeville, seems a world apart from its flashier counterpart. Earth-toned three-story buildings seem to blend into trees and ferns tumbling down a long, broad hillside past pools and tennis courts. The lobby, restaurant, and bar are subdued spaces where the view is far more important than sculpture or art. The 136 suites have an assortment of amenities, from full kitchens and multiple bedrooms to standard hotel rooms with balconies. A long trail winds down the hill past a small stream to a gorgeous beach beneath the Princeville Hotel. The Hanalei Bay has timeshare units, but the company uses a low-key sales approach that doesn't intrude on guests.

Moderate

Want to pretend you actually live in paradise? Book a full apartment at the **Hanalei Colony Resort** ((808) 826-6235 TOLL-FREE (800) 628-3004 FAX (808) 826-9893 WEB SITE www.hcr.com, PO Box 206, Hanalei. The property is spread over five acres (two hectares) along an idyllic beach at Haena, with 48 units in 13 modest buildings. Guests tend to settle in for a week or more, spreading their play gear through two bedrooms, a large living room, kitchen, and lanai. Amenities include maid service and a pool, but there are no televisions, stereos or phones in the units. Thus, the resort is blissfully peaceful, the perfect island escape.

Just outside the town of Kilauea and 10 minutes from Princeville is **Makai Farms** ((808) 828-1874 FAX (808) 828-0148, a little slice of paradise in a country setting. This private two-story cottage is a vacation hideaway with mountain views set amidst avocado, mango, banana, papaya, lychee and star fruit trees. The property has majestic Cook pines, unusual tropical flowers and an orchid nursery that can be explored at leisure. The bedroom is upstairs and can accommodate four people. The kitchen is on the ground floor, and a private sitting area outside with

a shower makes for a quick clean up when you come in off the beach.

Hanalei North Shore Properties ((808) 826-9622 TOLL-FREE (800) 488-3336 FAX (808) 826-1188, Princeville Center, Hanalei, represents everything from inexpensive cottages to grand estates on the North Shore.

WHERE TO EAT

Kauai's restaurants match its quirky, independent attitude. Several excellent establishments offer cutting-edge Hawaiian cuisine at typically high prices. But the island is filled with small, casual eateries favored by locals and visitors who prefer squandering on other pleasures. Many of the hotels have reasonable theme-oriented buffets that can fill you up for at least a day, and Kauai is filled with wonderful little markets and fruit stands offering a tempting array of picnic fare from sushi to pineapple smoothies.

LIHUE

Expensive

Located on the Kilohana Plantation, **Gaylord's** ((808) 245-9593, at 3-2087 Kaumualii Highway, looks across the estate's sweeping lawns to the majesty of the Kilohana crater. Though it's essentially part of a tourist attraction, the restaurant offers fine dining in a wonderful 1930s house filled with Hawaiian artifacts and antiques. The chef focuses on all-American favorites including prime rib, lamb, and barbecued ribs, all excellent. Consider having lunch here after touring the plantation's shops.

One of the better restaurants on the island is **Café Portofino** ((808) 245-2121, at 3501 Rice Street, Suite 208, in the Pacific Ocean Plaza across from the Marriott. Master chef Christian Risos was trained by both French and Italian chefs and restaurateurs. His forte is northern Italian cuisine, and the meals are light and fresh. Try *coniglio al vino bianco olive nere* (rabbit sautéed in white wine with black olives and herbs). His *osso buco all'arancio* (veal shank in orange sauce) and eggplant *parmigiana* are also tasty. Café Portofino also offers the best lunch deal in town: an all-you-can-eat buffet of pastas, frittatas, salads and desserts.

Moderate

Kauai's most famous chef, Jean-Marie Josselin, has finally turned his talents to those who appreciate his cooking but can't afford his other restaurants. The **Pacific Bakery and Grill** ((808) 246-0999, at 4479 Rice Street, highlights Josselin's pastry skills (don't miss the flaky *palmiers*) and serves casual Hawaiian fare including grilled *ahi* sandwiches and papaya salad. The pizzas and burgers are mighty fine as well. Like its counterpart on Oahu, **Duke's Canoe Club Barefoot Bar and Restaurant** ((808) 246-9599, at 3610 Rice

chow down on reasonably priced macadamia nut or pineapple pancakes with thick coconut syrup. The Ota family has run the Tip Top since 1916, and claims to have created the first macadamia nut cookie (whose successors are conveniently displayed by the cash register along with homemade papaya-pineapple jam). Local fare is also the draw at **Dani's Restaurant** ((808) 245-4991 at 4201 Rice Street. The papaya, pineapple, and banana pancakes offer the perfect sugar rush; *kalua* pig omelets provide enough protein to keep you hiking for hours.

Street, in the Kauai Marriott is a rowdy, happening spot filled with sunset revelers. The cheeriest waiters and waitresses imaginable deliver bountiful platters of chicken, grilled fish, and ribs. The salad bar is sufficient for light eaters, especially when followed by the utterly decadent hula pie.

Inexpensive

Not many tourists take the trouble to seek out the **Tip Top Motel and Bakery** ((808) 245-2333, 3173 Akahi Street, Lihue. But it's close to the Kauai Museum and gives visitors a glimpse at everyday island life. Regulars settle in at Formica-topped tables for Vienna sausage omelets, oxtail soup, corned beef hash, Spam, or fried noodles. Tourists

SOUTH SHORE

Expensive

Roy's Poipu Bar and Grill ((808) 742-5000 dominates the Poipu Shopping Village at 5022 Lawai Road with its open-air restaurant and adjacent bar. Hawaiian chef Roy Yamaguchi adapts his highly successful Oahu approach with a more casual air, though the din from merry diners is still deafening. Cooks rush about inside the glassed-in kitchen preparing *kalua* pork and cabbage ravioli, red pepper tomato soup, seafood potstickers, and an ever-changing array of innovative fare. The bar, across the

Hikers experience Kauai's natural beauty at its best along trails on the Na Pali coast.

sidewalk from the restaurant, is a bit quieter and a perfect spot for sampling Roy's appetizers without breaking the bank on a full meal. Equally popular and wildly successful is Jean-Marie Josselin's **Beach House** ((808) 742-1424, at 5022 Lawai Road right on the sand. A new menu is created daily with dishes such as sushi tempura, Pacific snapper with ginger and scallions, Caesar salad, Chinese pesto noodles with mustard dressing, or tumbleweed shrimp. Parking becomes horrendous at sunset; arrive a bit early and take an appetite-stimulating walk on the beach before claiming your dinner reservation.

Moderate

Piatti Italian Restaurant ((808) 742-2216, in the Kiahuna Plantation Resort at 2253 Poipu Road, is tucked amid ferns and a pond filled with water lilies at the edge of a quiet resort. The Italian fare draws regulars from all over the island who crave the smoked salmon and fresh *ahi* timbale, barbecued duck, and lobster linguini. Lighter fare includes a superb sesame chicken pizza and fresh spinach salad. The mood is simultaneously laid back and upbeat at **Brennecke's** ((808) 742-7588, at 2100 Hoone Road, overlooking Poipu Beach Park. Surf paraphernalia and T-shirts hang on the walls and ceiling in the second-story restaurant and bar, where it seems most of the diners are regulars, even if they only stop by on their annual holidays. Try the burgers, fish sandwiches, and steaks.

You're either going to love or hate this one. Waterfalls, fern grottos, and fishponds create a pseudo-tropical setting at **Keoki's Paradise** ((808) 742-7534 in Poipu Shopping Village. Some might find the South Pacific theme a bit hokey, but the portions of koloa ribs, pesto shrimp, and ice-cream filled hula pie are bodacious. Kids like the *keiki* menu with child-sized burgers; those on a budget enjoy the less expensive sandwiches and salads on the café menu. Beyond the tourist compounds several entrepreneurs have opened fine restaurants in the small towns along Highway 50 (Kaumualii Highway). The **Green Garden** ((808) 335-5422, on Highway 50 at the entrance to Hanapepe, is a local favorite. True to its name, the restaurant is nearly buried in ferns and flowers and con-

sists of a labyrinth of small dining rooms and porches. Local patrons descend on the place for Sunday breakfast immediately after church; tourists on their way to Waimea Canyon stop by for inexpensive plate lunches. Fresh fish dinners are a bit more expensive than the rest of the fare. Nearby, the **Hanapepe Café and Espresso Bar** ((808) 335-5011, at 3830 Hanapepe Road, is a haven for vegetarians. Multi-grain breads are used for the French toast and sandwiches, veggie burgers come with a wide array of toppings, and grilled portobella mushrooms are as satisfying as a steak. The chef works wonders with grains, cheeses, and vegetables, and the fare far exceeds the standard vegetarian brown rice and steamed broccoli routine. Just before the turnoff to the canyon, the **Waimea Brewing Company** ((808) 338-9733, 9400 Kaumualii Highway, pours its own brew — one of the best in the ever-increasing list of Hawaiian beers. The food surpasses standard pub fare; try the goat cheese dip, chicken quesadillas, and *kalua* pork.

Inexpensive

Several unique and inexpensive eateries line Kaumualii Highway, which passes through the South Shore's small towns leading to the turnoff to Waimea Canyon. The tiny town of Kalaheo, inland from Poipu, is home to the immensely popular **Kalaheo Coffee Company and Café** ((808) 332-5858, 2-2436 Kaumualii Highway. Owners John and Kris Ferguson satisfy java junkies with a wide range of Hawaiian and international coffees accompanied by delicious pastries, waffles, and omelets. In Eleele, **Grinds Espresso** ((808) 335-6027 serves bountiful veggie and chili omelets and a bodacious pizza skillet with rice or fried potatoes covered with salami, pepperoni, peppers, tomatoes, melted cheese and eggs — easily enough to feed two. Salads, sandwiches, and pizzas make equally satisfying lunches and dinners. Grilled hot dogs and sausages are the specialty under the peaked roof at **Mustard's Last Stand** ((808) 332-7245, at the corner of Highway 50 and Koloa Road in Lawai. **Tomkats Grille** ((808) 332-8887, 5404 Koloa Road in Koloa, fuels hearty appetites with steak, chicken, burgers, and ribs. Hearty imported beers are accompanied by spicy buffalo chicken wings and fried onion rings, and the camaraderie among regulars and tourists encourages all to linger about the bar and front porch long into the night. The ice-cream treats at **Lappert's Factory** ((808) 335-6121, 1-3555 Kaumualii Highway (Highway 50), are rich and flavored with the delicacies of the island, such as macadamia nut, guava and mango. **Jo-Jo's** ((808) 338-0056, 9734 Kaumualii Highway in Waimea, is little more than a shave-ice stand, but you'll stand in line on busy days. The 53 versions of shave ice, some with ice cream and azuki beans,

ginger butter sauce is his most famous dish, closely followed by his deep-fried tigereye sushi with wasabi *buerre blanc*. Try to dine with a group of friends so you can sample a wide selection, including the baked potato soup with smoked marlin and sour cream, the rack of venison with caramelized shallots, and the firecracker salmon. You may well return again and again.

Moderate

Talk about fern bars... the **Kapaa Fish and Chowder House** ((808) 822-7488, 4-

are the big draw, but the stand also offers hot dogs, popcorn, and other snacks.

THE EAST COAST

Expensive

French chef Jean-Marie Josselin of **A Pacific Café Kauai** ((808) 822-0013, 4-831 Kuhio Highway, in the Kauai Village, combines the flavors of Japan, China and other East Asian countries with those of his native land. The Kauai restaurant was his first, and remains my favorite for its casual yet chic ambience. Reservations are a must, as this may well be the most popular restaurant on the island — it's usually packed and noisy. Josselin's *mahimahi* with a sesame-garlic crust and lime-

1639 Kuhio Highway in Kapaa, looks like a giant indoor nursery filled with ferns and palms rustling under ceiling fans. Passionfruit margaritas are the drink of choice, and fresh fish the best dish. The portions are immense, and come with excellent rice pilaf and salad. This is the place to try sweet fried coconut shrimp. Steaks and prime rib top the bill at the **Bull Shed** ((808) 822-3791, 796 Kuhio Avenue in Waipouli. The oceanfront location is a major plus, as is the extensive salad bar. Beef also reigns at **Buzz's Steak and Lobster** ((808) 822-0041, 484 Kuhio Highway, where happy-hour drinks and appetizers pull in the after-work crowd.

Whales spout just offshore along Poipu's Mahaulepu Beach.

Inexpensive

If you're into omelets and big breakfasts, then the **Kountry Kitchen** ((808) 882-3511, 1485 Kuhio Avenue, Kapaa, is the place. The Kitchen boasts an 18-item omelet bar and claims to serve the finest banana pancakes on the island. The Hungryman's Breakfast is served on a huge tin plate. At lunchtime, the Kitchen specializes in plate lunches — complete meals featuring everything from grilled *mahimahi* to "Kountry" chicken served with hot cornbread. At lunch and dinner, Kountry Kitchen offers down-home, country-style dining. It's a good place to take hungry kids. Looking like little more than a rundown shack, the **Aloha Diner** ((808) 822-3851, 971 Kuhio Highway, Waipouli, is a haven for those who love real Hawaiian food. The plate lunches cover all the basics; saiman noodle soup soothes the stomach; and the menu delights locals in search of fried fish and squid in coconut milk. Those craving burritos and tacos head for **Norberto's El Café** ((808) 822-3362, 4-1373 Kuhio Highway in Kapaa. All the standard favorites are available, along with great fish tacos and unusual taro-leaf enchiladas. For meal-sized desserts, head across the street to **Beezers** ((808) 822-4411, 1380 Kuhio Highway, Kapaa. Slide into a bright orange booth and order a banana split, peppermint sundae, or pineapple malt. They serve more wholesome food, too, including 1950s-style sloppy joes, with ground beef smothered in barbecue sauce, which drips from a burger bun. Located between Kapaa and the North Shore, **Duane's Ono-Char Burger** ((808) 822-9181 on the Kuhio Highway in Anahola, is an island institution. This simple roadside stand with outdoor tables is renowned for its smoky-flavored charred burgers and crisp fries.

THE NORTH SHORE

Expensive

Casa di Amici ((808) 828-1555, 2484 Keneke Street in Kilauea, stands out for its garden setting and authentic Italian cooking. Match homemade pastas and sauces to suit your taste, or sample the sublime veal, shrimp, or lamb. Though all the standards shine, the chef takes great pleasure is jazzing up traditional dishes with unusual ingredients, such as the chili verde risotto and lamb with fruit sauce. Locals consistently end their North Shore excursions with dinner here. Italian cuisine is also featured at the Princeville **La Cascata** ((808) 826-9644, Ka Haku Road, overlooking Hanalei Bay. The views of emerald mountains and the sparkling ocean add a natural beauty to the restaurant's opulent decor. Outstanding Mediterranean dishes include baked island snapper with Kauai sweet basil, and sautéed veal medallions with lemon butter and capers. La Cascata also has an excellent wine cellar.

The **Bali Hai Restaurant** ((808) 826-6522 at the Hanalei Bay Resort has an expansive open-air lanai providing unrestricted views of the mystical mountain Makana—known as Bali Hai ever since *South Pacific* was filmed there. Watching the vibrant colors of sunset strike this lovely peak from the restaurant named in its honor is a real joy. The chefs create wonderful fresh tastes with their homegrown herbs and spices. Try the crab cakes served on a crisp corn tortilla with lime buerre blanc and black bean and corn salsa. *Poi* pancakes and *loco moco* (fried eggs with a hamburger patty and white rice smothered in brown gravy) add a local touch to the breakfast menu.

Moderate

Downtown Hanalei seems to have a restaurant on every corner these days, and the best are often crowded. The **Hanalei Gourmet** ((808) 826-2524 in the Hanalei Center, tops its burgers with Gorgonzola or avocado, and serves a savory roasted eggplant sandwich. The Old Hanalei Schoolhouse, built in 1926, serves as the dining room, complete with blackboards and creaking wood floors. Satisfy salad cravings with the Waioli Salad, filled with vegetables and goat cheese; at dinner try the pasta with mussels, clams, and feta cheese. **Postcards Café** ((808) 826-1191 on Kuhio Highway at the entrance to Hanalei, claims the loveliest building in town, the plantation style old Hanalei Museum. The red roof, green walls, and bright white railings serve as a landmark for the town, and the restaurant is one of its finest. A blend of Hawaiian, Japanese, and Thai ingredients add a gourmet touch to the fresh fish dishes; don't miss the taro fritters. Try to snag a table on the deck at **Zelo's Beach House** ((808) 826-9700 Kuhio Highway at Aku Road, during Happy Hour for a good view of locals and tourists partying after yet another great day. Zelo's serves something for everyone — pastas, steaks, salads, tacos — and the bar offers at least 50 brands of beers and 30 tropical drinks. Though it really should be on the sand, the beach house decor fits in well on Hanalei's main street, and half the diners look like they just got off the waves.

The Bakery turns out superb breads and pastries. As for the pizzas, they'd pass any taste test. It's good food at good prices.

NIGHTLIFE

Given Kauai's abundance of daytime activities, most folks are content to sleep rather than party all night. The swinging **Tahiti Nui** ((808) 826-6277 on Kuhio Highway presents a family-style luau and show on Wednesday nights, with lots of good local food and plenty of family fun. The larger hotels (Marriott,

Inexpensive

Swimmers head straight from the beach to **Bubba's Burgers** ((808) 826-7839 in the Hanalei Center on Kuhio Highway. This offbeat burger stand offers an attitude with its meals, boasting that the burgers don't need lettuce and tomatoes (you pay extra for such niceties) and are just fine with their traditional catsup and sweet pickle relish. In reality, you can get what you want from a plain burger to one topped with beer-flavored chili and join the gang at a picnic table on the lawn. The Kong Lung Center on Lighthouse Road may be an unlikely place for one of the best Italian restaurants and pizza places on the island, but this is the home of the **Kilauea Bakery and Pau Hana Pizza** ((808) 828-2020.

Hyatt, Sheraton, Princeville) usually have live music in their lounges on weekend nights at least.

HOW TO GET THERE

Aloha Airlines TOLL-FREE (800) 367-5250 WEB SITE www.alohaair.com and **Hawaiian Airlines** TOLL-FREE (800) 367-5320 offer interisland flights to Kauai's main airport at Lihue. **United Airlines** TOLL-FREE (800) 225-5825 is the only carrier that has direct flights from the mainland, departing from Los Angeles daily.

A rainbow adds to the color and serenity of the verdant Hanalei Valley.

Maui

MAUI IS HAWAII'S SECOND MOST POPULAR DESTINATION, surpassed only by Waikiki. For many visitors, Maui *is* Hawaii. It has all the right elements — a towering volcano, rainforest, palm-fringed beaches, crashing waterfalls — and all the right amenities. Lavish resort hotels, first-class restaurants, and classy art galleries satisfy sybaritic visitors. Nature lovers are more than happy with the island's outstanding underwater scenery and the endless hiking trails in Haleakala National Park. Escapists find serenity in rural Hana, one of the loveliest small towns in the islands. And everyone falls under Maui's languid spell.

Thus far, Maui has successfully isolated its tourist belt to a sweeping stretch of coastline that extends from Makena in southwest Maui to Kapalua in the northwest, without interfering with the charm of upcountry Maui, the lush grandeur of the East Haleakala Range, and the ruggedly beautiful coastline. But popularity has its drawbacks. Bumper-to-bumper traffic is common in the old whaling town of Lahaina and on the scenic road to Hana. Parking lots at popular beaches are often full before noon. Reservations are essential at the trendiest restaurants, and Maui's most popular resorts feel like small cities when they're full. But you can easily escape the crowds and find your own version of paradise on the beach or in the mountains.

BACKGROUND

Maui was formed by two volcanoes. Where their lava flowed together is today the isthmus or valley from which Maui derives its nickname, the "Valley Isle."

The greater part of the island's history is turbulent. Around 1700, a warrior chief named Kekaulike, "The Just," established control over the island. His son and successor, Kamehamehanui, ruled Maui for 29 peaceful years. On his death bed, he handed the reins of power to his brother Kahekili, "The Thunder King."

Kahekili was aptly named. During the next 25 years, he was constantly at war, either with the chiefs on his own island or with his mortal enemy, Kalaniopuu, fighting chief of the island of Hawaii, who also happened to be Kahekili's brother-in-law.

Kahekili succeeded in conquering the islands of Molokai, Lanai and Oahu. He even managed to establish his brother Kaeo as ruling chief of Kauai, but he was never able to conquer Hawaii and fulfill his dream of a united kingdom.

When Big Island chief Kalaniopuu died, his nephew Kamehameha the Great became chief of Hawaii and the enemy of Kahekili. The battles between the forces of these two chiefs were terrible, with the climax at Maui's Iao Valley in 1790. Kamehameha the Great sailed across from the Big Island and

beached his huge fleet of war canoes at Kahului. But Kamehameha now had the advantage of Western weapons and advisors and the Maui warriors were driven back from the coast and up into Iao Valley, where those who weren't slaughtered had to flee for their lives.

This defeat represented a major step in Kamehameha's master plan to unite the islands under one monarch.

Kahekili died on Oahu in 1794 at the age of 87. Kamehameha, meanwhile, had fallen in love with Kaahumanu, granddaughter of

OPPOSITE: A spectacular sunset on the Maui coast is the perfect romantic setting. ABOVE: Pineapples sprout from red earth in neat furrows, but economic conditions are gradually forcing the disappearance of Maui's plantations.

Kekaulike, and made her his queen, thus establishing a royal line that lasted 100 years.

Kaahumanu, born in a cave in Hana, stamped her name indelibly on the history of these islands — first as favorite wife of Kamehameha the Great and later as simultaneously wife of both Kaumualii, chief-king of Kauai, and his son and heir, Kealiiahonui. In this one act of double-marriage, Kaahumanu accomplished what Kamehameha could not — the conquest of Kauai.

Kaahumanu was immensely popular with the people. With another of Kamehameha's wives, Keopuolani (the sacred wife), she led Hawaii into the era of Christianity after first breaking the sacred *kapus* of the old ways. The legacies of both these extraordinary women can be seen at the many historic sites throughout the islands.

Maui's prosperity was founded on the sugar industry. The early Polynesians brought the cane to the islands, where it grew wild. Many attempts were made to turn it into a cash crop. Some plantations were started, and several failed, but the history of Maui is sprinkled with the names of businessmen who helped found the industry — none more famous than Claus Spreckels, who came to be known as the Sugar King.

Spreckels had a reputation for wheeling and dealing and political meddling, but he contributed greatly to the development of Maui's economy. The sugar industry has since fallen on hard times, but the great plantations remain; many today are in the process of diversification.

It was the Baldwins, who while developing sugar plantations, discovered that pineapples flourish under similar conditions to sugar. Henry Perrine Baldwin, who succeeded Spreckels as Maui's Sugar King, established the Maui Pineapple Company at Kapalua on the northeast coast of Maui. The company was later bought by the heirs of J. Walter Cameron, who married Baldwin's granddaughter. The Maui Land and Pineapple Company went into real estate, constructing a resort complex at Kapalua.

Their timing was obviously right. Today tourism fuels the economy of Maui as it does the economy of the entire state. It is this island that, after Oahu, attracts the most visitors on an annual basis.

GENERAL INFORMATION

The **Maui Visitors Bureau** ((808) 244-3530 TOLL-FREE (800) 525-6284 FAX (808) 244-1337 WEBSITE www.visitmaui.com, is at 1727 Wili Pa Loop, Wailuku. Brochures, coupon books, and tourist magazines are available at the airport and in most hotels.

WHAT TO SEE AND DO

You could visit Maui a half-dozen times and still not fully explore its distinct neighborhoods. Most visitors opt to divide their stays between two or more resort areas rather than commuting about the island. They begin at the southwest in Wailea, for example, before

MAUI

PACIFIC OCEAN

Hookipa Beach Park
Kuau
Lower Paia
Kuiaha
Haiku
Hoelo
Paia
Kailua
Haleakala
Halimaile
Kokomo
Puohokamoa Falls
Keanae Peninsula
Pukalani
Makawao
Keanae
Wailua
Waikani Falls
Nahiku
Makawao
Forest
Reserve
Olinda
Koolau
Forest
Reserve
Upper Nahiku
Waianapanapa
State Park
MAKAWAO   DISTRICT
Kaeleku
Maui Enchanting
Gardens
Cloud's Rest Protea Farm
Hanawi
Natural Area
Reserve
Hana
Hana
Forest
Reserve
Alau
Island
University of Hawaii
Agricultural
Research Center
Kula
Leleiwi Overlook
Kula Botanical Gardens
Hamoa
Kamaole
Keokea
Puu Ulaula
10,023 ft
3,055 m
Magnetic
Peak
10,008 ft
(3,050 m)
Haleakala
Haleakala National Park
HANA
Kakio
Kula
Forest
Reserve
Haleakala
8,201 ft
(2,500 m)
DISTRICT
Muolea
Wailua
Kahikinui Forest Reserve
Virgin Mary Shrine
Makena
Waimoku Falls
Kipahulu
Ahihi-Kinau
Natural
Area
Reserve
Ulupalakua Ranch
Tedeschi Winery
Kaupo Ranch
Mokulau
Pilani Highway
Bay
Hoapa (King's) Trail
Alenuihaha Channel

KAHULUI-WAILUKU

Maui, viewed from above, has the appearance of a kneeling figure — the north side of the neck dominated by the twin towns of Kahului and Wailuku. This is the business center of the island and one of its major residential districts. The main airport is at busy Kahului. Wailuku is the commercial center and the seat of the county government, yet there's a homespun feeling to the place.

Though business supersedes nature in Kahului, one of Maui's best birdwatching spots is the **Kanaha Wildlife Sanctuary** ((808) 984-8100 across from K-Mart in Kahului's business park. Follow the 50-yard (46-m) trail to a shade shelter and lookout. If you're lucky you'll be able to see endangered Hawaiian Koloa ducks, black-neck Hawaiian stilts, coots and other shorebirds. On the cultural side, the **Alexander and Baldwin Sugar Museum** ((808) 871-8058, at the intersection of Puunene Avenue and Hansen Road (10 minutes from Kahului Airport), offers a peek at Maui history.

heading to the wild east coast at Hana. Or they hang around the west shores at busy Lahaina, then retreat to mountain cabins on the misty slopes of Haleakala Crater. If you're planning to do a lot of exploring, choose your hotel's location wisely — you can spend a lot of time on the road here.

Housed in a sugar plantation superintendent's residence, the museum's exhibits tell the story of Maui's sugar industry as well as interesting facts about the island's geography and water system. If you've got kids along, finish the educational touring with a burst of energy at **Maui Go Karts (** (808) 871-7619, at the corner of Kane and Vevau streets in Kahului.

Tropical Plantation ((808) 244-7643, 1670 Honoapiilani Highway, Waikapu, has a narrated tram ride through working plantation fields, and offers fresh fruit dishes in their restaurant.

Many of Maui's oldest buildings are located in Wailuku. On South High Street, you'll find Maui's oldest church, the **Kaahumanu Church**, built in 1837; the **Territorial Building**; the 1928 **Wailuku Public Library**; the 1911 **Wailuku Union Church** and the 1904 **Wailuku Public School**. Across the street is the **Old County Building** and the **Circuit Courthouse** — which dates back to 1907. Turn off High street onto West Main Street and you'll soon see the sign for the **Bailey House Museum (** (808) 244-3326, 2375-A Main Street, Wailuku. This small museum is set in an 1833 mission home and has furnishings, artifacts, paintings and crafts on display.

After all that exploring, a massage might be in order. Try **No Ka Oi Associates (** (808) 242-7111, 1129 East Lower Main No. 205.

One of Maui's most captivating sights lies just three miles (five kilometers) west of Wailuku along Io Valley Road. The drive into **Iao Valley State Park (** (808) 984-8109 FAX (808) 984-8111 leads from the business center into a moist green rainforest world of ti leaf plants, tree ferns, wild orchids and ohia trees. A natural amphitheater lies at the head of the valley in the caldera of the volcano that formed the island. The road ends at the **Iao Needle**, a 2,250-ft (685-m) forested cinder cone that is often shrouded by misty rain. I've been known to drive straight from the airport to the park for an instant immersion into Maui's natural soul; islanders consider it a local park filled with diversions. Waterfalls, streams, walking trails and extraordinary views make Iao one of the most enjoyable urban parks in the islands. You can obtain more information and maps at

the visitors' center at 54 High Street, RM 101, in Wailuku.

Within the park, the **Hawaii Nature Center (** (808) 244-6500, 875 Iao Valley Road, is a wonderful place to learn about Hawaii's unique environment, and there are enough interactive displays to keep kids of all ages interested. Daily guided nature walks are offered, but advanced reservations are required. Beside the nature center at the **Kepaniwai Heritage Gardens** the island's various cultures are represented with pavilions (which could do with a bit of TLC).

LAHAINA AND THE NORTHWEST COAST

West of Wailuku across the West Maui Mountains lies Lahaina, a little town steeped in Hawaiian history. Once the capital of the islands and one of the most famous whaling ports in the world, Lahaina was a focal point for the missionaries who shaped "modern" Hawaii. The arrival of the missionaries forever changed the relationship between traditional Hawaiians and early sailors and traders. While subduing the sinful nature of this paradisiacal port of call, the missionaries introduced Western-style schools, installed Hawaii's first printing press, and helped change the course of Hawaiian history. Today, Lahaina's narrow streets are lined with trendy stores, restaurants, and art galleries. But it hasn't lost touch with its roistering past; Lahaina still swings, especially when the sun goes down.

Before you go out on the town, avail yourself of the *Lahaina Historical Guide* (at the visitor center kiosk) and tour the many sites of historical interest. Be sure to visit the **Baldwin Home Museum ⦅** (808) 661-3262, 696 Front Street, home of the Protestant medical missionary, Dwight Baldwin; the next-door **Master's Reading Room**, the oldest building in Maui which is now headquarters for

historic buildings include the waterfront courthouse, the old jail and the Seamen's Hospital. Whale-buffs shouldn't miss the **Lahaina Whaling Museum ⦅** (808) 661-4775, 865 Front Street, which recalls the rough and tumble days of whaling and the effects of the missionaries coming to town.

If you have absolutely nothing better to do (or if you are really keen on vintage steam locomotives and don't mind tourist traps), take the **Sugar Cane Train ⦅** (808) 661-8389 FAX (808) 661-8389, 975 Limahana Place #203, Lahaina, on the six-mile (10-km) ride between

the **Lahaina Restoration Foundation ⦅** (808) 661-3262; and the nearby **Richards House**, which was the first coral stone house in the islands and home to the first Protestant missionary to Lahaina. Perhaps the most noticeable landmark of the town is the **Banyan Tree** at the courthouse building, 649 Wharf Street. It is more than 60 ft (18 m) high, casts shade on two-thirds of an acre (a quarter hectare), and was planted in 1873 to mark the fiftieth anniversary of the arrival of missionaries in Lahaina.

At the edge of the town square at Lahaina Harbor is a replica of the brigantine *Carthaginian II* ⦅ (808) 661-8527, a floating museum and a reminder of the days when Lahaina was a great whaling port. Other

Lahaina and Kaanapali. Most of the ride is parallel to the road, but you do have a few glimpses of what's left of Maui's sugar cane fields, some old homes (and some large new ones), and a golf course. The **Hawaii Dome Theater ⦅** (808) 661-8314, 824 Front Street, shows the movie *Hawaii: Islands of the Gods*, throughout the day. You sit in planetarium seating to watch this spectacular 40-minute movie, but the theater is quite small and the close proximity to the screen made me feel a bit ill.

The lava cliffs and idyllic bays northwest of Lahaina are home to two of Maui's most

OPPOSITE: The Iao Needle remains one of the most visited sights on the Valley Isle. ABOVE: Historic buildings line the busy streets of downtown Lahaina.

exclusive resort areas. **Kaanapali**, with three-mile-long (five-kilometer) white-sand beach was a favorite of Hawaiian royalty and is now home to high-end hotels and golf courses. Like a self-contained village, Kaanapali is a 1,200-acre (480-hectare) master-planned resort lining gorgeous beaches; snorkeling and scuba tours often cruise along this area.

Within the development at the Whalers Village Shopping Mall, the **Whalers Village Museum** ((808) 661-5992, 2435 Kaanapali Parkway, G-8, is well worth a visit. The exhibits tell the story of Lahaina's whaling

history and include a large scale model of a whaling ship. Part of the same complex and right next-door is the **Hale Kohola**, a natural history science museum featuring interactive displays that showcase the history of Hawaii's humpback, baleen and toothed whales. There are also computer terminals to access information and a cinema to view movies about these gentle giants. At the entrance to Whalers Village is the Whale Pavilion, housing the skeleton of a 40-ft (12-m) sperm whale.

Two significant scenic features make nearby **Kapalua** (another master-planned resort area) special. First are the five splendid bays that lie sheltered by an imposing lava peninsula. Then there's the grandeur

of the West Maui Mountains looming behind the 23,000-acre (9,200-hectare) pineapple plantation, of which the resort is a small part. In a bow to the past, the **Maui Pineapple Company** ((808) 669-8088 has twice daily two-and-a-half hour tours of Hawaii's largest pineapple cannery, led by honest-to-goodness plantation workers.

A focal point of the Kapalua development is the **Ritz-Carlton Kapalua** (see WHERE TO STAY, below), which rises beside an ancient Hawaiian burial ground. The graves were discovered during excavations for the hotel. As a result, the buildings were moved inland and the sacred areas roped off. Guests and visitors can enjoy the hotel's **Aloha Friday** festivities from 10 AM to 1 PM in the amphitheater and main lobby. A member of the Hawaii Council heads the A Sense of Place tour of the hotel's site, as it pertains to the ancient Hawaiians and the Hawaiian community today, while employees head up activities such as lei making, pineapple carving and performances of *Hui Mele*. All activities are complimentary and open to the general public.

Adjacent to the Kapalua Resort is **Fleming's Beach**, access to which is gained by walking through a thick grove of trees. The beach has more pebbles than sand, and while the clear waters and range of marine life make it a tempting place to snorkel and dive, caution should be exercised. The **Kapalua Discovery Center** at the Kapalua Shops has displays on the island's culture, environment and history. Admission is free. The Kapalua Shops also hosts a number of performances and workshops weekly, from slack key guitar and ukulele performances to beginner hula lessons. The **Art School of Kapalua** ((808) 665-0007 FAX (808) 665-0212 E-MAIL kapaluart@aol.com, 800 Office Road, offers daily and weekly classes and workshops for people of all ages and experience levels in ceramics, dance, yoga, painting and more. Private instruction is also available. For more information about activities in Kapalua area, call the **Kapalua Nature Society** ((808) 669-0244, 800 Kapalua Drive.

North of Kapalua, the *heiau* at **Pohaku Kani** is a place of solitude. You may decide to turn back here, for the next few miles are still more rugged. The road winds past

Nakelele Point and a blowhole, and soon Highway 30 gives way to "Highway" 340 — an extremely narrow, heavily rutted road that demands reduced speeds, sometimes less than five miles per hour (eight kilometers per hour). Just when you think you are surely lost, you'll come across a hamlet with a quaint green church, a bridge across a rushing stream, children playing, and a few tiny houses. The road gradually improves after this, as it climbs into the high country before beginning its descent once again into Kahului. If you have the time, the courage and a sturdy four-wheel-drive vehicle, it is worth navigating this 18-mile (29-km) stretch of road.

THE SOUTHWEST COAST

The coastal highway (Highway 30) runs southwest from Lahaina to some of Maui's most popular tourism and residential centers. A 10-mile (16-km) stretch from Maalaea to Makena runs parallel to one of the longest and most beautiful beaches in the world — pure white sands, aquamarine waters, safe swimming and a staggering choice of hotel and condominium rentals at a variety of prices. **Maalaea**, with its small boat harbor, a smattering of condominiums and a couple of very good restaurants, marks the beginning of the tourist activity. Short of riding out in a boat, there are few better places to observe whales in their natural element than from the Maalaea shoreline as the sunset turns from pink to fiery red. The **Maui Ocean Center (** (808) 270-7000 FAX (808) 270-7070 E-MAIL info@mauioceancenter.com WEB SITE www.mauioceancenter.com, 192 Maalaea Road, Wailuku, has a wonderful array of native fish in this five-acre (two-hectare) facility. A highlight is the walk-through acrylic tunnel. Don't be put off by the lack of descriptive signage, the roving guides will soon find you and answer any questions you may have.

Nearby **Kihei** rivals Lahaina as a center of tourist activity and entertainment. Hotels, condominiums, restaurants, night spots, and karaoke bars proliferate. Budget travelers are particularly happy here, overlooking the town's unsightly jumble of buildings and taking advantage of reduced room rates.

Kealia Pond National Wildlife Preserve ((808) 875-1582, north of Kihei, is a 700-acre (283-hectare) preserve for endangered birds. You can take a stroll along the boardwalk (there are signs providing information).

The further south you go from Kihei, the larger your wallet should be; but if you care to spend the money, it won't be wasted in the splendid resort region of **Wailea**. Yet another master-planned resort area, Wailea is home to the opulent **Grand Wailea Resort and Spa** (see WHERE TO STAY, page 209), an attraction unto itself. Spread over 42 acres

(17 hectares) on the black lava shoreline, the resort looks like a Las Vegas rendition of Hawaii. Waterslides, waterfalls, gazebos, chapels, gardens, and pools are spread about in a mind-boggling array of excess worth visiting. The best way to check out the hotel (and the other lavish properties along the coast) is by walking the one-and-a-half-mile (two-and-a-half-kilometer) **Coastal Nature Trail**, which borders a few of Wailea's five perfect beaches. But don't think you'll be alone — the paved pathway is a veritable hive of activity, with coffee stands set up along the way by the various hotels.

Glitzy Wailea gives way to rural **Makena** at the end of Maui's southern shoreline. One of the driest areas on the island, Makena is a wild, remote place where recluses are pampered at the remote Maui Prince Hotel (see WHERE TO STAY, page 210). Beachgoers are fond of **Maluaka Beach** beside the hotel, while snorkelers find plenty of sea life around

Lahaina attractions: The *Carthaginian II* OPPOSITE, an ancient sailing vessel, is as beloved by visitors as is the historic Pioneer Inn ABOVE.

Makena Landing at the north side of the Makena Bay. The **Keawali Church** ((808) 879-5557, south of Makena Landing on Makena Road, was built in 1855 and has walls three feet (just under one meter) thick.

The **Puu Olai Cinder Cone** is a red-earth hillock that juts out to sea just beyond the Maui Prince Hotel. Puu Olai is one of Haleakala's craters, beneath which is a large cave said to be the sacred dwelling of the shark god Mano. During the whale-watching season, the Pacific Whale Foundation sets up a lookout station on top of the cinder cone.

Nearby are **Big** and **Little Beach**, favorites with swimmers and body surfers.

Further down the Makena Trail is the **Ahihi-Kinau Natural Area Reserve**, probably the finest body of water for snorkeling and scuba diving on this side of the island. **La Perouse Bay**, named after French explorer Admiral Jean François Galaup, Comte de la Pérouse, is the last bay accessible by car. The Frenchman, believed to be the first Caucasian to set foot on Maui, anchored his two frigates in the bay in 1786.

The two beaches at the end of the road are a reminder of old Maui — and the people of this island would love to keep it that way. **Oneloa** (Long Sands) may be the best undeveloped beach in all of Hawaii.

HALEAKALA CRATER AND UPCOUNTRY MAUI

At dawn or dusk, Haleakala Crater is an awesome sight. Within its 21-mile (38-km) circumference lie caves and caverns, patches of verdant forest, grassy plains and desert sands. The drive from Kahului on Maui's north shore up Mount Haleakala to the crater at an elevation of 10,023 ft (3,050 m) is one of the finest in the islands, taking you through pretty, rustic towns such as Pukalani, Kula and Makawao, often in mist and light rain, always through regions of scenic beauty and charm. From sea level at Kahului to the crater's edge is a distance of 40 miles (64 km), which should take you no longer than two hours to negotiate. The higher you go, the drier the landscape becomes, and if it's raining at lower altitudes, chances are that when you break through the clouds, Haleakala Crater will be bathed in sunshine.

The crater is only one part of **Haleakala National Park** ((808) 572-4400, with headquarters near the park entrance on Haleakala Crater Road. Restrooms and water are also available at the **Summit Visitor's Center**, near the crater's edge. The park extends southeast to the coast at Hana; there are hiking trails and campgrounds near the summit and on the coast. Most travelers with little time for exploring are content to tackle Haleakala Crater Road with its switchbacks and steep ascents, stopping at viewpoints along the way. The biggest rewards come at the top, especially if you arrive before sunrise or at sunset.

Driving to the crater before sunrise is a daring feat in itself; Haleakala Crater Road climbs 10,000 ft (3,048 m) in 37 miles (just over 59 km) in a series of twists and turns that terrify drivers in daylight. The weather changes drastically — it may be warm at the coast, but you'll long for a blanket and thermos of hot coffee once you reach the top. Be sure to bundle up and bring a flashlight. Drive all the way to the **Puu Ulaula Overlook**, the volcano's highest point, and find a perch on the rocks or inside the glassed-enclosed lookout where you're protected from the wind. As the first light dawns, the crater looks like a cloud-filled ocean with a rosy glow; when the sun climbs farther the view extends all the way to the snowy peak of Mauna Kea on the Big Island. Braver souls than I get their thrills by viewing the sunrise and then coasting down the mountain on bicycles (see SPORTS, page 200).

The eerie "Specter of the Brocken" draws the curious to **Leleiwi Overlook** at sunset. Haleakala is the only place other than in Scotland and Germany where you can experience this optical illusion. Created by a rare combination of sun, shadow and fog, the illusion causes the reflection of a person's shadow on the face of a cloud below the crater's edge. The image forms at sunset about 100 ft (30 m) from the crater's edge and 1,000 ft (300 m) above the ground, as clouds billow up the crater's face.

Upcountry Maui, on the slopes of Mount Haleakala, is home to farmers, vintners, artists, and entrepreneurs who enjoy the cool air and lush landscape of mountain climes. Coming down the mountain, your first landmark is the interesting little town of **Kula**. Portuguese immigrants were among the earliest foreign settlers in the area, and in 1894 they built a little octagonal church here, which, painted a bright white, is one of the town's landmarks.

Nearby is the village of **Keokea** which attracted many Chinese immigrants in the island's early days. Reminders of that era, and of the Chinese influence, are to be seen in the Kwock Hing Society Temple. Keokea is dotted with little farms growing a variety of flowers, such as the magnificent protea, roses and carnations, and vegetables such as the famous Maui onions so appreciated by chefs worldwide.

If you are interested in visiting one of the many flower gardens or flower farms in the area, try the **Enchanting Floral Garden of Kula (** (808) 878-2531 FAX (808) 878-1805, by the 10-mile marker on Highway 37. This eight-acre (three-hectare) garden is at an elevation of 2,500 ft (762 m) and promises 1,500 species of tropical and semitropical plants and flowers from around the world. **Kula Botanical Gardens (** (808) 878-1715, Highway 377, is a five-acre (two-hectare) garden with proteas, orchids, bromeliads and about 700 other native and exotic plants. There is also an aviary and a koi pond, a picnic area, and great views of Maui. **Cloud's Rest Protea Farm (** (808) 878-2544 and the 34-acre (13.5-hectare) **University of Hawaii Experimental Garden (** (808) 244-3242 are also open to the public.

About 15 miles (24 km) south of the Kula Lodge on Highway 37 is the Ulupalakua Ranch, now famed not only for its dairy herds, but also for the quality of the wines produced in its vineyard. The **Tedeschi Vineyard and Winery (** (808) 878-6058, PO Box 953, Ulupalakua, produces an excellent red wine, named La Perouse in honor of the French sea captain who sailed into the bay near Makena. More recently it began to make a fine *brut* champagne. Tedeschi's pineapple wine is also popular, and is served in restaurants from Lahaina to Kaanapali. You can tour the vineyard and sample wines.

Makawao is the liveliest of the upcountry towns and the site of an annual rodeo on July 4 (see FESTIVE FLINGS, page 76), one of the island's biggest attractions and one of

several rodeos held upcountry every year. Makawao was once purely a "cow town." Hawaiian *paniolos* (cowboys) from nearby ranches used to ride their horses down main street in search of a drink or some action. Today, Makawao has become something of a contradiction. Juxtaposing saddle and feed shops are thriving art galleries and clothing boutiques. Some of these new galleries lie tucked away in picturesque courtyards worth seeking out. The heart of much of this activity is the **Hui Noeau Visual Arts Center (** (808) 572-6560, 2841 Baldwin Avenue,

which organizes and holds workshops, classes and exhibitions by prominent artists on elegant estates in the area. Don't leave Makawao without spending a few minutes watching glassblowing in action at **Hot Island Glass (** (808) 572-4527, 3620 Baldwin Avenue, 101-A.

ROAD TO HANA AND HANA

You can't say you've explored Maui until you've driven to Hana along one of Hawaii's most idyllic hideaways. Sure, you can fly across the island to this remote paradise 50 miles (80 km) southeast of Kahului at the

This church in Kula is the legacy of early Portuguese settlers.

foot of the East Maui Mountains. But the true adventurer approaches Hana from ground level, preferably at the wheel of a convertible. Actually, the ideal way to visit Hana is to drive in and fly back — a workable proposition if you don't mind splurging on drop-off charges and the flight. Sensible travelers refrain from visiting Hana on a one-day, 100-mile (160-km) round trip road adventure. Instead, they spend at least one night at one of Hana's bed-and-breakfast establishments, camp out in one of the lovely state parks, or splurge on the beautiful,

onlookers with acrobatic stunts. If time permits, stop and watch. Soon after passing Hookipa, the scenery changes. As the road begins a gentle ascent away from the sand dunes and around the eastern flanks of Mount Haleakala, the traveler enters a zone where the eerie quiet is broken by the soft sound of rain on thick foliage and the rush of waterfalls.

Replenished by over 100 inches (255 cm) of rain annually, this area is lush with vegetation, the air heavy with the scent of wild flowers and tropical fruit. Wild heliconia, red,

secluded Hotel Hana-Maui (see WHERE TO STAY, page 212).

This lovely corner of Maui is so well known and so often written about that it has taken on nearly mystical proportions. Hana itself, however, is not the only attraction; what you encounter en route is equally fascinating. The road to Hana (Highway 360) has almost 15 curves to the mile (617 curves in all) and 56 one-lane bridges to negotiate. Check your gas tank before setting out — your last chance to fill up is at the little town of **Paia**. The scenery begins to weave its powerful spell almost immediately after you head east from Paia on Highway 36. Winds ripple the waves off **Hookipa Beach Park**, where windsurfers by the dozens dazzle

white, pink and yellow ginger and a variety of orchids are showcased against varying shades of green. Mountain apples, mango and guava grow alongside bamboo groves. In the summer, tulip trees, their scarlet blossoms in proud bloom, stand tall off the hillsides, often in the midst of thick carpets of moss and fern.

At the nine-mile marker the forest surrounds you. This is **Waiakmoi Ridge** where slender groves of bamboo compete for the dappled sunlight with eucalyptus, gingers, heliconia and vines. Here and there, pockets of ferns thrive in the dampness of miniature waterfalls. Drive another two miles (just over three kilometers) and you're at **Puohokamoa**. Take a break, stretch your legs and plunge

Maui

into one of the cool, deep pools in the area. The **Garden of Eden Arboretum and Botanical Garden** ((808) 280-1912, 10600 Hana Highway, Haiku, is between Kailua and Keanae at mile marker 10. Here both native and nonnative plants grow to extraordinary sizes. Gardeners beware — you can easily spend hours wandering the nature trails. Admission is charged, so you might as well take your time.

The **Keanae Peninsula** may be the best place of all to break your journey. The peninsula is a place of utterly wild beauty. Raging surf crashes on a shoreline of lava rock, or throws a tantrum, pounding the sea cliffs halfway up their sides — a scene that is even more dramatic by moonlight. At the summit of the hill leading away from the Keanae Peninsula is **Wailua Valley Lookout**, with views of one of the prettiest towns on the island.

As the road begins its ascent up to 1,275 ft (383 m), you'll hear before you actually see the many waterfalls cascading down Haleakala's flanks. Nearby **Waikani Falls** is one of the most romantic sites on this stretch of the highway. Both **Kaa**, with its waterfalls and cold pools, and **Waianapanapa**, famous for its black sand beach and sea caves, are popular attractions. Waianapanapa also has a thick native coastal forest, blowholes and hala trees that seem to sing in the wind.

The town of **Hana** — the ultimate destination on this rambling drive — is only a couple of blocks long. If you are seeking serenity and peace of mind, you have come to the right place. The silence is engulfing, broken only by the gentle slap of waves on the beach at Hana Bay. Hana's population numbers about 2,000 and most of these people either work for the 7,000-acre (2,834-hectare) Hana Ranch with its 9,000 head of cattle, or the Hotel Hana-Maui.

The town's focal point for commerce and socializing is the classic **Hasegawa General Store** ((808) 248-8231 on the Hana Highway past the hotel. The store has been around since 1910 and is Hana's oldest family-owned business. Besides being the best-stocked store in town, it is also a good place to get information about what's going on in town from the huge notice board out in front, and it has the only ATM machine in Hana. You should

also seek out this place as it will be the starting point for many directions given by locals. Take a stroll down Ulaino Road through forests of mango, guava, ilima, ferns, ginger, heliconia and impatiens to a 150-ft (45-m) waterfall tumbling down to **Blue Pond**. Dive into this gorgeous freshwater pool and enjoy the clean, invigorating water.

In the Hotel Hana-Maui, you'll find the **Hana Coast Gallery** TOLL-FREE (800) 637-0188 FAX (808) 248-7332 WEB SITE www.HanaCoast .com. This splendid gallery features the work of over 50 of the state's finest artists, from

native featherwork and *lau hala* jewelry to oil paintings and bronze sculptures. The **Hana Cultural Center** ((808) 248-8622 WEB SITE www.planet-hawaii.com/hana, 4974 Uakea Road, is a fascinating little museum dedicated to the preservation of the region's history. For a museum of its size, it displays an extraordinary range of Hawaiian artifacts including Hawaiian quilts, turtle shell fishhooks, koa canoe paddles, stone lamps, and woven fishing traps.

Legend has it that the demigod Maui hauled a mass of land off the bottom of the ocean using a magic fishhook. When the

OPPOSITE: Maui ice cream in Paia, the last major town on the way to Hana. ABOVE: Sugar cane factory equipment near Paia.

landmass shattered and formed the Hawaiian islands chain, what was left was a small shard, **Alau Island**, now standing off the Hana coast. A lane off County Road 31 a few miles south of Hana will take you to a spot from which to view the island.

Of the people who have come to Hana seeking to escape public attention, no one was as famous as aviator Charles A. Lindbergh. Nearing the end of his life — marked by triumph, and later the tragedy of the kidnapping and death of his young son — he chose to live out his years in Hana. He was

laid to rest in Kipahulu, 10 miles (16 km) south of Hana in the beautiful little churchyard of **Palapala Hoomau Congregational Church**.

Watch out for the **Virgin by the Roadside**, a pretty Catholic shrine on the way to the **Oheo Gulch** ((808) 248-7375 about 30 minutes southwest of Hana on Highway 31. Part of Haleakala National Park, the gulch is a natural wonderland of waterfalls, ponds, hiking trails, and forests. Its biggest attraction is the Seven Sacred pools, a misnomer for the nearly two dozen freshwater pools in the park. Many are located just beside the parking lot alongside the highway. On the inland side of the car park, a trail winds up the mountain through an exotic bamboo

forest to the 200-ft (61-m) **Waimoku Falls**. Sudden rain showers are common in this area, enhancing the experience of walking through bamboo clattering and whistling in the wind. Camping is permitted on the bluffs near the ocean, but while there are chemical and pit toilets, no drinking water is available. For further advice, seek out the park ranger; there is usually at least one ranger in the area during daylight hours. It's possible to complete your Hana journey by proceeding in the direction of Ulupalakua and upcountry Maui using a four-wheel-drive vehicle. But caution is advised. The road is narrow, unpaved and unstable in parts. On the way you'll pass through the hamlet of **Kipahulu** and near **Kaupo Ranch**, where beef cattle have been raised since the 1800s.

TOURS

Tour operators are scattered throughout the island, but many operators will arrange transportation from your hotel to their starting points. Give them a call and see what they can arrange for you.

Much of Maui is inaccessible; few roads traverse the interior. Thus, one of the best ways to see the island is from a helicopter. **Sunshine Helicopters** ((808) 871-0722 TOLL-FREE (800) 544-2520 FAX (808) 871-0682, 107 Kahului Heliport, provides helicopter tours of east and west Maui as well as the north shore of Molokai aboard their "black beauties." This is a great way to see hidden waterfalls and other wonders of nature inaccessible by road. A four-camera video system on board provides a unique souvenir of your flight. **Blue Hawaiian Helicopters** ((808) 961-5600 TOLL-FREE (800) 745-2583 WEB SITE www.bluehawaiian.com and **AlexAir** ((808) 871-0792 TOLL-FREE (888) 418-8458 WEB SITE www.helitour.com, also operate tours out of the Kahului Heliport. Airplane tours from Kahului Airport are available through **Volcano Air Tours** ((808) 877-5500.

Limousine tours to Hana from the south and northwest coast can be arranged through **Star Maui Limousine** ((808) 875-6900 WEB SITE www.limohawaii.com, PO Box 1609, Kihei. They also do airport arrival and

Two views of House of the Sun, Haleakala Crater.

departures, shopping excursions and private tours. Several companies offer nature excursions in the Hana area. Long time resident **Guy Aina** ((808) 248-8087 will take you on guided tours of the area. Caving trips to view stalactites, ledges and gorgeous skylights can be arranged through **Maui Cave Adventures** ((808) 248-7308 WEB SITE www.hanacave .com, at Kaeleku Caverns visitor center, Ulaino Road, off Highway 360 just past mile marker 31 in Hana. Fishing (including tag and release) and camping trips as well as off-road tours are offered by David Bloch of

Off-Road and Shorefishing Expeditions ((808) 572-3470.

In Upcountry Maui, experience a spectacular sunset at Haleakala National Park, followed by an incredible evening of stargazing with **Star Party** ((808) 281-0949 TOLL-FREE (877) 648-3759 E-MAIL info@starparty.net WEB SITE www.starparty.net. **Temptation Tours** ((808) 877-8888 FAX (808) 876-0155 WEB SITE www.temptationtours.net, 211 Ahinahina Place, Kula, has a range of tours including Haleakala at sunrise, Kaeleku Caverns and Hana, most in an eight-seat limo-van. **Adventures with the Gecko** ((808) 843-4325 TOLL-FREE (877) 843-4325, PO Box 574, Puunene, has multi-day excursions away from tourist buses: jungle hiking, swimming

in waterfalls, cave exploring and more. Camping equipment is included.

The **Kapalua Nature Society** ((808) 669-0244, 800 Kapalua Drive, leads the Puu Kaeo Nature Walk through a working pineapple plantation and an arboretum of exotic species.

You can't fully capture Maui's beauty without viewing it from the sea. **Boat tours** are abundant, especially during the winter months when whales spout just offshore. **Ocean Project** ((808) 667-6706 offers a marine education activity for kids which the whole family will enjoy. A selection of 12 themes are offered — from Turtles to the Reef and Touch the Sea, and a single family can go out with a researcher trained in marine education. Kids leave with an educational kit. In the Kaanapali area, the Hyatt Hotel has a 55-ft (17-m) catamaran, the *Kiele V* ((808) 667-4727, which goes out on sailing trips twice daily. **Gemini Charters** ((808) 661-2591 FAX (808) 669-2591 has whale-watching trip from Kaanapali Beach.

Maalaea Boat Harbor is headquarters for several tour boats. *Flexible Flyer* ((808) 244-6655 FAX (808) 879-4984, Slip 37, Maalaea Harbor, has daily excursions and private sailing charters aboard a 54-ft (16-m) ultra light displacement boat. The 65-ft (20-m) catamaran *Pride of Maui* ((808) 242-0955 leaves from Maalaea Boat Harbor for a fun trip which can include snorkeling, scuba, swimming, fishing and lots of turns on the two-story water slide. In Wailea, **Maui Classic Charters** ((808) 879-8188 TOLL-FREE (800) 736-5740 WEB SITE www.mauicharters.com has sailing charters aboard wooden pilot schooner the *Lavengro*, which has been plying the seas from Florida to Alaska since 1926.

In Lahaina, *SeaView Adventure* ((808) 661-5550, Lahaina Harbor, across from Pier One, is a 56-ft (17-m) semi-submersible, glass sided vessel that allows you to enjoy the ocean air up on deck or go below to view the underwater-scape. Another semi-submersible available in this area is the *Reefdancer* ((808) 667-2133, Slip 10, Lahaina Harbor. Or if you want to go deeper, the *Atlantis* **Submarine** ((808) 973-9811 TOLL-FREE (800) 548-6262 WEB SITE www.goatlantis.com/hawaii, Slip 18, Lahaina Harbor, will take you down 100 ft (30 m). Whale watching from a 118-ft (36-m) motor yacht is offered by the *Maui Princess* ((808) 661-8397, Lahaina Harbor.

The **West Maui Shopping Express** ((808) 877-7308 connects the Lahaina, Kaanapali, Honokowai, Napili and Kapalua areas with stops at shops as well as hotel and resort destinations.

SHOPPING

In busy Kahului, the malls cater mainly to the locals, although there are a few shops selling aloha wear and souvenirs. Maui's

Stop by **Aloha Poi Factory** ((808) 244-3536, 800 Lower Main in Wailuku.

Many of the best shops and galleries geared toward the tourist market are located around Lahaina. Works of America's most collected artist are available at the **Thomas Kinkade Gallery** ((808) 667-7171 TOLL-FREE (800) 303-8999, 780 and 855C Front Street, Lahaina, while **Gallerie Hawaii** ((808) 669-2783 FAX (808) 661-9299, 4405 Honoapiilani Highway #202, showcases a diverse mix of international and local artists. **Tuna Luna** ((808) 661-8662 FAX (808) 661-5932 E-MAIL

largest mall, with over 100 stores, restaurants and services is **Kaahumanu Center** ((808) 877-4325 WEB SITE www.kaahumanu.net, 275 West Kaahumanu Avenue, Kahului. Anchor department stores include Sears, JC Penney and Shirokiya. Don't knock it, you may need it. I replaced my broken clip-on sunglasses here. **Maui Marketplace**, 270 Dairy Road, Kahului, is a smaller place, but it has some good stores, including Old Navy, Border Books, The Sports Authority and a Samsonite Company Store. If you're looking for a bargain, look no further than the **Maui Swapmeet**, held each Saturday on the Kahului Fairgrounds, Highway 35, off Puunene Avenue. If you have a yearning for some *poi* to take home, you're in luck.

tunaluna@maui.net, Wharf Cinema Center, 658 Front Street #152, Lahaina, is a gift store stocked with unusual items — not the same old touristy stuff. **Lahaina Cannery Mall** ((808) 661-5304 has 50 shops, including Blue Ginger Designs, Crazy Shirts, Longs Drugs, FootLocker as well as free hula shows at 1 PM on Tuesdays and Thursdays. Stress-reducing spa essentials — oils to soaps — from all natural Hawaiian ingredients are available from **Lei Spa** ((808) 661-1178 FAX (808) 667-7727 WEB SITE www .planet-hawaii.com/leispa, 505 Front Street.

OPPOSITE: Aviator Charles A. Lindbergh is buried in this pretty churchyard in Kipahulu, eastern Maui. ABOVE: Clouds form over the West Maui Mountains.

A branch of **Hilo Hatties** ((808) 661-8457 is at the corner of Papalaua and Wainee streets. This is your one-stop source for Hawaiian fashions, souvenirs, jewelry and food.

In Kaanapali, **Whalers Village** ((808) 661-4567 WEB SITE www.whalersvillge.com, 2435 Kaanapali Parkway on Kaanapali Beach, has a large selection of luxury goods, souvenir and clothing stores, along with restaurants in a beachfront setting. From Gucci and Prada to Sgt. Leisure and an ABC Store. **Honokowai Farmers Market** is held

you can order more through their mail order services at ((800) 321-1180.

South Maui's largest shopping center is **Azeka Place** ((808) 874-8400, 1279 South Kihei Road, with over 50 shops and restaurants. **Coast Gallery** ((808) 879-2301 FAX (808) 879-2305, Wailea Shopping Village, 3750 Wailea Alanui, exhibits original works in a variety of media, including bronze sculptures, ceramic wall sculptures and blown glass.

The upcountry offers some great shopping opportunities. Wonderful protea and

on Monday, Wednesday and Friday from 7 AM to 11 AM in the Hawaiian Moons parking lot, on Lower Honoapiilani Highway, across from Honokowai Park. Locally grown fruit and vegetables, fresh baked goods, cheeses and tropical flowers are among the array of goods on sale.

The **Kihei Farmers Market** is held every Monday, Wednesday and Friday from 1:30 PM to 5:30 PM at Suda's Store and New Fish Market on South Kihei Road, with wonderful fresh fruit, vegetables and flowers, along with gourmet items. Can't find a swimsuit that will fit quite right? **Island Designer Swimwear** ((808) 891-1117, 1941 South Kihei Road, Kihei, will custommake one for you. And once you get home,

other exotic flowers can be bought or shipped from **Sunrise Farm** ((808) 876-0200 TOLL-FREE (800) 222-2797 FAX (808) 878-6796 WEB SITE www.sunriseprotea.com, on the slopes of Haleakala, Route 1, Box 416A, Kula.

Baldwin Avenue in Makawao is just packed with interesting shops. Books, music and gifts for self-discovery are available at **Miracles Bookery** ((808) 572-2317 FAX (808) 572-0963 WEB SITE www.miraclesbookery .com, 3682 Baldwin Avenue, Makawao. Chinese and Western herbs as well as other natural supplements can be found at the **Dragon's Den** ((808) 572-2424, 3681 Baldwin Avenue, Makawao. Further down Baldwin Avenue, in the Courtyard, **Hot Island Glass** ((808) 572-4527, blows and sells glass works of art. Also in the Courtyard is **Viewpoints Gallery** ((808) 572-5979 E-MAIL vpmaui@ viewpointsmaui.com WEB SITE www.view pointsmaui.com, 3620 Baldwin Avenue, Suite 101, which features paintings from local artists including Martha Woodbury, George Allan, Margaret Leach, Terry McDonald and Diana Dorenzo.

Similar one-of-a-kind shops are tucked along the Hana highway. **Maui Crafts Guild** ((808) 579-9697 WEB SITE www.maui-crafts-guild.com, 43 Hana Highway, Paia, is an artist-owned cooperative gallery which has been around for 15 years, with a large selection of art and craft items. Artists work at the store daily. **Biasa Rose Boutique** ((808) 579-8602 E-MAIL biasaros@mauigateway.com, 104 Hana Highway in Paia, has handmade dresses and Island apparel for women and girls, plus vintage aloha shirts for men and boys. **Bounty Music** ((808) 871-1141 WEB SITE www.ukes.com, 111 Hana Highway, Kahului, has a great selection of ukuleles and other musical instruments for sale and they also rent. **Hana Coast Gallery** TOLL-FREE (800) 637-0188 FAX (808) 248-7332 WEB SITE www .HanaCoast.com, at Hotel Hana-Maui, offers regional fine art and Hawaiian cultural handiwork (see WHAT TO SEE AND DO, above). Also at this hotel is **Susan Marie** ((808) 248-7231, which is your best bet for resort-wear shopping on this side of the island. Shipment of flowers back to the mainland United States and elsewhere can be arranged through **Hana Flower Company** TOLL-FREE (800) 952-4262 FAX (808) 646-6077 WEB SITE www .hanaflowers.com, PO Box 534, Hana, or **Hana Tropical Nursery** ((808) 248-7533, on the Hana Highway, just after the Hana School and Library.

SPORTS

Maui is a haven for sports enthusiasts, especially those who enjoy exploring the ocean. The options for **scuba** and **snorkeling** adventures are seemingly endless, and are especially exciting in the winter months when you can hear the songs of humpback whales reverberating through the water. A large and well respected ocean sports outfit which has been around for over 20 years is Trilogy ((808) 879-8811 TOLL-FREE (888)

628-4800 WEB SITE www.sailtrilogy.com, 180 Lahainaluna Road, Lahaina. They operate five catamarans on Maui and offer trips including snorkeling, scuba and an eco-marine mammal tour. The Maui Dive Shop ((808) 661-6166 has three shop locations in Lahaina (Maui): Honokowai Marketplace, Kahana Gateway Center and Lahaina Cannery Mall, from where you can arrange scuba and snorkeling trips. Scuba trips can also be arranged through Lahaina Divers ((808) 667-7496 TOLL-FREE (800) 998-3483 E-MAIL lahdiver@maui.net WEB SITE www .lahinadivers.com, 143 Dickenson Street, Lahaina. Snorkeling off Molokini and Turtle Reef is available on the *Lahaina Princess* ((808) 667-6165 TOLL-FREE (800) 275-6969 E-MAIL ismarine@maui.net, Slip 3, Lahaina Harbor. Dive Molokini and the Makena Coast with Makena Coast Charters ((808) 874-1273 TOLL-FREE (800) 833-6483 E-MAIL 75644,122@compuserve.com, PO Box 697, Puunene.

Take a highly personalized snorkeling trip through Ann Fielding's Snorkel Maui ((808) 572-8437 E-MAIL annf@maui.net, PO Box 1107, Makawao. A pioneer marine biologist, formerly with the University of Hawaii, Waikiki Aquarium and Bishop Museum, Ann is the author of three books on Hawaiian marine life and is an avid environmentalist. *Prince Kuhio* ((808) 242-8777 TOLL-FREE (800) 468-1287 FAX (808) 244-5890 WEB SITE www .mvprince.com, PO Box 516, Kahului, offers snorkeling to Molokini and Kalaeloa, as well as whale watching in season. Scuba excursions are offered by Ed Robinson's Diving Adventures ((808) 879-3584 TOLL-FREE (800) 635-1273 WEB SITE www .mauiscuba.com, PO Box 616, Kihei, or Bobby Baker's Maui Sun Divers ((808) 879-3337 FAX (808) 879-3631 E-MAIL sundiver@ maui.net, PO Box 565, Kihei. The ubiquitous Snorkel Bob's Maui outlet is in Kihei ((808) 879-7449 WEB SITE www.snorkelbob.com.

If you care to check out the **surfing** scene, there is an outlet for surf school Maui Waveriders ((808) 875-4761 by the cove on South Kihei Road, opposite Ahuana Street. Surf lessons for all shapes, sizes and ages are given by the Nancy Emerson School of

A stroller enjoys the solitude of a Maui beach.

Surfing ((808) 244-7873 E-MAIL ncesurf@ maui.net, Lahaina; Andrea Thomas' Maui Surfing School ((808) 875-0625 WEBSITE www .mauisurf.com; and Puuene and Maui Waveriders ((808) 875-4761, Lahaina Harbor. All offer group or private lessons.

Windsurfing lessons, from beginner to jumping and looping, are given by Action Sports Maui ((808) 283-7913 FAX (808) 244- 9760, 360 Papa Place, Kahului.

Kayaking and rafting gear and tours are available through South Pacific Kayaks and Outfitters ((808) 875-4848 WEB SITE WWW .mauikayak.com, Rainbow Mall, 2439 South Kihei Road, Kihei. The company has been around since 1991, offering kayaking and snorkeling ocean adventures for the beginner to the expert. Blue Water Rafting ((808) 879-7238 WEB SITE www.BlueWaterRafting .com, PO Box 1865, Kihei, takes small groups into the sea caves and lava arches of a hidden volcanic coastline. They also offer whale watching and snorkeling. Ocean Activities ((808) 875-1234, at the Grand Wailea Hotel, can arrange surfing, windsurfing and hobie cat lessons as well as kayak tours. The Ocean Activities Center desk at the Maui Prince Hotel ((808) 879-7218 will arrange a number of activities, including whale watching aboard the *Kai Kanani* catamaran. Hawaii Ocean Rafting ((808) 667-2191 TOLL-FREE (888) 677-7238 WEBSITE www.maui.net/~ocnraftn, PO Box 381, Lahaina, has ocean rafting trips to Lanai for small groups for whale watching and snorkeling. The activity desk at the Hotel Hana-Maui can book you on a number of trips, including Hana Kayak ((808) 248-8211. Kayak and snorkel tours start at Makena Landing with Makena Kayak ((808) 879-8426. Owner Robert "Dino" Ventura, also has trips to La Perouse Bay and Ahihi-Kinau Marine Reserve. Alternatively, Maui Eco-Tour ((808) 891-2223 WEBSITE www .mauiecotours.com, offers kayak/snorkel trips from Makena Landing, La Perouse Bay and Ahihi Bay.

Jet Skis are available for rent from Pacific Jet Sports ((808) 667-2066, at the south end of Kaanapali Beach, in front of the Hyatt Regency Hotel.

Sport Fishing trips can be arranged aboard the *Hinatea* ((808) 667-7548, Lahaina Harbor, Slip 27, or Luckey Strike Charters

((808) 661-4606 WEB SITE www.luckeystrike .com, Lahaina Harbor, Slip 50.

Parasailing for all ages is offered by West Maui Parasail ((808) 661-4060, Slip 15, Lahaina Harbor. For wonderful views and to get that adrenaline pumping, try Parasail Kaanapali ((808) 669-6555 or UFO Parasail ((808) 661-7836 WEB SITE www.ufoparasail .com. You could also choose to paraglide off the volcano with Proflyght ((808) 874-5433 WEB SITE www.paraglidehawaii.com, PO Box 1286, Kula. Tandem flights mean no experience is necessary. You can hang glide from the Hana airport with **Hang Gliding Maui** ((808) 572-6557 E-MAIL hangmaui@ maui.net.

Biking reaches new heights during a sunrise cruise down Mount Haleakala, one

of the most popular activities on Maui. Even the most timid souls are tempted by this thrilling ride, descending the 10,000-ft-tall (3,000-m) mountain in just 37 miles (59 km). Maui Downhill ((808) 871-2155 is the largest operator of these tours on the island, and offers top-notch bikes with excellent brakes. Hana Adventure Outfitters ((808) 248-7476 FAX (808) 248-7467 E-MAIL hanabike@shaka .com, 5210 Hana Highway, rents all manner of bikes, snorkling equipment and body boards, and will also take you on guided mountain bike tours.

Hiking is particularly popular in the mountains. About once a month multi-day backpacking and volunteer service trips are arranged by the Haleakala National Park ((808) 572-4400 and Hawaii Natural History Association. A lottery is held to allocate places. Parties are limited to two and applications must be sent by mail only to Hike Kaupo Gap, Haleakala National Park, PO Box 369, Makawao, HI 96768. Around since 1983, Hike Maui ((808) 879-5270 FAX (808) 893-2515 WEB SITE www.hikemaui .com, PO Box 330969, Kahului, have trained naturalist guides who lead 5- to 10-hour hikes all over the island from central Maui. LATAtudes & ADAtudes Adventure Tours, also known as Maui Eco-Adventures TOLL-FREE (877) 661-7720 FAX (808) 661-7199, 180 Dickenson Street, Suite 208, Lahaina, offer hiking trips in the west Maui mountains with highly educated, humorous guides.

Visions such as this one over Maui have earned Hawaii its title as the "Rainbow State."

Eco-cultural hikes for the experienced or casual hiker are the forte of Paths in Paradise ((808) 573-0094 FAX (808) 572-1584, PO Box 667, Makawao. See THE GREAT OUTDOORS, page 23 in YOUR CHOICE, for more on hiking.

Mendes Ranch ((808) 871-5222, 3530 Kahekili Highway, Kahakuloa, is a family-owned and operated business which organizes **horseback riding** along trails on their 3,000-acre (1,200-hectare) ranch, across rolling pastures, into rainforest and down into the Eke Crater. A wonderfully relaxing horseback ride on the Haleakala Ranch, and more invigorating rides to the Haleakala Crater with expert, interesting guides, are offered by Pony Express Tours ((808) 667-2200 E-MAIL ponex@maui.net, PO Box 535, Kula, at the Pony Express Corral, inside the Haleakala Ranch Ride on Highway 378. Inland from mile marker 29, off Highway 30, the Ironwood Ranch ((808) 669-4991, offers excursions on horseback lasting from three to five hours on restricted farmlands through Maui's largest pineapple plantation, lush valleys and a remote bamboo forest.

Adventures on Horseback ((808) 242-7445, Makawao, on the Hana Highway, two and a quarter miles (just over three and a half kilometers) past the intersection of highways 36 and 365, offers rides at Haleakala, in a eucalyptus and fern forest and across streams on the way to Haiku Falls. Further west, Hana Ranch Stables ((808) 248-8211 has rides along the Hana coast and Ohe'o Stables ((808) 667-2222, about 25 minutes past Hana in Kipahulu on County Road 31, will take you on rides through Oheo Gulch and the Kipahulu district of Haleakala National Park.

The biggest challenge in playing **golf** on Maui is the scenery — it's hard to keep your eye on the ball when whales are spouting just offshore (see SPORTING SPREE, page 42). Duffers have excellent courses at most of Maui's resort areas. Kaanapali has the North and South Golf Courses ((808) 661-3691, 2290 Kaanapali Parkway, Lahaina. Kapalua has three golf courses to choose from: the Plantation, Village and Bay Courses. For more information contact Kapalua Golf ((808) 669-8812 WEB SITE www.kapalua maui.com, 300 Kapalua Drive. The new

Kapalua Golf Academy TOLL-FREE (877) 527-2582, at the entrance to the Kapalua Resort, features grass tee areas, a multiple putting and chipping green and practice bunkers. Wailea is deep in golf country. It boasts 54 championship holes on courses that are as good as any anywhere in the world. The Makena Resort Golf Club ((808) 879-3344, 5415 Makena Alanui, Makena, has two world-class courses.

Kapalua also has a range of top-class **tennis** facilities at the Tennis Garden and the Village Tennis Center ((808) 669-5677. The courts are available to resort guests as well as the public and private and semiprivate lessons are on offer.

WHERE TO STAY

Maui offers a wide range of accommodations, including some of Hawaii's most celebrated luxury hotels. Those on moderate budgets find plenty of options as well, especially in the Kihei area.

KAHULUI AND WAILUKU

Moderate

Kahului's main hotel, **Maui Beach Hotel** ((808) 877-0051 TOLL-FREE (888) 649-3222 FAX (808) 871-5797, 170 Kaahumanu Avenue, Kahului, is a 10-minute drive from the airport and provides a free airport shuttle. Its rooms are basic with air-conditioning, refrigerator and telephone.

The **Old Wailuku Inn at Ulupono** ((808) 244-5897 TOLL-FREE (800) 305-4899 FAX (808) 242-9600 E-MAIL MauiBandB@aol.com WEB SITE www.mauiinn.com, 2199 Kahookele Street, Wailuku, is one of my favorite bed and breakfasts in the islands. The house was built by banker Charles Lufkin, who spared no expense in creating this historic 1924 Wailuku home. Innkeepers Janice and Tom Fairbanks are both Hawaii born and raised, and have decorated each of the seven guest rooms in honor a flower in Hawaii's poet laureate Don Blanding's *Old Hawaii Garden*. The centerpiece in each room is an heirloom quilt. Much thought has also been put into extra convenience and comfort touches, like in-room VCRs, modem jacks, and a wonderful variety of herbal bath salts and Aveda toiletries.

My favorite room is the Ilima, where the Jacuzzi tub is open to the bedroom.

Inexpensive

Banana Beach Bungalow and Maui North Shore Inn offer hostel-type accommodation (see BACKPACKING, page 52 in YOUR CHOICE).

LAHAINA AND THE NORTHWEST SHORE

Lahaina

VERY EXPENSIVE

Puunoa Beach Estates ((808) 667-1666 TOLL-FREE (800) 642-6284 FAX (808) 661-1025 WEB SITE www.classicresort.com/unit_puunoa, 50 Nohea Kai Drive, has 10 exclusive townhouses on a three-acre (just over one-acre) estate with pool, spa, sauna and paddle tennis courts. There is daily maid and personalized concierge services. Rates include a full size rental car and welcome grocery package.

MODERATE

Perched above Lahaina town, the remodeled 7,000-sq-ft (650-sq-m) **House of Fountains (** (808) 667-2121 TOLL-FREE (800) 789-6865 FAX (808) 667-2120, 1579 Lokia, off Fleming Street, offers six spacious bedrooms, all furnished island-style with queen-sized beds and all conveniences. Amenities include a swimming pool, Jacuzzi, barbecue area, and outdoor showers. The views of Lahaina and the islands of Lanai and Molokai from this elevation are inspiring. Your hosts are Thomas and Daniela Clement.

Lahaina Shores Beach Resort ((808) 661-4835 TOLL-FREE (800) 628-6699 FAX (808) 661-1025 WEB SITE www.lahaina-shores.com, 475 Front Street, is a perfect place to vacation if you want to absorb both the history and the culture of this old whaling port without sacrificing holiday excitement. You're on the ocean, in the heart of Lahaina, in a resort that boasts 199 studio and one-bedroom apartments. Each unit features a full kitchen and spacious lanai. It's not a typical resort because the beach isn't private and there's no golf or tennis, but the price is reasonable.

Aston Maui Islander ((808) 667-9766 FAX (808) 661-3733 WEB SITE www.aston-hotels.com, 660 Wainee Street, is a low-rise Hawaiian-style hotel on a quiet side street in town with studio to three-bedroom suites

with full kitchens and daily maid service. Hotel rooms with mini-refrigerators also available. On the 10-acre (four-hectare) property is a pool and tennis courts.

The 50-room **Pioneer Inn (** (808) 661-3636 TOLL-FREE (800) 457-5457 FAX (808) 667-5708 E-MAIL pioneer@maui.net, 658 Wharf Street, across from the harbor, is a hotel whose architecture reflects the town's seafaring history. Rooms and pool have been recently renovated. Reserve well in advance if you want to stay here.

The **Plantation Inn (** (808) 667-9225 TOLL-FREE (800) 433-6815 FAX (808) 667-9293 WEB SITE www.theplantationinn.com, 174 Lahainaluna Road, is a Victorian-style hostelry noted for its grace, elegance and old world charm. Its wicker chairs, broad lanais and large airy rooms are reminders of an age past, but, for my taste, not all the furniture goes together. The pool is a nice feature. Great breakfast is served at the on-site Gerard's restaurant.

The **Lahaina Inn (** (808) 661-0577 TOLL-FREE (800) 669-3444 FAX (808) 667-9480 WEB SITE www.lahainainn.com, near Front Street at 127 Lahainaluna Road, has 12 guest rooms furnished with wonderful antiques and oriental carpets. At the low end of the moderate price range, this is true value accommodation. Children over 15 are welcome. Downstairs is the Lahaina Grill.

INEXPENSIVE

Guest House ((808) 661-8085 TOLL-FREE (800) 621-8942 FAX (808) 661-1896, 1620 Ainakea Road, off Fleming Road, north of Lahaina town, has four rooms, each with a hot tub, and there is a garden pool and deck. Your hosts, the Brandons, love to dive and may well invite you to go diving for your dinner. The large kitchen is available for guests to use.

The **Aloha Lani Inn (** (808) 661-8040 TOLL-FREE (800) 572-5642 FAX (808) 661-8045 E-MAIL tony@maui.net, is a Hawaiian-style guesthouse located across from a neighborhood beach, and within walking distance of Lahaina town with its shopping, dining and nightlife. Your host is Melinda Mower.

An upscale residence with panoramic views, **Blue Horizons (** (808) 669-1965 TOLL-FREE (800) 669-1948 FAX (808) 665-1615 E-MAIL chips@maui.net, is at 3894 Mahinahina Street, between Kaanapali and Kapalua and only minutes from the ocean and golf courses. You can choose between an apartment with a separate bedroom and living room, a studio (both with kitchens), or the traditional bed-and-breakfast room with a queen-sized bed. All units have private bath facilities. There's a lap pool on the property. Your hosts are Jim and Beverly Spence.

A little oasis minutes from the beach, the **Garden Gate** (/FAX (808) 661-8800 E-MAIL Garden@maui.net, 67 Kaniau Road, includes a garden with fountains and a waterfall. Choose from the Garden Studio with queen-sized bed and sofa-sleeper, sitting area, kitchen, and private deck; or the Molokai Room with double bed and private bath. There's a hot tub too. Your hosts are Ron and Welmoet Glover.

Just a few steps away from a quiet beach, yet two blocks from Lahaina town, **Old Lahaina House** ((808) 667-4663 TOLL-FREE (800) 847-0761 FAX (808) 667-5615 WEB SITE www.mauiweb.com/maui/olhouse, PO Box 10355, is tucked away in a tropical garden with local birds and plants and a good-sized pool. You have a variety of accommodations to choose from and can elect to have either a private or shared bath. Your hosts are John and Sherry Barbier.

Wai Ola (/FAX (808) 661-7901 TOLL-FREE (800) 492-4652 E-MAIL tai@maui.net, 1565 Kuuipo Street, PO Box 12580, is an elegant, tastefully furnished private house located between Lahaina and Kaanapali, and a stone's throw away from Wahikuli Beach. The rental units have their own entrances and pool access.

Kaanapali to Napili

VERY EXPENSIVE

Embassy Vacation Resort ((808) 661-2000 TOLL-FREE (800) 669-3155 FAX (808) 661-1353, 104 Kaanapali Shores Place, Lahaina, is an easy-to-spot, bright pink resort in Honokowai with one- and two-bedroom suites. The rate includes full breakfast and a daily two-hour cocktail party; children under 18 stay free. And it is a great place for kids, with a one-acre (nearly half-hectare) pool with a 24-ft (over seven-meter) water slide, a good swimming and snorkel-

ing beach, plus an extensive entertainment system in every unit.

The **Royal Lahaina** ((808) 661-3611 TOLL-FREE (800) 447-6925 WEB SITE www.2maui .com, 2780 Kekaa Drive, Lahaina, has 592 rooms and cottages. A premier tennis destination, its three pools, free scuba instruction, and adjacent golf courses make this a good bet for the active.

Sheraton Maui ((808) 661-0031 FAX (808) 661-0458 WEB SITE www.sheraton-hawaii .com, 2605 Kaanapali Parkway, Lahaina, on what is perhaps the best beach in Kaanapali, recently went upscale and upmarket after undergoing a major facelift. The 510 guest rooms combine tropical furnishings, Hawaiian art and deluxe amenities. It is a particularly interesting hotel with a variety of elevations. Don't miss the sunset ceremony when divers swan dive into the rolling surf off the torch-lit cliffs.

Westin Maui ((808) 667-2525 TOLL-FREE (800) 937-8461 FAX (808) 661-5764 WEB SITE www.westin.com, 2365 Kaanapali Parkway, Lahaina, is another large hotel. It stands out from the others in the area with its 87,000 sq-ft (over 8,000-sq-m) playground area/pool, complete with waterfalls, slides and grottoes.

EXPENSIVE

The **Outrigger Maui Eldorado** ((808) 661-0021 TOLL-FREE (800) 688-7444 FAX (808) 667-7039 WEB SITE www.outrigger.com, 2661 Kekaa Drive, Lahaina, is on the northern end of Kaanapali. The studio, one- and two-bedroom condos come with full kitchens, washer/dryers and daily maid service. Lots of space and great views make this a special property.

At one end of the Kaanapali beach "tourist alley" is the **Hyatt Regency Maui** ((808) 661-1234 TOLL-FREE (800) 233-1234 FAX (808) 667-4498 WEB SITE www.hyatt.com, 200 Nohea Kai Drive, Lahaina. It is set on 40 acres (16 hectares) with flamingos, pelicans, swans and parrots mulling around, along with nine cascading waterfalls and a 150-ft (45-m) waterslide. Not the most natural surroundings you can find, but don't miss the rooftop astronomy program.

The torch-lighting ceremony is a nightly ritual at the Sheraton Maui Hotel in Kaanapali.

New in 2000, the Hyatt's Spa Moana has oceanfront cabanas for spa and beauty treatments.

The **Marriott Maui** ((808) 667-1200 TOLL-FREE (800) 228-9290 FAX (808) 667-8300 WEB SITE www.marriott.com, 100 Nohea Kai Drive, Lahaina, is a large, nondescript hotel catering to conventions, and offers all the usual amenities including pools, tennis courts, and a game room.

The **Whaler** ((808) 661-4861 TOLL-FREE (800) 367-7052 FAX (510) 939-6644, 2481 Kaanapali Parkway, Lahaina, is next to

Whalers Village shopping center and offers 360 studio to two-bedroom units with full kitchens, washer/dryer, marble baths and daily maid service; facilities include pool, spa and tennis courts.

MODERATE

Napili Kai Beach Resort ((808) 669-6271 TOLL-FREE (800) 367-5030 FAX (808) 669-0086 WEB SITE www.napilikai.com, 5900 Honoapiilani Road, Napili Bay, has its own white-sand cove, which is safe for swimming. The 163 studio to two-bedroom units are furnished in contemporary plantation-style with kitchenettes available. Free children's activities during peak seasons are offered along with complimentary sports equipment. This charmingly traditional, Hawaiian-style low-rise resort is the recipient of the 1999 World's Best Value Hawaii Region award from *Travel and Leisure*.

Very close to Napili Bay is a Hawaiian-owned beachfront low-rise, the **Mauian Hotel** ((808) 669-6205 TOLL-FREE (800) 367-5034 FAX (808) 669-0129 E-MAIL mauian@ maui.net WEB SITE www.mauian.com, 5441 Lower Honoapiilani Road, Lahaina. A place to kick back and relax, there are no phones or televisions in the bamboo-style furnished rooms, but there is a communal television, VCR and library. Continental breakfast included.

The **Noelani Condominium Resort** ((808) 669-8374 TOLL-FREE (800) 367-6030 FAX (808) 669-7904 E-MAIL noelani@maui.net WEB SITE www.noelani-condo-resort.com, 4095 Lower Honoapiilani Road, Lahaina, has 50 privately-owned studio to three-bedroom units for rent; they are furnished in standard rattan fare with kitchens and laundry facilities. There are two pools, Jacuzzi, a barbecue area and an adjacent sandy cove. Children under 18 stay free.

A great place for families lies at the northern end of Kahana, almost in Napili. **Kahana Sunset** ((808) 669-8011 TOLL-FREE (800) 669-1488 FAX (808) 669-9170 E-MAIL sun2set@ maui.net, 4904 Lower Honoapiilani Highway, Lahaina, is a low-rise wooden condo development with one- and two-bedroom units as well as executive oceanfront townhouses. Units have full kitchen with dishwasher and washer/dryer. What makes it great for the family is the wonderful white-sand beach that is safe for swimming, along with a large grassy area for children to romp on and a kids' pool.

Next to the Sheraton is the **Kaanapali Beach Hotel** ((808) 661-0011 TOLL-FREE (800) 262-8450 FAX (808) 667-5978 E-MAIL info@ kaanapalibeachhotel.com WEB SITE www .kaanapalibeachhotel.com, 2525 Kaanapali Parkway, Lahaina. This hotel isn't as modern as many of its neighbors, but because of this it exudes a more-authentic Hawaiian charm. The rooms aren't fancy, but they're clean and the beach is fabulous. There are lots of Hawaiian activities to get involved in.

Maui Kai ((808) 667-3500 TOLL-FREE (800) 367-5635 FAX (808) 667-3660 E-MAIL reservations@mauikai.com WEB SITE www .mauikai.com, 106 Kaanapali Shores Place, Lahaina, is a good-value condo block with individually decorated studio to two-bedroom units (all oceanfront) with full kitchens and private lanais. There is a recreation area with barbecue grills, a pool, a cabana with a kitchen, and a lending library.

INEXPENSIVE

Napili Bay is rented by Maui Beachfront Rentals ((808) 661-3500 TOLL-FREE (888) 661-7200 FAX (808) 661-5210 E-MAIL beachfrt@maui.net WEB SITE www.mauibeachfront.com/prop1.htm, 256 Papalaua Street, Lahaina, but is located at 33 Hui Drive, off Lower Honoapiilani Highway in Napili. This small, two-story complex has furnished beachfront studios in a prime location. A real

find! Near Napili Bay is **Napili Sunset** ((808) 669-8083 TOLL-FREE (800) 447-9229 E-MAIL info@napilisunset.com WEB SITE www.napilisunset.com, 46 Hui Drive, Lahaina, which has one- and two-bedroom beachfront and poolside (across the street) apartments with kitchens. You can't beat this location at this price.

Yet another Napili find is the **Hale Napili** ((808) 669-6184 TOLL-FREE (800) 245-2266 FAX (808) 665-0066 E-MAIL halenapi@maui.net, 65 Hui "H" Drive, Lahaina, which has 18 ocean-side studio and one-bedroom units which are standard motel-fare but good value. **Napili Village** ((808) 669-6228 TOLL-FREE (800) 336-2185 FAX (808) 669-6229 WEB SITE www.napilivillage.com,

5425 Lower Honoapiilani Road, Lahaina, does not have a beach but its close enough. There is a pool, coin-operated laundry, a general store and barbecue on the premises.

Maui Sands ((808) 669-1902 TOLL-FREE (800) 367-5037 FAX (808) 669-8790, 3600 Lower Honoapiilani Road, is a condo block next to the Papakea, at the north end of Kaanapali Resort. The 76 units are on a three-acre (just over one-hectare) property, each with kitchen and large lanai. There is a swimming pool and a beach nearby.

Kapalua
VERY EXPENSIVE

The **Ritz-Carlton Kapalua** ((808) 669-6200 TOLL-FREE (800) 262-8400 FAX (808) 665-0026 WEB SITE www.ritzcarlton.com, 1 Ritz-Carlton Drive, Kapalua, has 548 guest rooms and suites overlooking the ocean (80%) or tropical gardens. All the luxury rooms have private lanais and marble bathrooms with separate showers. The grounds sport three championship golf courses, 10 tennis courts, a 10,000 sq-ft (930-sq-m), three-level pool, two hydrotherapy pools, sun deck, spa, fitness center and a white-sand beach with ocean activities. There is an extensive kids program and a Ritz-Carlton Club. This luxury plantation-style hotel is set back from the beach because an ancient burial ground was discovered during its construction — the whole hotel was moved back so as not to disturb the site. Perhaps the best feature of the Ritz-Carlton is its staff, who are attentive, friendly and helpful, but unobtrusive.

The **Kapalua Bay Hotel and Villas** ((808) 669-5656 TOLL-FREE (800) 367-8000 FAX (808) 669-4690 WEB SITE www.luxurycollection hawaii.com, 1 Bay Drive, Lahaina, is situated on what has been described as "the best beach in America" — an accolade bestowed by the University of Maryland's Laboratory of Coastal Research, which surveyed 650 beaches in the nation. With 194 rooms, the Kapalua is modest in size, which contributes to its intimacy — and it's chic. From its impressive, vaulted lobby that captures

OPPOSITE: Amateur astronomers and heaven watchers get a chance to view the stars through some high powered equipment at the Hyatt Regency at Kaanapali. ABOVE: The pool area at the Hyatt Regency in Kaanapali.

the ocean breeze, to its black-marbled water-fall, the Kapalua Bay Hotel emphasizes luxury. Villas, which may be rented by the day, week or month, are scattered around the hotel complex on the fringe of the two Arnold Palmer-designed golf courses. These huge, well-appointed houses are beautifully de-signed—all with stunning ocean and mountain views.

Kapalua Villas ℂ (808) 669-8088 TOLL-FREE (800) 545-0018 FAX (808) 669-5234 E-MAIL kapaluavillas@kapaluamaui.com WEB SITE www.kapaluavillas.com, 5000 Office Road, Kapalua, offer a range of privately-owned, high-end one- and two-bedroom villas as well as three- and five-bedroom homes tucked into beautifully landscaped clusters.

THE SOUTHWEST COAST

Maalaea to Kihei

EXPENSIVE

The **Maalaea Surf Resort ℂ** (808) 879-1267 TOLL-FREE (800) 423-7953 FAX (808) 874-2884 E-MAIL msurf@maui.net, 12 South Kihei Road, is a five-acre (two hectare) resort set on a swimming beach. It has 34 luxury town houses, all with kitchens and maid service. Amenities include tennis, swimming pool, and barbecues.

Aston Maui Hill ℂ (808) 879-6321 TOLL-FREE (800) 922-7866 FAX (808) 922-8785 E-MAIL astonrest@aston-hotels.com WEB SITE www.aston-hotels.com, 2881 South Kihei Road, on the hill above Kihei, has 140 one-, two- and three-bedroom condos with full kitchens. The Spanish-style resort has a pool, tennis court, putting green, and barbecues.

MODERATE

Aston Maui Lu ℂ (808) 879-5881 TOLL-FREE (800) 922-7866 FAX (808) 922-8785 E-MAIL astonres@aston-hotels.com WEB SITE www.aston-hotels.com, 575 South Kihei Road, Kihei, is at the northern end of Kihei with a beachfront and 28-acre (11 hectare) garden setting. Some rooms are across the road around a Maui-shaped pool. It offers an old-Hawaiian ambience.

While it is not on the beach, the **Maui Coast Hotel ℂ** (808) 874-6284 TOLL-FREE (800) 426-0670 FAX (808) 875-4731 E-MAIL mch@

maui.net WEB SITE www.westcoasthotels .com, 2259 South Kihei Road, Kihei, offers plenty of value for money. The rooms are nothing fancy but come with a lot of extras like free coffee, free laundry, refrigerators, ironing boards, and hair dryers. Facilities include lit tennis courts, pool, hot tub, and a restaurant.

Another area hotel offering good value is the **Maui Oceanfront Inn ℂ** (808) 879-7744 FAX (808) 874-0145 WEB SITE www.castle-group.com, 2980 South Kihei Road, Kihei. On the beach, its rooms have air-conditioning, color cable television and refrigerators.

Among the better condo deals in this area is **Punahoa ℂ** (808) 879-2720 TOLL-FREE (800) 564-4380 FAX (808) 875-9147 E-MAIL PunahoaRes@aol.com, 2142 Iliili Road. It is a bit difficult to find (from South Kihei Road turn on Kaiau Place, 100 yards or about 90 m from Kamaole Park, then on to Iliili), but offers 15 oceanfront studio, one-bedroom and two-bedroom units with fully equipped kitchens. Snorkeling is fantastic just offshore. The rates drop to the inexpensive category in low season.

INEXPENSIVE

Island Sands ℂ (808) 244-7012 TOLL-FREE (800) 367-6084 FAX (808) 242-7476 WEB SITE www .maalaebay.com, Maalaea Village, near Maui Ocean Center, has large one- and two-bed-room apartments with full kitchens and washer/dryers in a pink, oceanfront build-ing. If you are planning to stay for at least five nights, the **Hono Kai Resort ℂ** (808) 244-5627 TOLL-FREE (800) 367-6084 FAX (808) 242-7476, 280 Hauoli Street, Wailuku, is a great deal. There are 32 one- to three-bedroom units, with a beautiful sandy beach activity harbor and pool.

Nona Lani Cottages ℂ (808) 879-2497 TOLL-FREE (800) 733-2688 E-MAIL nonalanicotttages @maui.net WEB SITE www.nonalanicottages .com, 455 South Kihei Road, Kihei, has eight 400-sq-ft (37-sq-m) cottages spread out over two acres (just under a hectare) of gardens, across from a white-sand beach. Each cot-tage has a full kitchen, bedroom and living room.

Another gem is the **Aloha Pualani ℂ** (808) 874-9127 TOLL-FREE (800) 782-5264 FAX (808) 874-9127 E-MAIL pualani@mauigateway.com

WEBSITE www.alohapualani.com, 15 Wailana Place, Kihei, which is across the street from Maalaea Bay with a heated pool and five two-story suites with fully equipped kitchens, washers and dryers, and one and a half bathrooms each. There is also a studio with a kitchenette which is rented on a bed and breakfast basis.

Babson's Bed and Breakfast ((808) 874-1166 TOLL-FREE (800) 824-6409 FAX (808) 879-7906 WEB SITE www.mauibnb.com, 3371 Keha Drive, Kihei (in Maui Meadows), has two rooms in the house and a

one-bedroom suite downstairs as well as a two-bedroom cottage, surrounded by a beautifully landscaped half acre with great views.

Eva Villa (/FAX (808) 874-6407 TOLL-FREE (800) 884-1845 E-MAIL pounder@maui.net, 815 Kumulani Drive, Kihei, in Maui Meadows is a bit complicated to find, so call ahead for directions. This bed and breakfast has a suite, studio and cottage for rent and there is a pool, Jacuzzi, rooftop deck and barbecue facilities.

Wailea and Makena
Within Wailea's lush 1,450 acres (590 hectares) are dozens of magnificent resort hotels and condominiums.

VERY EXPENSIVE

Renaissance Wailea Beach Resort ((808) 879-4900 TOLL-FREE (800) 992-4532 FAX (808) 874-5370 WEB SITE www.renaissancehotels.com, 3550 Wailea Alanui, Wailea, is a resort of quiet elegance with the accent on intimacy and exceptional service. The Renaissance has 345 units, its own beach with private coral reef and a pool surrounded by waterfalls. For even more luxury, the Mokapu Beach Club is a two-story building adjacent to the resort with personal concierge, private pool and all sorts of upgraded amenities.

Grand Wailea Resort and Spa ((808) 875-1234 FAX (808) 874-2411 E-MAIL info@grandwilea.com WEBSITE www.grandwailea.com, 3850 Wailea Alanui, Wailea, is a spectacular addition to the luxuries offered at Wailea. Over $500 million was spent on this 787-room hotel set in 42 acres (17 hectares) of oceanfront. The Grand Wailea consists of five wings plus the Napua Tower, an exclusive resort within a resort. What is great about this resort is there is so much to discover and everything is large and dramatic — such as the lovely beachside 15,000-sq-ft (1,400-sq-m) formal pool and the 2,000-ft-long (600-m) river pool that has an elevation drop almost equivalent to a five-story building, with enough slides, waterfalls, caves, whitewater rapids and grottos to keep the whole family entertained for hours. The Spa Grande is the ultimate in luxury, while the seaside chapel is a totally unexpected feature that appears to float above a lagoon.

Experienced travelers rate the **Four Seasons Maui Resort** ((808) 874-8000 TOLL-FREE (800) 334-6284 FAX (808) 874-2222 WEB SITE www.fourseasons.com, 3900 Wailea Alanui, Wailea, as one of the best in the world. What sets the Four Seasons apart is its understated elegance and exceptional service. The $160 million hotel sits on 15 acres (six hectares) of beachfront property and offers pools, water sports, a health club, a club floor and a children's program. The extra-large rooms (85% with ocean views) have expansive marble bathrooms with deep tubs and showers for two.

Hawaii's indigenous protea.

The **Kea Lani** ((808) 875-4100 TOLL-FREE (800) 882-4100 FAX (808) 875-1200 WEB SITE www.kealani.com, 4100 Wailea Alanui, Wailea, Hawaii's only luxury all-suites resort, is consistently highly ranked in the "best resort" lists of the likes of *Condé Nast Traveler* and *Travel and Leisure*. It sits on 22 acres (nine hectares) of prime Wailea oceanfront with views across the water to the islands of Lanai, Molokai and Kahoolawe. The startlingly white Mediterranean-ish architecture of the hotel is in sparkling contrast to the brilliant variety of bougainvillea and other flowers, shrubs and trees that dress the landscaped gardens. Four cascading fountains and seven waterfalls enhance the ambience. Kea Lani offers 413 one-bedroom suites, as well as 37 exclusive one-, two- and three-bedroom villas, each with its private plunge pool and sunning lanai. The villas are separated from the beach by a lawn shaded with coconut palms.

The **Maui Prince Hotel** ((808) 874-1111 TOLL-FREE (800) 321-6248 FAX (808) 879-8763 WEB SITE www.westin.com, 5400 Makena Alanui, Makena, with its splendid golf course, is the only development of any significance in the area. The V-shaped hotel sits on the edge of a pretty and secluded quarter-mile (half-kilometer) white-sand beach, with views of either the ocean or Haleakala from each of the hotel's 310 rooms. Its Japanese theme makes it obvious who its clientele is.

EXPENSIVE

Outrigger Wailea Resort ((808) 879-1922 TOLL-FREE (800) 688-7444 FAX (808) 875-4878, 3700 Wailea Alanui, Wailea, has a wonderful, open-air feel to its common areas, and 22 acres (about nine hectares) of well-manicured lawns (half a mile or just under a kilometer along the ocean) on which to stroll. But the rooms are in dire need of re-modeling (carpets you don't want to walk on barefoot and bathroom fixtures older than me!).

Maui Polo Beach Club ((808) 879-1595 TOLL-FREE (800) 367-5246 FAX (808) 874-3554 WEB SITE www.destinationresortshi.com, 3750 Wailea Alanui, Wailea, is a condominium block with one- and two-bedroom units with full kitchen, washer/dryers and

daily housekeeping. Facilities include oceanfront swimming pool and barbecues. Three-night minimum stay.

MODERATE

Wailea Ekahi ((808) 879-3043 TOLL-FREE (800) 222-7011 FAX (808) 874-6113 E-MAIL oewarufw@ccmaui.com WEB SITE www.prestige-mauirentals.com, 300 Ohukai Street #C-324, Kihei, is on Wailea's Keawakapu Beach and has one- and two-bedroom townhouses with full kitchens. On the complex are four pools, a beachfront pavilion and barbecues.

Destination Resorts' **Wailea Villas** ((808) 879-1595 TOLL-FREE (800) 367-5246 FAX (808) 874-3554 E-MAIL drh@maui.net WEB SITE www.destinationresortshi.com, at 3750 Wailea Alanui, Wailea, offer luxurious accommodation in four distinct townhouse villages. These are one-, two- and three-bedroom condominiums, each with a kitchen and lanai. Each village has its own swimming pool, barbecue grill and other amenities, including golf and tennis facilities.

INEXPENSIVE

Makena Landing ((808) 879-6286, 5100 Makena Road, Makena, is in a wonderful location right on the ocean next to the county beach, which has great snorkeling. The Hawaiian Luuwai family is your host. They are really nice and love to dive, so you may even be able to persuade them into a few lessons. The rental units are on either end of the large cedar house with their own entrances, full kitchens and private bathrooms.

UPCOUNTRY

Moderate

I recently saw the **Silver Cloud Ranch** ((808) 878-6101 TOLL-FREE (800) 532-1111 FAX (808) 878-2132 E-MAIL slvrdd@maui.net WEB SITE www.silvercloudranch.com, RR 2 Box 201, Kula, described as a mix between a turn-of-the-century cottage and college dorm, which is a perfect description for this bed and breakfast. The view is wonderful, the living area cozy and the breakfasts wonderful. The bedrooms are missing a few creature comforts and the walls are thin.

Olinda Country Cottages and Inn ((808) 572-1453 TOLL-FREE (800) 932-3435 FAX (808)

573-5326 E-MAIL olinda@mauibncottages .com WEB SITE www.mauibnbcottages.com, 536 Olinda Road, Makawao, is 15 minutes straight up the crater slope from Makawao, on an eight-and-a-half-acre (three-and-a-half-hectare) protea flower farm which is surrounded by the 35,000-acre (14,000-hectare) Haleakala Ranch. It exudes serenity, space and natural beauty. This bed and breakfast's 5,000-sq-ft (over 460-sq-m) Tudor mansion and two cottages have been lovingly decorated with antiques and collectibles by co-host Ellen Unterman, who owned an

Haleakala at sunrise is to stay overnight at the lodge and set out at about 4:30 AM for the crater.

Hula Kula Inn ((808) 572-9351 TOLL-FREE (888) 485-2466 FAX (808) 572-1132 E-MAIL kulahula@maui.net, 112 Hoopalua Drive, Makawao, is a homey, island-style pole house bed and breakfast at an elevation of 2,300 ft (700 m). There is a room, a three-room suite and a two-bedroom cottage (with king-sized waterbed) to choose from at this large estate property which offers wonderful mountain and ocean views.

antique shop in Santa Monica for 15 years. With her keen decorator's eye, every detail has been thought of. Perhaps the most special of the wonderful accommodations is the 950-sq-ft (88-sq-m) Hidden Cottage, which is in a secluded spot surrounded by protea plants, with full kitchen, washer/dryer, wood stove and deck complete with a hot-tub for two.

Well known to devotees of upcountry Maui, **Kula Lodge** ((808) 878-1535 TOLL-FREE (800) 233-1535 FAX (808) 878-2518, 475 Kula Highway, is a romantic hotel and restaurant where the views of the Kihei Coast and the West Maui Mountains are matched by the hearty food. Fires are lit in the hearth at night. A smart way to see

A single cottage is offered on the grounds of the hosts' home at **Pilialoha Bed and Breakfast Cottage** ((808) 572-1440 FAX (808) 572-4612 E-MAIL cottage@pilialoha.com WEB SITE www .pilialoha.com, in Haiku. It's equipped with everything you need for a home away from home and there is lots of privacy.

Inexpensive

If you have the time, book one of the three primitive cabins available in Haleakala Crater through **Maui National Park** ((808) 572-4400 WEB SITE www.nps.gov/hale, PO Box 369, Makawao, HI 96768. The cabins are assigned by lottery two months in advance,

Wild, remote Makena Beach is the perfect spot for solitary sunset viewing.

with group sizes limited to 12 and a maximum of three nights stay per month.

Giant banyan and monkeypod trees dominate the property of **Banyan Tree House** ((808) 572-9021 FAX (808) 573-5072 E-MAIL info @banyantreehouse.com WEB SITE www .banyantreehouse.com, 3265 Baldwin Avenue, Makawao, for a real laid-back, country atmosphere. For rent is the 1920s plantation manager's three-bedroom main house plus four cottages, each with their own charm, at a really good price.

The **Sunrise Garden Suite** ((808) 572-1440 FAX (808) 572-4612 E-MAIL cottage@ pilialoha.com WEB SITE www.pilialoha.com, Haiku, has a one-bedroom unit with kitchenette, attached to a residence which opens up to a fairy-tale like vine-covered pergola.

Hale Peno ((808) 572-1896 TOLL-FREE (800) 645-0431 E-MAIL halepeno@yahoo.com WEB SITE www.vrbo.com/vrbo/1038.htm, in Pukalani, has two wonderful 700-sq-ft (65-sq-m) cottages with full kitchens, washer/dryer and lanais with ocean views surrounded by beautiful gardens.

ROAD TO HANA AND HANA

Very Expensive

The **Hotel Hana-Maui** ((808) 248-8211 TOLL-FREE (800) 321-4262 FAX (808) 248-7202, PO Box 9, Hana, was built by Paul Fagan, owner of the San Francisco Seals, and soon gained an international reputation as one of the most romantic hotels. Once Hawaiian chiefs repaired to Hana to recover from the rigors of battle. More recently celebrities found their way here to escape the glare of publicity. The hotel and its one-story Sea Ranch cottages are spread out over the property's 66 lushly planted acres (27 hectares). The cottages, located on a coastal bluff, feature generous decks, most with hot tubs, and floor-to-ceiling glass with views of the shoreline and mountain top. The interiors of the cottages have oversized tropical furniture with original Hawaiian art and quilts.

However, the whole property has been suffering from terrible neglect of late, which makes you wonder how they dare to charge such prices. However, the hotel has recently been bought and hopefully a massive renovation project will soon be underway.

Moderate

Mama's Beachfront Cottages ((808) 579-9764 TOLL-FREE (800) 860-4852 FAX (808) 579-8594 E-MAIL info@mamasfishhouse.com, 799 Poho Place, Paia, has comfortable duplex cottages on the beach at Kuau Cove, which is a good swimming, snorkeling and windsurfing beach. But my overall feeling is that this place is overpriced, rather like the complex's beach house restaurant.

Huelo Point Flower Farm ((808) 572-1850 E-MAIL huelopt@maui.net, Huelo Church Road, is located on an organic farm and offers units ranging from a freestanding room with glass walls on three sides to a cliff-edge 1,300-sq-ft (120-sq-m) gazebo. Facilities include pool with waterfall and Jacuzzi.

Huelo Point Lookout ((808) 573-0914 E-MAIL dreamers@maui.net, Door of Faith Church Road, Huelo, has three guest cottages on the opposite side of the property from the owner's home. In the middle is a 44-ft (13-m) swimming pool with waterfalls, surrounded by rock gardens and a hot tub.

There are two units for rent at **Maui Dream Cottages** ((808) 575-9079 FAX (808) 575-9477 E-MAIL gblue@aloha.net WEB SITE planet-hawaii.com/haiku, 265 West Kuiaha Road, Haiku, each fully equipped and comfortably furnished, surrounded by fruit trees and lots of lawn.

The name, **Heavenly Hana Inn** (/FAX (808) 248-8422 WEB SITE www.places togo.com, Hana Highway PO Box 790, Hana, is not an exaggeration. This Japanese-style masterpiece has four suites each with a futon and couch in the living area and separate bedroom with raised platform bed. The black marble bathrooms have large tubs.

Hana Hale Malamalama ((808) 248-7718 FAX (808) 248-7429 E-MAIL hanahale@ hanahale.com WEB SITE www.hanahale.com, Uakea Road, Hana, is located on Popolana Beach (dramatic but not safe for swimming), with a rebuilt historic fishpond dominating the grounds. All units are constructed from Philippine hardwood and comfortably equipped with largely Filipino furnishings. All have full kitchens and many have Jacuzzi tubs for soaking and skylights for stargazing.

Next door (same owners) is the **Bamboo Inn at Hana Bay** ((808) 248-7718 FAX (808) 248-7429 E-MAIL hanahale@hanahale.com

WEB SITE www.hanahale.com, PO Box 374, Hana, which is a new offering with an ocean-front studio with kitchenette and two-story villa with full kitchen, large covered deck on both levels with a hot tub on the upper level.

Further up the same street, you'll also find the **Hana Kai Maui Resort** ((808) 248-8426 TOLL-FREE (800) 346-2772 FAX (808) 248-7482 WEBSITE www.hanakaimaui.com, 1533 Uakea Road, Hana. The 18 studio and one-bedroom units of this resort have completely equipped kitchens and private lanais and there is a barbecue area and spring-fed lava rock pool.

are on a five-acre (two-hectare) flower farm, both with hot tubs on private decks.

Hana Plantations ((808) 248-8975 TOLL-FREE (800) 228-4262, near the airport and Waianapanapa State Park, has tropical homes on the coast with spas.

There are 12 rustic cabins for rent at **Waianapanapa State Park** ((808) 984-8109, Off Hana Highway, % State Parks Division, 54 South High Street, Room 101, Wailuku, from where you can take full advantage of the black sand beach on Pailoa Bay. This is just one step up from camping, but the

Hamoa Bay Bungalow ((808) 248-7884 FAX (808) 248-8642 E-MAIL jody@maui.net, PO Box 773, Hana, may be a bit difficult to find as there are no signs to guide you, but it's worth the effort. Look for the Balinese statues on the lane inside the property, about two miles (just over three kilometers) east of Hasegawa's general store. This cottage is beautifully decorated in magical Indonesian design, with bamboo furniture and batiks.

Inexpensive
Tradewinds Cottage ((808) 248-8980 TOLL-FREE (800) 327-8097 FAX (808) 248-7735, 135 Alalele Place, Hana, is situated on the airport road. These two secluded cottages

cabins come with kitchen, living area and bedroom with hot water and linens.

If you are really traveling on a budget, and just need somewhere clean to spend the night, try **Joe's Place** ((808) 248-7033, opposite the Bamboo Inn on Uakea Road. There is a shared parlor with a television and kitchen, and maid service.

WHERE TO EAT

Maui's restaurant scene rivals that in Oahu, where many of Hawaii's top chefs have opened their own restaurants. Several of these famed chefs have restaurants on

Vegetable and flower gardens etch the hillsides in the West Maui Mountains.

Maui as well, and many a hotel kitchen is commandeered by a rising star. Reservations are a must at the big-name spots.

KAHULUI AND WAILUKU

Moderate

Sam Choy's ((808) 893-0366 WEB SITE www .samchoy.com, Kaahumanu Shopping Center, 275 Kaahumanu Avenue, will give you a good sampling of Hawaiian cuisine. His signature favorites include Maui fisherman's stew over pasta; char siu barbecue spareribs

and macadamia nut-crusted island catch. His lunchtime specials are very reasonable, not to mention delicious. **Marco's Grill and Deli** ((808) 877-4446, 444 Hana Highway, Suite M, Kahului, is a comfortable Italian restaurant, near the intersection of roads going west, south and to upcountry Maui. The house specialty is *pasta e fasio* (smoked ham hock simmered for hours in tomato with red and white beans, served with penne), but also consider the homemade ravioli with prosciutto, garlic and ricotta. When there is not much competition, I guess you can afford to be a bit cocky: **Saigon Café** ((808) 243-9560, 1792 Main Street, doesn't even have a sign, and, because of the bridge overpass, it's not easy to find by the street address. If you want

to eat here, get specific directions from a local. But it may not be worth the effort. This is very mediocre Vietnamese-ish food.

Inexpensive

If you've come off the plane starving and need some quick food before heading to your resort, stop by the food court at **Kaahumanu Center** ((808) 877-4325 WEB SITE www .kaahumanu.net, 275 West Kaahumanu Avenue. You'll find many of the fast food favorites: Panda Express, Edo Japan, Maui Tacos, McDonalds. At Maui Mall, try **Siu's Chinese Kitchen** ((808) 871-0828 for eat-in and take-away Chinese favorites. This is not gourmet, but it's okay and it's open seven days a week. In Wailuku, good local food is available at **Mushroom** ((808) 244-7117, 2080 Vineyard. The pork dishes are particularly good. Also on Vineyard, at 2130, is a vegetarian restaurant **Simple Pleasures** ((808) 249-0697, with wonderful homemade soup. For dessert, try the Kona coffee tiramisu.

NORTHWEST COAST

Lahaina may well be dining central, given its abundance of chain and one-of-a-kind eateries. Meanwhile, if you want a break from the Kapalua prices, drive down the road to Napili, where there is more variety of reasonable to inexpensive restaurants (alongside some more expensive ones).

Very Expensive

The **Anuenue Room** ((808) 669-1665 at the Ritz-Carlton Hotel in Kapalua is an elegant but laid-back Hawaiian Provençal restaurant with wonderful views. The food is worth the price as well. Appetizers include sugar cane cured salmon and crispy veal sweetbread, while for entrées its a hard choice between such dishes as curry-coriander roasted *poussin,* pan roasted *onaga,* and barbecue rack of lamb.

Expensive

French Provençal restaurant **Chez Paul** ((808) 661-3843, Olowalu, four miles south of Lahaina, has seatings at 6:30 PM and 8:30 PM and has been a Maui institution for the past 20 years. Entrées include caramelized Pacific salmon with Grand Marnier and shoyu and a star-anise butter sauce and boneless crispy duck with exotic fruit sauce bigarade.

The current stars of the Lahaina dining scene are chef James McDonald's **Pacific 'O** ((808) 667-4341 and **I'O** ((808) 661-8422, both at 505 Front Street, Lahaina. Pacific 'O is open for lunch and dinner with contemporary Pacific cuisine like Asian gravlox which has slices of salmon on a warm potato applejack with wasabi chive sour cream, kiawe sprouts and caviar for an appetizer; while the vegetarian dish of roasted marinated steak of tofu with a crown of sautéed quinoa, red lentils, and shitake mushrooms is unbelievably good. I'O has dishes like a wok stir-fry of lobster, sweet potato, pineapple and bamboo shoots flamed with dark cane rum and a mango Thai curry sauce. Vegetarians are not forgotten here either with a green Thai curry risotto.

Avalon ((808) 667-5559, 844 Front Street, Lahaina, is the domain of Chef Mark Ellman whose cooking is always an adventure for the palate. He has combined his affinity for the curries of Asia with the soul food of America and comes up with combinations that constantly surprise and delight his growing circle of devotees. Like other practitioners of Hawaiian regional cuisine, he works with local homegrown produce. Ellman's specialties include wok-fried *opakapaka* with a spicy black bean sauce; macadamia nut *mahimahi* salad; fruits de mer flambé and chili salmon tiki style.

One of the most honored chefs on Maui is David Paul of the **Lahaina Grill** ((808) 667-5117, 127 Lahainaluna Road, Lahaina. Paul specializes in "new American cuisine" and the popularity of this exceptional restaurant attests to his culinary skills. Specialties include tequila shrimp, Kona coffee-roasted rack of lamb and lobster/crab cakes. Chef Gerard Reversade of **Gerard's** ((808) 661-8939, 174 Lahainaluna Road, Lahaina, at the Plantation Inn, has a near 20-year history of winning awards at this French jewel of a restaurant. Escargots ragout, seared duck foie gras with passionfruit and kiawe honey, and rack of lamb with mint crust are just some of the favorites.

In Kaanapali, one restaurant you should certainly try is the **Swan Court** ((808) 661-

1234 at the Hyatt hotel. This airy, elegantly appointed room opens onto an ocean view and a miniature lake and Japanese garden inhabited by flamingos, peacocks and swans. The food is continental with a Pacific Rim flair. Dominating the center of the Kaanapali Beach Resort is the **Whalers Village**, a shopping complex with over 100 shops, two whaling museums and two fine places to eat on the beachfront — **Leilani's on the Beach** ((808) 661-4495 with fish, steak, chicken and ribs and the superb establishment of master chef Peter Merriman called the **Hula Grill**

Restaurant ((808) 661-1148. For starters, have the Tahitian *poisson cru* (raw fish marinated in lime and coconut with Maui onions and tomato). For a main course try the macadamia-nut roasted fresh island *opakapaka*.

A Pacific Café ((808) 667-2800, Honokowai Marketplace, is the sixth eatery in Hawaii for chef Jean-Marie Josselin, and is sure to add a few more awards to his burgeoning list. The menu changes daily but examples of his appetizers include a salmon roll with green papaya salad with hot and sour dip, and red Thai curry coconut soup. Specialties include Chinese roasted duck

The road to Hana reveals many quiet spots such as Red Sand Cove OPPOSITE and the beach near Hotel Hana-Maui ABOVE.

with baked sour cherry "*manapua*" and charred baby eggplant with *lilikoi*-star anise sauce; and pan seared *ono* "local boy" style with soba noodles and nori-soy vinaigrette and sizzling peanut oil.

Sansei Seafood Restaurant ((808) 669-6286, 115 Bay Drive, at Kapalua, has a highly creative and delicious Pacific Rim fusion menu that includes panko-crusted *ahi* sashimi; Asian tostada with fresh fish over crispy won ton with umeboshi vinaigrette for starters and Asian rock shrimp cake and spinach and gorgonzola cheese stuffed chicken breast. And, as it is open to 2 AM on Thursdays and Fridays, this is the place for late night dining.

Jameson's Grill and Bar ((808) 669-5653, 200 Kapalua Drive, located on the eighteenth hole of the Kapalua Bay Golf Course, is a typical country-club restaurant with unimaginative but well-prepared dishes like rack of lamb, New York steak and pan-sautéed, grilled or oven-braised fish. At lunch they offer reasonably-priced sandwiches.

The brewery part of the **Fish and Game Brewing Company and Rotisserie** ((808) 669-3474, 4405 Honoapiilani Highway, at Kahana Gateway Shopping Center, features eight handcrafted beers by brewmaster Thomas Kerns of Oregon, while the rotisserie prepares succulent duck, beef, chicken and lamb. But there is also quite an extensive menu that includes Italian favorites like *cioppino* and pasta, plus an oyster bar which also offers fish prepared in a multitude of ways. It's been around for seemingly ever, but the **Bay Club** ((808) 669-8008, 1 Bay Drive, still maintains its high standards: great view, impeccable service and good food. The menu includes salads, seafood, lamb, and steak. The seafood lunch buffet is a particularly good deal.

Moderate

In Lahaina, there's a party going on at **Kimo's** ((808) 661-4811, 845 Front Street, most nights of the week. You might start with a tropical cocktail, then opt for any of the delicious Hawaiian fish, chicken or beef dishes. At the far end of Front Street (No. 888) is the European-style **Longhi's** ((808) 667-2288, founded by New Yorker Bob Longhi in the mid-1970s. Since then the restaurant has gained a reputation for style, quality and atmosphere. There are no menus at Longhi's; the staff describes what's available, such as fresh strawberries, country-style ham and eggs and Kona coffee for breakfast. Cheese is flown in from New York, homemade pasta is from their own kitchen and bread and pastries fresh from their bakery. **Woody's Oceanfront Grill** ((808) 661-8788, 839 Front Street, has a good selection of sandwiches (from tuna melt to *mahimahi*), as well as fish tacos, ribs, grilled pork chops and specialty drinks. Assuming you take the incredible views for granted, then the reasons for visiting the **Chart House** ((808) 661-0937, 1450 Front Street, are limited. All you are going to get is standard fare of steak, fish and prime rib. But the desserts are good.

Two reasonably priced family Italian restaurants in the Kaanapali area are **Luigis** ((808) 661-4500, at the entrance to Kaanapali Resort, and **Basil Tomatoes** ((808) 662-3210, on the fourteenth green of Kaanapali's north golf course, at the entrance to the Royal Lahaina Resort. For plentiful, inexpensive meals for the whole family, try the daily breakfast, lunch and dinner buffets at the **Kaanapali Mixed Plate** restaurant at the Kaanapali Beach Hotel ((808) 661-0011.

Roy's Kahana Bar and Grill and **Roy's Nicolina Restaurant** ((808) 669-6999, Kahana Gateway, 4405 Honoapiilani Highway, are both owned by local celebrity chef Roy Yamaguchi and are situated side by side. The styles of their executive chefs — Tod Kawachi of Kahana Grill and Jacqueline Lau of Nicolina — make each place unique. These chefs create 20 nightly specials of "Euro-Asian" seafood, steak, and chicken treats as well as serving a mean pizza.

Orient Express ((808) 669-8077, Napili Shores Resort, is a Thai/Chinese mix restaurant serving up traditional favorites like tom ka gai (Thai coconut chicken soup), sweet and sour shrimp, and combination seafood clay pots. They promise no MSG.

Inexpensive

Good food is not only reserved for the expensive restaurants in Lahaina. The **Aloha Mixed Plate** ((808) 661-3322, 1285 Front Street, across from the Lahaina Cannery Mall, has some of the best local food: from *kalua* pig to *mahimahi* and noodles. Another equally good Hawaiian plate eatery to try is **Hoonokowai Okazuya and Deli** ((808) 665-0512, 3600D Lower Honoapiilani Road.

If you're on Front Street and get a craving for a really good smoothie (or a pastry), stop by **Groovy Smoothies** ((808) 661-8219, 708 Front Street. It's takeout only. The **Lahaina Bagel Café** ((808) 667-5225, 910 Honoapiilani Highway #16, is another good stop for smoothies, bagels, coffee and cookies. They also deliver locally. **Sir Wilfred's** ((808) 667-1941 WEB SITE WWW

Maui Tacos ((808) 665-0222, Napili Plaza, 5095 Napili Hau Street, is another of the chain of high quality Mexican food — from fish tacos to chimichangas — at takeout prices. Across the same plaza is another find: **Mama's Ribs 'N Rotisserie** ((808) 665-6262. The teriyaki citrus chicken is amazing and the ribs are pretty good too. Takeout only and it's closed on Sundays.

Honolua Store ((808) 669-6128, Office Road, in Kapalua, is the place to go for local plate lunches or a quick sandwich, while the **Maui Coffee and Espresso Bar** ((808) 669-

.sirwilfred.com, Lahaina Cannery Mall, offers coffee, tea, tobacco and sandwiches with courtyard seating. For more substantial fare, **Lahaina Coolers** ((808) 661-7082, 180 Dickenson Street, has pasta, pizza, fish and daily specials in a lively atmosphere. The full menu is available until midnight.

Besides the expensive restaurants, Whalers Village in Kaanapali also has some cheap eateries in their Food Court — **Ganso Kawara Soba** ((808) 667-0815, **Pizza Paradiso** ((808) 667-0333 (free area delivery), **Village Korean BarBQ** ((808) 661-9798 and for dessert, **Maui Yogurt** ((808) 661-8843. **Jonny's Burger Joint** ((808) 661-4500, at the entrance to Kaanapali Resort, has burgers and fries and will deliver in the area.

9667 at Kapalua Shops has sandwiches to go with their cappuccinos and lattes.

THE SOUTHWEST COAST

The southwest coast has a restaurant in every price range, with choices from gourmet establishments to pancake houses that serve wholesome, hearty food.

Very Expensive

Executive chef Pierre Albaladejo presides over **Seasons** ((808) 874-8000, a dramatic, open-design establishment at the Four Season's Hotel in Wailea. Offering great

The rugged grandeur of the northwest Maui shoreline.

ocean views and a distinctly Mediterranean cuisine, signature dishes include roasted Colorado rack of lamb with baby artichoke and *petite raviole* with a fennel sauce, and seared *opakapaka* with marinière vegetable *bouillabaisse jus.*

Expensive

The **Maalaea Waterfront Restaurant** ((808) 244-9028 WEBSITE www.waterfrontrestaurant .net, Maalaea Harbor, 50 Hauoli Street, Maalaea, serves excellent seafood in subdued surroundings. There are between five and eight fresh fish selections daily, with nine choices of preparation. There is also game *du jour* (exotic game prepared classically or in progressive ways).

Jean-Marie Josselin's **A Pacific Café Maui** ((808) 879-0069 WEBSITE www.pacific-cafe .com, Azeka Place 11, 1279 South Kihei Road, Kihei, is another in this Frenchman's highly successful chain of island restaurants, serving clever blends of Indian, Mediterranean and Hawaiian flavors. Try the wok-charred *mahimahi* with garlic sesame crust and lime ginger sauce. This restaurant also has a wood-burning grill and a tandoori oven for those great Indian breads and spicy chicken dishes.

Carelli's on the Beach ((808) 875-0001 , Keawakapu Beach, near Wailea is in a wonderful location for sunset viewing. The food is on par with the view: from *bruschetta paesana* to *cioppino* and pasta to specialties like *mahimahi* stuffed with crab meat or veal with fontina cheese and white truffle fondue. If you crave a more simple affair, the brick-oven pizzas are excellent too. But (boo, hiss) there is a table minimum for some seating.

Humuhumunuknukuapuaa ((808) 875-1234, The Grand Wailea Resort, 3850 Wailea Alanui, is named after Hawaii's state fish and known as the Humu Humu for short. A cluster of thatched roof huts which appears to float above a fish-stocked lagoon, this restaurant serves the most wonderful Polynesian and Hawaiian regional cuisine with seafood a specialty. Delicious food in a fun setting not to miss. Open for dinner only. **Nick's Fishmarket Maui** ((808) 875-7224 at the Kea Lani Hotel, 4100 Wailea Alanui, has a magical tropical setting and

serves the freshest seafood cooked imaginatively: chopped Maui onions with tomatoes, avocados, feta cheese and rock shrimp; Hawaiian pink snapper sautéed with rock shrimp and served with lemon butter and capers.

Moderate

Buzz' Wharf ((808) 244-5426, Highway 30, Maalaea Harbor, 50 Hauoli Street, Maalaea (look for the bright blue roof), serves up okay food on the high side of moderate pricing. The best part of this restaurant, by far, is the view, so it is worth a visit for a drink and a burger or salad. The desserts are good. Try the mango crème brûlée or the house specialty of baked papaya Tahitian.

There's a surprisingly good Greek restaurant in Kihei. I say "surprisingly" because there aren't many authentic Greek restaurants anywhere in the islands. But the **Greek Bistro** ((808) 879-9330, 2511 South Kihei Road, makes up for that. With its series of terraced open-air cabanas, this restaurant has a pleasant atmosphere, as well as tasty and moderately priced food. The fare at **Stella Blues Café** ((808) 874-3779, 1215 South Kihei Road, Kihei, is a simple affair. This is where to go for a quick and satisfying meal served amidst bright decor and high ceilings. A good choice here is the grilled eggplant sandwich accompanied by cucumbers, feta, sweet peppers and pesto mayonnaise, but the Thai sweet chili chicken is good too. Spicy Thai food is the order of the day at **Thai Chef** ((808) 874-5605, Rainbox Mall, 2439 South Kihei Road, Kihei. Recommendations include green papaya salad, Thai yellow curry and sweet and sour vegetables.

Joe's Bar and Grill ((808) 875-7767, Wailea Tennis Club, 131 Wailea Ike Place, in Wailea, serves up American food with more than a hint of the islands added. The menu includes lobster, steak and more exotic fare like crispy calamari with Thai sauce and *ahi* tartar. This restaurant has an amazing view of the golf course, tennis courts and Haleakala. The Kea Lani Hotel in Wailea has a bakery and deli as well as three restaurants, including the **Caffe Ciao**, a gourmet Italian delicatessen with oven-fresh pizzas, and the **Polo Beach Grill and Bar**, famous for its kiawe burgers.

Inexpensive
Da Kitchen ((808) 875-7782, Rainbow Mall, 2439 South Kihei Road, Kihei, has good local food including pork butt cooked in ti leaves and noodles with char siu, egg, kamaboko and vegetables. A cheap and cheerful Mexican restaurant, **Café Navaca** ((808) 879-0717, Kalama Village, 1945 South Kihei Road, serves up huevos rancheros for breakfast, *ahi* tacos for lunch and crawfish enchiladas for dinner. There is live entertainment every night. **Pita Paradise** ((808) 875-7679, Kihei Kalama Village, 1913 South Kihei Road, Kihei, has gourmet grilled pita wraps, from lamb to teriyaki chicken. A popular spot on the main drag is **Alexander's Fish and Chicken and Chips** ((808) 874-0788, 1913 South Kihei Road, across the street from Kalama Park. It's basically a takeout stand, but there is some patio seating outside. Very tasty food, if you are willing to wait in the inevitable line.

UPCOUNTRY

Expensive
The **Haliimaile General Store** ((808) 572-2666, 900 Haliimaile Road, is housed in a nondescript building with plantation-style architecture. Don't be fooled by the exterior. On closer inspection what looked like your basic country store turns out to be an elegant, well-designed restaurant — one of the best in all of Hawaii — with beautiful decor and great art adorning the walls. The ambience is matched by the food, superbly prepared by chef Beverly Gannon, a Texan who co-owns this eatery with her husband Joe. Beverly is one of the new wave of local chefs specializing in Hawaiian regional cuisine, but she leans less towards Asian flavors than do her peers. The emphasis is on local produce, which she turns into surprising and exotic dishes — duck salad with warm goat cheese and chive crêpes, or *opakapaka* baked in parchment with leeks, herbs and lobster. The menu is extensive and the helpings are huge. Make sure you book early.

Kula Lodge ((808) 878-2517, 377 Kula Highway, is famous for its cinnamon-apple-raisin French toast and banana-macadamia nut pancakes for breakfast as well as its range-fed beef and seared *ahi* sashimi for lunch

and dinner. If going for dinner, get there in time to see the magnificent view down to Haleakala, and then cozy up to the roaring fire as night descends.

Moderate
There's also good eating in Makawao. Try the **Makawao Steak House** ((808) 572-8711, 3612 Baldwin Avenue, where the setting is rustic yet elegant. The chops, ribs and fish are done to perfection, while the steaks might well be the best in Maui. **Casanova Italian Restaurant and Deli** ((808) 572-0220,

1188 Makawao Avenue, is one of the livelier places to hangout in Makawao. It offers good pasta, pizza, seafood and classy entertainment on weekends.

Inexpensive
Look out for the cows on the exterior of the **Upcountry Café** ((808) 572-2395 Andrade Building, 7-2 Aewa Place, just off Haleakala Highway, Pukalani. Once inside, the cow motif continues, everywhere. On the walls, menus and chairs. But don't be put off, the comfort food here is just too good to pass up: from meatloaf to roast pork with soups, salads and enormous burgers.

Hamoa Beach is but one of the many highlights along the Hana Highway.

Café O Lei ((808) 573-9065, Paniolo Court-yard, 3673 Baldwin Avenue, Makawao, has soups, sandwiches (grilled eggplant, turkey breast) and enormous salads (like lentil and brown rice, Caesar, or curried chicken).

A bit difficult to find but worth the effort is **Pukalani Country Clubhouse Restaurant (** (808) 572-1325, 360 Pukalani Street, which serves Hawaiian food, ribs and steaks and offers a delightful view of the Valley Isle across a beautiful golf course.

Situated on a busy intersection, **Polli's Mexican Restaurant (** (808) 572-7808, 1202 Makawao Avenue, Makawao, is a favorite with residents and tourists alike who like the healthy versions of favorites like seafood enchiladas, quesadillas, fajitas. The vegetarian fare is very good also.

Café 808 ((808) 878-6874, Lower Kula Road, across from Morihara Street, Kula, is a wonderful find to get just a hint of real Hawaiian life. Residents flock here for the homestyle cooking in completely unpreten-tious surroundings: plastic chairs, linoleum-tile floor and formica-clad tables. Many styles of noodles, lasagna, taro burgers, and stews are on offer, but check out the daily specials before making your selection. They are usu-ally excellent. There is no liquor license here, but if you want a drink with your dinner you can go across the road to the general store and bring back whatever you'd like to drink.

Grandma's Coffee House ((808) 878-2140, at the end of Highway 37 in Keokea, is a wonderful little roadside establishment which serves up coffee, soup, sandwiches, pasta, garden burgers and plate lunch specials.

ROAD TO HANA AND HANA

Expensive

The **Dining Room** at the Hotel Hana-Maui is where guests take most of their meals. A 35-ft-high (over 10-m) exposed-beam ceiling and a covered outdoor lanai give this res-taurant a wonderful blend of country el-egance and modern sophistication. The food served here is equally intriguing—a mélange of Pacific Rim, American and Oriental cui-sine prepared with great flair. Three miles (five kilometers) away, on Hamoa Beach, which author James Michener called "the most perfect crescent-shaped beach in the world," the hotel serves a buffet lunch daily. Once a week this beach is also the site of a luau.

Hana Ranch Restaurant ((808) 248-8255, Hana Highway, is also part of the Hotel Hana-Maui group but is a less formal alternative to the dining room. The prices are still high and the menu uninspired: steak, prawns, pasta. Lets hope for a major renovation here with the hotel's new owners.

Moderate

A lively, fun place to spend happy hour (won-derful margaritas) and stay for a meal is **Milagros Food Company (** (808) 579-8755, on the corner of Hana Highway and Baldwin Avenue in Paia. The southwestern/seafood menu includes dishes like blackened *ahi* taquitos, chiles-rellenos plate and a daily *ahi* special. Across the street is the **Paia Fish Market (** (808) 579-8030, 110 Hana Highway, is a real fish market that serves wonderfully fresh cooked fish as well as burgers.

Exiting Paia, the road meanders along the coast, passing by **Mama's Fish House (** (808) 579-8488, 799 Poho Place, a large private residence converted into a restaurant where the food is good but pricey.

Three miles (five kilometers) before Hana is a five-acre (two-hectare) slice of heaven that includes the **Hana Gardenland Café** — specializing in dishes made from organi-cally grown produce — and a botanical garden and gift shop. All the produce used on the menu here comes from local farms, so the food is as fresh as possible. It is now part of Hana legend that First Lady Hillary Rodham Clinton discovered the Gardenland Café in 1993 and liked it so much that she returned on two other occasions to dine there.

Inexpensive

If you are making a very early start on a trip to Hana, contact **Picnics Restaurant (** (808) 579-8021, 30 Baldwin Avenue, where you can pick up some tasty food at a reasonable price. Alternatively, get your picnic from **Anthony's Coffee Co. (** (808) 882-6509 WEB SITE www.anthonyscoffee.com, 90 Hana Highway #C. This is also a wonderful place for a leisurely breakfast with choices including eggs benedict, "catch of the day" benedict, Belgian waffles, granola and fruit.

The cheapest place for a hot meal in Hana is the takeout stand adjoining the Hana Ranch Restaurant, which offers noodles, burgers, fish plates, hot dogs, ice cream. Beware, they even charge for the tap water here. A little further up the road, the **Hana Ranch Store** ((808) 248-8261 sells hot dogs and other snacks and drinks (and also rents videos).

NIGHTLIFE

The **Maui Arts and Cultural Center** ((808) 242-7469, off Kahului Beach Road, is home to the Maui Symphony, Maui Philharmonic and the Maui Academy of Performing Arts. Call them to find out what's on.

Lahaina is the nightlife center of Maui. Most all the action on the island happens right here. If you only had one evening to spend in Lahaina, I would recommend **Ulalena** ((808) 661-9913, at the Myth and Magic Theatre, 878 Front Street. This theatrical presentation weaves together Hawaiian mythology and history through dance and acrobatics with original music and song, creating powerful images that will leave you with a new appreciation of the islands.

Old Lahaina Luau ((808) 667-1998, at the northern edge of Lahaina town near Mala Wharf is the least kitsch-touristy of the luaus on Maui (held nightly). There is also the **Feast of Lele** ((808) 667-5353, 505 Front Street, which is put on by the creators of the Old Lahaina Luau and Pacific 'O Restaurant.

There is live music nightly until 2 AM at **Maui Brews** ((808) 667-7794, 900 Front Street in the Lahaina Center. As the name implies, they also have a wide selection of beverages, from cocktails to beer, plus a full bistro menu from 11:30 AM to 10 PM and a late-night light menu from 10 PM to 11:30 PM. **Moose McGillycuddy's Pub and Café** ((808) 667-7758, 844 Front Street, is another nighttime hotspot, with sporting events shown live via satellite.

Windjammer Cruises ((808) 661-8600, 505 Front Street, has all-you-can-eat salmon and prime rib dinner cruises aboard a three-masted schooner from Slip 1, Lahaina Harbor. **Pacific Whale Foundation Eco Adven-**

tures ((808) 879-8811 WEB SITE www.pacific whale.org, does a sunset cruise aboard the *Manutea*, or try a champagne and chocolates sunset sail aboard the **Scotch Mist 11** ((808) 661-0386 FAX (808) 667-2113, Lahaina Harbor, Slip 2; or a champagne and gourmet *pu pus* sunset sail on Saturday with **Trilogy** ((808) 879-8811 TOLL-FREE (888) 628-4800 WEB SITE www.sailtrilogy.com.

The **Marriott Luau** ((808) 661-5828, at the Maui Marriott on Kaanapali Beach, features the triple knife dance in its Hawaiian/Polynesian music and show, along with the usual

shell leis greeting, *imu* ceremony, buffet dinner and open bar. The Renaissance Wailea Beach Resort ((808) 879-4900 has their version called the **Wailea's Sunset Luau**.

The **Outrigger Wailea Resort** ((808) 879-1922 has a luau on Monday, Tuesday, Thursday, and Friday.

HOW TO GET THERE

Maui's main airport is in Kahului on the north side of the island. Several airlines fly directly to Maui from the mainland United States. Interisland flights serve the main airport and smaller airfields in Kaanapali and Hana.

Early morning strollers on a Maui beach.

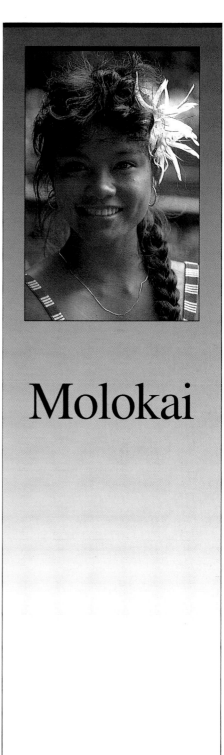

Molokai

MOLOKAI IS GENUINELY OLD HAWAII, laid back and free from the traumas that sometimes afflict the tourist centers of the other islands. The island has few modern trappings and the people who live here like it that way.

Molokai's population has the highest percentage of native Hawaiians among those of the major islands in the chain, and many of them guard their heritage jealously. Efforts to modernize the island have run into fierce resistance. Its potential as a tourist destination has only been scratched. To see it now in its pristine state is an opportunity not to be missed.

Molokai has three distinct touring zones to explore: the southeastern portions of the island from the town of Kaunakakai via Kamehameha V Highway to Halawa Valley; western Molokai; and central Molokai up to the northerly Kalaupapa Peninsula. The latter must be reached by helicopter, on foot (for which a permit is required), or on the back of a mule.

BACKGROUND

The island of Molokai, fifth largest in the Hawaiian chain, has a unique history. Like Maui, Molokai's main body was formed by two volcanoes, which flowed together to create a common plain. But Molokai, created by lava spewing from the ocean floor more than one and a half million years ago, is much older than Maui. Over the centuries, rain and seas have worked on the land, smoothing its jagged peaks, forming profound gorges along the eastern plains, and carving immense sea cliffs, the world's highest, on her northeastern flank, which render the island inaccessible from her windward shores.

Much later in its history, another eruption produced a remote and forbidding stretch of land along the base of the sea cliffs on the island's northern shores. This isolated peninsula was to become a prison for thousands of people afflicted with Hansen's Disease, or leprosy.

On the eastern tip of Molokai is Halawa Valley which, until recently, was regarded by some historians and archaeologists as the earliest recorded Polynesian settlement in the Hawaiian chain. But this remains in dispute, for others believe that Kau, on the Big Island, is older still.

Polynesians from the Marquesas were the first to arrive on Molokai, with Tahitians emigrating many years later. These early residents grew taro, sweet potato and other staples and fished extensively, developing an early aquaculture. As many as 58 fishponds were constructed of lava rock and coral along the shallow waters of the southern coast, possibly before the thirteenth century. Many of them remain today.

Evidence of the island's rich religious heritage also remains; Molokai's *heiaus* include some of the largest and most impressive to be found in the Hawaiian Islands. An aura of mysticism remains on this island, as does the traditional importance placed on the land and family.

In the mid-1800s ranching came to the island, dominated by the Molokai Ranch which today covers some 54,000 acres (nearly 22,000 hectares), or over a third of the island. It is Hawaii's second largest ranch and is currently owned by a New Zealand company, Brierley Investments Limited.

GENERAL INFORMATION

The **Molokai Visitors Association** ((808) 553-3876 TOLL-FREE (800) 800-6367 FAX (808) 553-5288 E-MAIL mva@molokai-hawaii.com WEB SITE www.molokai-hawaii.com is in Kaunakakai on Kamehameha V Highway (also known as Kam Highway), at the zero-mile highway marker.

GETTING AROUND

Traveling around Molokai is very difficult without a rental car. These are in very limited supply, so it's best to reserve one when you purchase your air ticket. **Budget** ((808) 567-6877 FAX (808) 567-6306 and **Dollar** ((808) 567-6156 have offices at Molokai Airport. A third alternative, **Island Kine Auto Rentals** ((808) 553-5242 FAX (808) 553-3880 E-MAIL fishin@aloha.net, have their office in Kaunakakai, but they will meet you at the airport and take you back. They also offer vans and pickup trucks.

Lone jogger beside the creamy surf of Kepuhi Beach at Kaluakoi Resort.

Alternatively, you can contact **Molokai Off-Road Tours and Taxi** ((808) 553-3369 FAX (808) 533-1233, who offer regular taxi service along with all-island tours, or **Kukui Tours and Limousine** ((808) 552-2282 FAX (808) 552-2443, who have an airport shuttle and offer two tours.

WHAT TO SEE AND DO

KAUNAKAKAI AND SOUTHEAST MOLOKAI

Kaunakakai is Molokai's largest town — all three blocks of it. This former canoe landing hasn't changed much over the past half century. Though small, the village has some well-stocked grocery stores, restaurants and bakeries to supply all your needs.

In recent years, the town has also become the center of the island's arts and crafts activities, and designers specializing in native jewelry, glass art, quilt making, silk screening and leis have all taken up residence here. **Kaunakakai Wharf** offers a mile-long stroll over the water and a vantage point from which to look back at Molokai. What remains of Kamehameha V's summer house is near the canoe house.

Nene O Molokai ((808) 553-5992 FAX (808) 553-9029 E-MAIL nene@aloha.net, in Kaunakakai on Kamehameha V Highway, is a nonprofit breeding and educational facility for Hawaii's state bird, the nene. Free educational tours are offered here. Just beyond the nene facility you'll come to the **Kakahaia Pond**, which is an ancient inland fishpond, now a wetland bird sanctuary.

Near Kamalo, on the right-hand side of the road just after mile marker 10 on Kamehameha V Highway, is **Saint Joseph's Catholic Church**, constructed in 1876. It was the second church built on the island by Father Damien. Less than a mile past the church, also on the right, is the Smith-Bronte landing site where pilots Ernie Smith and Emory Bronte crash-landed in 1927, after completing the first commercial, nonstop trans-Pacific flight. The journey took more than 25 hours to complete.

All along the southern shores are scenic beaches and ancient fishponds such as **Keawanui**, approximately 13 miles (21 km) out of Kaunakakai. On the left you will find the ruins of **Kaluaaha Church**, once one of the largest Western-style structure in the islands. Built in 1844, the church was used

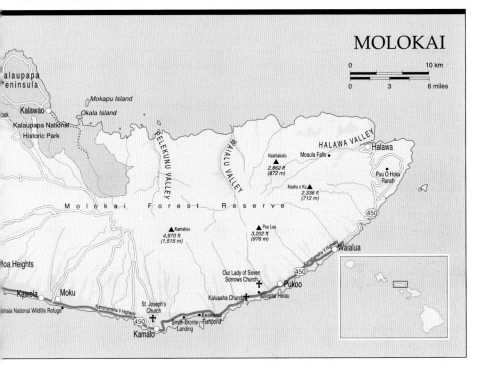

MOLOKAI

for worship until the 1940s. Farther along on the left is **Our Lady of Seven Sorrows Church**, Father Damien's first church, built in 1874.

The area has great religious significance for native Hawaiians, dating from well before first contact with westerners. Hidden from sight in the hills on the left is **Iliiliopae Heiau**, an important Hawaiian temple dedicated to the highest gods. The temple is on private land but an excursion can be arranged through **Molokai Horse and Wagon Ride** (/FAX (808) 558-8132 E-MAIL wgnride@aloha.net WEB SITE www.visitmolokai.com/wgnride, Kaunakakai. They also offer a range of other tours including overnight horseback riding trips and hiking tours.

Nearby is the beginning of the rugged **Wailau Trail**, which cuts clear across to the northern coast of Molokai. The Neighborhood Store at Pukoo is the last "watering hole" before you reach Halawa Valley, so don't forget to stock up.

At the crest of the hill of the Puu O Hoku Ranch you will see **Kaulukukuiolanikaula** on the right, the sacred grove of kukui where the prophet Lanikaula is said to be buried.

THE EAST

When you spot Halawa Valley, stop the car at a suitable vantage point and take in the view. This large and beautiful northern valley is one of the most stunning areas on the island. Lantana flowers and hale koa bushes line the hillsides, which sweep down into the fertile valley where houses snuggle in little coppices against the base of jungle slopes, almost hidden from view. Halawa Valley was home to the island's earliest settlers, and the beach was a favorite playground of the chiefs because of its fine surfing conditions. A tidal wave struck the valley in 1946 causing extensive damage. Today only about 20 people live here, without electricity or telephones.

Once in the valley itself, you can hike to **Moaula Falls** in about one hour. This is private property, however, so you'll need to hire a guide. Try guides Pilipo and Kawaimaka at **Pilipo's Halawa Falls and Cultural Hike** ((808) 553-4355 FAX (808) 567-6244 E-MAIL pilipo@visitmolokai.com WEB SITE www.molokai-hawaii.com, PO Box 96748, will lead you to Moaula Falls and teach you a little about Halawa's sacredness on the way.

Wavecrest General Store ((808) 558-0222 FAX (808) 558-0223, at mile marker 13, is a convenience store with local arts and crafts and an activities desk.

THE WEST

Ancient teachings speak of lush forests in the west, where ohia trees bore lehua blossoms so beautiful that a lei of the flowers would inspire love. Now the land is nearly devoid of trees. Just beyond Kaluakoi Resort lies **Kawakiu Beach**, one of the best swimming beaches on the island. The beach also has some important archaeological ruins. Look along the shoreline and you can see the remains of house platforms and a temple structure that mark the location of an ancient fishing village.

Within the Kaluakoi Resort is the imposing **Kaiaka Rock**, and further on, the vast expanse of **Papohaku Beach**, Hawaii's largest white-sand beach. Past Kepuhi Beach to the north lies the **Pohakumauliuli Cinder Cone**, formed in the vent of a volcano. The cone changes hue with the shifting sunlight, from a dull black to chocolate to reddish brown.

Eight miles (just under 13 km) from the Kaluakoi turnoff, down the road to the right, is the old pineapple plantation town of **Maunaloa**. Much has changed here in the past few years with the town undergoing a major facelift by the landowners of Molokai Ranch. Among the new offerings are a movie theater and new retailers.

THE CENTER AND NORTH

Just past the Kalae Highway turnoff is the state forest reserve road, leading off to the left to the **Kamakou Preserve**, a refuge for rare and endangered forest birds. The roads are accessible only by four-wheel-drive vehicle, but monthly tours are conducted by the **Nature Conservancy of Hawaii (** (808) 553-5236 FAX (808) 553-9870, PO Box 220, Kualapuu, HI 96757. For information on the Kamakou hiking trails, see THE GREAT OUTDOORS, page 30 in YOUR CHOICE.

Atop Maunaloa's neighboring hill, **Kaana** is said by some to be the birthplace of hula,

the site where the goddess Laka was taught to dance by her sister Kapo.

A spectacular hula festival takes place every year in May at the Papohaku Beach Park at Kaluakoi. The annual **Molokai Ka Hula Piko** attracts hula *halau* (schools), singers and musicians from Molokai as well as the other Hawaiian islands and Japan. For information contact the **Molokai Visitors Association (** (808) 553-3876 TOLL-FREE (800) 800-6367 FAX (808) 553-5288 E-MAIL mva@molokai-hawaii.com WEBSITE www.molokai-hawaii.com.

Running along the bluff above Kalaupapa is the **Palaau State Park**. This cool, beautifully wooded area is ideal for a picnic and casual strolls. The **Kalaupapa Overlook** provides an aerial view of the peninsula and

the colony below. A short walk away from the lookout is the phallic stone of **Nanahoa**. Hawaiians believe that a stone has certain powers related to its form. Thus, the phallic rock was a place of pilgrimage for barren women seeking children. It was said that if a woman sat at the base of the stone, where rainwater collected, she could absorb the power of the rock and become fertile.

Nearby are the **Molokai Museum and Cultural Center** ((808) 567-6436, Kalae Highway, and the **R.W. Meyer Sugar Mill** ((808) 567-6436. The Friends of the Meyer Sugar Mill have restored this historic site. Powered by steam and animals, the mill was built in 1878. It is, today, the only mill of its kind remaining in the United States. Meyer Sugar Mill is open for guided tours.

Kualapuu is the site of a relatively new industry on Molokai — coffee. The bean has been grown with such success in Kona on the Big Island that it was inevitable that other islands would be encouraged to experiment. At the **Malulani Estate** ((808) 567-9241 TOLL-FREE (800) 709-2326 E-MAIL coffee@aloha.net, some 450 acres (180 hectares) are under cultivation. There is an espresso bar and wagon tours are available.

In Hoolehua on Lihipali Avenue is **Purdy's Natural Macadamia Nut Farm** ((808) 567-6601 E-MAIL macnuts@molokai-aloha.com. This 70-year-old farm offers free tours and sells fresh fruits, nuts, and Molokai's famous macadamia-blossom honey.

Bathers enjoy the sun-dappled waters near Pukoo on the southeastern coast of Molokai.

KALAUPAPA PENINSULA

The Kalaupapa Peninsula is an isolated strip of land on the northern shores of Molokai. Here, 20-ft (six-meter) breakers thunder in from the open sea, past the tiny islands of Mokapi and Okala, dashing themselves in a frenzy on the pebbly shores at the feet of towering sea cliffs. The cliffs are too high to climb and the waters too rough to swim. Standing on the bluff high above the ocean, you may imagine hearing in the wind the

ghostly cries of terror and anguish from the thousands of sufferers of leprosy (Hansen's Disease, named after the Norwegian scientist who discovered the bacillus causing the condition), then believed to be highly contagious. They were sent here in 1866 following an act signed into law by King Kamehameha V. Shipped to Molokai in cages, these unfortunate men, women, and children were cast into the raging waters of Waikolu Bay and left to sink or swim to the forbidding shore. If they survived this ordeal, they faced an inhospitable environment and the predatory tendencies of their fellow sufferers.

A young Belgian priest named Father Damien Joseph de Veuster, came to the colony

in 1873 and gave back to the people both their dignity and their will to live. The patients assisted in building a settlement at Kalawao, which included a primitive hospital and a church. During the nineteenth century, the settlement shifted from Kalawao to the town of Kalaupapa on the leeward side of the peninsula.

Father Damien eventually contracted the disease. He died from pneumonia in 1889, at the age of 49, after living 16 years in the colony — weakened by his condition. His work, however, continued. Eventually, Hansen's Disease on the island was halted by the drug sulfone. After treatment, many patients moved back to live with their families in a free society. But a handful chose to remain in the colony.

Kalaupapa ((808) 567-6802 WEB SITE www.nps.gov/kala is now a national historic park and is administered by the State of Hawaii jointly with the National Park Service. But it remains a restricted area. **Damien Molokai Tours** ((808) 567-6171, run by Richard Marks, has the only blanket permit to bring the general public to the peninsula and is the only tour service operated by patients. On the tour you will be taken to Kalawao, the site of the first settlement, and the church of **St. Philomena's** —

now a pilgrimage shrine — which Father Damien started, and patients completed after his death.

THE MULE TRAIL

The mule trail is in the central northern coast of Molokai, running from the top of Highway 470 down to Kalaupapa. A Portuguese immigrant named Manuel João Farinha cut the mule trail in 1886. In some places, Farinha and his fellow workers had to be suspended by ropes secured to the cliff's face in order to complete their Herculean task.

The trail down the 1,800-ft (540-m) cliff meanders through a forest splashed here and there with wildflowers and fruit trees. Each bend in the trail opens up vistas of the ocean below and the cliffs above.

The **Molokai Mule Ride** ((808) 567-6088 TOLL-FREE (800) 567-7550 FAX (808) 567-6244 E-MAIL muleman@aloha.net WEB SITE www.muleride.com, Mule Route 1, Box 200, Kualapuu, began in the 1970s and became the must-do adventure for tourists visiting this island.

TOURS

Hawaiian Connection Tours ((808) 558-8396, HC01 Box 960, Kaunakakai, HI 96748, offers a range of tours of the island with guide Eddie: aka "The Happy Hawaiian."

Alternatively, you can take a plane to Kalaupapa airport with **Molokai-Lanai Air Shuttle** ((808) 567-6847 or **Island Air** TOLL-FREE (800) 652-6541 from Molokai Airport and be met by **Damien Molokai Tours** ((808) 567-6171, PO Box 1, Kalaupapa, HI 96742, for an area tour.

Waterfall Adventures ((808) 558-8464 offers hiking, rock climbing, bird watching and photography tours of East Molokai for beginners through to heavy-duty outdoor adventurers.

For a first-rate overview of East Molokai, take an air tour that will fly you past the cliffs, the 1,765-ft-high (535-m) Kahiwa Falls, Hawaii's tallest waterfall, and on to Kalaupapa. Try **Paragon Air/Wings Over Hawaii** TOLL-FREE (800) 428-1231 WEBSITE www.maui.netwings/index.htm.

SHOPPING

Kite expert Jonathan Socher and his wife, designer Daphne Socher, have combined their interests into two adjoining shops in the heart of Maunaloa. The **Big Wind Kite Factory** ((808) 552-2364 is next to the post office and features kites in all shapes and sizes, turning the interior of this charming store into a blaze of color. The reputation of the Big Wind Kite Factory for quality design and workmanship has brought the creations of other great kite

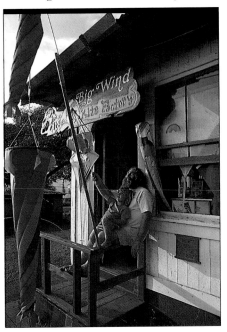

makers into the store. There are daily tours of the factory and free kite-flying lessons. The **Plantation Gallery** sells delicate deer horn and coral scrimshaw souvenirs and gift items created by Molokai's finest artists and craftspeople. Ex-surfer Butch Tabanao, for instance, creates magnificent deer horn cribbage boards (measuring less than four inches, or 10 cm long), notebooks, cards and paintings. The store also stocks casual wear, post cards, books, Old Hawaii coins and much more.

Molokai Fish and Dive (/FAX (808) 553-5926, in Kaunakakai town, offers a wide

OPPOSITE: Youngsters examine a statue of Father Damien. ABOVE: Houses of worship on "Church Row" leading into Kaunakakai. RIGHT: Big Wind Kite Factory in the sleepy plantation town of Maunaloa.

variety of merchandise, from cowboy boot tips to T-shirts to fishing tackle, and everything in between. They also have a large selection of books on Hawaii. Another shop in Kaunakakai town that offers nothing short of one-stop shopping is **Imports Gift Shop** ((808) 553-5734 FAX (808) 553-3017. Merchandise here runs the gamut from clothes to quilts, jewelry, snacks and frozen food.

A network of local artists who create contemporary and traditional Hawaiian works that include jewelry, woodwork, paintings and sculptures owns the **Artist Society of Molokai** ((808) 553-3461, PO Box 610, Kaunakakai. Studio visits are arranged by appointment to **Designs Pacifica** ((808) 553-5363 FAX (808) 553-5727, PO Box 1365, Kaunakakai, where local artist Jule Patten creates paper cast Hawaiian quilt designs. **Haku Designs** ((808) 558-8419, PO Box 900, Kaunakakai, offers nature-inspired original silk screen designs on clothes and bags.

SPORTS

The outfitters and check-in for **Molokai Ranch** ((808) 552-2741, extension 286 TOLL-FREE (888) 729-0059 FAX (808) 552-2773 WEB SITE www.molokai-ranch.com, PO Box 259, Maunaloa, is in Maunaloa town. This is the virtual epicenter of outdoor adventures on Molokai. A range of imaginative activities is offered to guests and non-guests alike with no expense spared on equipment, but always with a strong commitment to environmentally responsible tourism.

Activities at the ranch are geared to a variety of experience levels; from an Introduction to **Horsemanship** course to the Paniolo Roundup, where experienced horsemen can compete in traditional rodeo games. There is also **mountain biking** — you can ride on the road or on a challenging single-track terrain carved out by horses. The ranch also offers **hiking**, **kayaking**, Zodiac **rafting**, **whale watching**, **snorkeling**, and **canoeing**.

Another all-around rental company is Molokai Outdoor Activities ((808) 553-4477 TOLL-FREE (877) 553-4477 FAX (808) 553-4303 E-MAIL mosher@aloha.net. It is situated at Hotel Molokai and has kayaks, windsurfing equipment, bikes, snorkel equipment and more for rent. Alternatively, Lani's Kayak

((808) 558-8563 E-MAIL kayak@aloha.net, PO Box 826 Kaunakakai, has kayak, fishing and snorkeling equipment and will provide tour guide service.

For those interested in **cycling**, Molokai Bicycle ((808) 553-3931 FAX (808) 553-5740 E-MAIL molbike@aloha.net WEB SITE www.bikehawaii.com/molokaibicycle, 80 Mohala Street, Kaunakakai, has a large selection of mountain and road bikes, along with child carriers, kids' trailers, jogging strollers and car racks for rent. They also offer drop-off and pickup services.

Sailing and **snorkeling** trips can be arranged with Richard and Doris Reed aboard the sloop *Satan's Doll* at Molokai Charters ((808) 553-5852, at Kaunakakai Wharf, PO Box 1207, Kaunakakai. Alternatively, there is Bill Kapuni's Snorkel and Dive ((808) 553-9867. Bill is a professional PADI instructor and will provide all the necessary gear. Fun Hog Hawaii ((808) 567-6789, Molokai Ocean Recreation, PO Box 424, Hoolehua, offers body board excursions, sunset cruises, whale watching, and other custom charters from the Hale O Lono Harbor.

Fishing charters can be arranged through Captain Joe Reich ((808) 558-8377 and Alyce C ((808) 558-8377 WEBSITE www.worldwidefishing.com, Kaunakakai.

Those looking for **hunting** will be glad to learn that Maa Hawaii-Molokai Action Adventure ((808) 558-8184, PO Box 1269, Kaunakakai, provides a guide service for hunting deer, wild boar and goats using bows or rifles. A range of other activities including hiking, snorkeling and spear fishing can also be arranged.

If **golf** is your game, Kaluakoi Golf Course ((808) 552-2739 TOLL-FREE (800) 435-7208 FAX (808) 552-0144, PO Box 26, Maunaloa, offers 18 challenging holes designed by Ted Robinson (see SPORTING SPREE, page 42 in YOUR CHOICE). The Ironwood Hills Golf Course ((808) 567-6000, PO Box 182, Kualapuu, has nine holes at a 1,200-ft (365-m) elevation.

Information on **hiking** opportunities can be found in THE GREAT OUTDOORS, page 30 in YOUR CHOICE.

WHERE TO STAY

EXPENSIVE

Never before has Molokai offered such elegant accommodation. Opened in September 1999, the **Molokai Ranch Lodge** ((808) 552-2791 TOLL-FREE (877) 726-4656 WEB SITE www.molokai-ranch.com, Maunaloa, is fashioned after a ranch owner's private home and offers 22 luxury rooms overlooking vast pastures and the ocean. Most rooms have private lanais and some have skylights. Off the front desk is a comfortable "great room," featuring a huge fireplace and there is also a reading room, a fine dining room, a game room and a lounge. For the mind and body there is a day spa, fitness center and a heated "infinity" pool.

MODERATE

In a cluster of three-story buildings, **Molokai Shores Suites** ((808) 553-5954 TOLL-FREE (800) 535-0085 FAX (808) 553-5954 WEB SITE www.marcresorts.com, PO Box 1037, Kamehameha V Highway, has 100 one- and two-bedroom units with kitchens. The units aren't fancy, but are bright and clean. There are communal laundry facilities.

One mile (one and a half kilometers) east of Kaunakakai town is **Biljac Condos** (/FAX (808) 553-5006 E-MAIL biljac@aloha.net.

These fully equipped one-bedroom and one-bedroom with loft units have an ocean view, and there is a pool on the property.

Wavecrest Resort ((808) 558-8103 FAX (808) 558-8206, Kaunakakai, is the last accommodation on the southeastern shores before Halawa. Here there are one- and two-bedroom suites with kitchens. On-site there are tennis courts and a pool.

At the far western end of the island, just a 25-minute drive from the airport, is Kaluakoi Resort, encompassing the **Kaluakoi Villas/Quality Resorts** ((808) 552-2721

TOLL-FREE (800) 272-5275 FAX (808) 552-2201 WEBSITE www.castle-group.com, 1131 Kaluakoi Road, Maunaloa, which has villas and studios with kitchenettes, and the **Kaluakoi Hotel and Golf Club** ((808) 552-2555 TOLL-FREE (800) 552-2550 FAX (808) 552-2821 E-MAIL kaluakoi@juno.com WEB SITE www.aloha.net/kmkk, Maunaloa, which has cottages and suites. The **Ke Nani Kai** ((808) 922-9700 TOLL-FREE (800) 535-0085 FAX (808) 552-0045, Maunaloa, is the resort's condominium complex and is a block from Kepuhi Beach. It has one- and two-bedroom units with full kitchen and washer/dryers. Facilities include pool, spa, tennis, and barbecue.

The resort is superbly situated on a 6,800-acre (2,750-hectare) oceanfront property with five and a half miles (nine kilometers) of beautiful coastline, with an plenty of white-sand beaches, though not all are recommended for swimming. The vast majority of visitor accommodation units on the island are right here. Most of the rooms and cottages have

OPPOSITE: Kalaupapa muleteer. ABOVE: Post Office in the sleepy plantation town of Maunaloa.

superb views of the ocean and the 18-hole championship Kaluakoi Golf Course.

Another recommended condominium complex next door to the Kaluakoi Resort is the **Paniolo Hale Resort Condominiums** ((808) 552-2731 TOLL-FREE (800) 367-2984 FAX (808) 552-2288 WEB SITE www.lava.net/paniolo, Maunaloa, which has garden- and ocean-view studios, one- and two-bedroom condominiums with private lanais (some with hot tubs), and a pool and barbecue.

Alternative accommodation is offered at the **Camps at Molokai Ranch** ((808) 534-9515

are self-composing. All meals are served in communal, open-sided pavilions. Breakfast is included. Children under 12 stay free. A large diversity of activities are on offer here, from cattle trail drives to kayaking (see SPORTS, page 232).

INEXPENSIVE

Hotel Molokai ((808) 553-5347 TOLL-FREE (800) 553-5347 WEB SITE www.castle-group.com, PO Box 1020 Kaunakakai, Molokai, Kamehameha V Highway, has 45 modified

TOLL-FREE (877) 726-4656 FAX (808) 534-1606 WEB SITE www.molokai-ranch.com, Maunaloa. This environmentally friendly adventure travel resort offers three camps: Paniolo, on the hillside offering ocean views and a nearby rodeo arena; Kolo Cliffs, on a bluff overlooking the ocean and perfect for couples and those seeking absolute privacy; and Kaupoa Beach, nestled between two white-sand beaches, just right for families. Accommodation at all camps is in "tentalows" or "yurts"—bungalow-like, one- and two-unit permanent tents mounted on a wooden platform, each with a queen-sized bed, ceiling fan and wooden locker. Each tentalow has a large wooden lanai and an outside (but private) bathroom. Lights and hot water are solar powered and toilets

A-frames which are basic but comfortable and have private bathrooms, refrigerators, televisions and phones. The hotel is on a very thin beach, but swimming is not great here; it's better to use this area for kayak launching. There is a swimming pool, mediocre bar and restaurant that is popular with the locals as well as an activities desk and gift shop. This is a good place to relax and really get away from it all, but don't expect too much (like receiving phone messages).

Ka Hale Mala Bed and Breakfast (/FAX (808) 553-9009 E-MAIL cpgroup@aloha.net, 7 Kamakana Place, Kaunakakai, has a four room, ground-floor apartment for rent with full kitchen, private lanai and Jacuzzi just outside. **A'Ahi Place Bed and Breakfast**

((808) 553-5860 E-MAIL mitty@aloha.net, Kaunakakai, offers a cedar cottage with full kitchen and bathroom in a tropical garden setting.

To experience true Hawaiian hospitality, rooms are available inside a private home right in Kaunakakai town at **A Hawaiian Getaway** (/FAX (808) 553-9803 TOLL-FREE (800) 274-9303 E-MAIL mcai@aloha.net, 270 Kaiwi Street. You share utilities with the rest of the household. **Kamalo Plantation Bed and Breakfast** (/FAX (808) 558-8236 E-MAIL kamalo plantation@aloha.net WEB SITE WWW

mountains, gardens and a 75-ft (22.5-m) lap pool. Breakfast is served either on the deck or in a sunny dining room in the main house. Your hosts are Dorothe and David Curtis.

Puu O Hoku Ranch ((808) 558-8109 FAX (808) 558-8100, Kaunakakai, at mile marker 25 on Kamehameha V Highway, is located on the working cattle ranch that engulfs most of east Molokai. The vacation cottage with a full kitchen has two bedrooms and sleeps up to six. The ranch also accommodates up to 22 for business retreats and seminars.

.molokai.com/kamale, Kaunakakai, is across from Father Damien's St. Joseph's Church and has a cottage with kitchen nestled in an tropical garden hideaway at the foot of the Molokai mountain. Rooms in the main house are also available. The property has a working fruit orchard and even its own ancient *heiau* ruin in the front yard.

Kamueli Farms Bed and Breakfast (/FAX (808) 558-8284 E-MAIL dcurtis@aloha .net, PO Box 1829, Kaunakakai, is tucked away at the base of the Kaapahu Mountain. This is country living at its finest. The property is situated within an eight-acre (three-hectare) fruit orchard with Axis deer in the nearby pastures. The guest suite has a private entry and opens onto great views of the

WHERE TO EAT

EXPENSIVE

The **Maunaloa Room** ((808) 552-2791 TOLL-FREE (877) 726-4656, at the Molokai Ranch Lodge, Maunaloa, offers traditional recipes and cooking styles in a simple, yet elegant manner. The menu runs the gamut from baby back ribs with a coffee barbecue sauce and a mini Hawaiian *pu pu* plate, potless venison pot pie, to steak, chicken, seafood as well as salads and burgers.

OPPOSITE: Wild surf pounds the edges of the Kaluakoi Resort Golf Course. ABOVE: Molokai Ranch Wildlife Park provides an ideal habitat for a variety of island deer.

MODERATE

The **Ohia Lodge** ((808) 552-2555, found at the edge of Kepuhi Beach, is the main dining room at the Kaluakoi Hotel and features island cuisine.

The **Village Grill** ((808) 552-0012, beside the Plantation Gallery in Maunaloa offers Continental "ranch-style" dishes with a local flair in a paniolo setting. Favorites here include the Molokai shrimp, which are served with Brazilian-style pesto and Szechuan cream sauce and the veggie stir-fry. They now also serve a selection of "stone-grill" dishes (like mixed seafood) which are cooked on a heated stone at your table.

INEXPENSIVE

Kanemitsu's Bakery ((808) 553-5855, 79 Ala Malama Street, in the town of Kaunakakai, makes delicious Molokai bread (don't miss the macadamia-nut bread) and pastries and serves breakfast and lunch — omelets, burgers, sandwiches, fried chicken. Neighbor island visitors to Molokai rarely go home without some delicacy from this family bakery. Closed Tuesdays.

Molokai Pizza Café ((808) 553-3288, Kahua Center on the old Wharf Road, Kaunakakai, serves a plain cheese as well as six other varieties of pizza, which are all named after Hawaiian islands, and all delicious. Don't feel like pizza? The menu also includes pasta, salads, sandwiches, fish, chicken, ribs and daily specials. **Molokai Drive-inn** ((808) 553-5655, has been an institution in town since 1960, serving up fish, burgers, sandwiches, chicken and noodles (almost all fried). Air-conditioned dining or takeout. Healthier food can be had at the tiny lunch counter at the back of **Outpost Natural Foods** ((808) 553-3377, 70 Makaena. Vegetarian selections include tofu-spinach lasagna, meatless meatloaf and tempeh sandwiches. **Kamoi Snack-N-Go** ((808) 553-3742, Kamoi Professional Center, features Dave's Ice Cream (of Oahu fame), with all the shakes and floats offshoots, together with snacks, candy and cold drinks.

About the only game in the east is the **Neighborhood Store N' Counter** ((808)

558-8498, near mile marker 16, in Pukoo. The lunch counter here offers omelets, sandwiches, salads, vegetarian and local dishes as well as daily specials.

Like it or not, Molokai now has its first fast food chain outlet: **KFC** (Kentucky Fried Chicken) ((808) 552-2625, in the heart of Maunaloa, beside the new movie complex. Trust me, you may end up eating here on a Sunday when not much else is open.

On the way north, **Coffees of Hawaii** ((808) 567-9241, is an espresso bar which serves 100% Molokai coffee straight or in lattes, espressos, cappuccinos. It also has a gift shop. **Kualapuu Cook House** ((808) 567-6185, Kualapuu, is a local hangout for farmers and cowboys, so the meals are hearty

and the servings enormous. Steak and eggs, *mahimahi* omelet, chili and prime-rib.

HOW TO GET THERE

Molokai has two airports, but **Hoolehua Airport** is more popular and is commonly referred to as Molokai Airport. **Hawaiian Air** TOLL-FREE (800) 882-8811 has daily scheduled flights from Honolulu, Kahului, Lihue, Hilo and Kona. **Island Air** TOLL-FREE (800) 652-6541 has daily flights to and from Lanai, Honolulu, Kajului, Hana and Kapalua. **Molokai Air Shuttle** ((808) 567-6847 has flights between Molokai and Oahu, and Lanai and provides tours to Kalaupapa and Molokai's north shore. **Pacific Wings** ((808)

567-6814 TOLL-FREE (888) 575-4546 E-MAIL info @pacificwings.com WEB SITE www.pacific wings.com, has scheduled daily flights to and from Kahului, Honolulu and Hana. **Paragon Air/Wings Over Hawaii** TOLL-FREE (800) 428-1231 WEB SITE www.maui .netwings/index.htm offers charter flights and tours.

You can also cruise to Molokai, aboard the *Maui Princess* ((808) 667-6165 TOLL-FREE (800) 275-6969 FAX (808) 661-5729 WEB SITE www.maui.net/ismarine, 113 Prison Street, Lahaina, Maui, for a single-day, fully narrated tour on Wednesday and Saturday.

The Molokai Mule Ride snakes down the sea cliffs on the way to the settlement far below.

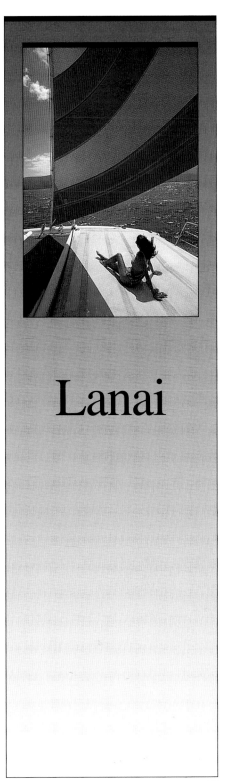

Lanai

TINY LANAI IS BOTH WILD AND LUXURIOUS. In little more than a decade, the third smallest island in the Hawaiian chain has evolved from a pineapple plantation into a secluded getaway for the rich and famous (along with everyday folk). Two world-class resorts — the Lodge at Koele and the Manele Bay Hotel — attract most of the attention, though nature is a major draw as well. Within its 140 sq miles (363 sq km) lie steep lava cliffs, petroglyphs, isolated beaches, forested mountains, and several natural reserves protecting seabirds, tropical fish, and endangered native plants. White spotted axis deer, Moulton sheep, and goats roam the undeveloped hills and canyons. Spinner dolphins, sea turtles and humpback whales gather offshore. Paved roads travel only 30 miles (48 km) through the most populated areas, home to some 2,800 inhabitants. The largest settlement, Lanai City, is but a collection of small businesses framing a central park. A few side streets are lined with plantation-style wood houses with tin roofs and front lanais. Residents automatically wave to anyone passing by, and think nothing of driving newfound friends to secret beaches and lookouts. Lanai is blissfully quiet, slow paced, and mystical. At times it seems half the visitors are residents of other Hawaiian islands seeking a drastic change of scenery and a sense of total escape. With just the right combination of unspoiled nature and creature comforts, Lanai is the perfect destination for adventuresome narcissists.

BACKGROUND

Ancient Hawaiians regarded Lanai as a sinister place inhabited by malevolent spirits. The island was shunned for five decades as Polynesian settlers colonized the friendlier islands. Legend has it that a mischievous young prince from Maui was banished to the evil island when he offended his father and the gods. Challenged to survive on an island where no human had lived overnight, the prince tricked the hostile spirits and killed them off. Maui's leaders took control of the island and a peaceful settlement was soon established. After warriors from the Big Island conquered Lanai it became a favored retreat for King Kamehameha the Great.

Lanai was the sleepiest backwater in the Hawaiian chain until 1922, when Boston businessman Jim Dole bought the land and planted 15,000 acres (6,070 hectares) of pineapples. Later, the Dole Company, a subsidiary of Dole Food Company Inc., purchased the island and expanded the pineapple acreage. In its prime, Lanai was the world's largest pineapple plantation, with 16,000 acres (6,475 hectares) of the prickly fruit. Its only town, Lanai City, and the surrounding residential district consisted of weatherworn, gaily painted buildings, one hotel, one public golf course, and lots of stately Cook Island pines. The sweet scent of pineapple permeated the air.

In 1985, David Murdock purchased 98% of Dole's island interests, and Lanai took on the moniker "The Private Island." Eight years later the pineapple industry ran into tough economic times, and pineapple production stopped in 1993. Castle & Cooke Properties now controls the Lanai Company, with Murdock remaining at the helm. Former pineapple fields have been turned into resorts and golf courses, and many of the plantation workers who remained on the island now work in the hospitality industry and its support services.

Lanai's residents were forced to make a swift transition from planting and harvesting pineapples to working in fancy hotels where guests expect excellent service and pampering. In 1989, the Lanai Company encouraged locals to become involved in the design of the Lodge at Koele, which opened in 1990. Over two dozen local artists worked on the elaborate stenciled paintings of local flora and fauna on the lodge's walls, ceilings, and floors. Artists have continued to thrive, creating ukuleles and carvings from island woods, painting local scenes in watercolors and pastels. Entrepreneurs have opened galleries, gift shops and restaurants. Young adults who left Lanai for more exciting and profitable territories are returning to the quiet island where their children are nurtured, educated and supervised by the entire community. Over 30 babies were born on the island in 1998, and the local schools educate

Bougainvillea adds a splash of color to the Lanai brush on an island where tourism has replaced pineapple cultivation as the main industry.

over 700 children and teens. There's even a small community college branch, and a hospital. Locals speak of their island with a reverential fervor, as if there's nowhere else in the world they'd rather live.

GENERAL INFORMATION

Lanai's major resorts, golf courses and restaurants are all controlled by the Lanai Company; reservations for accommodations and most activities can be arranged by calling **central reservations** ((808) 565-7300 TOLL-FREE (800) 321-4666 FAX (808) 565-3868 E-MAIL reservations@lanai-resorts.com WEB SITE www.lanai-resorts.com, Lanai Company Inc., PO Box 310, Lanai City, HI 96763. The concierge desks serve as tourist information bureaus for visitors. A shuttle runs from early morning to late night between the Manele Bay Hotel, Lanai City, and the Lodge at Koele; there is no public transportation. Van service is provided to the Manele Bay small boat harbor for a fee, and can be

arranged through the hotels. Private transportation is available through **Rabaca's Limousine** ((808) 565-6670.

WHAT TO SEE AND DO

Most of the residents of Lanai live in or around **Lanai City**, seven miles (11 km) north of Manele Bay in the central highlands. While the sun shines at the beach, the city is often shrouded in a fine, cool mist. Though hardly bustling, the town center has all the necessities one requires—a library, post office, bank, gas station and several small shops. You can easily meander through town in an hour or two, though you may end up in conversations that last much of the day. Many of the businesses around the central Dole Park are housed in older, plantation-style buildings; modern architecture would be totally out of place. Street addresses are shunned as well. Nearly everyone has a post office box, and locals see little reason to bother with street numbers, or even names.

Dole park is bordered by Seventh and Eighth streets on its longest sides, and Lanai and Frasier avenues on the shorter. The **Lanai Theatre** ((808) 565-7500 anchors the intersection of Seventh and Lanai and presents first-run movies. Also on Seventh is the **Lanai Arts and Culture Center** ((808) 565-7503 showcasing local arts and crafts and housing two restaurants. **Gifts with Aloha** ((808) 565-6589, 363 Seventh Street, is packed with locally made jellies and jams, wood carvings and ceramics, along with books, resort wear, straw hats, greeting cards and all manner of unusual treasures.

Eighth Street's businesses meet the daily needs of islanders; a scan through the merchandise provides insight into life on Lanai. Small markets are stocked with Asian and Hawaiian specialties from smoked squid legs to frozen green mussels. The **Pine Isle Market** ((808) 565-6488 displays a curious jumble of fishing gear, tackle boxes, televisions and groceries. **Richard's Shopping Center** ((808) 565-6047 adds camouflage hunter's clothing and hardware to the mix, while **Akamai Trading Company** ((808) 565-6587 serves as the town's espresso bar, ice-cream stand and used-clothing shop. Herbal teas and trail mix and other supplies for the healthy traveler are sold at **Pele's Garden** ((808) 565-9629 right behind **Pele's Other Garden** ((808) 565-9629 health-food deli. Some of these shops close for lunch from noon to 1:30 PM. Two banks, two restaurants and the police station (complete with a small wooden shack that serves as the jail) finish up the town's offerings. The Lanai Company, which literally owns the island, tries to support this spirit of entrepreneurship among the local people. Chain stores and restaurants are taboo.

Exploring beyond Lanai City is best accomplished in a four-wheel-drive vehicle able to handle the island's rutted (and often muddy) trails. Though the island is only 13 miles (21 km) long and 18 miles (29 km) wide, it can take several days to explore its geographic and archaeological wonders. Jeep rentals are available from the only gas station, **Lanai City Service** ((808) 565-7227 TOLL-FREE (800) 533-7808 FAX (808) 565-7087. They also have a few cars available for rent, but they're hardly worth the expense since the hotel shuttle reaches most places along the paved roads. Be sure to pay attention to the instructions on using four-wheel drive — if you're much of an adventurer you're likely to get stuck in sand or mud at least once.

When you have wheels, all of Lanai's attributes are within reach. The rental company provides drivers with a valuable guide to the most important attractions; reaching most involves a slow bumpy ride up mountains rising to 4,000 ft (1,427 m) above sea level. Polihua Road runs northwest from the Koele through the center of the island to the **Kanepuu Reserve** where the Nature Conservancy protects native Hawaiian plants. A hiking trail leads through a small part of the 590-acre (239-hectare) native dryland forest, home to rare sandalwood trees. The road continues on to **Garden of the Gods**, an area of eerie rock pinnacles, canyons, boulders and buttes, seven miles (11 km) from Lanai City. The red earth looks as though it has been seared, tumbled and molded by unseen, powerful hands. At sunrise or sunset, the stones glow in tones of amber and canyons leading to the blue Pacific turn a deep reddish gold. A side trail off Polihua Road leads to **Shipwreck Beach**, a favorite haunt for escapists and beachcombers. The beach gets its name from a World War II liberty ship stuck on offshore reefs, and it faces Molokai and the deep Kalohi Channel. All sorts of debris washes ashore here, including driftwood and colored Japanese glass buoys. Branching east from Shipwreck Beach, a dirt road meanders along the coast past isolated beaches to the site of what was once the Maunalei Sugar Company. All that remains of the little village of **Keomuku** is its old Hawaiian church and a grove of coconut palms.

The 8.8-mile-long (14.1-km) **Munro Trail** rises east of Lanai City with a crest of tall Cook Island pines standing like sentinels atop stark mountains. Legend has it the pines were planted to tickle the clouds and bring rain to the pineapple fields. The trees, planted in the early 1900s at the behest of rancher George Munro, have become as much a logo for the island as the pineapple. Several lookouts along the trail offer amazing views of up to six other islands. The best is from **Lanaihale Summit** at 3,370 ft (1027 m). The trail also leads to **Hookio Ridge**, an ancient battlefield and the island's only fortifications.

Kaunolu Bay, southwest of town, is the site of King Kamehameha's summer residence, now one of the most complete archaeological sites in Hawaii. Kamehameha spent many summers here in the early 1800s, and archaeologists from the Bishop Museum have found evidence of an ancient Hawaiian settlement in **Kaunolu Archeological Interpretive Park** at the end of Kaunolu Trail. Signs mark the foundations of several *hales* (houses) and the **Halulu Heiau**, a place of worship. **Kahekili's Leap** at the sea's edge was a popular site for athletes and warriors practicing *lele kawa* (cliff jumping). Kamehameha's warriors are said to have tested their courage by sprinting down a narrow path and leaping more than 60 ft (18 m) into the sea after clearing a 15-ft (4.5-m) ledge which protrudes from the cliff's base.

Several petroglyphs have been discovered in **Luahiwa**, southeast of the city, though they're difficult to see. They're more visible when the sun is not directly overhead, and they consist of human forms and animals carved in stone. Most of the images date back to the seventeenth century.

Tour boats and ferries to Maui tie up in Manele Bay Harbor at the end of the paved road to the Manele Bay Hotel. The waters offshore are considered among Hawaii's best scuba diving spots, protected in the Manele-Hulopoe Marine Life Conservation Area. Lobster, octopus and tropical fish thrive in abundance in lava tubes and coral gardens. Concierges at the resort hotels can arrange dive and snorkel trips with the Maui-based **Trilogy Ocean Sports (** (808) 879-8811 TOLL-FREE (888) 628-4800 WEB SITE www.sailtrilogy.com. In the winter, whale-watching trips are available through Trilogy and **Spinning Dolphin Charters of Lanai (** (808) 565-6613. **Lanai EcoAdventure Service (** (808) 565-7737 offers kayak, snorkel and whale-watching tours; they also have mountain bike, jeep and hiking tours in the backcountry.

Other island diversions keep visitors busy. The **Stables at Koele (** (808) 565-4424 offers guided horseback rides on the wooded trails around the Lodge and in the countryside. Floating discs draw hunting enthusiasts to **Lanai Pine Sporting Clays (** (808) 563-4600, where targets are launched at 14 stations tucked in the woods. Golfers find plenty of challenges at the 18-hole **Experience at Koele (** (808) 565-4653 course designed by Greg Norman and the **Challenge at Manele (** (808) 565-2222 Jack Nicklaus course. Locals putt about on the nine-hole **Cavendish Golf Course**, while amateurs treat the 18-hole putting green in front of the Lodge at Koele like a miniature golf course. Hikers have over 100 miles (160 km) of unpaved trails to explore, with the promise of a soothing massage for sore muscles at Manele Bay's spa.

Lanai's **Visiting Artist Program (** (808) 548-3700 TOLL-FREE (800) 321-4666 is one of

the finest programs of culture and the arts in the islands. Introduced in 1993, the Visiting Artist Program brings nationally renowned writers, musicians, filmmakers, artists and chefs to the two resort hotels. Locals and visitors meet and mingle with the talent during performances, gourmet meals and informal chats in the hotels' libraries and lounges.

Some guests plan their visits to Lanai to coincide with a visiting artist. Schedules of upcoming appearances are available from the hotels. The list is an eclectic one, featuring writers Paul Theroux, Jane Smiley, Jay McInerney, and Anne Lamont; humorists Garrison Keillor and Dave Barry; pianists Andre Watts and Roger Taub; jazz singer Cleo Laine; Ensemble Galilei (performing Celtic chamber music); and Chef Alfred Portale of New York's Gotham Bar & Grill.

WHERE TO STAY AND EAT

Lanai's visitors have just three options for accommodations. The two main resorts are among the most expensive and luxurious in the islands, while the third is modest and comfortable. All three have great restaurants, and there are a couple of inexpensive dining options in town. Advance reservations are essential for the hotels and the more expensive dining rooms. **Camping** is allowed in the backcountry and by Manele Bay; call ((808) 565-3982 for information and reservations.

VERY EXPENSIVE

Unlike any other resort on the islands, the **Lodge at Koele** ((808) 565-7300 TOLL-FREE (800) 321-4666 FAX (808) 565-4561 WEB SITE www.lanai-resorts.com, Lanai Company Inc., PO Box 310, Lanai City, HI 96763, resembles an English country manor with Hawaiian overtones. Set amid banyans and pines 1,700 ft (500 m) above sea level in the island's cool highlands, the lodge is surrounded by gorgeous formal gardens and lawns. The grounds alone are worth exploration, from the croquet and lawn bowling courts to the greenhouse filled with rare orchids.

The Great Hall at the Lodge's front door is far more than a lobby. Sunlight streams through the slanted glass and timber ceiling onto Chinese antiques and plush couches arranged before two huge stone fireplaces. Hardwood floors and banisters, oriental carpets, and sprays of orchids add warmth to the massive room and the corridors leading to several sitting rooms filled with books and musical instruments. Four-poster beds with hand-carved pineapples at each corner are the focal point in the 102 rooms and suites, some with fireplaces.

The Lodge's **Formal Dining Room** (very expensive) is one of the finest restaurants on the islands, always at the top of best-restaurant lists. The cuisine is described as Pacific Rim or rustic American; the best starter is "marble" of *ahi* and snapper with radish, fennel and mustard seed. Fresh venison is usually in abundance on this island, and the

Formal Dining Room offers roasted venison with a *lilikoi* (passion-fruit) marinade. Rack of Colorado lamb is served with a goat cheese potato cake, pan-roasted Maine lobster sits atop English pea and morel risotto. As befits the name, the dining room exudes elegance; men are required to wear jackets here.

The setting is slightly less formal at the **Terrace Dining Room**, where breakfast selections include omelets filled with Japanese and Chinese vegetables accompanied by sausage made of Lanai axis deer meat, or sweet rice waffles with *lilikoi*-coconut chutney and warm Vermont maple syrup. For lunch you might want to start with fresh pineapple cider and dine on grilled pastrami of striped marlin served with pineapple salsa, or seared *ahi* (yellowfin tuna) on a bed of greens with cilantro dressing; fresh seafood and local game are featured at dinner. Afternoon tea replete with irresistible pastries is presented in the quiet Tea Room; salads and sandwiches are served alfresco at the **Experience at Koele Clubhouse** (moderate).

The **Manele Bay Hotel** ((808) 565-7700 TOLL-FREE (800) 321-4666 FAX (808) 565-3868 WEB SITE www.lanai-resorts.com, Lanai Company Inc., PO Box 310, Lanai City, HI 96763, opened in 1991 as a seaside counterpart to the Lodge. A shuttle runs between the two hotels, stopping in Lanai City enroute, and guests are able to sign tabs and use the facilities at both properties. Manele Bay Hotel sits on a slight rise above the beach; the 250 rooms, suites and villas all have private lanais with spectacular ocean or garden views, and are decorated in a tropical style with palms, floral fabrics, and original paintings. Like the Lodge, the hotel is filled with artwork. Wall-sized murals depicting ancient Hawaiian legends fill the lobby with color; paintings of island petroglyphs appear on hallway ceilings; elaborate stenciled paintings of starfish and birds wind around doorways and stairwells. Gardens with Asian themes, gazebos, bridges and koi ponds fill courtyards between the low-lying buildings with green-tile roofs. Hawaiian and Chinese artifacts are displayed in the public areas, and the library is stocked with history and nature volumes.

Boulders and sharp pinnacles lie in a jumble along the red earth of the Garden of the Gods.

A gravel trail leads from the hotel's swimming pool and lawns to **Hulopoe Beach**. Hulopoe was once a bustling Hawaiian fishing village where people worshipped native gods, and worked the land. Traces of an ancient past at Hulopoe are being carefully preserved. Nearby is the tomb of Pehe, and just offshore is the rocky islet of Puu Pehe, also known as Sweetheart Rock, which played a role in a bittersweet romantic legend. Snorkeling off the hotel beach is good when the water is calm; when it isn't, surfers ride the waves with aplomb.

There are several dining options at Manele Bay. **Ihilani** (very expensive), the hotel's signature restaurant, is designed in the style of a grand salon of the Hawaiian monarchy. Here, at linen-covered tables set with silver and crystal, diners sample veal loin with kalamata olives, vine-ripened tomatoes and anchovies, thyme-marinated salmon with leeks, or fresh *mahimahi* and other local fish made with French preparations. Men are asked to wear jackets at Ihilani, though on a typical evening diners sport everything from aloha shirts to tuxedos.

Patio tables overlook the pool at **Hulopoe Court** (expensive)—open for breakfast and dinner. Hawaiian regional cuisine is featured in dishes including fennel-cured salmon and green lentil salad, buckwheat pasta with vegetable vermicelli, tiger prawns in tangerine olive oil with garlic cloves and Italian parsley, and roast saddle of rabbit with porcini mushrooms, fava beans and olives. Fish sandwiches and bountiful Cobb salads are served at the **Pool Grille** (moderate); *pupus* and burgers top the menu at the Challenge at **Manele Bay Clubhouse** (moderate).

The **Spa at Manele Bay** serves as the island's best beauty salon. Guests have complementary use of the fitness studio and steam rooms, and massages are reasonably priced. Daily clinics and private lessons are available at the Tennis Club's six courts.

MODERATE

The **Hotel Lanai** ((808) 565-7211 TOLL-FREE (800) 795-7211 FAX (808) 565-6450 E-MAIL hotellanai@aloha.net, overlooks Lanai City from a slight rise above the park. Built in 1923

in the plantation style, the white wood hotel's 11 rooms have ceiling fans, hardwood floors, and comfy beds covered with Hawaiian quilts. A glass-enclosed lanai connects the rooms and provides a cozy sitting area for guests and locals visiting after work. The restaurant, **Henry Clay's Rotisserie**, fills the center dining room and patio. Dinner is served nightly with the menu featuring Maui onion soup, moist rotisserie chicken, local pâtés and Louisiana-style barbecued ribs. Locals and visitors enjoy sampling excellent, hearty dishes outside the resort hotels, and Henry Clay's is a favorite gathering spot.

INEXPENSIVE

Many locals begin their days with breakfast at the **Blue Ginger Café** ((808) 565-6363 in a blue and white cottage on Seventh Street. Omelets stuffed with Portuguese sausage, cheese and vegetables are served with white or fried rice and white toast; customers help themselves to coffee and share the newspapers and gossip with friends. Breakfast leads into lunches of saiman, burgers, and carne asada tacos; dinners feature local fish. The owners are building a larger dining room and bar next to the original restaurant to accompany their ever-growing following. A few doors away, **Tanigawa's** ((808) 565-6537 on Seventh Street is the island's version of a mainland diner serving burgers and noodle dishes.

HOW TO GET THERE

Lanai lies 50 miles (80 km) southeast of Honolulu and nine miles (just over 14 km) west of Maui, and is served by inter-island flights on **Island Air** ((808) 565-6744 TOLL-FREE (800) 652-6541 and **Hawaiian Air** ((808) 565-6977 TOLL-FREE (800) 652-6541. Daily ferry service between Maui's port at Lahaina and Lanai's Manele Bay boat harbor is provided by **Expeditions** ((808) 661-3756 TOLL-FREE (800) 695-2624.

Overlooking the stunning white-sand Hulopoe Beach from Manele Bay Hotel.

Hawaii: The Big Island

HAWAII, OR THE BIG ISLAND, is larger than all the other Hawaiian islands put together. It has the highest mountains, the most active volcanoes, an abundance of desert and lush rainforests. It even has snow, which during the winter months drapes the summits and shoulders of Mauna Kea and Mauna Loa.

This combination of fire and ice creates a wealth of astonishing scenery. Beaches with sand as soft and white as talcum powder contrast with beaches that are black or even green, all washed by waters so blue and clean as to look supernatural. Deep brown and

ebony lava fields provide a constant reminder of how this island was created and why it continues to grow.

The Big Island's magic lies in its contrasts. The east coast is very wet, with rampant vegetation and a riot of colorful flowers. The west coast is barren and dry. There are secluded tropical valleys where time has virtually stood still, mountain pastures reminiscent of Switzerland, and sprawling resorts that rank among the best in the world.

If you want to hike trails traversing lunar landscapes and rainforests draped in mist,

ABOVE: South Point, the windswept and sea-lashed southernmost point in the United States.
RIGHT: A hala tree clings to the barren earth of Lapakahi State Park.

plunge into the waters of a marine wonderland, or witness the dancing curtain of fire which only a volcano such as Kilauea can kick up, then you've come to the right place.

But it's not just the scenery and the drama of Kilauea that have made Hawaii famous. Because of the clarity of the skies above Mauna Kea, the mountain has become the center of an international astronomical research program. The island's perfect blend of soil conditions and the hot dry climate have enabled the Kona region on the west side of the island to produce high-quality macadamia nuts and some of the finest coffee in the world.

And here's one other remarkable fact about this island: over 90% of its native flora and fauna is found nowhere else on earth. Bearing in mind that this was once a barren island, the astounding diversity of life that now flourishes here is testimony to the force of evolution — and the tenacity of nature.

GENERAL INFORMATION

The **Big Island Visitors Bureau** ((808) 961-5797 TOLL-FREE (800) 648-2441 FAX (808) 961-2126 E-MAIL thinkbig@gte.net web site www .bigisland.org, is at 250 Keawe Street in Hilo. There is another office in Kona ((808) 329-7787 FAX (808) 326-7563 at 75-5719 West Alii Drive.

There are many free tourist information publications available throughout the island at racks positioned outside shops, restaurants and attractions. If you want to check your e-mail or just keep in touch with the folks back home, you can stop in at the cybercafé **Bytes & Bites** ((808) 935-3520 FAX (808) 935-4435 E-MAIL bytes1@hotmail.com, 223 Kilauea Avenue, in Hilo, which offers superfast connections and coffee.

GETTING AROUND

The Big Island lives up to its name. You need a car, unless you want to spend most of your vacation lying on the beach at your hotel. A few of the towns have trams, and taxis are readily available and expensive. Driving is easy and rewarding. The coastal roads are in good condition, well marked and rarely congested. It is a violation of most car rental

Hawaii: The Big Island

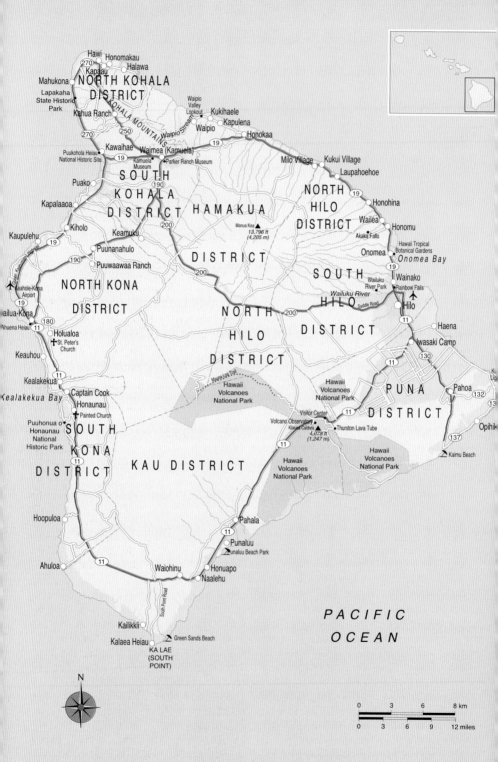

PACIFIC OCEAN

contracts to drive on secondary roads, so keep off the Saddle Road, which cuts through the center of the island. Public buses reach most important areas, though the rides can be lengthy; for schedules call ((808) 961-8744.

WHAT TO SEE AND DO

HILO

Hilo is a classic, laid-back tropical town where the tempo of life hasn't changed much in the last 50 years. The town has two main streets, Kilauea and Kinoole. Kilauea merges with Keawe Street and runs one way toward the Wailuku River. Kinoole runs one way away from the river and feeds into Kilauea creating a large loop. Running along the bay in front of the town is Kamehameha Avenue.

Hilo's cultural highlights can be toured in a few hours. To get a good insight into the Big Island's multi-cultural heritage, stop by the **Lyman Mission House Memorial Museum** ((808) 935-5021 E-MAIL lymanwks@ interpac.net, 276 Haili Street, which is housed in an early nineteenth-century house, built for the first Christian missionaries to arrive in Hilo. The havoc caused by the awesome *tsunami* (tidal waves) that struck in 1946 and 1960 are on display at **Pacific Tsunami Museum** ((808) 935-0926, 130 Kamehameha Avenue in downtown Hilo. The **East Hawaii Cultural Center** ((808) 961-5711, 141 Kalakaua Street in Hilo's historic old police station, directly across from Kalakaua Park, is the focal point of the Big Island's theater, dance, music and art. Call ahead and ask what's on when you're in town.

The daily **Suisan Fish Auction**, on Lihiwai Street, is the best free show in town. In a warehouse near the waterfront, restaurant chefs gather at around 7 AM to bid on the day's catch. It's a colorful ritual that has been going on in Hilo for generations and presents a sampling of island life. Local farmers and crafts persons set up stands under canvas on a lot bounded by Kamehameha and Mano streets every Wednesday and Saturday at the **Hilo Farmers' Market**. Here you can buy everything from arts and crafts to fresh fruit and vegetables, food products such as goat cheese, and a dazzling variety of cut flowers.

Beer aficionados may want to check out the **Mehana Brewing Company** ((808) 934-8211 E-MAIL ber@mehana.com WEBSITE www .mehana.com, 275 East Kawili Street, which is Hilo's first microbrewery; it has a tasting room and gift shop. Tours are available on request. If you are able to resist the sights and smells at **Big Island Candies** ((808) 935-8890, 585 Hinano Street, you are a stronger person than I am. Owner Alan Ikawa and his team will overwhelm your senses as you watch them make a large variety of cookies from local ingredients and premium chocolate, with no preservatives.

The Big Island is renowned for its orchids and anthuriums, and the best place to see them is at one of the many tropical gardens in and around the city. In Hilo check out the **Nani Mau Gardens** ((808) 959-3541, 421 Makalika Street.

Though the 80-ft (24-m) Rainbow Falls in the **Wailuku River Park**, along Waianuenue Avenue past Kaumana Drive, aren't as spectacular as those on Kauai, they're worth a visit while you're cruising in the area.

EASTERN HAWAII

Traveling north out of Hilo, take the scenic route off Highway 19 and you'll follow the tracks of a former sugar cane train through lush jungle, passing waterfalls and gorges on the way. You'll pass the former sugar port of **Onomea Bay** and the wonderful **Hawaii Tropical Botanical Garden** ((808) 964-5233 FAX (808) 964-1338 WEB SITE www.htbg.com, which I think is best visited early in the morning. Just after you return to the highway, take a left on Highway 220 to **Honomu**, an artists' colony. On the charmingly renovated main street you'll find coffee shops, cafés and galleries. Past the main street, follow the signs to **Akaka Falls State Park** and follow the paved route past the breathtaking 400-ft (122-m) Kahuna Falls and 420-ft (128-m) Akaka Falls — the tallest straight drop of water in the state.

Still on the east coast, but now south of Hilo, free samples of glorious macadamia nuts are offered in the visitors center at **Mauna Loa Macadamia Nut Factory and Orchards** ((808) 982-6562, 1 Macadamia Road, just five minutes south of Hilo on

Highway 11. It's really just a tourist trap but if you want a quick, one-stop selection of all kinds of macadamia nuts (from sour cream and onion to chocolate covered) it might be worth a visit.

Beyond that is the region of **Puna**. Since the Chain of Craters Road was closed in 1988 due to a lava flow, you can now only get to and from Puna on Highway 130. It's worth the detour just to see the small town of **Pahoa**, which seems to be well stuck in the 1960s, complete with flower children and the smell of incense filling the air.

Past Pahoa is the **Wood Valley Temple and Retreat Center** ((808) 928-8539. Just the most tranquil place imaginable, it is now a Tibetan Buddhist spiritual center.

Orchid fans may like to stop at the **Akatsuka Orchid Gardens** ((808) 967-8234, south on Highway 11, left past the 22-mile marker, in Volcano.

Tasting of local wines is offered at **Volcano Winery** ((808) 967-7479 WEB SITE www .volcanowinery.com, Pii Manua Drive, off Highway 11 at the 30-mile marker. One unique wine is made with 100% honey (no grapes), while more traditional varieties from grape and tropical fruit blends.

VOLCANOES NATIONAL PARK

Few sights are as awesome and overwhelming as Hawaii Volcanoes National Park ((808) 985-6000; 24-hour eruption report ((808) 967-7977. Located 29 miles (47 km) from Hilo off Highway 11, the park encompasses rainforests, steaming craters, fields of lava, and the only active volcano in a national park. Explore it leisurely. To rush through the park would be to miss out on an experience that could be the most memorable of your Hawaiian vacation.

Hawaiians past and present believe the fire goddess Pele rules all the volcanoes that formed the islands. These days, believers feel her presence in the cathedral-like silence of the vast, smoldering lava fields, sense her impatience in the hissing steam vents, and see her wrath in the sudden eruptions of the park's active volcano, Kilauea. Many leave offerings to appease the goddess, scattering flowers on her lava fields and leaving bottles of gin (her favorite beverage) beside lava

flows. Kilauea, about 4,078 ft (1,247m) in height, is on the southeast flank of Mauna Loa, but is a completely independent volcano. It has been almost continuously active since January 1983, with intermittent bursts of energy developing into a series of violent outbursts.

For the past several years, lava has poured out of Kilauea's Puuo'o vent in an orange and red river of fire, scorching the terrain and destroying all before it. In 1990, lava snaked its way towards the southern end of Chain of Craters Road, buried part of the road, then destroyed the picturesque little town of Kalapana and houses in some subdivisions, including Kalapana Gardens, Royal Gardens, and Kalapana Shores. Some residents reacted before the lava reached their properties, lifting entire houses onto trailers and transporting them away. But most had no choice but to watch in stoic silence, resigned to their fate, as lava crawled to the foot of houses, causing the timbers to explode in sheets of flame. Several tourist attractions were buried under the huge flows, including the famous Kaimu Black Sand Beach, which was completely covered over. At times, the lava surges toward the sea and seems to explode in a cloud of steam. Other times, it appears as a shimmering orange stream slithering through the blackened ground. No matter how many times one visits this park — box seat to one of nature's most magnificent shows — the sights inspire awe.

The national park encompasses 377 sq miles (610 sq km) of a seemingly extraterrestrial landscape fringed by forests and extraordinary plant life. A good portion of the land is inaccessible, but there are enough sights to fill at least one full day. I have found it is best to spend a night or two in the town of Volcano (see WHERE TO STAY, page 273) and tour the park at both dawn and dusk, when the roads are free of tour buses and a sense of solitude prevails.

Begin your tour at the Kilauea Visitor's Center just inside the park entrance. An exciting film of volcanic eruptions is shown throughout the day, and maps of the park and volcano-theme souvenirs are available for sale. Crater Rim Road circles the park's most accessible area and attractions, beginning with the stinking Sulfur Banks — one whiff and you know you're atop an active volcano. Nearby, clouds seem to form atop the ground at the Steam Vents, best seen in early morning. The Thomas A. Jaggar Museum at the edge of Halemaumau Crater, is packed with exhibits that explain the legend of Pele and the amazing force of volcanoes. Cool and tranquil, the Thurston Lava Tube is surrounded by rainforest and towering tree ferns. Steep stairs descend a hillside to what at first looks like a cave but is actually a long tunnel formed when magma flowed through a crust of hardened lava. Dripping with con-

certainly much less taxing, are the 3.6-mile (5.8-km) round-trip Mauna Iki Trail (Footprints Trail) across the Kau Desert, or the Halemaumau Trail into the Kilauea Caldera (6.4 miles or 10.2 km round trip). The pseudonym comes from the footprints embedded in lava by 80 fleeing warriors who were trapped by the 1790 eruption and died six miles (10 km) southwest of the summit. These warriors were returning to the Kau district to defend it from an attack by Kamehameha. Their death was seen as a sign that Pele favored Kamehameha, who ultimately

densation, the tube extends for a quarter-mile (just under half a kilometer) under the earth's surface. The most fascinating man-made attraction in the park is the Puu Loa Petroglyphs carved in stone. The human figures are filled with small holes formed by air pockets in the lava. The early Hawaiians placed their babies' umbilical cords in these holes to ensure good fortune.

The park has several hiking and walking trails. The most challenging is the 18-mile (29-km) hike to the summit of Mauna Loa. It can take two days to get there, but the rewards for those who make the effort are a feast of shapes and colors created by the intermingling of lava and snow, found nowhere else in the islands. No less fascinating, and

united and ruled the islands. Devastation Trail, with its sulfur banks, creates the illusion of a dead planet. It is a landscape of trees singed by the heat of a Kilauea eruption — bleak yet fascinating.

Every day, hundreds of visitors make their way down Chain of Craters Road, a spectacular drive across a landscape that reveals in detail the various eruptions that have occurred in the park. There are great lookout points over old craters and from atop the mountain down to the plains and ocean far below. The road ends abruptly after a run along the coast to a point where a recent flow surged across the road on its way to the ocean.

The rugged Halemaumau Trail.

From here it's a walk across the freshest lava on the island to a point where magma continues to tumble into the ocean, occasionally creating huge clouds of yellow-white steam. The sometimes swirling, often chocolate mousse-smooth lava is liberally laced with patterns of brilliant blue and gold crystals that glint in the hot sun. The smooth lava, called pahoehoe, has the appearance of dark chocolate fudge that has been smoothed out and then seemingly raked over with a fork. A'a is the rough-edged lava, which looks like coal slag and usually trails off into channels.

popular spot from which to view green sea turtles. Every year the turtles nest and lay their eggs in the sands on this beach; they are present most of the year. Beware of strong offshore currents if you swim here.

Situated in the Kau district, close to South Point Road is the town of **Waiohinu**, where author Mark Twain planted a monkeypod tree in 1866. Twain's tree was blown over in a 1957 storm, but a new tree has now sprouted from the original trunk.

The residential community of Oceanview is your landmark for the turnoff for **South**

Be careful when walking on either type, as air holes may have formed beneath a thin layer of lava — your foot could end up in a deep hole. If you happen to fall, the sharp a'a lava leaves nasty scratches and cuts. In nearly two decades, the lava from Kilauea has created several acres of new land on the Big Island.

WESTERN HAWAII

If you exit Hawaii Volcanoes National Park and join Highway 11 going west, you'll continue to drive through lava fields and scrub forest until you reach the **Punaluu Beach Park**. This stunning beach is composed mostly of lava rocks and black sand and is a

Point (**Ka Lae**), the southernmost tip of the United States, where the first Polynesians are said to have landed around AD 140. It's 11 miles (18 km) of rough riding from Highway 11 down a straight-as-an-arrow road to the ocean. On the way you'll pass a wind farm that generates electricity. Finally you'll reach the rugged cliffs and the ancient canoe mooring site carved out of the rock. The right fork in the road takes you to a favorite fishing spot where fishermen haul their catch up the cliff by rope. There's also a huge blowhole in the vicinity. The **Kalalea Heiau** is the other landmark of interest in this area.

East of South Point, you can park your car and hike to the **Green Sand Beach** (**Papakolea**), which gets its distinct color from a cinder cone of olivine that poured into the ocean. The large grains of this semiprecious mineral have a beautiful, glassy luster. This is one of the most exposed beaches in the world and is pounded by heavy seas and rough surf. Use extreme caution when swimming or surfing in this area.

Follow Highway 11 up the western coast to Highway 160, which begins with a swift descent to the coast and ends at **Puuhonua O Honaunau National Historic Park ℂ** (808) 328-2326, PO Box 129, Honaunau. When ancient Hawaiians broke a sacred law, or were on the run from an enemy, the system decreed that if they could reach a designated refuge, their lives would be spared. Puuhonua O Honaunau is one of the best examples of such a sanctuary.

Further along Puuhonua Road heading north, you'll come to **Kealakekua Bay**. It was here that explorer Captain Cook, the first European to land on the islands, dropped anchor. The Hawaiians heralded Cook as a reincarnation of the shark god Lono and greeted him with much respect. But an altercation on the beach led to Cook's untimely. Across the bay, a white marker indicates the site where Cook was slain.

Kealakekua Bay is one of the island's best scuba and snorkeling sites. You can jump in from the pier or take a boat to the area.

If you double back around Puuhonua Road, you'll come across the **Painted Church** that Father John Berchmans Velghe decorated with stories from the bible for the benefit of illiterate parishioners.

On Highway 11, between markers 111 and 112, you'll find the tiny **Kona Historical Society Museum ℂ** (808) 323-3222 FAX (808) 323-2398 WEB SITE www.ilhawaii.net/~khs, in the historic Greenwell Store in Captain Cook. Here you'll find a selection of everyday items from the last century.

COFFEE COUNTRY

Kona coffee is saluted around the world for its sweetness and intense aroma, and this is the area of its origin, starting from the town of Honaunau. Today coffee farms exist on a 15-mile (24-km) stretch of hill country above the coast, starting from the town of Honaunau all the way to Kailua-Kona.

A few of these coffee estates are open to the public for tours and/or sampling. These include **Bay View Farm ℂ** (808) 328-9658 TOLL-FREE (800) 662-5880 FAX (808) 328-8693 E-MAIL bayview@aloha.net WEB SITE www.bayview farmcoffees.com, on Painted Church Road, Honaunau; **Greenwell Farms Estate Coffee** ℂ (808) 322-2862 FAX (808) 323-2050 E-MAIL tomgr@aloha.net WEB SITE www.greenwell farms.com, on Highway 11, next to the Greenwell Historical Museum; and **Royal Kona Museum and Coffee Mill ℂ** (808) 328-2511 TOLL-FREE (800) 669-5633, 83-5427 Mamalahoa Highway. For more information on touring this area, pick up a free copy of *Coffee Country Driving Tour* from the Hawaii Visitors and Convention Bureau.

One of the fascinating little towns in the heart of coffee country is **Holualoa**, which sits above Kona along Highway 180. This former plantation town now has a seen-better-days charm, with great views of the ocean and the lava fields of the Kona-Kohala Coast. Holualoa has, in recent years, attracted a colony of artists and now has several galleries selling some of Hawaii's best woodwork and pottery. One of the older stores on the street is **Kimura Lauhala Store**, specializing in arts and crafts made from coconut fronds and the hala tree. In the heyday of sugar, this was the town's general store.

KONA

There is no way to dress it up. Kona is an in-your-face resort town, chock-full of hotels, restaurants, T-shirt shops and timeshare sales offices. Yet for all its garishness, no one can deny that the two-mile (three-kilometer) Alii Drive is a fun place to hang out.

In the days of the ancient Hawaiians, Kailua was more than a prominent fishing village and the seat of the government of Kamehameha the Great. Evidence of the royal past is to be found on the grounds of the **Hotel King Kamehameha**, at the beginning of Alii Drive. There is a compound of thatched-roof huts and fishponds, which has been declared a National Historical Monument, and the **Ahuena Heiau** from where

OPPOSITE: The summit of Mauna Kea.
OVERLEAF: Rainbow Falls, near Hilo.

Kamehameha ruled his kingdom during the last seven years of his reign. There is also a little museum in the hotel's mall.

Not far down Alii Drive is **Mokuaikaua Church** ((808) 329-1589, the first Christian church in the islands, built in 1836. Its lava-rock and coral structure have weathered the years well.

Across the street is the **Hulihee Palace** ((808) 329-1877, 75-5718 Alii Drive. Built in 1838 by the island's governor, John Adams Kuakini, the palace served as King David Kalakaua's summer residence through the 1880s. There are daily tours through this two-story building. And if you are lucky, you can catch young Hawaiian girls having hula lessons on the lawn outside.

St. Peter's Catholic Church, at Kahaluu was built in 1889 on the site of a *heiau*. It is also known as the little blue church, as blue is the dominant color both inside and outside. It has seating for a congregation of 26.

At Keahole-Kona International Airport is the **Ellison S. Onizuka Space Center** ((808) 329-3441 FAX (808) 326-9751. Dedicated to Big Island-born Ellison Onizuka who died in the *Challenger* space shuttle disaster, it houses some genuine moon rock and other memorabilia. There are also some fun interactive exhibits for the kids (big and small) to play with.

Technology geeks should make a point of visiting the **Natural Energy Laboratory of Hawaii Authority** ((808) 329-7341, one mile (about one and a half kilometers) south of the airport at 73-4460 Queen Kaahumanu Highway, at 10 AM on Thursdays. At this time they offer a free tour explaining how they are working towards their mission of "developing and diversifying the Hawaii economy by providing resources and facilities for energy and ocean-related research, education and commercial activities in an environmentally sound and culturally sensitive manner." It's more interesting than it sounds.

Motorbikes, from mopeds and scooters to big twin Harley Davidsons, are available to rent at **DJ's Rentals** ((808) 329-1700 TOLL-FREE (800) 993-4647 E-MAIL harleys@kona.net WEBSITE www.harleys.com, 75-5663 Palanai Road, across from the King Kamehameha Hotel.

KOHALA COAST

Ho'okamaha'o — something wondrous that takes on a new and more splendid form — is the word used to describe the northwest's Kohala Coast. Kohala is all that, and more. Once the playground of Hawaiian royalty, their legacy remains; you see it in the trails they carved, the fishponds they created for their pleasure, and the *heiaus* they built for worship and sacrifice.

If you land at Keahole-Kona International Airport in Kona and turn left going north up the coast, your route along Queen Kaahumanu Highway (Highway 19) will take you past seven exceptional resort hotels. These hotels occupy a stretch of coastline from eight miles (13 km) north of the airport to Kawaihae, 28 miles (45 km) further up the coast.

The most remarkable aspect about these resorts is that unless you saw a sign, you would never know they were there. Viewed from the highway, they blend discreetly with the landscape. Very little interrupts the magnificent expanses of lava fields, peppered with white-stone graffiti, and the variegated blue of the ocean.

The **Kalahuipuaa Fishponds** at the Mauna Lani Resort ((808) 885-6622 and the **Kuualii** and **Kahapapa Fishponds** at the Outrigger Waikoloa Beach Resort ((808) 886-6789 are wonderful examples of ancient fishponds, giving a clear indication of the aquaculture practiced by ancient Hawaiians.

The largest concentration of ancient petroglyphs in the Pacific — more than 3,000 — are found in the **Puako Petroglyph Archaeological Preserve**, which is situated near the Manua Lani resort. Within **Puukohola Heiau National Historic Site** near Kawaihae Harbor, on Highway 270 is the Temple on the Hill of the Whale, one of the last major sacred structures constructed in Hawaii before outside influences reached the islands. It was built by Kamehameha I in 1790–1791 with mortarless stone. A prophet told him that if he did this, he would conquer and unite the islands. The prophecy came true in 1810, through conquest and treaties.

Giant wooden idols stand watch at Puuhonua O Honaunau, the City of Refuge.

Mauna Kea Divers ((808) 882-1477 E-MAIL mkdivers@interpac.net WEB SITE www .maunakeadivers.com, is a one-stop source of a range of watersport activities — from scuba to snorkeling, fishing charters, whale watching and the like. All trips depart from Kawaihae Harbor.

NORTH KOHALA

Leaving luxury behind, you rejoin the workaday world on Queen Kaahumanu Highway.

Kawaihae, once an important harbor for Big Island cattle and later for the sugar industry, lapsed into neglect when the industry declined. But now as tourist traffic through the town grows, drawn by the beauty of the North Kohala District, a few interesting shops and restaurants are sprouting up.

Enjoy the panoramas of rolling pastures and ocean as you climb the rise past Kawaihae, and keep a lookout for **Lapakahi State Historic Park (** (808) 889-5566, Highway 270, Mahukona, a fishing village preserved as it was 600 years ago. Park your car at the top of the village, pick up a brochure at the gate, and walk its trails, reflecting on the lives of the people who lived here.

Picnic and camping grounds abound in this area. One of the best is at **Keokea Beach Park**, which will evoke memories of the Monterey Bay Peninsula for those who know that corner of California. Ocean breakers thunder into caves carved in the cliffs below well-forested bluffs, and the entire area of North Kohala is punctuated by waterfalls, forests, and pretty streams. Tiny wooden churches and small communities dot the area.

The **Original King Kamehameha Statue** is now guarding a senior citizens center, housed in the New England-style courthouse on Highway 270 in the town of Kapaau. The eight-and-a-half-foot (two-and-a-half-meter) bronze statue by Thomas R. Gould was cast in Europe in 1880 but was lost at sea and was not placed at this site until 1912. King Kamehameha ruled Hawaii from 1810 to 1819. (It is the replica of this statue opposite Iolani Palace in Honolulu that most visitors see and photograph.)

WAIMEA AND MAUNA KEA

Waimea is no ordinary mountain town. It has prospered because of the Parker Ranch, a property developed by John Palmer Parker, a ship's clerk from Massachusetts who is said to have jumped ship in 1809 in the harbor at Kawaihae.

As his herds of cattle and horses grew, Parker brought in Native American, Mexican and Spanish cowboys to work the ranch. The Hawaiians who were also recruited

Parker Ranch **Visitor's Center** ((808) 885-7655 is in the Parker Ranch Shopping Center and houses the Parker Ranch Museum, which has items that have been used on the ranch throughout its history. There is also a Parker family tree and a video of daily ranch life.

Half a mile (just under a kilometer) out of Waimea on Highway 190 going towards Kailua are the old Parker houses, Puupelu and the Mana House. About 500 yards (455 m) from these historic houses is **Paniolo Park** ((808) 885-7655, where every July 4 the

quickly adopted the trappings of the cowboys — the bandannas, ponchos and lassos — and called themselves *paniolos*, after *españoles*, Spaniards. A free brochure on Big Island's *paniolo* history and present day activities can be obtained from the Hawaii Island Economic Development Board ((808) 966-5416 FAX (808) 966-6792 WEB SITE www .rodeohawaii.com, 200 Kanoelehua Avenue, Suite 103, Hilo.

Today, **Parker Ranch** sprawls over 227,000 acres (about 92,000 hectares), the largest privately owned ranch in the United States. Some 50,000 head of cattle now graze these ranges. The name Parker is therefore much in evidence in the town of Waimea (sometimes referred to as Kamuela). The

Parker Ranch Rodeo takes place (see FESTIVE FLINGS, page 76 in YOUR CHOICE).

Today, the mist-draped town of Waimea has an air of affluence, much of it brought about by a group of mainland artists who discovered it and came to stay. They transformed this farming town into a charming enclave where antique shops, art galleries and excellent restaurants rub shoulders with feed and grain stores and shops selling fresh farming produce.

Kamuela Museum ((808) 885-4724, at Waimea-Kamuela junction, has an interest-

OPPOSITE: Rich and colorful tropical foliage surrounds the spectacular Akaka Falls not far from Hilo. ABOVE: Old West-style stores line the streets of Hawi, North Kohala. OVERLEAF: Cattle dot the green expanse of the Parker Ranch lands.

ing private collection of royal Hawaiian artifacts and other treasures from around the world.

At an elevation of over 13,000 ft (over 3,960 m), 11 nations have set up enormous telescopes on the top of the Big Island's tallest peak — **Mauna Kea** — to peer into the heavens, and are currently rewriting the theory of the cosmos as we know it (see WINDOW TO THE HEAVENS, page 19 in TOP SPOTS). Mauna Kea is considered the world's best astronomical observation point, as it is near the equator, offers pollution-free skies and has little or no interference from urban light. To get to the true summit one must walk a few hundred yards up a narrow footpath to a cairn of rocks. At this altitude it's hard to make the short trip, but words cannot explain the 360-degree view that rewards you.

At 9,300 ft (2,835 m) there is the **Onizuka Center for International Astronomy** ((808) 961-2190 (for programs) or (808) 969-3218 (for weather), which has a lecture and stargazing (usually on Thursday, Friday, Saturday and Sunday nights). If you are going to visit the summit at night, dress warmly and take plenty of liquids. Altitude sickness is a very real possibility if you don't take the necessary precautions. As car rental companies don't want you taking anything but four-wheel-drives up to the summit, its best to take a tour (see TOURS, below).

A model of the world's largest telescope (which is on the top of Manua Kea) can be found at **Keck Observatory** ((808) 885-7887, 65-1120 Highway 19.

HONOKAA

Honokaa, founded by Chinese immigrant labor, is a charming old town of quaint and colorful timber-framed stores on wooden boardwalks along Mamane Street. Once the town's economy depended on the Hamakua Sugar Company, but since the plantation shut down, the town has spruced up to attract more tourists.

The **Honokaa People's Theater**, built in 1930, has been restored over the last decade and has become the focal point for a Hawaiian music festival. Organizers are hoping it will become an annual event to support the town's Western week (usually held the last

week of May), the high point of which is the rodeo. There are plenty of little gift and antique stores in this town, but the **Hawaiian Shop** of the venerable James Rice is definitely worth browsing. It's a sort of musty treasure trove, with items from all over the world.

WAIPIO VALLEY

Leave Highway 19 at this point, and branch left onto Highway 240, which will take you past the town of Kapulena to the Waipio Lookout. From this vantage point you get your first view of the legendary valley where King Kamehameha the Great lived until he was 15 years old.

It isn't merely the history of Waipio that makes it worth visiting. It is one of those idyllic, secret valleys for which the Hawaiian chain is so famous.

Tucked deep in the furthest recesses of a horseshoe-shaped canyon are the 2,000-ft (610-m) twin falls of **Hiilawe**, the tallest in the Big Island. The waters of Hiilawe feed a crystalline pool — refreshing on hot, humid days when clothes cling to the body, as they often do in this valley.

Waipio Valley is a giant orchard. Guava, mango, mountain apple and java plum trees grow wild, and the air is alive with birdsong. A river meanders through the valley and spills out past the black sand beach into the ocean. The only way down into the valley is by four-wheel drive, traversing a steep one-lane road. If you don't want to risk the drive, take a tour (see TOURS, below).

THE HAMAKUA COAST

The drive from Honokaa to Hilo along further stretches of the Hamakua Coast offers more picture-book scenery. In springtime the hillsides and valleys in this area leap out at you, so rich are they in colors and textures. Waterfalls tumble over rocks polished by centuries of pounding. The roar of the falls on one side of the highway blends with the crash of waves on rocks on the other side.

A self-guided tour of the Hamakua Coast is a breeze armed with a copy of the *Hilo-Hamakua Heritage Coast Drive Guide* from the Hawaii Island Economic Development Board ((808) 966-5416 FAX (808) 966-6792 WEB

SITE www.rodeohawaii.com, 200 Kanoele-hua Avenue, Suite 103, Hilo.

TOURS

Helicopter tours from the Kona coast are offered by **Island Hoppers** ℂ (808) 969-2000 TOLL-FREE (800) 538-7590 FAX (808) 331-2079 E-MAIL info@fly-hawaii.com WEB SITE www.fly-hawaii.com, Kona Airport. Flights also depart from Hilo Airport.

Blue Hawaiian Helicopters ℂ (808) 961-5600 TOLL-FREE (800) 745-2583 WEBSITE www

.polyad.com will take you on a whirlwind one-day tour of the Big Island, among many others.

To explore the Waipio Valley, the guides and drivers of the **Waipio Valley Shuttle** ℂ (808) 775-7121, PO Box 5128, Kukuihaele, will be happy to take you on a tour of this verdant area, or just provide transportation in and out of the valley. **Waipio Valley Wagon Tours** ℂ (808) 775-9518 E-MAIL pwagon@aloha.net, PO Box 1340, Honokaa, will give you lots of information about the area aboard a mule-drawn wagon.

.bluehawaiian.com, is also based at Hilo International Airport, directly across from the first parking lot inside the main terminal, and offer three tours out of Hilo. They have been in operation for over 13 years and have been used in the filming of such films as *Jurassic Park*, *George of the Jungle* and *Six Days, Seven Nights*.

Or if you prefer to see the sights from a fixed-wing plane, try **Island Hoppers** ℂ (808) 969-2000 TOLL-FREE (800) 538-7590 FAX (808) 331-2079 E-MAIL info@fly-hawaii.com WEBSITE www.fly-hawaii.com. They are at gate 29 of Hilo Airport.

Polynesian Adventure Tours ℂ (808) 329-8088 TOLL-FREE (800) 622-3011 FAX (808) 531-1357 E-MAIL sales@polyad.com WEBSITE www

And for those who want a more sedentary trip, but still want to explore the area, **Waipio Rim Backroad Adventures** ℂ (808) 775-1122 has trips in a four-wheel drive to waterfalls, pools, vistas and historic sites. Don't let the word "adventures" put you off. This is no rough and tumble ride — just a drive through the countryside.

To get your bearings around the Kona Coast, as well as a cheap means of sightseeing transportation, a trip on the **Kona Coast Express** ℂ (808) 331-1582, King Kamehameha Hotel Lobby, is highly recommended. There are two routes: Kohala Coast to Waikoloa Resort and Kona Town, with about eight

Colorful Alii Drive in downtown Kailua-Kona.

stops on each. The fare includes an all day pass on their trolleys and buses, and you can also buy a combination, system-wide pass. They also have an express bus running between King Kamehameha Hotel and King's Shopping Center.

One of the larger scuba and snorkeling outfits is **Eco-Adventures** ((808) 329-7116 TOLL-FREE (800) 949-3483 FAX (808) 329-7091 E-MAIL ecodive@kona.net WEBSITE www.eco-adventure.com, King Kamehameha's Beach Hotel, Kailua-Kona. Among the various options they offer is a three-day Open Water

Certification and pretty scary night (manta ray) dives. They also book a range of other tours, from whale watching to hiking, fishing charters to golf packages.

Fair Wind ((808) 322-2788 TOLL-FREE (800) 677-9461 E-MAIL snorkel@fair-wind.com WEB SITE www.fair-wind.com, has fun snorkeling cruises from Keauhou Bay to Kealakekua Bay with scuba as an option. The 15-ft (four-and-a-half-meter) waterslide slide off the top deck of their catamaran, straight into the water, is worth the trip alone.

Body Glove Cruises ((808) 326-7122 TOLL-FREE (800) 551-8911 WEB SITE www.bodyglove hawaii.com, North Kona Shopping Center, is another outfit that offers snorkeling and dolphin/whale-watching cruises, but they go to Pawai Bay.

UFO Parasails ((808) 325-5836 E-MAIL ufomaui@mauigateway.com WEB SITE www.ufoparasail.com, will take you to 400 ft (122 m) for seven minutes or 800 ft (244 m) for 10 minutes, for bird's-eye views of the area.

Dolphin Discoveries ((808) 322-8000 E-MAIL dolphindiscoveries@aloha.net WEB SITE www.dolphindiscoveries.com, offers dolphin and whale-watch snorkeling tours in small, personal groups with certified naturalist guides.

Captain Zodiac ((808) 329-3199 FAX (808) 329-7590 E-MAIL seakona@interpac.net, PO Box 5612, Kailua-Kona, has two trips a day from Honokohau Marina on a 14-mile (22-km) trip to Kealakekua Bay, past sea caves, lava tubes and wildlife above and below the water.

Ocean Safaris ((808) 326-4699 TOLL-FREE (800) 326-4699 FAX (808) 322-3653 E-MAIL kayakhi@gte.net, PO Box 515, Kailua-Kona, rents open cockpit kayaks for self-guided tours. Guided tours also available.

Glass-bottom boat cruises are offered by **Kailua Bay Charter Co**. ((808) 324-1749 E-MAIL kbcc@gte.net WEB SITE www.home1 .gte.net/kbcc, PO Box 112, Holualoa. The boat takes up to 44 passengers and the crew will share much knowledge about Hawaii's fish and Kona lore.

If you want to explore the amazing underwater world off the Big Island, but scuba diving just doesn't appeal to you, **Atlantis Kona** TOLL-FREE (800) 548-6262 WEBSITE www .goatlantis.com/hawaii might be your answer. You'll descend 100 ft (over 30 m) in their 48-passenger submarine and will be taken over an 18,000-year-old, 25-acre (10-hectare) coral reef.

At **Hawaii Earth Guides** ((808) 324-1717 FAX (808) 324-1182 E-MAIL vbright@kona.net WEB SITE www.hawaiiearth.com, guide and naturalist Valerie Bright leads groups of three to seven people on "real hiking for fitness." Tours include a four-hour jaunt to 7,200-ft (2,195-m) elevation up Hualalai Mountain three times a week, past craters, wild animals and birds. The rest of the week she is available for custom hikes and four-wheel-drive adventures on private land to waterfalls, Akoakoa Point, Makalawena and the Mauna Kea Volcano summit. Valerie also offers Hawaii Adventure Spa for those who want to balance body, mind and spirit through a packaged vacation program that includes adventure fitness, yoga, meditation and massage.

Hawaii Forest and Trail ((808) 322-8881 TOLL-FREE (800) 464-1993 FAX (808) 322-8883 E-MAIL hitrail@aloha.net WEB SITE www

.hawaii-forest.com, 74-5035B Queen Kaahumanu Highway, Kailua-Kona, offers a range of "eco-friendly" tours. Excursions offered include bird watching, mule trails, cave adventures, hiking, working cattle ranch and a waterfall adventure where you walk behind the Kapoloa Falls about halfway down its 500-ft (152-m) cascade.

Kona Coast Cycling Tours ((808) 327-1133 FAX (808) 327-1144 E-MAIL bikeinfo@ cyclekona.com WEB SITE www.cyclekona .com, 691 Kuakini Highway, Kailua-Kona, is a new outfit offering van-supported road

tours, as well as mountain bike tours where you have to make it on your own.

Multi-sport kayaking and backpacking trips for a day or a week can be arranged with **Hawaii Pack and Paddle (** (808) 328-8911 E-MAIL gokayak@kona.net WEBSITE www .hawaiipackandpaddle.com, 87-3187 Honu Moe Road, Captain Cook.

For a tour where you won't see any tour buses and will benefit from the insight of a longtime Hawaii resident, take the horse-back-snorkeling tour offered by **King's Trail Rides (** (808) 323-2388 E-MAIL sales@ konacowboy.com WEB SITE www.kona cowboy.com, 15 miles south of Kailua-Kona on Highway 11 in Kealakekua. The tour takes you from a 1,000-ft (300-m) elevation down

the Kaawaloa Trail, past some amazing vistas, to the Captain Cook Monument and snorkeling at Kealakekua Bay. No riding experience is needed, but the trail gets quite rough at times.

Mauna Kea Summit Adventures ((808) 322-2366 offers experienced guides for their six-hour sunset stargazing tour to Mauna Kea summit. This is a trip not to be missed.

Watch the breathtaking spectacle of lava flowing into the ocean as well as dolphins, whales and flying fish by taking a cruise with **Kilauea Volcano Yacht Cruises (** (808) 935-5070, 111 Banyan Drive, Hilo.

SHOPPING

In Kona there are a few shopping centers where you will surely be able to pick up the required resort wear and souvenirs. Try **Keauhou Shopping Center (** (808) 322-3000 WEB SITE www.hawaiishopper.com, 78-6831 Alii Drive, has over 40 shops and restaurants, with free Keauhou Resort shuttle, or **Lanihau Center (** (808) 329-9333, 75-5595 Palani Road.

For a one-shop stop for souvenirs, from exotic wood to jewelry, hats and more, check out **Kealakekua's Grass Shack (** (808) 323-2877, Kealakekua, Kona.

Beyond the hotel lobbies, the best place to shop in Kohala is **Kings' Shops (** (808) 886-8811, in the Waikoloa Beach Resort. Here you'll find a full-blown shopping center with stores, restaurants, galleries and activity desks. To stock up on coffee, macadamia nuts and other souvenirs and food products, without paying tourist prices, visit **Waikoloa Village Market (** (808) 883-1088, Waikoloa Highlands Shopping center, about six miles (10 km) east of the Kohala Coast.

In the Hilo area, visit **Sig Zane Designs (** (808) 935-7077, 122 Kamehameha Avenue, a low-key store, packed with Hawaiian craft, woods, aloha wear, bed coverings and every-thing in between. Partner in this store is well-known hula master Nalani Kanaka'ole whose understanding and appreciation of Hawaiian arts and culture is obvious in the store's merchandise.

OPPOSITE: A cowboy at the Waikoloa Rodeo near resort areas on the Kona Coast. ABOVE: St. Benedict's Painted Church, in Kailua-Kona.

As soon as you have spent your first few days on the Big Island, there is little doubt you'll notice the logo for **Hilo Hattie** ((808) 961-3077, on the Kanoelehua Avenue in the Prince Kuhio Plaza, as they are an ubiquitous advertiser. Regardless, they are a good source for those vibrant island fashions (100 styles in 800 exclusive prints) as well as jewelry, souvenirs and foodstuff such as coffee and macadamia nuts. The staff will also teach you how to tie your sarong in 14 different ways! Just call for free transportation from all Hilo hotels.

But if you'd prefer to make your own creations, **Discount Fabric Warehouse** ((808) 935-1234, 933 Kanoelehua Street has the island's largest selection of fabric, including over 1,000 Hawaiian prints, all at warehouse prices.

For stylish, good quality T-shirts that will last far beond the first wash, visit **Crazy Shirts** WEB SITE www.crazyshirts.com, in the Kona Market Place and Waterfront Row.

If you want to take home some of Hawaii's most beautiful flowers, in the form of a lei, tropical arrangement or orchid spray, drop by **Flowers of Hawaii** ((808) 959-5858 FAX (808) 959-2121. They have been around since 1946 and will ship for you.

If wood is more to your taste, **Winkler Wood Products** ((808) 961-6411 E-MAIL winkler@interpac.net WEBSITE www.interpac .net/-winkler, 261 Kekuanaoa Street, has exquisite koa and native hardwood items.

The original **Black Pearl Gallery** ((808) 935-8556 is in Hilo on the bayfront on Kamehameha Avenue. Here you'll find one of the largest collections of certified Tahitian pearls in the world.

Visit the home workshop **Ukuleles by Kawika Inc.** ((808) 969-7751 E-MAIL kawika@ ilhawaii.net, 1626 Kino'ole Street, for a fascinating insight into how these instruments are still being handmade. While there, don't miss taking a peak at their collection of antique ukuleles.

While waiting to set off on your tour of Waipio Valley, look inside **Waipio Valley Artworks** ((808) 775-0958 TOLL-FREE (800) 492-4746, Kukuihaele, a mile (a kilometer and a half) from Waipio Valley. You'll discover a little Aladdin's cave of a gallery that sells the works of some of the most talented artists in the island chain. The selection of wood here is spectacular.

SPORTS

Kayaking, sailing, scuba, snorkeling tours, instructions and rentals are available at Aquatic Perceptions ((808) 933-1228, 111 Banyan Drive, Hilo.

Scuba charters along the eastern Hawaii coastline, as well as four-day certification classes, kayak and boogie board rentals, are offered by Nautilus Dive Center (/FAX (808) 935-6939, 382 Kamehameha Avenue, Hilo. They've been around forever and really know the area.

Mauna Lani Sea Adventures ((808) 885-7883, at the boathouse at the Mauna Lani Bay Hotel, Kohala, can arrange a number of sailing, snorkeling and scuba adventures.

Surfing lessons, as well as scuba instructions and hiking trips can be booked though Ocean Eco Tours ((808) 937-0494 E-MAIL info@oceanecotours.com WEB SITE www .oceanecotours.com, PO Box 652, Kailua-Kona.

Scuba lessons and dives are also offered by Kona Coast Divers ((808) 329-8802 WEB SITE www.konacoastdivers.com, 74-5614 Palani Road, Kailua-Kona, and Sandwich Isle Divers ((808) 329-9188 FAX (808) 326-5652, 75-57921 Alii Drive, Kailua-Kona.

The Kohala Mountain Kayak Cruise ((808) 889-6922 FAX (808) 889-6944 WEB SITE www .kohala.net/kayak has guided tours in double-hulled, inflatable kayaks through the Kohala Sugar Plantation irrigation system, followed by a swim in a waterfall-fed mountain pool. For some, this two-and-a-half-hour "cruise" gets just plain boring, but others find it fascinating just sitting back and enjoying the ride and the lore imparted by the guides.

For the **fishing** enthusiasts in the group, Captain Ronne Grabowiecki ((808) 329-4025 FAX (808) 331-8159 E-MAIL ronho@kona.net will customize a half- or full-day sport-fishing trip just for you, aboard his fully-equipped 34-ft (10-m) Hatteras, *Dorado II*. Captain Bob's Kona Coast Fishing (/FAX (808) 322-7815 E-MAIL captbobs@gte.net, Kailua-Kona, has over 20 boats in four classes to fit all your fishing needs. Bottom Fishing Hawaii ((808) 329-4900, PO Box 821, Kailua-Kona, is a family-owned business that caters to people who aren't really interested in Blue Marlin fishing and would rather go after *aku*, *ono* and *mahimahi*.

The Naniloa Country Club ((808) 935-3000, 120 Banyan Drive, Hilo, is set in the middle of town and, with its narrow fairways and small greens, offers a very challenging nine-hole **golf** course. The Hilo Municipal Golf Course ((808) 959-7711, 340 Haihai Street, Hilo 96720, is just three miles (just

under five kilometers) from Hilo airport. This lush course is easily walked.

The Kona coast offers two golf courses: the Alii Country Club ((808) 322-2595, which has wonderful coastal vistas, and the Billy Bell-designed, Kona Country Club ((808) 322-2595, within the Keauhou Resort.

There are nine golf courses to choose from in the Kohala area. Among the best are the Jack Nicklaus-designed Hualalai ((808) 325-8480; the Waikoloa Beach ((808) 886-6060; with its stunning views; the North and South Courses at the Mauna Lani Resort ((808) 885-6655, which sit on lava flows from two different geological ages; and the world-famous Mauna Kea Beach ((808) 882-5400 (see SPORTING SPREE, page 42 in YOUR CHOICE).

Hamakua Country Club ((808) 775-7244, Highway 19, Honokaa, is worth a visit for novelty value alone. This nine-hole golf course was built in the 1920s on a very steep hill with holes crisscrossing fairways to fit them all into the limited land space. This is probably the cheapest round of golf you'll find on the island, open to nonmembers on weekdays.

Offering **horseback riding**, Mauna Kea Resort Stables ((808) 885-4288 FAX (808) 885-4288, 62-100 Mauna Kea Drive, will take you on open range riding on the spectacular Parker Ranch, and Kohala Naalapa Stables ((808) 885-0022, Highway 250 at mile marker 11, has unforgettable rides into Kahua and Kohala ranches. Kohala Naalapa Trail Rides ((808) 889-0022 E-MAIL pwagon @aoloha.net, Honokaa, offers an impressive horseback ride on a working cattle and sheep ranch.

Waipio on Horseback ((808) 775-7291, Honokaa, will take you on a trail ride on Mooiki Ranch, while Waipio Naalapa Trail Rides ((808) 775-0419 E-MAIL pwagon@ aloha.net, Honokaa, will give you a fully narrated horseback tour of the surrounding lush area. Waipio Naalapa tours leave from the Waipio Artworks, a mile (a kilometer and a half) from Waipio Valley.

Hawaii Horse Owners Association ((808) 959-8932, 591 Alawaena Street, Hilo, arranges fun family trail rides and campouts. Paniolo Riding Adventures ((808) 889-5354 E-MAIL pwagon@aoloha.net, mile marker 13.2 on Highway 250, Honokaa, offers open range horseback riding on an working cattle ranch on Kohala Mountains as well as ATV (all terrain vehicles) rides — the modern cowboy's horse.

Promoting **biking**, the Big Island Mountain Bike Association ((808) 961-4452 WEB SITE www.interpac.net/~mtbike, Hilo, is a nonprofit organization. Contact them for information on how you can get going on two wheels.

Mauna Kea Mountain Bikes Inc. ((808) 883-0130 TOLL-FREE (888) 682-8687 E-MAIL mtbtour@aol.com, Kamuela, offers tours for all level of mountain bike riders, including the advanced Mauna Kea Kamakaze, which

Petroglyph field on the edge of the Sheraton Waikoloa Golf Course.

starts at 13,796 ft (4,205 m) and features a 7,276-ft (2,218-m) descent in just 13 miles (21 km).

If **hiking** is more your speed, Arnott's Hiking Adventures ((808) 969-7097 FAX (808) 961-9638 E-MAIL info@arnottslodge.com WEB SITE www.arnottslodge.com, 98 Apapane Road, will take you off the beaten path where no bus tours go. Tours offered include Puna, Mauna Kea and Hilo Waterfalls.

Leaving from Waipio Artworks are hiking tours by Hawaiian Walkways ((808) 775-0372 TOLL-FREE (800) 457-7759 E-MAIL hiwalk@ aloha.net WEBSITE www.hawaiianwalkways .com, on the Waipio Rim Trail and Parker Ranch, to the Kilauea Volcano as well as custom trips. For more information on hiking on the Big Island, see THE GREAT OUTDOORS, page 32 in YOUR CHOICE.

For those of you who don't have a **tennis** court at your hotel, contact the Big Island Tennis Academy ((808) 324-7072 TOLL-FREE (888) 386-5662, 78-7190 Kaleopapa Road, Kailua-Kona for private and semiprivate lessons.

Half- and full-day **hunting** trips on historic Hawaiian ranch land are arranged by Kealia Ranch ((808) 328-8777 E-MAIL McCandless@panworld.net WEB SITE www .kealiaranch.com, 86-4181 Mamalahoa Highway, Captain Cook.

WHERE TO STAY

HILO AND ENVIRONS

Expensive

You can experience the gracious elegance of Old Hawaii at the **Shipman House Bed and Breakfast** (/FAX (808) 934-8002 TOLL-FREE (800) 627-8447 E-MAIL bighouse@ bigisland.com WEB SITE www.hilo-hawaii .com, 131 Kaiulani Street, Hilo. You can choose to stay in the main house, which is a 1899 National Register mansion, or in the guesthouse with its private entrance. Either way, hosts Barbara Ann and Gary Anderson will go all out to ensure you enjoy the five surrounding acres (two hectares), oversized tubs, porch rockers and stunning views. This inn is almost a museum and is perhaps one of the most unusual bed and breakfasts on the island.

Moderate

Nestled in Hilo Bay is the **Hilo Hawaiian Hotel** ((808) 591-2235 TOLL-FREE (800) 363-9524 FAX (800) 477-2329 E-MAIL terry@catle-group.com WEBSITE www.castle-group.com, 71 Banyan Drive, Hilo. Built in 1974 and renovated in 1992, it has 286 well-appointed rooms and a swimming pool, and is within walking distance of the town, with its parks, golf courses and shopping center.

The oceanfront **Hawaii Naniloa Resort** ((808) 969-3333 TOLL-FREE (800) 367-5360 FAX (808) 969-6622 E-MAIL hinan@aloha.net WEB SITE www.naniloa.com, 93 Banyan Drive, Hilo, features two swimming pools, a golf driving range, a well-equipped fitness center, and seaside dining and entertainment. With 325 rooms, the Naniloa is the largest hotel on this side of the island.

Inexpensive

Ironwood House (/FAX (808) 934-8855 TOLL-FREE (888) 334-8855 E-MAIL ironwd@aloha.net WEBSITE www.wwte.com/hawaii/ironwood .htm, 2262 Kalanianaole Avenue, Hilo, offers three rooms in a 1939 country home, just 300 ft (about 90 m) from Richardson Beach. The inn is chock-full of hand-blown glass, handmade tiles and other artistic touches. **Dolphin Bay Hotel** ((808) 935-1466 E-MAIL johnhilo @gte.net WEBSITE www.dolphinbayhilo.com, 333 Iliahi Street, Hilo, has 18 clean apartments in a quiet garden setting.

Overlooking Hilo Bay, in a quiet, lush setting, just a two-minute walk from downtown Hilo, is the **Bay House** (/FAX (808) 961-6311 E-MAIL Bayhouse@interpac.net, 42 Pukihae Street, Hilo. This bed and breakfast has spacious rooms with ceiling fans, private baths and ocean-view lanai.

The **Inn at Kulaniapia** ((808) 966-6373 TOLL-FREE (888) 838-6373 FAX (808) 968-7580 E-MAIL waterfall@prodigy.net WEBSITE www .waterfall.net, Hilo, is a purpose-built bed and breakfast with four units on 22 acres (nine hectares) with a 120-ft (over 36-m) waterfall and a swimming pond, gardens and biking trails.

Thirteen miles (21 km) north of Hilo on Highway 220 in the old plantation community of Honomu Village, you'll find the delightful **Akaka Falls Inn** ((808) 963-5468 FAX (808) 963-6353 E-MAIL akakainn@gte.net, on the main street in the 1923 Akita Building. Host Sonia Martinez is a cooking-school professional, so you can be assured of the very best homemade pastries in the included continental breakfast. The bed and breakfast offers a vacation/cooking school package.

There are also a number of alternatives for backpackers in Hilo (see BACKPACKING, page 52 in YOUR CHOICE).

VOLCANOES NATIONAL PARK AND ENVIRONS

One hotel, several excellent inns and some great bed-and-breakfast establishments are available within or in close proximity to Hawaii Volcanoes National Park.

Expensive

Chalet Kilauea ((808) 967-7786 TOLL-FREE (800) 937-7786 FAX (808) 967-8660 or (800) 577-1849 E-MAIL Reservations@Volcano-Hawaii .com WEB SITE www.volcano-hawaii.com, Wright Road, Volcano Village, was the first AAA three-diamond inn in Hawaii. While it may be a little formal for some, other guests revel in the inn's theme rooms with marble bathrooms and personalized service, and packed with treasures from all over the world. Candlelight gourmet breakfast and fireside afternoon tea are offered.

Moderate

It began as a grass hut built on the crater rim by a sugar planter in 1846. If you wanted to spend the night in this shelter, the owner charged you a dollar. Today the **Volcano House (** (808) 967-7321 FAX (808) 967-8429, PO Box 53, Hawaii Volcanoes National Park, occupies this site. It has played host to kings, queens and writers such as Mark Twain. This hotel has the warm atmosphere of a large inn. It's perched on the lip of Kilauea Caldera providing some of the most dramatic views of the great crater. The rooms are cozy and well appointed. The main lobby has a huge fireplace that is always lit, where you can kick back, read or enjoy a drink on those cold, misty evenings.

Kilauea Lodge ((808) 967-7366 FAX (808) 967-7367 E-MAIL k-lodge@aloha.net WEB SITE www.planet-hawaii.com/k-lodge, Volcano, is only a mile (kilometer and a half) from the park entrance. Spacious, beautifully appointed rooms (six with fireplaces) with attached baths, Hawaiian country furnishings, and native art make the lodge a slice of heaven in the midst of one of nature's most spectacular settings.

There are nine units between the main house and the cottages at **Carson's Volcano Cottages (** (808) 967-7683 TOLL-FREE (800) 845-5282 FAX (808) 967-8094 E-MAIL carsons@ aloha.net WEB SITE www.carsonscottages .com, Maunaloa Estate, Volcano, some with wood-burning stoves and private hot tubs.

All exude tranquillity and privacy. Full breakfast is served fireside in the main dining room.

Inexpensive

Between Hilo and Volcanoes Park is **Mountain View Bed and Breakfast (** (808) 968-6868 TOLL-FREE (888) 698-9896 FAX (808) 968-7017 E-MAIL info@bbmtview.com WEB SITE www .bbmtview.com, 18-3717 South Kulani Road, Mountain View. Jane and Linus Chao, famous silk and watercolor artists, own this beautiful estate with a custom-designed 10,000-sq-ft (929-sq-m) fishpond. You'll find their paintings throughout the four bedrooms and common areas. The breakfast is

Lava eruption and fire pit of Kilauea Caldera, Volcanoes National Park.

amazing here, enough delicious hot food to set you up for the whole day.

The brick-red color of the historic Dillingham summer estate buildings and the surrounding lush gardens makes for a startling first impression at **Hale Ohia Cottages** ((808) 967-7986 TOLL-FREE (800) 455-3803 FAX (808) 967-8610 E-MAIL haleohia.com WEB SITE www.haleohia.com, Volcano Village. This charming and romantic hideaway, one mile (a kilometer and a half) from the park, offers suites and cottages from one to three bedrooms and has a small hot tub in the garden. One word of caution, you go here for the atmosphere, not the food, as the breakfasts are very basic.

Another inn, just a mile (a kilometer and a half) from the park, is **Volcano Country Cottages** ((808) 967-7960 TOLL-FREE (800) 967-7960, Volcano. Nestled among huge ancient trees on the grounds of one of Volcano's oldest family residences, the Artist's House and Ohelo Berry Cottage are comfortable and well-appointed. Expect a rate surcharge on stays of fewer than two nights.

The **Volcano Inn** ((808) 967-7293 TOLL-FREE (800) 997-2292 FAX (808) 985-7349 E-MAIL volcano@volcanoinn.com WEB SITE www .volcanoinn.com, 19-3820 Old Volcano Highway, is another great bet if you are looking for absolute peace and quiet. All units have exposed beam ceilings and overlook a forest of tree ferns. Some rooms have full cooking facilities.

Holo Holo Inn provides a hostel alternative for Volcanoes (see BACKPACKING, page 52 in YOUR CHOICE) .

SOUTH POINT

Moderate
Macadamia Meadows Bed and Breakfast ((808) 929-8097 TOLL-FREE (888) 929-8118 FAX (808) 929-8097, 94-6263 Kamaoa Road, Naalehu, is located on a working macadamia nut farm. Each room in this delightful bed and breakfast has its own entrance, and guests can use the swimming pool and tennis court.

Inexpensive
Becky's Bed and Breakfast ((808) 929-9690 TOLL-FREE (800) 235-1233 FAX (808) 929-

9690 E-MAIL beckys@interpac.net WEB SITE www.1bb.com/Beckys, Naalehu, on Highway 11, offers three comfortable units in a 57-year-old plantation house with a spa in the backyard. Come morning, owners Dave and Patti serve up an all-you-can-eat hot breakfast.

KAILUA-KONA AREA

Moderate
Keauhou Beach Hotel ((808) 322-3441 TOLL-FREE (800) 321-2558 FAX (808) 922-8785 WEB SITE www.aston-hotels.com, 78-6740 Alii Drive, Kailua-Kona, was the Big Island's happening resort in the 1970s and is now enjoying a rebirth after a recent $15 million renovation. The hotel, with its great oceanfront location and lush gardens, has 311 rooms, six tennis courts, exercise room and traditional Hawaiian *lomi-lomi* massage, plus two restaurants supervised by renowned local chef Sam Choy.

On the slopes of Mount Hualalai, you'll find **Holualoa Inn** ((808) 324-1121 TOLL-FREE (800) 392-1812 FAX (808) 322-2472 E-MAIL inn @aloha.net WEB SITE www.konaweb.com/ HINN, Holualoa. The contemporary 7,000-sq-ft (650-sq-m) house is finished with cedar and eucalyptus and located on a 40-acre (16-hectare) estate with sweeping coastline views. There are six elegant rooms with Polynesian and Asian themes and a pool and Jacuzzi as well as a barbecue grill for guests. This is an adult retreat, and children under 13 are not encouraged. The village of Holualoa is an eclectic blend of local coffee growers and artists and is just 10 minutes above Kailua-Kona.

On a massive lava field at the mouth of the Keauhou Bay is **Kona Surf Resort and Country Club** ((808) 322-3411 TOLL-FREE (800) 367-8011 FAX (800) 322-3245 E-MAIL konasurf @ihawaii.net, 78-128 Ehukai Street, Kailua-Kona. Two swimming pools, sweeping lawns and the wild surf constantly pounding the lava rocks compensate for its lack of beach. The terraced design and open-air lobby make the Kona Surf one of the more visually exciting resort hotels on the islands. Plenty of aquatic activities, as well as the splendid fairways of the Kona golf course, keep visitors busy.

Two miles (about three kilometers) east of Kailua-Kona and very near the airport is a real find: **Puanani Bed and Breakfast** (/FAX (808) 329-8644 TOLL-FREE (877) 950-9061 E-MAIL Puanani@aloha.net WEB SITE www.planet-hawaii.com/puanani, 74-4958 Kiwi Street, Kailua-Kona. Here, Michael and Christina Raymond host you at their contemporary inn, which is set in lush vegetation with Jacuzzi, a lap pool with waterfall, a weight room, and tennis court. There are three rental units, with a minimum two-night stay.

Inexpensive

With a charming country atmosphere (and great ocean views) the hillside **Merryman's Bed and Breakfast** ((808) 323-2276 TOLL-FREE (800) 545-4390, Kealakekua, is in the coffee country of the Kealakekua–Captain Cook area. Don and Penny Merryman are gracious hosts with a keen eye for detail, as well as being lots of fun.

Dragonfly Ranch Tropical Fantasy Retreat ((808) 328-2159 TOLL-FREE (800) 487-2159 FAX (808) 328-9570 E-MAIL dfly@aloha.net WEB SITE www.dragonflyranch.com, Honaunau, offers rustic lodging within three minutes of Puuhonua O Honaunau National Historic Park. Owner Barbara Moore has big plans to soon offer movement workshops (similar to yoga), and "rejuvenation retreats" for those who want to learn more about Hawaiian culture and reconnect with the land.

Reggie's Tropical Hideaway ((808) 322-8888 TOLL-FREE (800) 988-2246 FAX (808) 323-2348 E-MAIL bana@ilhawaii.net WEBSITE www.ilhawaii.net/~bana/bb, Kealakekua, is an unusual bed-and-breakfast lodging in the midst of an authentic tropical fruit farm and coffee plantation. Relax in a hot tub in your private sunbathing garden surrounded by banana, papaya and mango trees. This is the place to get away from it all.

Romantic and peaceful are the two words that best describe **Rosy's Rest** (/FAX (808) 322-7378 E-MAIL rosyrest@get.net, 76-1012 Mamalahoa, Holualoa. The charming two-cottage unit has panoramic views of the Kona coastline. In the morning a wonderful breakfast is delivered right to your door.

Hale Maluhia Country Inn ((808) 329-1123 TOLL-FREE (800) 559-6627 FAX (808) 326-5487 E-MAIL hawai-inns@aloha.net WEB SITE www.hawaii-bnb.com/halemal.html, 76-770 Hualalai Road, Kailua-Kona, is a lush, tree-shaded estate 900 ft (270 m) up in Holualoa coffee country. Set amidst tall trees, koi fishponds and waterfalls, the property has four spacious bedrooms, a cottage and a house that's just right for families. The proprietors are as knowledgeable about the island as anyone in the business and serve one of the best breakfasts on the Kona Coast.

Kiwi Gardens Bed and Breakfast ((808) 326-1559 TOLL-FREE (888) 326-1559 E-MAIL kiwi@ilhawaii.net WEB SITE www.kiwigardens.com, 74-4920 Kiwi Street, Kailua-Kona, has four rooms in a lovely Hawaiian-style home with ocean and sunset views. The surrounding garden is planted with fruit, nuts and spices as well as trees, flowers and shrubs.

KAILUA-KONA

Most of the Big Island's hotel and condominium rooms are along a five-mile (eight-kilometer) oceanfront stretch on Alii Drive. There's accommodation here to suit a wide range of budgets.

Moderate

One of the town's larger hotels, **King Kamehameha's Kona Beach Hotel** ((808) 329-2911 FAX (808) 329-4602 E-MAIL sales@hthcorp.com WEB SITE www.konabeachhotel.com, 75-5660 Palani Road, Kailua-Kona, is on Kamakahonu Beach and has a fine pool. The hotel is showing its age a bit but it's in a great location beside the Kailua Pier: the water sport epicenter of Kona. Rooms are clean and well equipped. Hawaiian music performances, craft shows and luaus are held in the gardens and there are a variety of shops and tour companies on the lobby level.

The **Royal Kona Resort** ((808) 329-3111 TOLL-FREE (800) 222-5642 FAX (808) 329-7230 E-MAIL cameron@royalkona.com WEB SITE www.royalkona.com, 75-5852 Alii Drive, Kailua-Kona, was formerly the Kona Hilton. The name has changed, but not much else has; the handsome white edifice remains a landmark in the area, perched on the edge of rocky promontory. Each room has a private balcony, most with ocean views. As there is no natural beach, the hotel has built a saltwater lagoon with a manmade sandy edge. **Uncle Billy's Kona Bay Hotel** ((808) 961-5818 TOLL-FREE (800) 367-5102 FAX (808) 935-7903 E-MAIL resv@unclebilly.com WEB SITE www.unclebilly.com, 75-5739 Alii Drive, Kailua-Kona, is a no-frills hotel that is great for families, specially because of the daily, reasonably-priced buffet breakfasts and lunches. It's across the street from the ocean, but in a great central location.

Kona Seaside Hotel ((808) 329-2455 TOLL-FREE (800) 367-7000 FAX (808) 922-0052 E-MAIL sandsea@aloha.net WEB SITE www.sandseaside.com, 75-5646 Palani Road, Kailua-Kona, is another basic hotel with large, very adequate rooms, some with kitchenettes. Rooms near the road tend to be noisy.

If you're looking for luxurious accommodation with the coziness of a bed and breakfast, you might want to try **Kailua Plantation House** ((808) 329-3727 TOLL-FREE (888) 357-4262 FAX (808) 326-7323 E-MAIL kphbnb @ilhawaii.net WEB SITE www.kphbnb.com, 75-5948 Alii Drive, Kailua-Kona. Situated right on the water, you'll find elegance and privacy at Kailua Plantation House — yet you're only minutes away from all the action in Kailua-Kona. Your host is Danielle Berger.

Inexpensive

The **Kona Islander Inn** ((808) 329-9393 TOLL-FREE (800) 622-5348 FAX (808) 326-4137 E-MAIL konahawaii@hotmail.com WEB SITE www.konahawaii.com, 75-5776 Kuakini Highway, Kailua-Kona, has budget-priced studio condominiums with kitchenettes that can be rented by the day, week or month. It is not on the ocean but has a large swimming pool, spa and barbecue and is directly across the street from a white, sandy sunbathing beach (i.e. not for swimming). **Kona Billfisher Resort** ((808) 329-9393 TOLL-FREE (800) 622-5348 FAX (800) 326-4137 E-MAIL konahawaii @hotmail WEB SITE www.konahawaii.com, Alii Drive (opposite the Royal Kona Resort), offers up one-bedroom units (convertible to two-bedroom) to sleep two or four with full kitchens. No frills at a no-frills price.

Kona Magic Sand Resort ((808) 329-9393 TOLL-FREE (800) 622-5348 FAX (808) 326-4137 E-MAIL konahawaii@hotmail WEB SITE www.konahawaii.com, 77-6452 Alii Drive, is on the water with beaches on either side and has a pool and barbecue area and large studios with full kitchens.

KOHALA

Very Expensive

The first in this strand of luxurious accommodation is the **Four Seasons Resort Hualalai** ((808) 325-8000 TOLL-FREE (888) 340-5662 FAX (808) 325-8100 WEB SITE www.fourseasons.com, 100 Kaupulehu Drive, Kaupulehu-Kona. The 243-unit luxury property sprawls over 625 acres (253 hectares) of lava fields, with the white-capped ocean in front and a new Jack Nicklaus golf course in back. Architect Riecke Sunnland Kono has created a place with the spirit and feel of old Hawaii, with her design based on a typical Hawaiian coastal village, or *kauhale*. The two-story, 600-sq-ft (56-sq-m) units are arranged in horseshoe configurations around four distinctive features of the hotel — the palm grove, the pool, the children's pool and the King's pond. Additionally, there are 20 luxurious golf villas with unrestricted ocean views on the eighteenth fairway. Special features of the resort are its extensive spa and sports facilities as well as its art collection.

The **Kona Village Resort** ((808) 325-5555 TOLL-FREE (800) 367-5290 FAX (808) 325-5124 E-MAIL krv@aloha.net WEB SITE www.konavillage.com, Queen Kaahumanu Highway, Kailua-Kona, is as close to the traditional Polynesian style as you are likely to find anywhere on the island. Guests stay in individual thatched roof hales nestled among lagoons, black-sand beach or lava landscape. Each is spacious and secluded, some with private whirlpools. There are no televisions or telephones except at the office. In fact, this hotel doesn't even have room keys. The room rate includes meals, soft drinks, ocean activities, tours and children's program.

The **Mauna Lani Bay Hotel and Bungalows** ((808) 885-6622 TOLL-FREE (800) 367-2323 FAX (808) 885-1484 E-MAIL maunalani@maunalani.com WEB SITE www.maunalani.com, 68-1400 Mauna Lani Drive, Kohala Coast, is a large but gracious hotel that incorporates 29 acres (11 hectares) of historic park and 15 acres (six hectares) of fishponds set aside as archaeological preserves. The land area of the complex is extensive, covering around 3,200 acres (1,226 hectares) on the edge of a beach lined with coconut palms and milo trees, and a series of small lagoons. There are two championship golf courses, extensive tennis facilities and a fitness center for the active and a new spa that highlights acupuncture, Watsu and Hot Rocks. An action-packed kids program for ages 5 to 12, plus an "Eco-Teen Adventures" program entertains and challenges guests aged 13 to 17. The 350 comfortable rooms are designed for optimal ocean views. They have private lanais and are built around interior atriums, with fishponds where rays, sharks and endangered turtles roam. On July 4 each year, those turtles deemed large enough to survive in the wild are released into the ocean. Five, two-bedroom luxury bungalows have hosted the likes of Steven Spielberg, Celine Dion and Kevin Costner (for six months while he filmed *Waterworld*).

The **Orchid at Mauna Lani** ((808) 885-2000 TOLL-FREE (800) 845-9905 FAX (808) 885-5778 WEB SITE www.orchid-maunalani.com, 1 North Kaniku Drive, Kohala Coast, is a far more formal hotel. The lobby, with its colorful floral arrangements, sets the hotel's tone for style and elegance. There are carp pools, rushing waterfalls, tennis courts, a fitness center and spa and a kids program. Learn about Hawaii's history through the Orchid Beach Boys, a group of fellows who can teach you how to make fishhooks from bone or drums from coconut trees. Within the Puako Petroglyph Preserve are 3,000 rock carvings. But expect some service glitches at this hotel: undelivered messages, hanging around for a bell boy to show you to your room, waiting for restaurant tables while tables go unbussed. Also beware the daily "resort fee" and valet parking charges added to you bill.

The **Mauna Kea Beach Resort** ((808) 882-7222 TOLL-FREE (800) 882-6060 FAX (808) 882-5700 WEB SITE www.maunakeabeachhotel .com, 62-100 Mauna Kea Beach Drive, Kohala, is the legacy of millionaire hotelier Laurence Rockefeller. In 1960, Mr. Rockefeller selected a remote lava field with two lovely beaches and then went about sparing no expense in creating the resort. Opened in 1965, it does not offer the facilities of other hotels in the area and tends to attract an older clientele,

who have remained loyal over the years. Features include one of the best beaches on the Big Island, ocean and sunset views from the open-air lobby and wonderfully mature landscaped gardens. The Mauna Kea is worth a visit for the 1,000 or more pieces of art from Asia and the Pacific which decorate almost every corner of the 310-room complex.

Expensive

In keeping with the style and standards of resorts on this coast, the newly renovated **Outrigger Waikoloa Beach Resort** ((808) 886-

6789 TOLL-FREE (800) 922-5533 FAX (303) 369-9403 E-MAIL reservations@outrigger.com WEB SITE www.outrigger.com, 69-275 Waikoloa Beach Drive, Kamuela is lovely. Its petroglyph fields are well preserved, and its golf course, designed by Robert Trent Jones Jr., is another masterpiece of lava-field architecture. It sits on Anaehoomaulu Bay (or A-Bay as its locally known), which is the watersports center for the area.

The **Hilton Waikoloa Village** ((808) 886-1234 TOLL-FREE (800) 445-8667 FAX (808) 886-2900 E-MAIL waikoloa_rooms@hilton.com WEB SITE www.hilton.com/hawaii/waikoloa, 425 Waikoloa Beach Drive, Kamuela, is certainly not your typical area resort hotel. Described by some as Disneyland meets Asia meets Las Vegas, this place is just too big and too spread out for many. With on-site transportation choice of monorail or boat, the resort occupies 62 acres (25 hectares) of prime land on the edge of the ocean (no real beach). A key attraction here is the dolphin pool

The Orchid at Mauna Lani's pool and beyond it, the beach.

interaction program (guest participation is drawn by lottery). Art from Asia and the Pacific is scattered about the well-landscaped property.

On the bluffs above spectacular Hapuna Beach has risen the **Hapuna Beach Prince Hotel (** (808) 880-1111 TOLL-FREE (800) 882-6060 FAX (808) 880-3412 WEB SITE WWW.hapuna beachprincehotel.com, 62-100 Kauna'oa Drive, Kohala Coast. It has a contemporary feel with low-rise structures blending inconspicuously with the natural surroundings, trapping trade winds and providing unimpeded ocean views from each of the 350 rooms and suites. The rooms are comfortable but rather small. Japanese ownership acts as a magnet for upscale visitors from Japan who dominate the guest list of this rather formal hotel.

NORTH KOHALA AND WAIMEA

Moderate

Waimea Country Lodge ((808) 885-4100 FAX (808) 885-6711 E-MAIL terry@castle-group.com WEB SITE www.castle-group.com, 65-1210 Lindsey Road, Kamuela, was formally known as Parker Ranch Lodge and is located within walking distance to the town of Waimea, at the base of Mauna Kea. All rooms, which are standard motel-style fare, have mountain views. **Waimea Gardens Cottage (** (808) 885-4550 TOLL-FREE (800) 262-9912 FAX (808) 885-0559 E-MAIL bestbnb@ interpac.com WEB SITE www.bestbnb.com, Kamuela, is about two miles (about three kilometers) west of the center of Waimea town. On the property are two large and comfortable guest cottages. One has a kitchen and both are beautifully furnished and decorated with fine antiques with views of the green Kohala Hills. Your host is Barbara Campbell. There is a three-night minimum stay.

Belle Vue Bed and Breakfast (/FAX (808) 885-7732 TOLL-FREE (800) 772-5044 E-MAIL bellvue@aloha.net WEB SITE www.hawaii-bellevue.com, 1351 Konokohau Road, Kamuela, has contemporary suites and a cottage 15 minutes from the Kohala Coast. The decor is not my style, but rooms are meticulously maintained and the location is great, offering wonderful views of Waimea

town, Mauna Loa, and Mauna Kea. Hosts Viviane and Gayland Baker speak French and German.

Inexpensive

Kamuela Inn ((808) 885-4243 FAX (808) 885-8857, Kamuela, is a former motel that has been renovated into a comfortable inn with rooms and suites with private baths, some with kitchenettes. Complimentary continental breakfast is included. The hotel is just off Highway 19, and within walking distance of two of the best restaurants on the island.

Kohala Country Adventures ((808) 889-5663 E-MAIL lahi@pixi.com WEB SITE www .kcadventures.com, Kapaau, is on a working farm involved in livestock raising and taro growing. All rooms have baths and private entrances.

Kamuela's **Mauna Kea View Bed and Breakfast (** (808) 885-8425 FAX (808) 885-6514 WEB SITE www.hawaii-inns.com/bigisle/ kohala/maunakea, Kamuela, borders Parker Ranch and has an unobstructed view of Mauna Kea. There is a two-night minimum stay for either the two-bedroom suite or the cottage.

Hale Ho'onanea (/FAX (808) 882-1653 TOLL-FREE (877) 882-1653 E-MAIL jroppolo@ houseofrelaxation.com WEB SITE www .houseofrelaxation.com, Kamuela, offers all the privacy you could ever want, with three detached suites set among three rural acres (slightly over one hectare). Breakfasts of fruit, homemade bread, and nuts are served to your suite.

HAMAKUA COAST

Moderate

About midway between the two airports is **Mountain Meadow Ranch (** (808) 775-9376 FAX (808) 775-8033 E-MAIL wgeorge737@aol .com WEB SITE www.bnbweb.com/mountain-meadow.html, 46-3895 Kapuna Road, Honokaa. At an elevation of 2,000 ft (600 m) on the North Slope of Mauna Kea, this bed and breakfast offers cool air, green meadows and a chance to get in touch with nature.

Hale Kukui ((808) 775-7130 TOLL-FREE (800) 444-7130 E-MAIL retreat@halekukui WEB SITE www.halekukui.com, located in the village of Kukuihaele, Honokaa, overlooks

　　　　　　　　　　　　　　　　　　　　　Hawaii: The Big Island

the coastline, with a 600-ft (183-m) drop straight into the sea. To comply with state regulations, you must become a partner in the orchard enterprise to be able to stay in an "agricultural dwelling." The inn charges $5 for a year's membership, which allows you to pick as much as you can eat of the 26 varieties of fruit growing.

Inexpensive

Waipio Wayside Bed and Breakfast ((808) 775-0275 TOLL-FREE (800) 833-8849 E-MAIL wayside@bigisland.net WEB SITE WWW .waipiowayside.com, two miles (about three kilometers) west of the Honokaa Post Office, is a 1932 plantation home, restored to all its old Hawaii charm. A backyard lanai features comfortable hammocks, overlooking a variety of fruit trees. The inn specializes in delicious organic home-cooked food, and is well worth a visit for the breakfasts alone. A self-serve tea, chocolate and nut bar helps you fill those between-meal gaps. Host Jacqueline Horne is incredibly knowledgeable about the Big Island — she is involved in a range of local activities and is graciously willing to share her insight and opinions.

Hotel Honokaa Club offers hostel accommodations (see BACKPACKING, page 52 in YOUR CHOICE).

WHERE TO EAT

HILO

Expensive

Pescatore ((808) 969-9090, 235 Keawe Street, is about as fancy as it gets in Hilo. Southern Italian cuisine with a major emphasis, as the name implies, on seafood. The daily catch is offered five ways and there is also pasta, chicken and veal. Don't miss the excellent *cioppino classico*, a stew of clams, mussels, scallops and lobster, served with garlic bread.

Moderate

You could easily drive right by **Harrington's (** (808) 961-4966, 135 Kalanianaole Avenue. It is tucked away in an unassuming timber building about a mile (one and a half kilometers) out of town overlooking Reeds Bay.

New lava builds up the Big Island coastline.

Hawaii: The Big Island

But don't be fooled — the food is good. For starters, try the escargot en casserole. Main dishes include excellent seafood creations such as *calamari meunière* and Cajun prawns and scallops Chardonnay. There's live music from Wednesday to Saturday.

The decor might be plain at **Seaside Restaurant** ((808) 935-8825, 1790 Kalanianaole Highway, but the food is fresh and delicious and very popular with the locals who frequent the place. Much of the fish on the menu is reared right outside in the ponds beyond the large glass windows. Each menu item is served as a complete dinner, with salad, rice, vegetables, dessert and coffee.

Reubens ((808) 961-2552, 336 Kamehameha Avenue, is an earthy restaurant specializing in Mexican cuisine. Colorful cloth paintings give Reubens the feel of a tavern, but it is more than that. The portions here are lavish and matched only by the size of the margarita pitchers.

Inexpensive

There are only four tables and a small counter at **Honu's Nest** ((808) 935-9321, 270 Kamehameha Avenue, so count yourself lucky if you get in to taste the delicious home-cooked Japanese dishes with a sashimi plate that should not be missed. The *teishoku* dishes, featuring chicken, beef, squid, fish or tofu are a good value as they come with salad, miso and rice.

Slightly away from town, **Ken's Pancake House** ((808) 935-8711, 173 Kamehameha Avenue, is a Hilo institution. This restaurant is open 24 hours a day and specializes in local as well as standard American fare. The food is inexpensive and very good. As its name implies, pancakes are a specialty, but there's a large menu to choose from. Ken's serves breakfast, lunch and dinner — and a late supper.

High ceilings and neat tile floors contribute to the pleasant atmosphere at **Café Pesto** ((808) 969-6640 WEBSITE www.cafepesto.com, 380 Kamehameha Avenue. They specialize in excellent open-faced sandwiches, "provocative" pizzas and organic salads. The shrimp Milolii is good value. The restaurant is famous for its *calzones* — folded pizzas full of inventive fillings such as Japanese eggplant and artichokes, or lime-marinated fish.

For those with big appetites, try the paella with lobster and Calabrese sausage.

Royal Siam Thai Restaurant ((808) 961-6100, 70 Mamo Street, is often the first stop of residents returning to the island after trips abroad. Don't be put off by the simple decor, the food is consistently good. Try the garlic shrimp in coconut sauce.

Home-cooked healthy breakfasts and lunches are on offer at **Bears' Coffee** (808) 935-0708, 106 Keawe Street. The fruit and yogurt is just right if you don't want too heavy a start to your day, and the fresh muffins and bagels are wonderful. For those of you suffering from jet lag, they open at 5:30 AM with coffee to go, while breakfast is served from 7 AM. They'll also pack you a picnic lunch, with large orders requiring two hours notice.

All the food is homemade at **Happy Cats Café** ((808) 935-0595, 55 Mamo Street. The emphasis is on vegetarian dishes but there are some sandwiches and salads that contain turkey, steak, corned beef and tuna. My favorite? The coconut French toast.

On the four-mile (six-kilometer) scenic drive off Highway 19, you can't miss **What's Shakin'** ((808) 964-3080, 27-999 Old Mamalahoa Highway, for healthy fare including fresh fruit smoothies, tamales and veggie burgers. The plantation-style wooden house is sprightly painted in yellow and white, surrounded by lush fruit trees, with a winning ocean view.

VOLCANO

Expensive

The **Kilauea Lodge's** main building ((808) 967-7366, Highway 11 (Volcano Village exit), houses one of the island's finest restaurants, operated with obvious pride by owner-chef Albert Jeyte, who runs the lodge and restaurant with his wife Lorna. Jeyte's cooking style reflects his European training. Homemade soups, superb main courses ranging from duck to fish and venison, and wonderful desserts complemented by an excellent wine list make for a memorable meal. When you make your lodge reservations, remember to book a table at the restaurant, there aren't too many other fine dining outlets for miles around, and this one fills up quickly.

Moderate

Surf's ((808) 967-8511, Old Volcano Road, is a cozy bistro with fusion Asian-European specialties like boneless stuffed chicken wings, beef panang and chicken eggplant linguini. Nightly specials also include steak and the freshest of local seafood, cooked to perfection.

Inexpensive

Gourmet sandwiches, salads, homemade soup, freshly baked goods and coffee are on offer at **Steam Vent Café** ((808) 985-8744, Haunani Road, behind Surf's. This small café also sells postcards, flashlights and rainwear. **Lava Rock Café** ((808) 967-8526, Volcano Village exit off Highway 11, serves comfort food like fried chicken, lasagna steak and shrimp combos, and grilled fish. Wednesday is Mexican, Friday is Hawaiian specialties. You can get sandwiches to go here, perfect for hiking trips.

SOUTH OF KONA

Inexpensive

Shaka Restaurant ((808) 929-7404, Highway 11, Naalehu, is a large restaurant (52 seats) with a laid-back, family atmosphere, popular with local residents. The servings are huge and the plate lunches are particularly popular. Burgers, dogs, Reubens, burritos and great fries.

Mark Twain Square ((808) 929-7550, Highway 11, Waiohinu has sandwiches, coffee and homemade breads on a verandah shaded by the Mark Twain tree.

Ted's Kona Theater and Café ((808) 328-2244, Captain Cook, just before the 109-mile marker from Kona, is open from 7:30 AM to noon Tuesday through Sunday for delicious breakfasts. Order Ted's specialty of Greek-style eggs (scrambled with feta cheese, kalamata olives and sun dried tomatoes), Italian frittata (scrambled eggs with potatoes, peppers and Italian cheese), or fresh catch of the day and eggs any style.

KAILUA-KONA

Expensive

Sam Choy, of **Sam Choy's Restaurant** ((808) 326-1545, 73-5576 Kauhola Street, in the Kaloko Light Industrial Park, is a local whose distinctive style combines the subtleties of Italian cooking with the ingredients of Hawaii and the flair of Asian cuisine. Try, for example, Papa's Island pig's-feet soup with

Performers uncover an underground oven, an *imu*, at a luau in Kona.

wild mountain mushrooms, mustard cabbage, peanuts and ginger. Or if you're not so adventurous, try the South Pacific seafood stew with Tahitian spinach-dill cream. This is delicious food.

La Bourgone ((808) 329-6711, Kuakini Plaza South, 77-6400 Nalani Street No. 101, three miles (five kilometers) south of Kailua on Highway 11, is an intimate and authentic French restaurant. Its excellent appetizers include escargot and baked Brie. On its soup menu are traditional lobster and French onion soups. Entrées include the customary fish dishes, as well as saddle of lamb with garlic and rosemary, and venison in sherry with a pomegranate glaze.

Chart House ((808) 329-2451, Waterfront Row, 75-5770 Alii Drive, serves traditional grill fare of steak and seafood in an open-air restaurant on Kailua Bay.

Huggo's ((808) 329-1493 WEB SITE www .huggos.com, 75-5828 Kahakai Street, is a pleasant restaurant with good atmosphere and a large lanai on the water's edge. The Pacific Rim cuisine includes island-bred Maine lobster, pan-charred ahi, pasta and grilled lamb chops as well as burgers, pizza and Caesar salad. There's live entertainment most evenings, karaoke on Monday and Tuesday, and the adjacent **Huggo's on the Rocks** is a happening sunset meeting place.

Moderate

Oodles of Noodles ((808) 329-9222, in the Crossroads Shopping Center, 75-1027 Henry Street, serves dishes from all over the world — providing they include noodles. The grilled chicken with rice noodle salad is the best. Don't leave out the shave-ice for dessert.

LuLu's ((808) 331-2633, on the main drag at 75-5819 Alii Drive, is a place you go to for the atmosphere more than anything. It's loud, lively and intentionally tacky, serving tacos, burgers, salads, and sandwiches. The bar is open until 2 AM.

Quinns almost by the Sea ((808) 329-3822, 75-5655A Palani Road, is another happening place with a bar and lounge inside and a garden lanai for dining. This local favorite serves lots of dishes with chips — shrimp, calamari, fish, as well as steak, burgers and chicken.

If you've got a hankering for a microbrew and a hand-tossed gourmet pizza, head for **Kona Brewing Pub** ((808) 329-2739 at the corner of Kuakini and Palani Road. The organic salads are good too, and the balmy outdoor setting is just right for Hawaii.

Inexpensive

There are some surprisingly good Thai restaurants in Kona, and **Thai Rin** ((808) 329-2929, 75-5799 Alii Drive, is one of them. Dinners include a variety of spicy *tom yum* soup, fine curries made with or without coconut milk, satays, and a selection of vegetarian dishes.

Sibu Café ((808) 329-1112, in the Banyan Court, 75-5695 Alii Drive, offers *laksa* (noodles and vegetables in a rich coconut milk soup), *gado gado* salad, satays and other Indonesian favorites in a casual setting at reasonable prices.

For a quick bagelwich, wrap, or pita pocket, and 100% Kona coffee, try **Island Lava Java** ((808) 327-2161 WEB SITE www .islandlavajava.com, at 75-5799 Alii Drive #A1.

For the best breakfast in Kona, head to the **Kona Ranch House** ((808) 329-7061 at the corner of Kuakini and Palani on Highway 11. Huge portions of eggs any way you want them, plus pancakes, waffles and more. Family-style dining for lunch and dinner, including spaghetti, chicken, steak, ribs, and fish.

KOHALA

Expensive

At the Four Seasons Resort, the **Pahuia** ((808) 325-8000 is an elegant oceanfront restaurant which serves dishes that are a magical blend of East and West, and it features an extensive range of fish dishes. The Asian dishes are particularly good.

One of the best dining experiences on the Kohala Coast is a meal at the **Canoe House** ((808) 885-6622, one of the Mauna Lani's fine restaurants located on a beautiful site just steps from the sea. You can dine by candlelight or the light of the moon, and savor great food. The restaurant features the

A page-turner at the Mauna Lani Hotel Beach.

Pacific Rim cuisine of chef Pat Saito, with starters including the signature nori-wrapped tempura *ahi* with soy mustard sauce and tomato-ginger relish. For the main course there are dishes like whole Kona-raised lobster with mushroom stuffing or Thai curry risotto in a passionfruit chili sauce. For dessert, you can't pass up the ice cream pie — coffee and vanilla ice cream layered with fudge on a chocolate-chip cookie crust. The Mauna Lani has two other restaurants, the informal **Bay Terrace** and the poolside **Ocean Grill**.

The most formal of the three restaurants at the Orchid Hotel is the **Grill** ((808) 885-2000, which is only open for dinner, serving seafood and game including pan-roasted loin of Colorado lamb and rosemary and thyme-crusted swordfish steak. But for ambience you can't top **Brown's Beach House** where tables are set under the stars, you are serenaded with haunting Hawaiian music, and the food includes dishes like macadamia honey-mustard crusted lamb chops and miso-teri glazed swordfish.

The **Batik** ((808) 882-6060 is the sedate, elegant restaurant at the Mauna Kea Beach Resort, with classical European dishes, influenced by Provence. Among the best dishes are the *ahi* carpaccio and the lobster and avocado napoleon. Many of the meals here are cooked at your table. For Sunday brunch, go nowhere else but to this hotel's **Terrace** for an extravagant spread.

Yes, there is dining life beyond the hotels in this area, with most of the better restaurants situated at the Kings' Shops. **Roy's Waikoloa Bar and Grill** ((808) 885-4321 serves imaginative dishes which blend East and West with a little Polynesia thrown in, like ginger chicken and sesame shrimp tower salad, lemongrass chicken and Mongolian grilled rack of lamb. They serve great vegetarian dishes and the chocolate soufflé is worth all the calories.

Moderate

Good Chinese food is available at **Grand Palace** ((808) 886-6668, King's Shopping Center, where you can order hot pots and sizzling platters, plus your favorite seafood, pork, beef and poultry dishes. The set meal for four is good value.

Don't be surprised to see many hotel staff at **Café Pesto** ((808) 882-1071, Suite 101, Kawaihae Center, Kawaihae. It is a refreshing alternative to resort food. The menu includes exotic pizza, pasta fresh organic greens and seafood including crab cakes, and wok-fired shrimp and scallops.

Good old dependable Mexican fare is served at **Tres Hombres** ((808) 882-1031, also in Kawaihae Center. Quesadillas, carnitas, tacos… they are all here. El grande burrito is enough for two really hungry adults.

NORTH KOHALA AND WAIMEA

Expensive

Peter Merriman, chef and owner of **Merriman's** ((808) 885-6822, Opelo Plaza, 65-1227A Opelo Road, emphasizes organic produce in his cooking. His dinner appetizers include wok-charred *ahi* and steamed clams. Entrées feature fresh fish done in a wide variety of styles and steak and veal T-bones, including an amazing *ono* with a sesame crust and a passionfruit sauce. The coconut crème brûlée is my favorite dessert. Lunch is a simpler yet no less tasty affair with grilled shrimp salad among the choices.

Moderate

For being in a semi-remote area, **Bamboo** ((808) 889-5555, Highway 270, Kapaau, in North Kohala, is tremendously popular and the turn-of-the-century building is a major attraction in itself. The Hawaiian atmosphere is very friendly and the vegetables served are mainly from nearby gardens, with fish caught personally by the chef, and the pork slow-roasted in the *imu* in the backyard. Try the passionfruit margarita. Thursday night is karaoke night, while on weekends there is Hawaiian music from 7 PM.

It is not entirely out of character to find an alpine chalet in this Hawaiian town. It certainly gets cold enough in the months of December through April to enjoy dining on German and Austrian fare at **Edelweiss** ((808) 885-6800, opposite Kamuela Inn, Highway 19, in a room of dark-hued woods.

Once the playground of Hawaiian royalty, the Kohala Coast now attracts surfers and swimmers.

This is a very good restaurant with a long history of quality. You can order a simple yet tasty lunch of bratwurst and sauerkraut, or sandwiches and burgers. The menu may look limited but the specials are seemingly endless. Edelweiss specializes in *Wiener schnitzel* (breaded veal cutlets), filet mignon, sautéed calf's liver and the finest green-peppercorn steak this side of the Rocky Mountains.

Parker Ranch Grill ((808) 887-2624, Parker Ranch Center, 65-1185A Mamalahoa Highway, Kamuela, serves down-home cooking with hearty helpings: prime rib, meatloaf, pork chops, and a few fancier dishes like lobster pot pie and chili crusted shrimp and crab stir-fry. There is live music on Friday and Saturday nights. It has a *paniolo* décor, with two fireplaces and a lounge with board games. This is the sister restaurant of Huggo's in Kona.

Inexpensive

Jen's Kohala Café ((808) 889-0099, across from King Kamehameha's statue in Kapaau, is a great little spot for healthy, homemade daily soups, salads, deli sandwiches, wraps, burgers and smoothies.

Don't be put off by the size of the kitchen, **Maha's Café** ((808) 885-0693, in the old Spencer Building in Waimea on Highway 19, turns out some mouth-watering food. Try the smoked *ahi* with passionfruit chutney or corn bread with tomatoes and feta. For breakfast, hotcakes and granola are the order of the day.

Paniolo Country Inn ((808) 885-4377, next to Parker Ranch Lodge, serves large meals at reasonable prices, so bring your appetite. Breakfasts are particularly good — try the eggs Benedict. The inn serves good Mexican burritos and quesadillas for dinner.

HAMAKUA COAST

Inexpensive

Café Il Mondo ((808) 775-7711, 45-3626-A Mamane Street, in the Andrade Building, Honokaa, is a place to sit back, read a newspaper, or admire the local art hanging on the walls. The menu ranges from pizza (pesto with marinated artichokes and mushrooms or *quatro fromage* with blue cheese are my favorites) to *calzone*, lasagna, fresh pasta and gourmet sandwiches.

Tex Drive Inn ((808) 775-0598, Highway 19, Honokaa, has an extensive selection of tasty soups, stews, salads, sandwiches, burgers, wraps as well as lunch and dinner plates, all at very reasonable prices. But their specialty is *malasada* (a sort of doughnut without the hole) filled with cream, papaya or pineapple, and strawberry or pepper jelly. Owner Ada Lamme says she now sells about 50,000 of these treats a month. Many tourist buses make the stop, so it can get crowded.

NIGHTLIFE

Let's face it, the Big Island is not the nightlife capital of the world. But there are a few places that see a little action past midnight (on weekends anyway), notably in the Kona-Kohala area.

The bar at **LuLu's** ((808) 331-2633, 75-5819 Alii Drive, is open until 2 AM; **Quinns Almost by the Sea** ((808) 329-3822, 75-5655A Palani Road, stays open until 2 AM on Monday to Saturday and until midnight on Sunday. **Kona Brewing Pub** ((808) 329-2739 at the corner of Kuakini and Palani Road and **Hard Rock Café** ((808) 329-8866, 75-5815 Alii Drive, are other good bets for some night action.

For an evening of dining on the water and Polynesian entertainment, its **Captain Beans' Polynesian Cruise** ((808) 329-2955 TOLL-FREE (800) 831-5541, 73-4800 Kanalani Street. This is an adults-only cruise and the price includes dinner and drinks. Look for the distinctive orange sails when the boat is tied up at Kona pier.

Kona' only oceanfront luau, **Drums of Polynesia** is put on by the Royal Kona Resort ((808) 331-1526 WEB SITE www.royalkona .com, on Monday, Friday and Saturday. If you get past the fact that this is a "for tourists only" event, the food is okay, the entertainment amusing and the setting quite nice.

Without doubt, Hawaii's most authentic luau is the **Ahaaina** (feast), held on Friday nights at the Kona Village Resort ((808) 325-6787 WEB SITE www.konavillage.com.

The evening starts with a walking tour of the fishponds at Kaupulehu, followed by the *imu* ceremony and dinner. Hawaiian music plays throughout dinner, followed by hula and a Polynesian revue. Book early, it's usually difficult to get reservations for this luau. If you can't get reservations for Kona Village, try the **Luau** on Tuesdays at the Mauna Kea Beach Hotel ((808) 882-5801 WEB SITE www.maunakeabeachhotel.com. Kumu Hula Nani Lim and her award-winning hula troupe perform the after-dinner entertainment.

direct flights from Los Angeles and San Francisco, and **Japan Airlines** TOLL-FREE (800) 525-3663 has daily direct flights from Tokyo.

Scheduled connections from Honolulu to both Kona and Hilo are offered by **Aloha Airlines** TOLL-FREE (800) 367-5250 WEB SITE www.alohaair.com and **Hawaiian Airlines** TOLL-FREE (800) 367-5320.

American Hawaii Cruises TOLL-FREE (800) 513-5022 E-MAIL ahcresdesk@uucp .deltaqueen.com, makes weekly trips to Hilo Harbor and Kailua Bay in Kona.

Each Friday, a dinner show, **Legends of the Pacific**, is held at the Hilton Waikoloa Village. Produced by Tahiti Productions, there is dancing and music to go with the buffet dinner.

HOW TO GET THERE

The Big Island has two airports, one on either side. On the east coast is the **Hilo International Airport** ((808) 934-5838, and on the west coast the **Keahole-Kona International Airport** ((808) 329-3423. As most visitors are heading to the Kona coast, this airport handles most traffic and has the most direct flights. **United Airlines** TOLL-FREE (800) 241-6522 has daily

There are two routes you can take from Hilo to get to the West Coast of the island. The shorter route carries you north along the picturesque Hamakua Coast through towns with names such as Laupahoehoe, Papaikou, Honomu, Honokaa and Waimea. The other route is to proceed along the edge of Hawaii Volcanoes National Park around the southern end of the island via South Point.

A Big Island helicopter operator flies sightseers high over a remote coastline.

Hawaii: The Big Island

Travelers' Tips

GETTING THERE

The main airport for Hawaii is Honolulu International Airport on Oahu, which receives flights from throughout the world. Some carriers have direct flights from mainland United States to Keahole-Kona Airport on the Big Island, Kahului Airport on Maui, and Lihue Airport on Kauai. Along with these major airports, interisland carriers also serve the smaller islands.

MAINLAND CARRIERS

American Airlines ((808) 833-7600 TOLL-FREE (800) 433-1790.
Continental Airlines TOLL-FREE (800) 523-3273.
Delta Airlines TOLL-FREE (800) 221-1212.
Northwest Orient ((808) 955-2255 TOLL-FREE (800) 225-2525.
United Airlines TOLL-FREE (800) 241-6522.

INTERNATIONAL CARRIERS

All Nippon ((808) 838-0190 TOLL-FREE (800) 235-9262.
Japan Airlines ((808) 521-1441 TOLL-FREE (800) 525-3663.
Korean Airlines ((808) 836-1717 TOLL-FREE (800) 438-5000.

INTER-ISLAND CARRIERS

Many travelers to Hawaii fly to Honolulu and connect with inter-island shuttles, which run frequent daily flights to most islands. Travel between the islands is a bit more complicated; at times, you may have to make connections in Oahu to reach your destination, particularly if you're flying to Molokai or Lanai. Multi-island passes are available through Aloha Airlines and Hawaiian Airlines; both offer considerable savings over individually booked flights, though flexibility is hampered since the passes are usually only good for a limited time.
Aloha Airlines TOLL-FREE (800) 367-5250; Hawaii ((808) 935-5771; Kauai ((808) 245-3691; Lanai ((808) 244-9071; Maui ((808) 244-9071; Molokai TOLL-FREE (800) 652-6541; Oahu ((808) 484-1111 WEB SITE www.alohaair.com.

Hawaiian Airlines TOLL-FREE (800) 367-5320.
Island Air TOLL-FREE (800) 323-3345; Maui ((808) 484-2222; Molokai ((808) 484-2222; Oahu ((808) 484-2222.
Pacific Wings Maui ((808) 873-0877.

ARRIVING AND LEAVING

VISA AND TRAVEL DOCUMENTS

Most citizens of Australia, Canada, and New Zealand, and Britain, France, Germany, Italy, the Netherlands, Spain and many other Western European nations qualify for a visa exemption. They may enter the United States without a visa if they are traveling for holiday or business and staying fewer than 90 days. A valid passport and return ticket are also required.

Citizens of many other countries do require a tourist visa to enter the United States, however. Tourist visas can vary from single entry to multiple entry; length of stay also varies. Telephone a United States embassy or consulate before you leave home to find out if you need one.

CUSTOMS

You are allowed to bring into the United States, duty free, gifts valued at no more than $100. Two hundred cigarettes, or 50 cigars, or three pounds (1.35 kg) of tobacco are allowed, as is one quart (one liter) of alcohol. Nonprescription narcotics are, of course, strictly prohibited.

CONSULATES

The following foreign consulates are on Oahu:
Australia ((808) 524-5050, 1000 Bishop Street.
Germany ((808) 946-3819, 2003 Kalia Road, Suite 1.
Italy ((808) 531-2277, 735 Bishop Street.
Japan ((808) 536-2226, 1742 Nuuanu Avenue.
New Zealand ((808) 547-5117, 900 Richards Street #414.

The following consulates can be found on the mainland, in California:
Canada ((415) 495-6021, 50 Fremont Street, San Francisco.

Boogie boarders exit the surf on an isolated Maui beach.

France ((310) 235-3200, 10990 Wilshire Boulevard, Los Angeles.
Netherlands ((310) 268-1598, 11766 Wilshire Boulevard, Los Angeles.
United Kingdom ((310) 477-3322, 11766 Wilshire Boulevard, Los Angeles.

TOURIST INFORMATION

The best source for tourist information on Hawaii is the **Hawaii Visitors and Convention Bureau** (HVCB). They publish a 122-page vacation planner, *Islands of Aloha*, which

contains much of the information you will need before your trip. You can request it by mail from any of the bureaus, or online at their WEB SITE www.gohawaii.com. Some islands also have their own web site (see below). The Maui HVCB also covers Lanai and Molokai.

The HVCB has branches on each of the islands:
Big Island ((808) 961-5797 FAX (808) 961-2126, 250 Keawe Street, Hilo, HI 96720; or ((808) 329-7787 FAX (808) 326-7563, 75-5719 West Alii Drive.
Kauai ((808) 245-3971 FAX (808) 246-9235 WEB SITE www.kauai-hawaii.com, 3016 Umi, Suite 207, Kauai, HI 96766.
Lanai ((808) 565-7600, PO Box 700, Lanai City, HI 96763.
Maui ((808) 244-3530 TOLL-FREE (800) 525-6284 WEB SITE www.visitmaui.com, 1727 Wili Pa Loop, Maui, HI 96793.
Molokai ((808) 553-3876 TOLL-FREE (800) 800-6367 WEB SITE www.molokai-Hawaii.com, Kamehameha V Highway, Kaunakakai, PO Box 960, Molokai, HI 96748.

Oahu ((808) 524-0722 FAX (808) 521-1620, 733 Bishop Street, Suite 1872, Honolulu, HI 96813.

As a rule, these offices are situated in areas that are not too easy to get at. Most of the information you need on restaurants, shops, nightlife and the like can be found on the tourist information racks found in most strip malls, hotel lobbies and other tourist destinations.

The HVCB also has a mainland office in **San Francisco** ((415) 248-3800 FAX (808) 248-3808, 180 Montgomery Street, Suite 2360, California 94104.

GETTING AROUND

Renting a car is by far the easiest way of getting around most of Hawaii, except in Honolulu where it is probably better to rely on public transportation. Most islands only have a few main roads, so it's difficult to get lost and the roads are generally in good condition.

CAR RENTAL

The following is a list of national car rental agencies in Hawaii:
Alamo TOLL-FREE (800) 327-9633 WEB SITE www.alamo.com.
Avis TOLL-FREE (800) 331-1212 WEB SITE www.avis.com.
Budget TOLL-FREE (808) 527-0700 WEB SITE www.budget.com.
Dollar TOLL-FREE (800) 342-7398 WEB SITE www.dollar.com.
Hertz TOLL-FREE (800) 654-3131 WEB SITE www.hertz.com.
National TOLL-FREE (800) 227-7368 WEB SITE www.nationalcar.com.
Thrifty TOLL-FREE (800) 367-5238 WEB SITE www.thrifty.com.

As a general rule, Avis seems to offer the best service, and Alamo the most threadbare vehicles.

Taxes on rental cars in Hawaii include a 50-cents-a-day vehicle licensing fee, a 7.56% concessionary recovery fee and a $3-a-day road tax, so make sure you find out what's included when you get a package deal.

If you are looking for a vehicle with a bigger statement, try **Hawaiian Riders** ((888)

527-9484 in Kaui or (888) 527-0075 in Maui WEB SITE www.hawaiianriders, which will fit you out with a Prowler, Viper, Porsche, convertible Corvette or a Harley. They also have more mundane offerings, from jeeps to mopeds. The same sort of exotic car offering is available at **Island Riders** ((808) 661-9966 in Lahaina or (808) 874-0311 in Kihei WEB SITE www.islandriders.com/maui.

OTHER FORMS OF TRANSPORTATION

Oahu is the only island where traveling by public bus is really a viable option. Traffic jams, parking problems and a modestly priced, reliable service makes this a good means of getting around. Service in Honolulu is operated by **Oahu Transit Services** ((808) 848-4501 WEB SITE www.thebus.org, 811 Middle Street, Honolulu, HI 96819. There is really not enough flexibility of service on the other islands, but in Kauai you could try **Kauai Bus** ((808) 241-6410, that island's public bus system, which runs along most major roads around the island, with routes from Kekaha to Hanalei.

Waikiki Trolley Tours ((808) 596-2199 TOLL-FREE (800) 824-8804, at 1050 Ala Moana Boulevard, offers a good way to explore Honolulu, Waikiki and the Makapuu Coast, with one ticket lasting all day and allowing for unlimited reboarding at 31 locations throughout the island. Likewise, Maui has the **West Maui Shopping Express** ((808) 877-7308 which connects Lahaina, Kaanapali, Honokowai, Napili and Kapalua areas with stops at shops as well as hotel and resort destinations. On the Big Island there is the **Kona Coast Express** ((808) 331-1582, King Kamehameha Hotel Lobby, that plies the major tourist sites on the western coast. Kona Coast Express also operates an express bus between King Kamehameha Hotel in Kona and King's Shopping Center in Kohala. The **Lanai Company** TOLL-FREE (800) 321-4666 FAX (808) 565-3868 E-MAIL reservations@lanai-resorts.com WEBSITE www.lanai-resorts.com, operates a shuttle from early morning to late night between the Manele Bay Hotel, Lanai City and the Lodge at Koele.

There is a myriad of taxi services on most islands, but this tends to be a very expensive option. So think of using taxis only for short

hops and maybe airport transportation if your hotel does not offer any shuttle service. A one-way trip in a taxi from the airport to some hotels is the same or more than a one-day compact car rental. Limousine and taxi alternatives on Oahu include **Exclusive Inc**. ((808) 772-1152, 955 Waimanu Street, Honolulu, and **Charley's** ((808) 531-2333 E-MAIL charleys@lava.net, 680 Ala Moana Boulevard, Honolulu. On Maui, **Maui Central Cab** ((808) 224-7278 WEBSITE www.mauicab.com, 895 Kekeona Loop, Wailuku, has metered taxis which let seven passengers ride for the

cost of one. The phone numbers for other taxis can be found on WEB SITE www.mauibound .com/taxi. A Limousine service is provided by **Maui Aloha Golf and Tours** ((808) 276-4592 E-MAIL limo@maui.net, 30 Alania Place, Kihei, or try **Town and Country Limousine** ((808) 572-3400. Airport shuttles in both Kona ((808) 329-5433 and Maui ((808) 875-8079 are provided by **SpeediShuttle** WEB SITE www.speedishuttle.com. Among the many other taxi companies available on the Big Island are **Ace One Taxi** ((808) 935-8303, 1403 Kinoole Street, Hilo, and **C&C Taxi** ((808) 329-0008, Kona Airport.

Detail of the palace gate at Kailua-Kona on the Big Island with the Mokuaikua Church in the background. ABOVE: The garden at Lanai's Lodge at Koele.

For more romance in your Big Island transportation, horse-drawn carriage tours of Kailua-Kona are offered by **Hawaiian Dreams Carriage Service** ((808) 325-2280 E-MAIL 4horse@gte.net, 73-1270 Mamalahoa Highway. Private transportation on Lanai is available through **Rabaca's Limousine** ((808) 565-6670, while on Molokai, you should try **Molokai Off-Road Tours and Taxi** ((808) 553-3369 or at Molokai Ranch, **Kukui Tours and Limousine** ((808) 552-2282.

Accessible Vans of Hawaii ((808) 879-5521 TOLL-FREE (800) 303-3750, 186 Mehani

The budget-conscious tourist would be well advised to check out tour packages that include air fare, accommodation and meals.

To give you some idea of the prices you might expect in Hawaii, accommodation has been categorized under the following headings, based on a standard double room. **Inexpensive** accommodation will cost under $100; **moderate** hotels will charge between $100 and $200; hotels listed as **expensive** will cost between $200 and $300; **very expensive** means you can expect to pay over $300.

Circle, Kihei, has wheelchair-accessible vans for rent on Oahu, Maui, Big Island and Kauai. **C. R. Newton Company** ((808) 949-8389, 1575 South Beretania Street, Honolulu, has scooters, crutches, walkers and wheelchairs for rent or sale. They also do repairs.

ACCOMMODATION

Hawaii is generally recognized as an expensive state. In fact, based on the price of residential accommodation and the price of food, Hawaii is one of the three most expensive states in the country. But when compared with prices in parts of Europe or Asia, prices in Hawaii are not unreasonable.

Condominiums are a popular option in Hawaii. Most of these apartments are well appointed, with full-sized kitchens. Many condominiums have well-equipped gyms, large pools, and the occasional racquetball or court tennis. Most important in the price equation is the proximity of the complex to the beach, and of course the view from the apartment.

EATING OUT

If you look off the main tourist track, there are many inexpensive eateries catering to budget-conscious tourists. Participating in the Hawaiian ritual of the plate lunch gets you a complete meal; they are available in a variety of cooking styles ranging from Japanese to Chinese to Hawaiian, at economical prices. American fast-food chains and noodle shops are another low-cost alternative.

Restaurants are divided into four categories according to the range of prices you can expect to pay for a three-course meal for one person without drinks. Restaurants listed as **inexpensive** cost up to $15 per person; **moderate** restaurants will generally charge between $15 and $30; an **expensive** meal cost between $30 to $50; and **very expensive** means your meal will cost $50 or more.

ian banks offer foreign currency exchange services. Credit cards are widely accepted.

TIPPING

When it comes to tipping, Hawaii is very much a part of the rest of the United States and gratuities are well-ingrained in the lifestyle. Waiters, bartenders, tour operators, cab drivers all expect about 15%. Bellhops at mid-range to luxury accommodation expect $1 to $2 a bag and valets $1 to $2 whenever your car is delivered to you.

BASICS

TIME

Hawaiian Standard Time is eleven hours behind Greenwich Mean Time, six hours behind Eastern Standard Time (United States East Coast) and three hours behind Pacific Standard Time (United States West Coast). Hawaii does not have daylight savings time, so reduce all time differences by an hour in the winter months.

MONEY

It is advisable to purchase travelers' checks in United States currency. Not many Hawai-

TAXES

Hawaii has a 4.16% excise tax on all goods and services. This tax applies to gifts, hotel rooms, clothing, medical services, rental cars, and all other goods and services. In addition, there is a 10% room tax on hotel and resort accommodations. For car rental taxes, see CAR RENTAL, above, under GETTING AROUND.

ELECTRICITY

Electricity in the United States is 110–120 volts AC.

OPPOSITE: Hula *halau* dance schools encourage respect for ancient traditions. ABOVE: Souvenir shoppers cruise the Kona streets.

WEIGHTS AND MEASURES

The United States uses ounces, pounds, gallons, miles, etc. It's an antiquated system, and if you're used to metric, it can be a bit confusing. Here are some conversions to help you along:

Distance and Length

1 inch = 2.54 centimeters
1 foot = 0.305 meters
1 mile = 1.6 kilometers

Weight

1 ounce = 28.35 grams
1 pound = 0.45 kilograms

Volume

1 gallon = 3.78 liters

Temperature

To convert Fahrenheit to Centigrade, subtract 32 and multiply by $\frac{5}{9}$. To convert Centigrade to Fahrenheit, multiply by 1.8 and add 32.

COMMUNICATION AND MEDIA

TELEPHONES

Calls within an island cost 35 cents. Calls between islands are considered long distance and are charged depending on the time of day: on Monday to Friday between 8 AM and 5 PM, it is 35 cents for the first minute and 25 cents for each additional minute or fraction thereof. To place long-distance calls, dial 1 + the area code and the number you are calling. All calls between Hawaii's islands are preceded by 808.

Toll-free numbers within the United States begin with area code 800 or 888. Local information is reached by dialing 1-411 and billed at 20 cents a call. United States nationwide information (including interisland) is reached by dialing 1 + (area code) 555-1212. For direct dialing of international numbers, dial 011 + country code + city code + telephone number. For local operator assistance dial 0.

MAIL

Most post offices are open Monday through Friday from 9 AM to 5 PM. Some postal branch offices are open on Saturdays until noon. First-class letters sent within the United States require a $0.33 stamp and postcards a $0.20 stamp. International rates vary according to country.

MASS MEDIA

Network television programming on broadcast stations originates in Honolulu and is retransmitted to relay stations on the other islands. The major United States networks have local affiliates in the islands, so check a local television guide. KITV has a digital broadcast on Channel 40 and will be joined by other stations by 2006.

Local news is transmitted in Oahu on channels 2, 8 and 9 at 6 PM and 10 PM.

Oahu has the most radio stations. Public radio, with classical music and news, is at 88.1 FM (KHPR) and 1380 (KIFO) on AM. At 650 AM, KHNR is Hawaii's only all-news station; 830 (KHVH) and 1080 (KWAI) have news and talk and 760 (KGU) is all sports. Big Island has a new talk and sports station at 670 FM (KPUA). Maui has public radio at 90.7 FM (KKUA) and on AM, news, talk and sports at 1110 (KAOI) and 1570 (KUAU). Kauai has community radio which includes news at FM 90.9 (KKCR) and 91.9 (KKCU). The rest of the stations are mainly music — there is a wide variety available on most islands.

ETIQUETTE

Even though Hawaii is largely a resort destination, try and be sensitive to the local people's customs and religious beliefs. Treat sacred sites with respect, ask for permission before taking photographs of people, don't join in local festivities uninvited. And just let common good manners prevail.

HEALTH

EMERGENCIES

If you are seriously ill or injured, dial (911, the emergency hotline, for help. In addition to the hospitals listed below, many fire stations have paramedics on hand who can administer emergency first aid.

The following hospitals offer 24-hour emergency service.

Big Island
Hilo Medical Center ((808) 969-4111, 1190 Waianuenue Avenue, Hilo.
North Hawaii Community Hospital ((808) 885-4444, 67-1125 Mamalahoa Highway, Kamuela.
Kona Community Hospital ((808) 322-9311, Kealakekua.

Kauai
Wilcox Memorial Hospital ((808) 245-1100, 3420 Kuhio Highway, Lihue.
West Kauai Medical Center ((808) 338-9431, 4643 Waimea Canyon Road, Waimea.

Lanai
Lanai Community Hospital ((808) 565-6411, 628 Seventh Street, Lanai City.

Maui
Maui Memorial Hospital ((808) 244-9056, 221 Mahalani, Wailuku.

Molokai
Molokai General Hospital ((808) 553-5331, Kaunakakai.

Oahu
Castle Medical Center ((808) 263-5500, 640 Ulukahiki Street, Kailua.
Kapiolani Medical Center ((808) 486-6000, 98-1079 Moanalua Road, Pearlridge.
Kapiolani Medical Center for Women and Children ((808) 973-8511, 1319 Punahou Street, Honolulu.
Queen's Medical Center ((808) 538-9011, 1301 Punchbowl, Honolulu.
Straub Clinic and Hospital ((808) 522-4000, 888 South King Street, Honolulu.
Wahiawa General Hospital ((808) 621-8411, 128 Lehua Street, Wahiawa.

DANGEROUS ANIMALS

Although Hawaii is fortunate to have few problems with the more dangerous and aggressive marine creatures that inhabit its waters, they are potentially harmful and should be avoided. Eels are frequently found in crevices and under coral. They are usually not aggressive, but if threatened can be dangerous. Observe them from a distance and never reach into holes or crevices where

you may risk being bitten. Above all, never try to feed an eel.

Another potential danger is the Portuguese Man-of-War, a bubble-shaped creature whose long tentacles contain poison cells that can inflict painful stings on anyone venturing too close. They are uncommon in island waters, but if encountered, dead or alive, they should never be handled.

Other hazards include cone shells, which can shoot off a poisonous dart used to capture prey, and spiny sea urchins (or *wana* as they are locally known), which can inflict painful puncture wounds through their brittle spines. Remember too that coral cuts and abrasions are slow to heal and often become infected.

TANNING

Since the difference between a suntan and sunburn can be the difference between a happy vacation and an unhappy one, it is well to remember that the Hawaii sun is intense and should be treated with respect. From 11 AM to 2 PM you are well advised to stay indoors. As we all now know that a suntan is just as bad for you as sunburn, my advice is simple: wear sunscreen at all times, even if the weather is overcast.

Another point to bear in mind is that some parts of the body are more sensitive to the sun's rays than others. Your nose, knees, and the tops of your feet should be particularly well protected by sunscreen, and your eyes should be protected by UV-protectively-coated, polarized sunglasses.

SECURITY

There is no real problem with crime in Hawaii, but you are well advised to take the normal precautions with your valuables, such as using hotel safes and security boxes whenever possible. Theft of rental cars is very low to nonexistent on most islands (where are they going to go?), but there are some instances of breaking windshields and windows just to see what's inside cars left in desolate areas. My advice? Don't leave valuables in your car, just leave it unlocked.

WHEN TO GO

The high seasons in Hawaii are winter, when everyone is trying to avoid bad weather elsewhere, and during the summer vacations, for kids on the mainland. The last week of April is also busy as it's Golden Week in Japan (when three public holidays run together).

Bargain rates are available from mid-April to mid-June and from September to mid-December. These are also the periods of best weather in Hawaii.

WHAT TO TAKE

The state of Hawaii is known for diverse climatic conditions over concentrated areas, so if you are planning to travel around, don't think you can get by with a swimsuit and flip-flops. You'll need to bring a good pair of shoes (for hiking, horseback riding) and a sweater and jacket for temperatures of about 40° Fahrenheit or about 5° Celsius (for trips up craters and upcountry); some rain gear may also be a good idea. Beyond that, Hawaii is very casual. A polo shirt and chinos (or the female equivalent) will do for most restaurants, except fine dining in the most exclusive resorts.

LANGUAGE BASICS

Spoken Hawaiian is a beautifully melodic language for which there was no written form until after the eighteenth century.

As part of the renaissance of Hawaiian art and culture, spoken and written Hawaiian is in midst of revival.

Hawaiian is not to be confused with pidgin, a dialect spoken widely by locals. Whereas Hawaiian is a Polynesian language that has its roots in the languages of Southeast Asia, pidgin evolved out of English, Japanese, Samoan and Chinese.

Hawaiian words are pronounced precisely as they are spelled. There are no silent letters, and words can be easily broken down into syllables as in "Waikiki" (Wai-ki-ki) or "aloha" (a-lo-ha).

Below are some of the words you'll hear in day-to-day conversations while in the islands.

Ahaiaina feast
A hui hou Until we meet again
aina land, earth; that from which plant food (*'ai*) comes
aloha lover; hello; good-bye
halau longhouse, such as used in hula instruction; school
haole white person, Caucasian; formerly any foreigner
hula traditional Hawaiian dance
kahakai seaside
kahuna priest or minister of old religion; expert in any profession
kai sea, salt water
kamaaina old-time resident; literally "child of the land"
kane man, male
kapu taboo, forbidden
keiki child
lanai porch, verandah
lomi-lomi massage
luau taro leaves; term used for Hawaiian feast
mahalo thank you
makai towards the sea
malihini stranger, newcomer; one unaccustomed to a place or its customs
mana spirit power
mauka towards the uplands
mele song, poem; to sing
moana ocean; deep sea
muumuu loose-fitting dress
nene official state bird, also called the Hawaiian goose
ono delicious; also wahoo
pau the end; finished, completed
wahine woman, female
wai fresh water

WEB SITES

There are literally thousands of web sites on all aspects of Hawaii. Just enter the search word *Hawaii* on any of the larger search engines and you can entertain yourself for hours, covering such topics as all you need to know about leis at **www.leisofhawaii.com** to up-to-the-minute surf reports at **www .surf-news.com**.

Some of the more interesting sites from a historical and cultural standpoint include **Bishop Museum**'s site www.bishop museum.org, which includes a natural history inventory of the archipelago with a searchable gallery and image gallery, and **www.surfart.com**, with its history of surfing. Basic Hawaiian language lessons with journal musings, language links and even the possibility of sending an aloha card are available at **www.geocities.com**, while **www.hookele.com** provides Hawaiian culture online, with a directory of cultural sites and Maui genealogies and stories.

For general, pre-travel tourist information, you may not need to go beyond the **Hawaii Visitors & Convention Bureau's** www.gohawaii.com and the official sites of the various islands. But other all-inclusive information sites that are easy to navigate and timely include **Hawaii State Vacation planner** www.hshawaii.com, which gives information on hotels, dining, entertainment, shopping, together with feature stories on activities, a bookstore and an extensive wedding site. **Best of Hawaii** www.bestofhawaii .com offers last minute discount package deals, general information, service links and even a shot of Hawaii from space. Discount package deals are also available at **Travel Zoo** www.travelzoo.com.

For more Oahu-oriented information, **Hawaii Attractions Association** www .HawaiiAttractions.com, gives a good overview of attractions, including a handy calendar of events. For more information on Maui, **Maui Information** www.maui.net includes a lot of what you need to know about accommodation, with an activities desk, professional services plaza, health and fitness corner, alternative lifestyle choices, real estate, a newsstand and more.

Looking for a specific business? Look no further than the **Hawaii Yellow Pages** www .surfhi.com. For **weather** updates, try www .weather.com/weather/us/states/hawaii or www.cnn.com/WEATHER/cities/us .hawaii.

Recommended Reading

ALLEN, HELENA G. *The Betrayal of Liliuokalani: Last Queen of Hawaii 1838–1917.* Mutual Publishing, 1991.

BALDWIN, JEFF. *Cycling Hawaii.* Motorbooks International, 1997.

BUCK, SIR PETER. *Arts and Crafts of Hawaii.* Honolulu: Bishop Museum, 1957.

CALDWELL, PETER. *Adventurer's Hawai'i.* Taote, 1992.

CARROLL, RICK and MARCIE. *Travelers' Tales Hawai'i.* Travelers' Tales, 1999.

CONGDON-MARTIN, DOUGLAS. *Aloha Spirit: Hawaiian Art and Popular Design.* Schiffer Publishing, 1998.

CUNNINGHAM, SCOTT. *Hawaiian Religion and Magic.* Llewellyn Publications, 1994.

JENKINS, BRUCE. *North Shore Chronicles: Big Wave Surfing in Hawaii.* North Atlantic Books, 1999.

JUVIK, SONIA P., JAMES O. *Atlas of Hawaii.* Honolulu: University of Hawaii Press, 1999.

KANE, HERB K. *Ancient Hawaii.* Honolulu: Kawainui Publishing, 1998.

KUHNS, GRANT. *On Surfing.* Rutland: C.E. Tuttle Co, 1963.

PENISTEN, JOHN. *Adventure Guide to Hawaii.* Hunter Publishing, 1999.

MICHENER, JAMES. *Hawaii.* 1959; New York: Fawcett Books, 1994.

MORGAN, JOSEPH R. *Hawaii.* Boulder: Westview Press Inc., 1983.

PUKUI, MARY KAWENA. *English–Hawaiian Dictionary.* Honolulu: University of Hawaii Press, 1964.

SMITH, ROBERT. *Hiking Oahu: The Capital Isle.* Boulder: Wilderness Press, 1980.

SOEHREN, RICK. *The Birdwatcher's Guide to Hawai'i.* Honolulu: University of Hawaii, 1996.

Quick Reference A–Z Guide to Places and Topics of Interest with Listed Accommodation, Restaurants and Useful Telephone Numbers

The symbols Ⓕ FAX, Ⓣ TOLL-FREE, Ⓔ E-MAIL, Ⓦ WEB-SITE refer to additional contact information found in the chapter listings.

A accommodation
  cabins 57
  camping 28, 50, 57
  condominiums 294
  general information 50, 294
  hostels 50, 52
  hotels with flair 53, 55
  room prices 294
  youth hostels 50
Ahihi-Kinau Natural Area Reserve (Maui) 190
  sports
    diving and snorkeling 190
Akaka Falls State Park (Big Island) 253
  attractions
    Kahuna Falls and Akaka Falls 253
Alakai Swamp (Kauai) 16–17, 149
Alau Island (Maui) 194
Alenuihaha Channel 102
Anahola (Kauai) 158, 178
  restaurants
    Duane's Ono-Char Burger
      ((808) 822-9181 178
Anahola Bay (Kauai) 158, 161
Anini Beach Park (Kauai) 162
  sports
    diving and windsurfing 162

B backpacking 50, 52, 201
Baldwin Beach Park (Maui) 30
  general information
    Maui County ((808) 243-7389 30
Bali Hai (Kauai) 162, 164, 178
Barking Sands (Kauai) 153, 157
  attractions
    Pacific Missile Range Facility 153, 157
Bellows Air Forces Base (Oahu) 127
Bellows Field Beach Park (Oahu) 28, 127
Big Island 11, 14–16, 19–20, 24, 32, 34, 36, 40,
  42, 45, 47, 50, 55–57, 63–66, 68, 70, 72–73, 75–76,
  78–79, 81, 87–88, 89, 91, 93, 99, 102–105, 151, 183,
  190, 225, 241, 250, 291, 294

C canoeing 40, 42
Captain Cook (Big Island) 57, 257, 269, 272, 281
  attractions
    Greenwell Farms Estate Coffee
      ((808) 322-2862 Ⓕ 257
    Kona Historical Society Museum
      ((808) 323-3222 257
    Royal Kona Museum and Coffee Mill
      ((808) 328-2511 Ⓣ 257
  general information
    Kealia Ranch (hunting)
      ((808) 328-8777 Ⓔ Ⓦ 272
  restaurants
    Ted's Kona Theater and Café
      ((808) 328-2244 281
Chain of Craters Road (Big Island) 11–12, 50,
  254–255

children, traveling with
  activities 57
    cowboy lifestyle ((808) 966-5416 Ⓕ Ⓦ 58
    go karts ((808) 871-7619 186
    marine education ((808) 667-6706 196
    surfing ((808) 742-8019 58
  festivals and special events 74–75
    Whalefest Week (March) ((808) 667-9175 73
  general information 56–57
  recommended places 56, 58–59, 204, 206–207
climate 102–103, 298
Coconut Coast (Kauai) 158
coffee 50, 81, 86–87, 229, 250, 257, 275
consulates
  in California 291
  on Oahu 291
cuisine 83, 140, 174, 177, 215
  beverages 86–87
  fruits 84–85
  general information 82
  luau 83, 86
  meat 86
  Portuguese influence 112
  seafood 85
  snacks 83–84
  vegetables 85
customs 291

D Diamond Head (Oahu) 24, 67, 125–126
Diamond Head Beach (Oahu) 36
  sports
    windsurfing 36
Dillingham Field (Oahu) 130, 134
  general information
    Skysurfing Glider Rides ((808) 256-0438 134
  sports
    glider riding 134
diving 36, 40
Dole Plantation (Oahu) 130
  attractions
    Pineapple Garden Maze 130
  general information
    plantation information ((808) 621-8408 130
Donkey Beach (Kauai) 161

E Ehukai Beach (Oahu) 34–35, 129
  sports
    surfing 34, 129
Eke Crater (Maui) 202
electricity 295
Eleele (Kauai) 154, 176
  restaurants
    Grinds Espresso ((808) 335-6027 176
etiquette 296
Ewa Beach (Oahu) 43
  general information
    West Loch Golf Course ((808) 296-2000 43
  sports
    golf 43
Ewa Plain (Oahu) 43, 117
extreme surfing 36

F festivals and special events   *70, 73, 75–76, 78–79, 81*
  Big Island Bounty (May) ((808) 845-9905   *75*
  Buddha Day, April   74
  hula festivals   70
  Kauai festival information ((808) 553-3876   *76*
  Kauai-Tahiti Fete, August   78
  King Kamehameha Day, June 11   76
  Kona Coffee Festival (November)
    ((808) 326-7820   *81*
  Lei Day, May 1   75
  Maui Triathlon (October) ((808) 579-9502   *79*
  Molokai festival information ((808) 553-3876   *76*
  Na Wahine O Ke Kai, (September)   *79*
  Oahu Aloha Festival (September)
    ((808) 885-8086   *79*
  Paradise Ride Hawaii (July) ((808) 242-4900   *78*
First and Second Cathedrals (Lanai)   *38*
fishing   *42*
Fleming's Beach (Maui)   *188*
flora and fauna   *12, 15–17, 24, 26–27, 29, 36, 40,
  149, 166, 185, 191–192, 241, 250, 256, 266*
Fort DeRussy Beach (Oahu)   *41, 79*
  festivals and special events
    Molokai Hoe, October   *41*

G geography   *23, 102, 149, 183, 225, 241, 250*
getting around
  by bus   293
  by car   *48, 118, 225, 250, 292*
    car rental   *48, 225, 292*
    driving recommendations   *118*
    special car rental   *292*
  by horse-drawn carriage   294
  by limousine   293294
  by plane   291
    interisland carriers   291
  by taxi   293–294
  by wheelchair accessible van   294
getting to Hawaii
  by plane   95, 291
    international carriers   291
    mainland carriers   95, 291
golf   *42, 44–45, 47*
Green Sand Beach (Big Island)   *256*
  attractions
    olivine   *257*

H **Haena (Kauai)**   *163, 166, 174*
Haena Beach Park (Kauai)   *29, 164*
Haiku (Maui)   *193, 211–212*
  accommodation   211
    Maui Dream Cottages ((808) 575-9079   *212*
    Sunrise Garden Suite
      ((808) 572-1440 Ⓕ Ⓔ Ⓦ   *212*
  attractions   193
Haiku Falls (Maui)   *202*
Halawa Valley (Molokai)   *50, 225, 227, 235*
  accommodation
    Puu O Hoku Ranch ((808) 558-8109 Ⓕ   *235*
  attractions
    Moaula Falls   227
    Puu O Hoku Ranch ((808) 558-8109 Ⓕ   *227*
  general information   227
  shopping
    Wavecrest General Store
      ((808) 558-0222 Ⓕ   *228*
Haleakala (Maui)   *14–15, 23–24, 29–30, 49, 68, 79,
  103, 183, 185, 190, 192, 200, 202*
Haleakala National Park (Maui)   *14, 29–30, 68,
  99, 183, 190, 196, 201–202, 211*

accommodation
  camping and cabins
    ((808) 572-4400 Ⓦ   *30, 211*
    Silver Cloud Upcountry Ranch   *68*
attractions
  Crater Loop Hike   *29*
  Haleakala Crater   *190*
  Halemauu Trail   *30*
  Leleiwi Overlook   *190*
  Paint Pot   *30*
  Puu Ulaula Overlook   *190*
  Sliding Sands Trail   *29*
  Sliding Sands-Halemauu Loop   *30*
  Specter of the Brocken   *190*
general information
  Maui Downhill ((808) 871-2155   *14, 201*
  Park Information ((808) 572-4400,
    7749   *30, 190*
  Summit Visitor's Center   *190*
  Temptation Tours ((808) 877-8888   *14*
sports
  biking   *14*
  hiking ((808) 572-4400   *14, 29–30, 183, 201*
  horseback riding   *202*
Haleiwa (Oahu)   *28, 48, 50, 67, 130, 134, 138, 143*
  accommodation   50
    Beach Homes North Shore
      ((808) 637-3507 Ⓣ Ⓕ Ⓦ   *138*
  attractions   67, 130
    Baywatch stage set   *130*
    M. Matsumoto Store ((808) 637-4827   *67, 130*
  general information
    Haleiwa Surf Center ((808) 637-5051   *134*
    Surf and Sea ((808) 637-9887   *134*
  restaurants
    Cholo's ((808) 637-3059   *143*
    Coffee Gallery ((808) 637-5355   *143*
    Haleiwa Joe's ((808) 637-8005   *143*
    Jameson's by the Sea ((808) 637-4336   *143*
    Kua Aina Sandwich ((808) 637-6027   *67, 143*
    Paradise Found Café ((808) 637-4540   *143*
  shopping
    H. Miura Store ((808) 637-4845   *130*
    Haleiwa Shopping Center   *130*
Haleiwa Alii Beach (Oahu)   *35*
Haliimaile (Maui)   *30, 56, 219*
  attractions
    Rainbow Park   *30*
  restaurants
    Haliimaile General Store
      ((808) 572-2666   *56, 219*
Halona Blowhole (Oahu)   *126*
Hamakua Coast (Big Island)   *69, 81, 266, 287*
  general information
    Hilo-Hamakua Heritage Coast Drive Guide
      ((808) 966-5416 Ⓕ Ⓦ   *266*
Hana (Maui)   *30, 54, 61, 74, 91, 183–185, 191,
  193–194, 199–202, 212, 220*
  access   192, 221
  accommodation
    Bamboo Inn at Hana Bay
      ((808) 248-7718 Ⓕ Ⓔ Ⓦ   *212*
    Hamoa Bay Bungalow
      ((808) 248-7884 Ⓕ Ⓔ   *213*
    Hana Hale Malamalama
      ((808) 248-7718 Ⓕ Ⓔ Ⓦ   *212*

Hana Kai Maui Resort
  ((808) 248-8426 Ⓣ Ⓕ Ⓦ   213
Hana Plantations ((808) 248-8975 Ⓣ   213
Heavenly Hana Inn
  (/FAX (808) 248-8422 Ⓦ   54, 212
Hotel Hana-Maui
  ((808) 248-8211 Ⓕ   192, 212
Joe's Place ((808) 248-7033   213
Tradewinds Cottage
  ((808) 248-8980 Ⓣ Ⓕ   213
attractions   193
  Blue Pond   193
  Hana Cultural Center
    ((808) 248-8622 Ⓦ   61, 193
  Hasegawa General Store
    ((808) 248-8231   193
  Kahanu Garden ((808) 248-8912   91
  Piilanihale Heiau   91
environs and excursions
  Alau Island   194
  Virgin by the Roadside   194
festivals and special events
  East Maui Taro Festival (March)
    ((808) 248-8972   74
general information
  Hana Adventure Outfitters
    ((808) 248-7476 Ⓕ Ⓔ   201
  Hana Kayak ((808) 248-8211   200
  Hana Ranch Stables ((808) 248-8211   202
  Hang Gliding Maui ((808) 572-6557 Ⓔ   200
restaurants
  Hana Gardenland Café   220
  Hana Ranch Restaurant ((808) 248-8255   220
  Hana Ranch Store ((808) 248-8261   221
  Hotel Hana-Maui Dining Room
    ((808) 248-8211   220
shopping   65, 193, 199
  Hana Tropical Nursery ((808) 248-7533   199
  Susan Marie ((808) 248-7231   199
Hanalei (Kauai)   36, 42, 48, 161–162, 165–166,
173–174, 178, 293
accommodation   174
  Hanalei Colony Resort
    ((808) 826-6235 Ⓣ Ⓕ Ⓦ   174
  Kilauea Lakeside Estate
    ((808) 379-7842 Ⓣ Ⓕ Ⓦ   173
attractions
  Black Pot   162
  Pine Trees Beach Park   162
general information
  Hanalei Surf Company ((808) 826-9000   166
  Kayak Kauai Outbound
    ((808) 826-9844 Ⓣ Ⓕ Ⓦ   42, 166
restaurants
  Bubba's Burgers ((808) 826-7839   179
  Hanalei Gourmet ((808) 826-2524   178
  Postcards Café ((808) 826-1191   178
  Zelo's Beach House ((808) 826-9700   179
shopping
  Ola's ((808) 826-693   165
  Tropical Tantrum ((808) 826-6944   165
  Yellowfish Trading Company
    ((808) 826-1227   65, 165
sports
  kayaking   42, 166
  surfing   166
Hanalei Bay (Kauai)   48, 54, 162–163, 166, 172
Hanalei River (Kauai)   42, 166

Hanapepe (Kauai)   153–154, 156, 176
attractions
  Hanapepe Canyon Lookout   154
  Salt Pond Beach   156
restaurants
  Green Garden ((808) 335-5422   176
  Hanapepe Café and Espresso Bar
    ((808) 335-5011   176
Hanapepe River (Kauai)   156
Hanauma Bay (Oahu)   38, 67, 118, 126
sports
  diving   38
Hapuna Beach (Big Island)   81, 278
Hawaiian Homelands (Oahu)   127
healing, traditional methods of
courses
  Pacific Adventures ((808) 324-1338 Ⓦ   88
general information   88
  Helping Hands ((808) 822-1715 Ⓔ   88
spas   53, 88, 90, 138
  Hawaii Adventure Spa
    ((808) 324-1717 Ⓕ Ⓔ Ⓦ   88
  Kohala Spa ((808) 886-1234 Ⓦ   89
  Mauna Lani Spa ((808) 885-6622 Ⓦ   89
  Spa Grande ((808) 875-1234 Ⓕ Ⓔ Ⓦ   90
  Spa Without Walls ((808) 885-2000 Ⓦ   89
health
  dangerous animals   297
  emergency numbers   296
  sunburns   297
Heeia State Park (Oahu)   128
Hilo (Big Island)   36, 52, 55, 63–64, 68–70, 76, 78,
250, 253, 263, 266–267, 269–273, 279–280, 287
access   287
accommodation   55
  Arnott's Lodge ((808) 969-7097 Ⓕ Ⓔ Ⓦ   52
  Bay House (/FAX (808) 961-6311 Ⓔ   272
  Dolphin Bay Hotel ((808) 935-1466 Ⓔ Ⓦ   272
  Hawaii Naniloa Resort
    ((808) 969-3333 Ⓣ Ⓕ Ⓔ Ⓦ   272
  Hilo Hawaiian Hotel
    ((808) 591-2235 Ⓣ Ⓕ Ⓔ Ⓦ   272
  Inn at Kulaniapia
    ((808) 966-6373 Ⓣ Ⓕ Ⓔ Ⓦ   272
  Ironwood House
    (/FAX (808) 934-8855 Ⓣ Ⓔ Ⓦ   272
  Shipman House Bed and Breakfast
    (/FAX (808) 934-8002 Ⓔ Ⓦ   272
  Wild Ginger Inn ((808) 935-5556 Ⓣ Ⓦ   52
attractions   63, 253
  Big Island Candies ((808) 935-8890   253
  East Hawaii Cultural Center
    ((808) 961-5711   253
  Malia Puka O Kalani Church   76
  Mehana Brewing Company
    ((808) 934-8211 Ⓔ Ⓦ   253
  Nani Mau Gardens ((808) 959-3541   253
  Pacific Tsunami Museum
    ((808) 935-0926   253
  Rainbow Falls   253
  Suisan Fish Auction   253
  Wailuku River Park   253
environs and excursions   91, 253
festivals and special events   76, 78
  Merrie Monarch Hula Festival, April   70
general information   250
  Aquatic Perceptions ((808) 933-1228   270
  Arnott's Hiking Adventures
    ((808) 969-7097 Ⓕ Ⓔ   272

Big Island Mountain Bike Association
((808) 961   *271*
Bytes & Bites ((808) 935-3520 Ⓕ Ⓔ   *250*
Hawaii Horse Owners Association
((808) 959-8932   *271*
Hawaii Island Economic Development Board
((808) 966-5416 Ⓕ Ⓦ   *263, 266*
Hilo International Airport
((808) 934-5838   *287*
Hilo Municipal Golf Course
((808) 959-7711   *271*
Naniloa Country Club ((808) 935-3000   *271*
Nautilus Dive Center
(/FAX (808) 935-6939   *270*
restaurants
Bears' Coffee (808) 935-0708   *280*
Bytes & Bites ((808) 935-3520   *250*
Café Pesto ((808) 969-6640 Ⓦ   *280*
Happy Cats Café ((808) 935-0595   *280*
Harrington's ((808) 961-4966   *279*
Honu's Nest ((808) 935-9321   *280*
Ken's Pancake House ((808) 935-8711   *280*
Pescatore ((808) 969-9090   *279*
Reubens ((808) 961-2552   *280*
Royal Siam Thai Restaurant
((808) 961-6100   *280*
Seaside Restaurant ((808) 935-8825   *280*
What's Shakin' ((808) 964-3080   *280*
shopping
Black Pearl Gallery ((808) 935-8556   *270*
Discount Fabric Warehouse
((808) 935-1234   *270*
Flowers of Hawaii ((808) 959-5858 Ⓕ   *270*
Hilo Farmers' Market   *253*
Hilo Hattie ((808) 961-3077   *270*
Sig Zane Designs ((808) 935-7077   *64269*
Ukuleles by Kawika Inc.
((808) 969-7751 Ⓔ   *270*
Winkler Wood Products
((808) 961-6411 Ⓔ Ⓦ   *270*
sports
golf   *271*
history
annexation   108, 117
coffee   87
Cook, Captain James   104–105, 257
earliest inhabitants   103
fiftieth US State   108, 118
immigrants   112–113, 191
independence movement   108, 109
Kaahumanu   105–106, 150, 183
Kalakaua   107–108
Kamehameha I   20, 105, 117, 126, 150, 183, 241,
  257, 260, 266
Kamehameha III   106, 111
Kauai   149, 152
Lanai   20, 241
Lunalilo   107
Maui   183–184
missionaries   106, 186
modern Hawaii   108–109, 118
Molokai   225
Oahu   117–118
Pearl Harbor   13, 60, 108, 118
Polynesians   103, 184, 225, 256
United States meddling   108, 117

Holualoa (Big Island)   *257, 274–275*
accommodation
Holualoa Inn ((808) 324-1121 Ⓣ Ⓕ Ⓔ Ⓦ   *274*
Rosy's Rest (/FAX (808) 322-7378 Ⓔ   *275*
attractions
Kimura Lauhala Store   *257*
Honaunau Bay (Big Island)   *40*
sports
diving   *40*
Honaunua (Big Island)   *73, 257, 275*
accommodation
Dragonfly Ranch Tropical Fantasy Retreat
((808) 328-2159 Ⓣ Ⓕ Ⓔ Ⓦ   *275*
attractions
Bay View Farm
((808) 328-9658 Ⓣ Ⓕ Ⓔ Ⓦ   *257*
Painted Church   *257*
Honokaa (Big Island)   *52, 81, 266, 271, 278,*
286–287
accommodation
Hale Kukui ((808) 775-7130 Ⓣ Ⓔ Ⓦ   *278*
Hotel Honokaa Club
((808) 775-0678 Ⓣ Ⓦ   *52*
Hotel Honokaa Club
((808) 775-0678 Ⓣ Ⓦ   *279*
Mountain Meadow Ranch
((808) 775-9376 Ⓕ Ⓔ Ⓦ   *278*
Waipio Wayside Bed and Breakfast
((808) 775-0275 Ⓣ Ⓔ Ⓦ   *279*
attractions
Honokaa People's Theater   *266*
Mamane Street   *266*
festivals and special events   81
general information
Hamakua Country Club ((808) 775-7244   *271*
Kohala Naalapa Trail Rides
((808) 889-0022   *271*
Paniolo Riding Adventures
((808) 889-5354 Ⓔ   *271*
restaurants
Café Il Mondo ((808) 775-7711   *286*
Tex Drive Inn ((808) 775-0598   *286*
shopping
Hawaiian Shop   *266*
sports
golf   *271*
Honokowai (Maui)   *215, 293*
restaurants
A Pacific Café ((808) 667-2800   *215*
Honolua Bay (Maui)   *36, 38*
sports
diving   *38*
surfing   *36*
Honolulu
festivals and special events   70, 81
Honolulu (Oahu)   *13–14, 20, 24, 26, 28, 42, 47–48,*
50–51, 59–60, 76, 79, 81, 87, 95, 99, 107–108,
117–118, 125, 134, 143, 150, 244, 262, 293
access   144
accommodation   50
Aloha Inns–Piikoi Arms
((808) 596-2080 Ⓕ Ⓔ Ⓦ   *51*
attractions   60, 124–125
Aloha Stadium   *65*
Aloha Tower   *117, 123, 134*
Aloha Tower Marketplace
((808) 528-5700   *74, 134*
Arizona Memorial ((808) 422-0561   *13–14,*
  60, 67, 124

Battleship Missouri Memorial
  ((808) 973-2494   125
Bishop Museum ((808) 847-3511 Ⓦ   59, 67,
  124, 244
Chinatown   66, 123
Contemporary Museum
  ((808) 526-1322   59, 125
Diamond Head   99, 125–126
Foster Botanical Gardens
  ((808) 533-3214   125
Harold L. Lyon Arboretum
  ((808) 988-7378   91
Hawaii Maritime Center
  ((808) 536-6373   16, 59, 74, 122
Herbarium Pacificum
  ((808) 847-3511   59, 124
Honolulu Academy of the Arts
  ((808) 532-8701   60, 122
Iolani Palace ((808) 522-0822   76, 108, 117,
  120–121
Iolani Palace ((808) 522-0822   262
Kapiolani Park   72–73, 76, 120
Kawaiahao Church ((808) 538-6267   107, 121
Kewalo Basin   123
Lady Columbia   125
Mauna Ala   107
Maunakea Marketplace ((808) 524-3409   123
Mission Houses Museum
  ((808) 531-0481   121
Moanalua Gardens   70
Pearl Harbor   13–14, 60, 99, 124–125
Planetarium ((808) 847-8201   59
Punchbowl Crater   125
Restaurant Row ((808) 538-1441   123
Royal Mausoleum ((808) 536-7602   125
State Capitol ((808) 586-2211   121
Statue of Kamehameha I   76, 121
War Memorials   122
Washington Place ((808) 587-0790   122
environs and excursions
  Makiki Valley   26
  Mount Tantalus   26
festivals and special events   72–76, 81
  Bankoh Kayak Challenge, May   40
  Honolulu City Lights (December)
    ((808) 527-5784   81
  Honolulu King Kamehameha Floral Parade,
    June   76
  Honolulu Marathon (December)
    ((808) 734-7200 Ⓦ   47, 81
  Intertribal Powwow (October)
    ((808) 734-5171   79
  King Kamehameha Day, June 11   121
  Oahu Aloha Festival (September)
    ((808) 885-8086   79
  Oahu Kite Festival (March)
    ((808) 735-9059   73
  Oahu Perimeter Relay (February)
    ((808) 486-2692   72
  Prince Lot Hula Festival (July)
    ((808) 839-5334   70
general information   134
  Bishop Museum ((808) 847-3511 Ⓦ   20
  City and County of Honolulu
    ((808) 523-4525   28
  Hawaii Kai Golf Courses ((808) 395-2358   42
  Hawaii Prince Golf Club ((808) 944-4567   43
  Honolulu International Airport   291
  Magnum Helicopters ((808) 833-1133   134

Navatek I ((808) 848-6360 Ⓣ Ⓦ   16
Oahu Visitor's Association
  ((808) 524-0722 Ⓣ   118
Rainbow Pacific Helicopters
  ((808) 834-1111   134
Roberts Hawaii Tours ((808) 539-9400 Ⓣ   95
Seaplane Service ((808) 836-6273   134
State of Hawaii Campgrounds
  ((808) 587-0300   28
TheBus ((808) 848-5555   118
history   13, 117
nightlife   144
  Hard Rock Café ((808) 955-7383   144
  Hula's Bar and Lei Stand
    ((808) 923-0669   144
  Ocean Club ((808) 526-9888   144
  The Row ((808) 528-2345   144
restaurants   67, 141–142
  3660 On the Rise ((808) 737-1177   56, 141
  A Taste of Saigon ((808) 947-8885   142
  Alan Wong's ((808) 949-2526   55, 140
  Aloha Tower Marketplace
    ((808) 528-5700   142
  Andy's Sandwiches and Smoothies
    ((808) 988-6161   142
  Big Island Steak House ((808) 537-4446   142
  Chai's Island Bistro ((808) 585-0011   141
  Chef Mavro ((808) 944-4714   55, 140
  Don Ho's Island Grill ((808) 528-0807   142
  Duc's Bistro ((808) 531-6325   142
  Indigo ((808) 521-2900   141
  Keo's Thai Cuisine ((808) 737-8240   142
  L&L Drive Inn ((808) 951-8333   142
  Mocha Java Café ((808) 591-9023   142
  Ono Hawaiian Food ((808) 737-2275   142
  Restaurant Row ((808) 538-1441   123
  River Street   123
  Roy's ((808) 396-7697   55, 67, 141
  Sam Choy's Diamond Head
    ((808) 732-8645   141
  Sushi King ((808) 947-2836   142
  Wo Fat ((808) 533-6393   142
shopping
  Aloha Flea Market   65
  Aloha Stadium Swap Meet
    ((808) 486-1529   134
  Aloha Tower Marketplace
    ((808) 528-5700   65, 123, 134
  Bailey's Antiques ((808) 734-7628   134
  Bishop Museum ((808) 847-3511 Ⓦ   65
  Hilo Hattie ((808) 537-2926   134
  Maunakea Street   66
  Russ K Makaha ((808) 951-7877,   134
sports
  fishing   134
  golf   42
Honomu (Big Island)   253, 272, 287
accommodation
  Akaka Falls Inn ((808) 963-5468 Ⓕ Ⓔ   272
Honopu Valley (Kauai)   157
Hookio Ridge (Lanai)   243
Hookipa Beach (Maui)   36, 79, 192
attractions
  Hookipa Beach Park   192
festivals and special events   79
sports
  windsurfing   36, 192

Hoolehua (Molokai) *229, 232, 237*
  access *237*
  attractions and shopping *229*
  general information *237*
    Budget ((808) 567-6877 Ⓕ *225*
    Dollar ((808) 567-6156 *225*
    Fun Hog Hawaii ((808) 567-6789 *232*
    Hawaiian Air TOLL-FREE (800) 882-8811 *237*
    Island Air TOLL-FREE (800) 652-6541 *237*
    Molokai Air Shuttle ((808) 567-6847 *237*
    Pacific Wings ((808) 567-6814 Ⓣ Ⓔ Ⓦ *237*
Hualalai Mountain (Big Island) *268, 274*
Huelo (Maui) *212*
  accommodation
    Huelo Point Flower Farm
      ((808) 572-1850 Ⓔ *212*
    Huelo Point Lookout ((808) 573-0914 Ⓔ *212*
hula *63, 70, 74– 76, 78–79, 81, 83, 111–112, 130, 132,*
  136, 144, 163, 170, 188, 197, 228, 260, 269, 287
Huleia National Wildlife Refuge (Kauai) *166*
Huleia River (Kauai) *166*
Hulopoe Beach (Lanai) *32, 78, 247*
  accommodation
    Lanai Company ((808) 565-3982 *32*

I **Iao Valley State Park (Maui)** *183, 186*
  attractions
    Iao Needle *186*
    Kepaniwai Heritage Gardens *186*
  general information
    Hawaii Nature Center ((808) 244-6500 *186*
    Visitor's Center ((808) 984-8109 *186*
  history *183*

K **Ka Lae (Big Island)** *See* South Point (Big Island) *256*
Kaa (Maui) *193*
Kaana (Molokai) *228*
Kaanapali (Maui) *16, 36, 45, 73–74, 78, 187–188,*
  196, 198, 202, 215–217, 221, 293
  access *221*
  attractions
    Hale Kohola *188*
    Whale Pavilion *188*
    Whalers Village Museum
      ((808) 661-5992 *16, 188*
  festivals and special events
    Maui Marathon (March) ((808) 871-6441 *74*
    Maui Onion Festival (August)
      ((808) 875-0457 *78*
    Whalefest Week (March) ((808) 667-9175 *73*
  general information
    North and South Golf Courses
      ((808) 661-3691 *45, 202*
    Parasail Kaanapali ((808) 669-6555 *200*
    UFO Parasail ((808) 661-7836 Ⓦ *200*
  nightlife
    Marriott Luau ((808) 661-5828 *221*
  restaurants *216*
    Basil Tomatoes ((808) 662-3210 *216*
    Ganso Kawara Soba ((808) 667-0815 *217*
    Hula Grill Restaurant ((808) 661-1148 *215*
    Jonny's Burger Joint ((808) 661-4500 *217*
    Leilani's on the Beach ((808) 661-4495 *215*
    Luigis ((808) 661-4500 *216*
    Maui Yogurt ((808) 661-8843 *217*
    Pizza Paradiso ((808) 667-0333 *217*
    Swan Court ((808) 661-1234 *215*
    Village Korean BarBQ ((808) 661-9798 *217*

  shopping
    Honokowai Farmers Market *198*
    Whalers Village
      ((808) 661-4567 Ⓦ *188, 198, 215*
  sports
    golf *45, 202*
    surfing *36*
Kaau Crater (Oahu) *27*
Kaena Point (Oahu) *131*
Kahakuloa (Maui) *202*
  general information
    Mendes Ranch ((808) 871-5222 *202*
  sports
    horseback riding *202*
Kahala (Oahu) *54–56, 126, 137, 143*
  accommodation
    Kahala Mandarin Oriental
      ((808) 739-8888 Ⓣ Ⓕ Ⓦ *54, 126, 137*
  children activities
    Keiki Club ((808) 739-8888 Ⓣ Ⓕ Ⓦ *56*
  restaurants
    Hoku's ((808) 739-8777 *55, 137, 143*
Kahana (Maui) *216*
  restaurants *216*
    Bay Club ((808) 669-8008 *216*
    Roy's Kahana Bar and Grill
      ((808) 669-6999 *216*
    Roy's Nicolina Restaurant
      ((808) 669-6999 *216*
Kahanamoku Beach (Oahu) *41*
  festivals and special events
    Na Wahine O Ke Kai, September *41*
Kahe (Oahu) *35*
Kahiwa Falls (Molokai) *231*
Kahoolawe Island *102, 109*
Kahului (Maui) *61, 63, 74, 185, 190–191, 194, 197,*
  199, 201–202, 214, 221, 291
  access *221*
  accommodation
    Maui Beach Hotel ((808) 877-0051 Ⓣ Ⓕ *202*
  attractions *61, 185*
    Kanaha Beach Park *30*
    Kanaha Wildlife Sanctuary
      ((808) 984-8100 *185*
    Maui Go Karts ((808) 871-7619 *186*
  cultural events
    Maui Arts and Cultural Center
      ((808) 242-7469 *63, 76, 81, 221*
  festivals and special events *74*
    Bankoh Ki-Ho Alu (June) ((808) 242-7469 *76*
    First Night Maui (December 31)
      ((808) 242-7469 *81*
    Maui Marathon (March) ((808) 871-6441 *74*
  general information
    Action Sports Maui ((808) 283-7913 Ⓕ *200*
    Hike Maui ((808) 879-5270 Ⓕ *201*
    Kahului Airport *291*
    Prince Kuhio (9808) 242-8777 Ⓣ Ⓕ Ⓦ *199*
  restaurants
    Kaahumanu Center Food Court
      ((808) 877-4325 *214*
    Marco's Grill and Deli ((808) 877-4446 *214*
    Saigon Café ((808) 243-9560 *214*
    Sam Choy's ((808) 893-0366 Ⓦ *214*
    Siu's Chinese Kitchen ((808) 871-0828 *214*
  shopping
    Bounty Music ((808) 871-1141 Ⓦ *199*
    Kaahumanu Center
      ((808) 877-4325 Ⓦ *74, 197*
    Maui Marketplace *197*
    Maui Swapmeet *197*

Kahului Bay (Maui)   63
Kaieie Waho Channel   150
Kailua (Big Island)   See Kailua-Kona
  (Big Island)   257
Kailua (Maui)   193
Kailua (Oahu)   28, 48, 67, 128, 134, 137
  accommodation   137
  general information   134
  restaurants
    Brent's Bestaurant ((808) 262-8588   143
  sports
    kayaking and sailboarding   134
Kailua Bay (Oahu)   128
Kailua-Kona (Big Island)   16, 34, 36, 40, 42, 47, 50,
  68–69, 73, 75, 78–79, 90–91, 93, 250, 257, 267–272,
  274–276, 281–282, 287, 291, 293
  access   287
  accommodation
    Hale Maluhia Country Inn
      ((808) 329-1123 ⓣ ⓕ ⓔ   275
    Kailua Plantation House
      ((808) 329-3727 ⓣ ⓕ ⓔ ⓦ   276
    Keauhou Beach Hotel
      ((808) 322-3441 ⓣ ⓕ ⓔ   274
    King Kamehameha's Kona Beach Hotel
      ((808) 329-2911 ⓕ ⓔ ⓦ   275
    Kiwi Gardens Bed and Breakfast
      ((808) 326-1559   275
    Kona Billfisher Resort
      ((808) 329-9393 ⓣ ⓕ ⓔ ⓦ   276
    Kona Islander Inn
      ((808) 329-9393 ⓣ ⓕ ⓔ ⓦ   276
    Kona Magic Sand Resort
      ((808) 329-9393 ⓣ ⓕ ⓔ ⓦ   276
    Kona Seaside Hotel
      ((808) 329-2455 ⓣ ⓕ ⓔ ⓦ   276
    Kona Surf Resort and Country Club
      ((808) 322-3411 ⓣ ⓕ ⓔ   274
    Kona Village Resort
      ((808) 325-5555 ⓣ ⓕ ⓔ ⓦ   55
    Kona Village Resort
      ((808) 325-5555 ⓣ ⓕ ⓔ ⓦ   276
    Puanani Bed and Breakfast
      (/FAX (808) 329-8644 ⓣ   275
    Royal Kona Resort
      ((808) 329-3111 ⓣ ⓕ ⓔ ⓦ   275
    Uncle Billy's Kona Bay Hotel
      ((808) 961-5818 ⓣ   276
  attractions   91
    Ahuena Heiau   257
    Ellison S. Onizuka Space Center
      ((808) 329-3441   260
    Hulihee Palace ((808) 329-1877   260
    King Kamehameha Hotelmuseum
      ((808) 329-2911 ⓕ ⓔ   257
    Mokuaikaua Church ((808) 329-1589   260
    National Historical Monument   257
    Natural Energy Laboratory of Hawaii
      Authority ((808) 329-7341   260
    St. Peter's Catholic Church   260
  children activities
    Kona Village Resort ((808) 325-5555   57
  festivals and special events   42, 47, 73, 78–79
    Bankoh Ki-Ho Alu (April)
      ((808) 239-4336   75
    Keauhou-Kona Triathlon (May)
      ((808) 329-0601   76
    King Kalakaua Keiki Hula Festival
      (November)   81
    Kona Stampede (March) ((808) 323-2388   73

  general information   287
    Alii Country Club ((808) 322-2595   271
    Big Island Tennis Academy
      ((808) 324-7072 ⓣ   272
    Big Island Visitors Bureau
      ((808) 329-7787 ⓕ   250
    Bottom Fishing Hawaii ((808) 329-4900   271
    Captain Bob's Kona Coast Fishing
      (/FAX (808) 322   270
    Captain Ronne Grabowiecki
      ((808) 329-4025 ⓕ ⓔ   270
    DJ's Rentals ((808) 329-1700 ⓣ ⓔ ⓦ   260
    Eco-Adventures
      ((808) 329-7116 ⓣ ⓕ ⓔ ⓦ   16
    Hualalai Golf Club ((808) 325-8480   47
    Hualalai Golf Club ((808) 325-8480   271
    Keahole-Kona International Airport
      ((808) 329-3423   260, 291
    Kona Coast Divers ((808) 329-8802 ⓦ   270
    Kona Country Club ((808) 322-2595   271
    Ocean Eco Tours ((808) 937-0494 ⓔ ⓦ   270
    Sandwich Isle Divers ((808) 329-9188 ⓕ   270
  nightlife   286
    Drums of Polynesia ((808) 331-1526 ⓦ   286
    Hard Rock Café ((808) 329-8866   286
    Kona Brewing Pub ((808) 329-2739   286
    Kona Village Resort (luau)
      ((808) 325-6787 ⓦ   286
    LuLu's ((808) 331-2633   286
    Quinns Almost by the Sea
      ((808) 329-3822   286
  restaurants
    Chart House ((808) 329-2451   282
    Huggo's on the Rocks   282
    Huggo's ((808) 329-1493 ⓦ   282
    Island Lava Java ((808) 327-2161 ⓦ   282
    Kona Brewing Pub ((808) 329-2739   282
    Kona Ranch House ((808) 329-7061   282
    La Bourgone ((808) 329-6711   282
    LuLu's ((808) 331-2633   282
    Oodles of Noodles ((808) 329-9222   282
    Quinns almost by the Sea
      ((808) 329-3822   282
    Sam Choy's Restaurant ((808) 326-1545   281
    Sibu Café ((808) 329-1112   282
    Thai Rin ((808) 329-2929   282
  shopping
    Crazy Shirts   270
    Kealakekua's Grass Shack
      ((808) 323-2877   269
    Keauhou Shopping Center
      ((808) 322-3000 ⓦ   269
    Lanihau Center ((808) 329-9333   269
  sports
    golf   47, 271
Kalaheo (Kauai)   154, 176
  attractions   154
  restaurants
    Kalaheo Coffee Company and Café
      ((808) 332-5858   176
Kalalau Beach (Kauai)   29, 167
Kalapaki Beach (Kauai)   152, 168
Kalapana (Big Island)   254
Kalaupapa (Molokai)   58, 63, 228, 230–231
  attractions   230
    Kalaupapa Overlook   228
    mule trail   231
    Nanahoa   229
  environs and excursions   63, 229

general information
    Damien Molokai Tours ((808) 567-6171 *230*
    Molokai Mule Ride
      ((808) 567-6088 Ⓣ Ⓕ Ⓔ Ⓦ *58*
history *230*
Kalaupapa Peninsula (Molokai) *225, 230*
Kalawao (Molokai) *230*
  attractions
    St. Philomena Church *230*
Kalihiwai Bay (Kauai) *162*
Kalihiwai River (Kauai) *162*
Kalihiwai Tree Tunnel (Kauai) *162*
Kalopa (Big Island) *34*
Kaluaaha (Molokai) *50, 226*
  attractions
    Kaluaaha Church *226*
    Our Lady of Seven Sorrows Church *50, 227*
Kaluakoi (Molokai) *40, 45, 70, 228, 233, 236*
  accommodation *233–234*
    Ke Nani Kai ((808) 922-9700 Ⓣ Ⓕ *233*
  attractions
    Kaiaka Rock *228*
    Kawakiu Beach *228*
    Papohaku Beach Park
      ((808) 553-3204 *32, 70, 228*
  festivals and special events *70, 228*
    Bankoh Kayak Challenge, May *40*
    Molokai Hoe, October *41*
    Na Wahine O Ke Kai, September *41*
  general information
    canoeing and kayaking races
      ((808) 261-6615 *41*
    Kaluakoi Golf Course
      ((808) 552-2739 Ⓣ Ⓕ *45, 233*
  restaurants
    Ohia Lodge ((808) 552-2555 *236*
  sports
    golf *45, 233*
Kamakou Mountain (Molokai) *30*
Kamakou Preserve (Molokai) *30, 228*
  access *32*
  attractions
    Waikolu Lookout *32*
  general information
    Nature Conservancy of Hawaii
      ((808) 553-5236 Ⓕ *32, 228*
  sports
    hiking *32*
Kamalo (Molokai) *50, 226, 235*
  accommodation *235*
  attractions
    Saint Joseph's Catholic Church *50, 226*
    Smith-Bronte landing site *226*
Kamaole Beach (Maui) *75*
Kamuela (Big Island) *47, 63, 76, 271, 277–278, 286*
Kanaha Beach Park (Maui) *30, 36*
  general information
    Maui County ((808) 243-7389 *30*
Kanaha Wildlife Sanctuary (Maui) *185*
Kaneohe (Oahu) *43, 128, 138*
  accommodation *138*
  general information
    Koolau Golf Course ((808) 236-4653 *43*
  sports
    golf *43*
Kanepuu Reserve (Lanai) *243*
Kapaa
  restaurants and nightlife
    Tahiti Nui ((808) 826-6277 *179*

Kapaa (Kauai) *44, 48, 56, 88, 93, 158, 161, 165–166, 168, 172, 177–178*
  accommodation *172*
    Hotel Coral Reef
      ((808) 822-4481 Ⓣ Ⓕ Ⓦ *172*
    Islander on the Beach
      ((808) 822-7417 Ⓣ Ⓕ *172*
    Lae Nani ((808) 822-4938 Ⓣ Ⓕ Ⓦ *172*
  children activities *57*
  general information *168*
    Bed-and-Breakfast Kauai
      ((808) 822-1177 Ⓣ Ⓕ Ⓦ *168*
    Bubbles Below Scuba Charters
      ((808) 822-3483 *166*
    Paradise Outdoor Adventures
      ((808) 822-0016 Ⓣ Ⓦ *166*
    Rental Warehouse ((808) 822-4000 *166, 168*
    Snorkel Bob's ((808) 823-9433 *166*
  restaurants
    A Pacific Café Kauai ((808) 822-0013 *56, 177*
    Beezers ((808) 822-4411 *178*
    Kapaa Fish and Chowder House
      ((808) 822-7488 *177*
    Kountry Kitchen ((808) 882-3511 *178*
    Norberto's El Café ((808) 822-3362 *178*
  shopping *166*
    Kauai Village *165*
Kapaa Stream (Kauai) *161*
Kapaau
  general information
    Kohala Mountain Kayak Cruise
      ((808) 889-6922 Ⓕ *270*
Kapaau (Big Island) *262, 278, 284, 286*
  accommodation
    Kohala Country Adventures
      ((808) 889-5663 Ⓔ Ⓦ *278*
  attractions
    Original King Kamehameha Statue *262*
  restaurants
    Bamboo ((808) 889-5555 *284*
    Jen's Kohala Café ((808) 889-0099 *286*
Kapalua (Maui) *44, 75, 78, 183–184, 188, 196, 202, 208, 214, 217, 293*
  accommodation *207*
    Kapalua Villas
      ((808) 669-8088 Ⓣ Ⓕ Ⓔ Ⓦ *208*
    Ritz-Carlton Kapalua
      ((808) 669-6200 Ⓣ Ⓕ Ⓦ *188, 207*
  attractions *188*
    Aloha Friday festivities *188*
    ancient burial ground *188*
    Fleming's Beach *188*
    Kapalua Discovery Center *188*
    Kapalua Shops *188*
    Maui Pineapple Company
      ((808) 669-8088 *188*
  children activities
    Ritz-Carlton Kapalua
      ((808) 669-6200 Ⓣ Ⓕ Ⓦ *57*
  festivals and special events *74, 78*
  general information *202*
    Kapalua Golf Academy
      TOLL-FREE (877) 527-2582 *202*
    Kapalua Golf Club ((808) 669-8044 *44, 202*
    Kapalua Golf ((808) 669-8812 Ⓦ *202*
    Kapalua Nature Society ((808) 669-0244 *188*
  history *184*

restaurants
  Anuenue Room ((808) 669-1665 *214*
  Honolua Store ((808) 669-6128 *217*
  Jameson's Grill and Bar ((808) 669-5653 *216*
  Maui Coffee and Espresso Bar
    ((808) 669-9667 *217*
  Sansei Seafood Restaurant
    ((808) 669-6286 *216*
sports
  diving and snorkeling *188*
  golf *44, 202*
  tennis *202*
Kapolei (Oahu) *43, 58*
  attractions *58*
  general information
    Koolina Golf Club ((808) 676-5300 *43*
  sports
    golf *43*
kapu (ancient system of laws) *104–105,*
  109–110, 184
Kapuaiwa Coconut Grove (Molokai) *73*
Kapulena (Big Island) *266*
Kau (Big Island) *225, 255*
Kauai *15–16, 23–24, 28–29, 36, 38, 42–43, 48, 54,*
  56, 60, 65–67, 72, 75–76, 78, 79, 81, 88, 94, 102,
  104–105, 149, 157, 164, 291, 293
Kaulukukuiolanikaula (Molokai) *227*
Kaunakakai (Molokai) *52, 70, 73, 225–226, 231,*
  233, 235
  accommodation *234–235*
  A Hawaiian Getaway
    (/FAX (808) 553-9803 ⓣ Ⓔ *235*
  A'Ahi Place Bed and Breakfast
    ((808) 553-5860 Ⓔ *235*
  Biljac Condos (/FAX (808) 553-5006 Ⓔ *233*
  Hotel Molokai ((808) 553-5347 ⓣ Ⓦ *234*
  Molokai Shores Suites
    ((808) 553-5954 ⓣ Ⓕ Ⓦ *233*
  Waialua Pavilion and Campground
    ((808) 558-8150 Ⓕ *52*
  Wavecrest Resort ((808) 558-8103 Ⓕ *233*
  attractions
    Kakahaia Pond *226*
    Kamehameha V's summer house *226*
    Kaunakakai Wharf *226*
    Nene O Molokai ((808) 553-5992 Ⓕ Ⓔ *226*
  environs and excursions
    Iliiliopae Heiau *227*
    Keawanui *226*
    Wailau Trail *227*
  festivals and special events
    Ka Molokai Makahiki (January)
      ((808) 553-3673 *70*
    Prince Kuhio Celebration, March *73*
  general information *225–227, 232–233*
    Alyce C ((808) 558-8377 Ⓦ *232*
    Captain Joe Reich ((808) 558-8377 *232*
    County of Maui ((808) 553-3204 *52*
    Department of Homelands
      ((808) 567-6104 *52*
    Island Kine Auto Rentals
      ((808) 553-5242 *225*
    Kukui Tours and Limousine
      ((808) 552-2282 Ⓕ *226*
    Lani's Kayak ((808) 558-8563 Ⓔ *232*
    Molokai Bicycle ((808) 553-3931 Ⓕ Ⓔ Ⓦ *232*
    Molokai Charters ((808) 553-5852 *232*
    Snorkel and Dive ((808) 553-9867 *232*

restaurants
  Kamoi Snack-N-Go ((808) 553-3742 *236*
  Kanemitsu's Bakery ((808) 553-5855 *236*
  Molokai Drive-inn ((808) 553-5655 *236*
  Molokai Pizza Café ((808) 553-3288 *236*
  Outpost Natural Foods ((808) 553-3377 *236*
shopping *226*
  Artist Society of Molokai
    ((808) 553-3461 *232*
  Designs Pacifica ((808) 553-5363 Ⓕ *232*
  Haku Designs ((808) 558-8419 *232*
  Imports Gift Shop ((808) 553-5734 Ⓕ *232*
  Molokai Fish and Dive
    (/FAX (808) 553-5926 *231*
Kaunolu Archeological Interpretive Park
(Lanai) *20, 244*
  attractions
    Halulu Heiau *244*
    Kahekili's Leap *21, 244*
Kaunolu Bay (Lanai) *20, 244*
  attractions
    Kaunolu Archeological Interpretive
      Park *20, 244*
    petroglyphs *21*
    royal residence *20*
Kaupo Ranch (Maui) *194*
Kawaihae (Big Island) *69, 75, 260, 262–263, 284*
Kawakiu Beach (Molokai) *228*
kayaking *40, 42*
Keahole Point (Big Island) *40*
  attractions
    Plane-Wreck Point *40*
  sports
    diving *40*
Keaiwa Heiau State Recreation Area (Oahu) *26*
  attractions
    Aiea Loop Trail *26*
    ancient healing heiau *26*
  sports
    hiking *26*
Kealakekua (Big Island) *40, 269, 275*
  accommodation
    Merryman's Bed and Breakfast
      ((808) 323-2276 ⓣ *275*
    Reggie's Tropical Hideaway
      ((808) 322-8888 ⓣ Ⓕ *275*
  sports
    diving *40*
Kealakekua Bay (Big Island) *91, 104–105, 257*
  history *104–105*
  sports
    diving and snorkeling *257*
Kealia Beach (Kauai) *161*
Kealia Pond National Wildlife Preserve
(Maui) *189*
Keanae (Maui) *193*
Keanae Peninsula (Maui) *193*
Keauhou (Big Island) *40*
Keawaula Beach (Oahu) *36, 131*
  sports
    surfing *36, 131*
Kee Beach (Kauai) *161, 163–164, 166*
  sports
    diving and snorkeling *166*
Kekaha (Kauai) *79, 152–154, 157, 293*
  attractions
    sugar plantation *157*
  festivals and special events
    Mokihana Festival (September)
      ((808) 822-2166 *79*

Keokea (Maui)   *191, 220*
attractions
  Kwock Hing Society Temple   *191*
restaurants
  Grandma's Coffee House
    ((808) 878-2140   *220*
Keokea Beach Park (Big Island)   *262*
Keomuku (Lanai)   *243*
Keoneloa Bay (Kauai)   *170*
Kepuhi Beach (Molokai)   *228, 233*
Kihei (Maui)   *16, 36, 68, 75, 93, 189, 194, 198–200, 202, 208, 218–219*
accommodation   *209*
  Aloha Pualani
    ((808) 874-9127 Ⓣ Ⓕ Ⓔ Ⓦ   *208*
  Aston Maui Hill
    ((808) 879-6321 Ⓣ Ⓕ Ⓔ Ⓦ   *208*
  Aston Maui Lu
    ((808) 879-5881 Ⓣ Ⓕ Ⓔ Ⓦ   *208*
  Eva Villa (/FAX (808) 874-6407 Ⓣ Ⓔ   *209*
  Island Sands ((808) 244-7012 Ⓣ Ⓕ Ⓦ   *208*
  Maalaea Surf Resort
    ((808) 879-1267 Ⓣ Ⓕ Ⓔ   *208*
  Maui Coast Hotel
    ((808) 874-6284 Ⓣ Ⓕ Ⓔ Ⓦ   *208*
  Maui Oceanfront Inn
    ((808) 879-7744 Ⓕ Ⓦ   *208*
  Nona Lani Cottages
    ((808) 879-2497 Ⓣ Ⓔ Ⓦ   *208*
  Punahoa ((808) 879-2720 Ⓣ Ⓕ Ⓔ   *208*
environs and excursions   *189*
festivals and special events
  Kihei Sea Festival (April) ((808) 874-9400   *75*
general information   *16, 199–200*
  Blue Water Rafting
    ((808) 879-7238 Ⓦ   *16, 200*
  Maui Waveriders ((808) 875-4761   *199*
  Snorkel Bob's ((808) 879-7449 Ⓦ   *199*
restaurants   *219*
  A Pacific Café Maui ((808) 879-0069 Ⓦ   *218*
  Café Navaca ((808) 879-0717   *219*
  Da Kitchen ((808) 875-7782   *219*
  Greek Bistro ((808) 879-9330   *218*
  Pita Paradise ((808) 875-7679   *219*
  Stella Blues Café ((808) 874-3779   *218*
  Thai Chef ((808) 874-5605   *218*
shopping
  Azeka Place ((808) 874-8400   *198*
  Island Designer Swimwear
    ((808) 891-1117   *198*
  Kihei Farmers Market   *198*
sports
  diving   *16*
Kilauea (Big Island)   *11, 24, 34, 70, 102–103, 250, 254, 256*
Kilauea (Kauai)   *56, 149, 161, 174, 178*
accommodation
  Makai Farms ((808) 828-1874 Ⓕ   *174*
attractions
  Christ Memorial Church   *161*
  Kilauea Lighthouse   *161*
environs and excursions
  Kalihiwai Road   *162*
restaurants   *161, 179*
  Casa di Amici ((808) 828-1555   *56, 178*
shopping
  Kong Lung ((808) 828-1822   *161, 165*

**Kilauea Point National Wildlife Refuge
(Kauai)**   *161*
attractions
  wildlife   *162*
Kilohana Plantation (Kauai)   *68, 152, 174*
Kipahulu (Maui)   *194, 202*
attractions
  Palapala Hoomau Congregational
    Church   *194*
general information
  Ohe'o Stables ((808) 667-2222   *202*
kite sailing   *36*
Kohala (Kauai)   *149*
Kohala Coast (Big Island)   *47, 56, 75, 78, 81, 89, 93, 99, 260, 271, 282, 284, 293*
accommodation   *55, 76, 78, 89*
  Four Seasons Resort Hualalai
    ((808) 325-8000 Ⓣ   *276*
  Hapuna Beach Prince Hotel
    ((808) 880-1111 Ⓣ Ⓕ Ⓦ   *81, 278*
  Hilton Waikoloa Village
    ((808) 886-1234 Ⓣ Ⓕ Ⓔ Ⓦ   *78, 89, 277*
  Mauna Kea Beach Resort
    ((808) 882-7222 Ⓣ Ⓕ Ⓦ   *277*
  Mauna Lani Bay Hotel and Bungalows
    ((808) 885-6622 Ⓣ Ⓕ Ⓔ Ⓦ   *260, 276*
  Orchid at Mauna Lani
    ((808) 885-2000 Ⓣ Ⓕ Ⓦ   *88–89, 277*
  Outrigger Waikoloa Beach Resort
    ((808) 886-6789   *260, 277*
attractions
  Kalahuipua Fishponds   *260*
  Kuualii and Kahapapa Fishponds   *260*
  Lapakahi State Historic Park
    ((808) 889-5566   *262*
  Mookini Heiau   *99*
  Puako Petroglyph Archaeological
    Preserve   *260*
  Puukohola Heiau National Historic Site   *260*
  Temple on the Hill of the Whale   *260*
  Waikoloa Stables   *72*
children activities   *57*
  Hilton Waikoloa Village
    ((808) 886-1234 Ⓣ Ⓕ Ⓔ Ⓦ   *69*
  Orchid at Mauna Lani
    ((808) 885-2000 Ⓣ Ⓕ Ⓦ   *57, 277*
festivals and special events   *75*
  Dolphin Days (July) ((808) 886-1234   *78*
  Great Waikoloa Rodeo, February   *72*
  Ka Hula Lea Festival (July)
    ((808) 886-6789   *78*
  Turtle Independence Day, July   *76*
  Winter Wine Escape (November)
    ((808) 880-3023   *81*
general information
  Francis I'i Brown Golf Course
    ((808) 885-6655 Ⓦ   *47, 271*
  Kohala Naalapa Stables ((808) 885-0022   *271*
  Mauna Kea Divers ((808) 882-1477 Ⓔ Ⓦ   *262*
  Mauna Kea Resort Golf Course
    ((808) 882-5400   *47, 271*
  Mauna Kea Resort Stables
    ((808) 885-4288   *271*
  Mauna Lani Sea Adventures
    ((808) 885-7883   *270*
  Waikoloa Beach Golf Club
    ((808) 886-6060 Ⓣ   *47, 271*

nightlife
Legends of the Pacific ((808) 886-1234   287
Mauna Kea Beach Hotel (luau)
((808) 882-5801 Ⓦ   287
restaurants
Batik ((808) 882-6060   284
Bay Terrace ((808) 885-6622   284
Brown's Beach House   284
Café Pesto ((808) 882-1071   284
Canoe House ((808) 885-6622   56, 282
Grand Palace ((808) 886-6668   284
Ocean Grill ((808) 885-6622   284
Orchid Hotel Grill ((808) 885-2000   284
Pahuia ((808) 325-8000   282
Roy's Waikoloa Bar and Grill
((808) 885-4321   56, 284
Terrace ((808) 882-6060   284
Tres Hombres ((808) 882-1031   284
shopping
Kings' Shops ((808) 886-8811   269
Waikoloa Village Market
((808) 883-1088   269
sports
golf   47, 271
Kohua Ridge (Kauai)   28
Kokee State Park (Kauai)   17, 28–29, 42, 48, 51,
67–68, 152, 157, 166–167, 171
accommodation
Kokee Lodge ((808) 335-6061   18, 157, 171
park cabins ((808) 335-6061   29
YWCA Camp Sloggett
((808) 245-5959 Ⓕ Ⓔ Ⓦ   51
attractions
Aakai Swamp Trail   18
Awaawapuhi Trail   18
Kalalau Lookout   158
Kokee Natural History Museum
((808) 335-9975 Ⓔ   17, 58, 157
general information   158
fishing licences ((808) 241-3400   42
shopping
Kokee Museum ((808) 335-9975   166
sports
fishing   42, 158
hiking   17, 28, 158, 167
hunting   158
Koloa (Kauai)   44, 52, 78, 149, 153, 166–167, 169–
170, 171, 175–176
accommodation   54, 57, 169–170
Coastline Cottages ((808) 742-9688 Ⓕ   170
Colony Poipu Kai Resort
((808) 742-6464 Ⓣ Ⓕ   170
Grantham Resorts
((808) 742-2000 Ⓣ Ⓕ Ⓦ   170
Kahili Mountain Park Cabins
((808) 742-9921   52
Kiahuna Plantation Resort
((808) 742-6411 Ⓣ Ⓕ   170
Poipu Kai Suite Paradise
((808) 742-1234 Ⓣ Ⓕ Ⓦ   170
Sheraton Kauai Resort
((808) 742-1661 Ⓣ Ⓕ Ⓦ   170
attractions
Old Koloa Town   153
Tunnel of Trees   153
festivals and special evens
Koloa Plantation Days, July   78

general information
Fathom Five Adventures
((808) 742-6991   166
Kiahuna Plantation Golf Course
((808) 742-9595   44, 167
history   149
restaurants
Beach House ((808) 742-1424   56, 176
Brennecke's ((808) 742-7588   176
Keoki's Paradise ((808) 742-7534   176
Lappert's Factory ((808) 335-6121   177
Piatti Italian Restaurant ((808) 742-2216   176
Roy's Poipu Bar and Grill
((808) 742-5000   175
Tomkats Grille ((808) 332-742-8887   176
sports
golf   44, 167
Koolau Mountains (Oahu)   27, 43, 125, 128, 134
attractions
Kaau Crater   27
Lanipo Trail   27–28
Wiliwilinui Trail   27
general information
Correa Trails Hawaii ((808) 259-9005   134
sports
hiking   27
horseback riding   134
Koolina (Oahu)   131, 138–139, 144
accommodation   53, 90, 131, 138
general information
Tod Robinson Course
((808) 679-0079 Ⓣ Ⓕ Ⓦ   139
nightlife
Germaine's Luau ((808) 949-6626   144
Paradise Cove Luau
((808) 842-5911   131, 144
restaurants
Azul ((808) 679-0079   138
Naupaka Terrace ((808) 679-0079   138
Ushio-Tei ((808) 679-0079   138
sports
golf   139
Kualapuu (Molokai)   58, 99, 229, 231, 233, 236
attractions
Malulani Estate ((808) 567-9241 Ⓣ Ⓔ   229
general information
Ironwood Hills Golf Course
((808) 567-6000   233
Molokai Mule Ride
((808) 567-6088 Ⓣ Ⓕ Ⓔ Ⓦ   231
restaurants
Coffees of Hawaii ((808) 567-9241   236
Kualapuu Cook House ((808) 567-6185   236
sports
golf   233
Kualoa Beach (Oahu)   134
sports
surfing   134
Kualoa Point (Oahu)   27
Kualoa Ranch (Oahu)   128, 135
general information
ranch information ((808) 237-8515 Ⓣ   128
sports
horseback riding   135
Kualoa Regional Park (Oahu)   128
sports
snorkeling   128
Kuhio Beach (Oahu)   35
Kukuihaele (Big Island)   278

Kula (Maui)   *57, 190, 196, 198, 200, 202, 210–211, 219–220*

accommodation
Kula Lodge ((808) 878-1535 Ⓣ Ⓕ   *68, 211*
Silver Cloud Ranch
((808) 878-6101 Ⓣ Ⓕ Ⓔ Ⓦ   *210*
attractions   191
Cloud's Rest Protea Farm
((808) 878-2544   *191*
Keiki (Children's) Petting Zoo   *57*
Kula Botanical Gardens ((808) 878-1715   *191*
general information
Ironwood Ranch ((808) 669-4991   *202*
Pony Express Tours ((808) 667-2200 Ⓔ   *202*
Proflyght ((808) 874-5433 Ⓦ ·   *200*
restaurants
Café 808 ((808) 878-6874   *220*
Kula Lodge ((808) 878-1535   *68, 211, 219*
shopping
Sunrise Farm ((808) 876-0200   *198*

L | La Perouse Bay (Maui)   *36, 190*
sports
surfing   *36*
Lahaina (Maui)   *16, 40, 44–45, 56, 58, 61, 73–74, 79, 93, 107, 183, 185–186, 189, 196–197, 199–201, 203–204, 206–207, 214–216, 221, 237, 293*
accommodation   203, 206
Aloha Lani Inn ((808) 661-8040 Ⓣ Ⓕ Ⓔ   *203*
Aston Maui Islander
((808) 667-9766 Ⓕ Ⓦ   *203*
Blue Horizons ((808) 669-1965 Ⓣ Ⓕ Ⓔ   *203*
Embassy Vacation Resort
((808) 661-2000 Ⓣ Ⓕ   *204*
Garden Gate (/FAX (808) 661-8800 Ⓔ   *204*
Guest House ((808) 661-8085 Ⓣ Ⓕ   *203*
House of Fountains
((808) 667-2121 Ⓣ Ⓕ   *203*
Hyatt Regency Maui
((808) 661-1234 Ⓣ Ⓕ Ⓦ   *204*
Kaanapali Beach Hotel
((808) 661-0011 Ⓣ Ⓕ Ⓔ Ⓦ   *206*
Kahana Sunset ((808) 669-8011 Ⓣ Ⓕ Ⓔ   *206*
Lahaina Inn ((808) 661-0577 Ⓣ Ⓕ Ⓦ   *203*
Marriott Maui ((808) 667-1200 Ⓣ Ⓕ Ⓦ   *206*
Maui Kai ((808) 667-3500 Ⓣ Ⓕ Ⓔ Ⓦ   *206*
Maui Sands ((808) 669-1902 Ⓣ Ⓕ   *207*
Mauian Hotel
((808) 669-6205 Ⓣ Ⓕ Ⓔ Ⓦ   *206*
Old Lahaina House
((808) 667-4663 Ⓣ Ⓕ Ⓦ   *204*
Outrigger Maui Eldorado
((808) 661-0021 Ⓣ Ⓕ Ⓦ   *204*
Pioneer Inn ((808) 661-3636 Ⓣ Ⓕ Ⓔ   *203*
Plantation Inn ((808) 667-9225 Ⓣ Ⓕ Ⓦ   *203*
Puunoa Beach Estates
((808) 667-1666 Ⓣ Ⓕ Ⓦ   *203*
Royal Lahaina ((808) 661-3611 Ⓣ Ⓦ   *204*
Sheraton Maui ((808) 661-0031 Ⓕ Ⓦ   *204*
Wai Ola (/FAX (808) 661-7901 Ⓣ Ⓔ   *204*
Westin Maui ((808) 667-2525 Ⓣ Ⓕ Ⓦ   *204*
Whaler ((808) 661-4861 Ⓣ Ⓕ   *206*
attractions
Baldwin Home Museum
((808) 661-3262   *187*
Banyan Tree   *187*
Carthaginian II ((808) 661-8527   *187*
Hale Kohola Whale Museum
((808) 661-9918   *61*

Hawaii Dome Theater ((808) 661-8314   *187*
Lahaina Cannery Mall ((808) 661-5304   *79*
Lahaina Restoration Foundation
((808) 661-3262   *187*
Lahaina Whaling Museum
((808) 661-4775   *16, 187*
Master's Reading Room   *187*
Richards House   *187*
Sugar Cane Train ((808) 661-8389 Ⓕ   *58, 187*
children activities
Hyatt Regency Maui
((808) 661-1234 Ⓣ Ⓕ Ⓦ   *58*
Kahana Sunset
((808) 669-8011 Ⓣ Ⓕ Ⓔ   *57, 206*
cultural events
Ulalena ((808) 661-9913   *221*
festivals and special events   79
Buddha Day (April) ((808) 661-4304   *74*
Halloween in Lahaina (October)
((808) 667-9175   *79*
Na Mele O Maui (December)
((808) 661-3271   *81*
Whalefest Week (March) ((808) 667-9175   *73*
general information   199–200
Atlantis Submarines ((808) 973-9811 Ⓣ Ⓦ   *40*
Hawaii Ocean Rafting
((808) 667-2191 Ⓣ Ⓦ   *200*
Hinatea ((808) 667-7548   *200*
Lahaina Divers ((808) 667-7496 Ⓣ Ⓔ Ⓦ   *199*
Lahaina Princess ((808) 667-6165 Ⓣ Ⓔ   *199*
Luckey Strike Charters
((808) 661-4606 Ⓦ   *200*
Maui Dive Shop ((808) 661-6166   *199*
Maui Eco-Adventures   *201*
Maui Princess
((808) 667-6165 Ⓣ Ⓕ Ⓦ   *16, 237*
Pacific Jet Sports ((808) 667-2066   *200*
Puuene and Maui Waveriders
((808) 875-4761   *200*
Trilogy ((808) 879-8811 Ⓣ Ⓦ   *199*
West Maui Parasail ((808) 661-4060   *200*
history   186
nightlife   221
Feast of Lele ((808) 667-5353   *221*
Maui Brews ((808) 667-7794   *221*
Old Lahaina Luau ((808) 667-1998   *221*
Scotch Mist 11 ((808) 661-0386   *221*
Trilogy ((808) 879-8811 Ⓣ Ⓦ   *221*
Windjammer Cruises ((808) 661-8600   *221*
restaurants
Aloha Mixed Plate ((808) 661-3322   *216*
Avalon ((808) 667-5559   *56, 215*
Chart House ((808) 661-0937   *216*
Gerard's ((808) 661-8939   *56, 203, 215*
Groovy Smoothies ((808) 661-8219   *217*
Hoonokowai Okazuya and Deli
((808) 665-0512   *217*
I'O ((808) 661-8422   *56, 215*
Kimo's ((808) 661-4811   *216*
Lahaina Bagel Café ((808) 667-5225   *217*
Lahaina Coolers ((808) 661-7082   *217*
Lahaina Grill ((808) 667-5117   *56, 215*
Lahaina Inn Grill ((808) 661-0577   *203*
Longhi's ((808) 667-2288   *216*
Pacific 'O ((808) 667-4341   *56, 215*
Sir Wilfred's ((808) 667-1941 Ⓦ   *217*
Woody's Oceanfront Grill
((808) 661-8788   *216*

shopping
Gallerie Hawaii ((808) 669-2783 Ⓕ   *197*
Hilo Hatties ((808) 661-8457   *197*
Lahaina Cannery Mall ((808) 661-5304   *197*
Lei Spa ((808) 661-1178 Ⓕ Ⓦ   *197*
Thomas Kinkade Gallery
((808) 667-7171 Ⓣ   *197*
Tuna Luna ((808) 661-8662 Ⓕ Ⓔ   *197*
Laie (Oahu)   *58, 75, 78, 113, 129*
attractions
Polynesian Cultural Center
((808) 293-3333 Ⓦ   *58, 67, 75, 78, 113, 129*
festivals and special events   *75, 78*
Lanai   *15–16, 20–21, 24, 32, 38, 42, 45, 48, 50, 52,*
55–56, 63, 66, 78, 86, 102, 105, 183, 200, 241
Lanai City (Lanai)   *20, 21, 55, 63, 66, 241–244*
access   *247*
accommodation
Hotel Lanai ((808) 565-7211 Ⓣ Ⓕ Ⓔ   *247*
Lodge at Koele ((808) 565-7300 Ⓣ Ⓕ Ⓦ   *55,*
66, 241–242, 245
Lodge at Koele ((808) 565-7300 Ⓣ Ⓕ Ⓦ   *293*
attractions
Dole Park   *242*
Lanai Arts and Culture Center
((808) 565-7503   *243*
Lanai Theatre ((808) 565-7500   *243*
Pine Isle Market ((808) 565-6488   *243*
environs and excursions
Garden of the Gods   *243*
Munro Trail   *32, 243*
general information
Cavendish Golf Course   *244*
Central Reservations
((808) 565-7300 Ⓣ Ⓕ Ⓔ Ⓦ   *242*
Experience at Koele
((808) 565-4653 Ⓣ Ⓔ Ⓦ   *45, 244*
Hawaiian Air ((808) 565-6977 Ⓣ   *247*
Island Air ((808) 565-6744   *247*
Lanai City Service
((808) 565-7227 Ⓣ Ⓕ   *21, 243*
Lanai Pine Sporting Clays
((808) 563-4600   *244*
Rabaca's Limousine ((808) 565-6670   *242*
Stables at Koele ((808) 565-4424   *244*
Visiting Artist Program
((808) 548-3700   *63, 244*
restaurants   *56, 245*
Akamai Trading Company
((808) 565-6587   *243*
Blue Ginger Café ((808) 565-6363   *247*
Experience at Koele Clubhouse
((808) 565-7300   *245*
Henry Clay's Rotisserie
((808) 565-7211 Ⓣ Ⓕ Ⓔ   *247*
Pele's Other Garden ((808) 565-9629   *243*
Tanigawa's ((808) 565-6537   *247*
shopping
Akamai Trading Company
((808) 565-6587   *243*
Gifts with Aloha ((808) 565-6589   *243*
Pele's Garden ((808) 565-9629   *243*
Richard's Shopping Center
((808) 565-6047   *243*
sports
golf   *45, 244*
hiking   *32*
horseback riding   *244*

Lanaihale Summit (Lanai)   *243*
language
Hawaiian and Pidgin   *298*
useful Hawaiian expressions   *298*
Lanikai Beach (Oahu)   *36, 67*
sports
windsurfing   *36*
Lao Valley (Maui)   *63*
Lapakahi State Historic Park (Big Island)   *262*
Laupahoehoe (Big Island)   *287*
Lawai (Kauai)   *91, 176*
attractions
Allerton Garden ((808) 742-2623   *91*
Lawai Garden   *91*
general information
National Tropical Botanical Garden   *91*
restaurants
Mustard's Last Stand ((808) 332-7245   *176*
Lawai Valley (Kauai)   *91*
Lehua Island   *166*
Lihue (Kauai)   *28–29, 44, 60, 72, 76, 152, 159,*
166–167, 179, 291
access   *179*
accommodation   *168*
Aston Kaha Lani ((808) 822-9331 Ⓣ   *169*
Garden Island Inn ((808) 245-7227 Ⓣ   *169*
Outrigger Kauai Beach
((808) 245-1955 Ⓣ Ⓕ   *169*
Tip Top Motel ((808) 245-2333 Ⓕ Ⓔ   *169*
attractions
Grove Farm Homestead Museum
((808) 245-3202   *61, 152*
Kalapaki Beach   *152*
Kauai Museum ((808) 245-6931   *60, 75, 152*
Kilohana Plantation ((808) 245-5608   *68, 152*
Wings Over Hawaii ((808) 245-8838   *153*
children activities   *56*
festivals and special events
Concert in the Sky (July 4)
((808) 245-5006   *76*
Keiki Fun Run (January) ((808) 246-9090   *72*
May Day Lei Contest   *75*
general information   *24, 152*
Island Adventures ((808) 245-9662   *166*
Kauai Bus ((808) 241-6410   *152*
Kauai Lagoons Golf Course
((808) 241-6000 Ⓣ   *44, 167*
Kauai State Parks Office ((808) 274-3445   *29*
Kauai Vacation Rentals
((808) 245-8841 Ⓣ Ⓕ Ⓦ   *168*
Kauai Visitors Bureau ((808) 245-3971   *152*
Lihue Airport   *291*
restaurants   *175*
Café Portofino ((808) 245-2121   *174*
Dani's Restaurant ((808) 245-4991   *175*
Gaylord's ((808) 245-9593   *153, 174*
Pacific Bakery and Grill ((808) 246-0999   *175*
Tip Top Motel and Bakery
((808) 245-2333   *175*
shopping
Kauai Museum ((808) 245-6931   *65, 166*
sports
golf   *44, 167*
Luahiwa (Lanai)   *20, 244*
attractions
petroglyphs   *20, 244*
Lucy Wright Park (Kauai)   *29*
Lumahai Beach (Kauai)   *163*

M **Maalaea (Maui)** *16, 36, 189, 196, 208, 218*
  attractions
    Maui Ocean Center
    ((808) 270-7000 Ⓕ Ⓔ Ⓦ *16, 58, 189*
    whale watching *16*
  general information
    Flexible Flyer ((808) 244-6655 Ⓕ *16*
  restaurants
    Buzz' Wharf ((808) 244-5426 *218*
    Maalaea Waterfront Restaurant
    ((808) 244-9028 Ⓦ *218*
  sports
    surfing *36*
Mahaulepu (Kauai) *154*
  sports
    horseback riding and mountain biking *154*
mail *296*
Maile Point (Oahu) *35*
  sports
    surfing *35*
Major's Bay Beach (Kauai) *157*
Makaha (Oahu) *35, 43, 131*
  attractions
    Cave of Kane *131*
    Makaha Beach Park *131*
  general information *43*
  sports
    golf *43*
    surfing *35*
Makaha Valley (Oahu) *43*
Makapuu (Oahu) *34, 126*
  attractions
    Sea Life Park ((808) 259-7933 *126*
  sports
    hang-gliding *126*
Makapuu Coast (Oahu) *293*
Makawao (Maui) *57, 61, 68, 76, 190–191, 198–199,*
  202, 210–212, 219–220
  accommodation *210*
    Banyan Tree House
    ((808) 572-9021 Ⓕ Ⓔ Ⓦ *211*
    Hula Kula Inn ((808) 572-9351 Ⓣ Ⓕ Ⓔ *211*
  attractions
    Hot Island Glass ((808) 572-4527 *191*
    Hui Noeau Visual Arts Center
    ((808) 572-6560 *61, 191*
  festivals and special events
    Makawao Rodeo (July)
    ((808) 573-0090 *76, 191*
  general information
    Adventures on Horseback
    ((808) 242-7445 *202*
    Ann Fielding's Snorkel Maui
    ((808) 572-8437 *199*
    Paths in Paradise ((808) 573-0094 Ⓕ *202*
  restaurants *219–220*
    Café O Lei ((808) 573-9065 *219*
    Makawao Steak House ((808) 572-8711 *219*
    Polli's Mexican Restaurant
    ((808) 572-7808 *220*
  shopping
    Dragon's Den ((808) 572-2424 *198*
    Hot Island Glass ((808) 572-4527 *198*
    Miracles Bookery ((808) 572-2317 Ⓕ Ⓦ *198*
    Viewpoints Gallery
    ((808) 572-5979 Ⓔ Ⓦ *198*

Makena (Maui) *38, 44, 183, 189–191, 200, 202, 210*
  accommodation
    Makena Landing ((808) 879-6286 *210*
    Maui Prince Hotel
    ((808) 874-1111 Ⓣ Ⓕ Ⓦ *189, 210*
  attractions
    Big and Little Beach *190*
    Five Caves *38*
    Keawali Church ((808) 879-5557 *190*
    Makena Landing *189*
    Maluaka Beach *189*
    Puu Olai Cinder Cone *190*
    whale-watching *190*
  general information
    Makena Kayak ((808) 879-8426 *200*
    Makena Resort Golf Club
    ((808) 879-3344 *44, 202*
    Maui Eco-Tour ((808) 891-2223 Ⓦ *200*
    Ocean Activities Center ((808) 879-7218 *200*
  sports
    diving *38*
    golf *44, 202*
    snorkeling and surfing *189*
Makiki Valley (Oahu) *26*
  attractions
    Makiki Valley Trail *26*
  general information
    Makiki Environmental Education Center *26*
  sports
    hiking *26*
Makua Beach (Oahu) *131*
Manele Bay (Lanai) *45, 52, 55, 242, 244*
  accommodation
    camping ((808) 565-3982 *52, 245*
    Manele Bay Hotel
    ((808) 565-7700 Ⓣ Ⓕ Ⓦ *55, 241, 242, 245*
    Manele Bay Hotel
    ((808) 565-7700 Ⓣ Ⓕ Ⓦ *293*
  attractions
    Manele-Hulopoe Marine Life Conservation
    Area *244*
    Spa at Manele Bay *247*
  festivals and special events
    Pineapple Festival (July) ((808) 565-7600 *78*
  general information
    Challenge at Manele ((808) 565-2222 *45, 244*
    Expeditions ((808) 661-3756 Ⓣ *247*
    Lanai EcoAdventure Service
    ((808) 565-7737 *16*
  restaurants
    Hulopoe Court ((808) 565-7700 Ⓣ Ⓕ Ⓦ *247*
    Ihilani ((808) 565-7700 Ⓣ Ⓕ Ⓦ *247*
    Manele Bay Clubhouse
    ((808) 565-7700 Ⓣ Ⓕ Ⓦ *247*
    Pool Grille ((808) 565-7700 Ⓣ Ⓦ *247*
  sports
    diving *38, 244*
    fishing *42*
    golf *45, 244*
Manniholo Cave (Kauai) *164*
Manoa Valley (Oahu) *50, 91*
Maui *14–16, 23–24, 29–30, 36, 38, 40, 44, 49, 54,*
  56–58, 61, 65–66, 68, 72, 74, 76, 79, 85, 102–103,
  105, 117, 151, 183, 241, 291
Maui Mountains (Maui) *186, 188, 191*

Mauna Kea (Big Island)   *14, 19–20, 24, 34, 40, 50,*
102–103, 190, 250, 266
attractions   19
Keck Observatory ((808) 885-7887   *266*
Observatory Hill   *19*
general information
Mauna Kea Mountain Bikes Inc.
((808) 883-0130 Ⓣ   *271*
Mauna Kea Summit Adventures
((808) 322-2366   *20*
Onizuka Center for International Astronomy
((808) 961-2190, 969-3218   *266*
sports
hiking   *19*
Mauna Loa (Big Island)   *14, 33, 40, 47, 102,*
250, 255
Maunaloa (Molokai)   *42, 55, 228, 231, 234, 236*
accommodation
Camps at Molokai Ranch
((808) 534-9515 Ⓣ Ⓕ Ⓦ   *234*
Molokai Ranch Lodge
((808) 552-2791 Ⓣ Ⓦ   *55, 225, 228, 233*
attractions
Kaana   *228*
children activities
Molokai Ranch Lodge
((808) 552-2791 Ⓣ Ⓦ   *57*
general information   42, 232
restaurants
Kentucky Fried Chicken ((808) 552-2625   *236*
Maunaloa Room ((808) 552-2791   *235*
Village Grill ((808) 552-0012   *236*
shopping
Big Wind Kite Factory ((808) 552-2364   *231*
Plantation Gallery   *231*
Maunalua Bay (Oahu)   *36, 38*
attractions
Turtle Canyon   *38*
sports
diving   *38*
windsurfing   *36*
Menpachi Cave (Lanai)   *38*
Mokapi Island (Molokai)   *230*
Mokolii (Oahu)   *129*
Mokuhookini Rock (Molokai)   *38*
sports
diving   *38*
Mokuleia (Oahu)   *130*
attractions
Dillingham Airfield ((808) 256-0438   *130*
Open Air Gallery ((808) 637-3442   *130*
Molokai   *15, 30, 32, 38, 40, 45, 48–49, 52, 55, 57, 63,*
65–66, 70, 73, 94, 99, 102, 105, 183, 225
Molokai Channel   *41*
Molokini Crater (Maui)   *38*
Molokini Island (Maui)   *23*
money   *295*
Mountain View (Big Island)   *273*
Ⓝ **Na Pali Coast (Kauai)**   *18, 23, 28–29, 38, 42, 48, 68,*
93, 99, 152–153, 157, 161–166
attractions
Hanakapiai Beach   *29*
Hanakapiai Falls   *29*
Kalalau Trail   *28, 167*
Na Pali Coast State Park (Kauai)   *167*
general information
Kauai State Parks Office ((808) 274-3445   *167*

sports
diving   *38, 166*
hiking   *23, 28–29, 167*
kayaking   *42, 166*
Na Pali Coast State Park (Kauai)   *68, 167*
Naalehu (Big Island)   *274, 281*
Nakelele Point (Maui)   *188*
Napili (Maui)   *206–207, 293*
accommodation
Hale Napili ((808) 669-6184 Ⓣ Ⓕ Ⓔ   *207*
Napili Bay ((808) 661-3500 Ⓣ Ⓕ Ⓔ Ⓦ   *207*
Napili Kai Beach Resort
((808) 669-6271 Ⓣ Ⓕ Ⓦ   *206*
Napili Sunset ((808) 669-8083 Ⓣ Ⓔ Ⓦ   *207*
Napili Village ((808) 669-6228 Ⓣ Ⓕ Ⓦ   *207*
restaurants
Mama's Ribs 'N Rotisserie
((808) 665-6262   *217*
Maui Tacos ((808) 665-0222   *217*
Orient Express ((808) 669-8077   *216*
Napili Bay (Maui)   *206–207, 216*
Niihau   *38, 65, 102, 105, 113, 152, 164, 166*
attractions
Niihau shells   *165*
Puuwai   *164*
general information
Niihau Helicopters ((808) 335-3500   *165*
history   164
shopping
leis and jewelry   *165*
sports
diving   *38, 166*
North Shore (Oahu)   *23, 34, 48, 67, 72, 75, 81, 113,*
129, 134, 138
accommodation
Backpackers Vacation Inn
((808) 638-7838   *138*
festivals and special events   35, 72, 81
Eddie Aikau Big Wave surfing meet   *35*
general information
Links at Kuilima ((808) 293-8574   *43*
sports
golf   *43*
surfing   *23, 34–35, 72, 81, 129, 134*
Nounou Ridge (Kauai)   *161*
Nuuanu Pali (Oahu)   *26, 66, 105, 117, 125*
attractions
Nuuanu Pali Lookout   *48, 66, 125*
Ⓞ **Oahu**   *15–16, 23–24, 28, 34, 36, 38, 40, 42–43, 48,*
53, 55, 58–59, 64–67, 72–73, 75, 79, 81–82, 91, 102,
104–105, 113, 117, 139, 149, 183, 293
Oasis Reef (Kauai)   *38*
sports
diving and snorkeling   *38*
Oheo Gulch (Maui)   *194, 202*
attractions
Seven Sacred Pools   *194*
Waimoku Falls   *194*
general information
Park Information ((808) 248-7375   *194*
Okala Island (Molokai)   *230*
Olowalu (Maui)   *214*
restaurants
Chez Paul ((808) 661-3843   *214*
One Alii Beach Park (Molokai)   *32*
general information
Park Information ((808) 553-3204   *32*
Oneloa Beach (Maui)   *190*
Onomea Bay (Big Island)   *91, 253*

P **Pahoa (Big Island)** *254*
  attractions *254*
Paia (Maui) *30, 36, 57, 68, 79, 192, 199, 212, 220*
  accommodation *212*
  attractions
    Baldwin Beach Park *30*
  festivals and special events
    Run to the Sun (September)
      ((808) 871-6441 *79*
  restaurants
    Anthony's Coffee Co. ((808) 882-6509 ⓦ *220*
    Mama's Fish House ((808) 579-8488 *220*
    Milagros Food Company
      ((808) 579-8755 *220*
    Paia Fish Market ((808) 579-8030 *220*
    Picnics Restaurant ((808) 579-8021 *220*
  shopping
    Biasa Rose Boutique ((808) 579-8602 ⓔ *199*
    Maui Crafts Guild ((808) 579-9697 ⓦ *65, 199*
Palaau State Park (Molokai) *228*
  general information
    Hawaii State Division of Parks
      ((808) 984-8109 *32*
Papaikou (Big Island) *287*
Papakolea (Big Island) *See* Green Sand
  Beach *256*
Papohaku Beach (Molokai) *228*
Pohaku Kani (Maui) *188*
Pohakumauliuli Cinder Cone (Molokai) *228*
Poipu (Kauai) *36, 38, 44, 58, 67–68, 93, 152–154,*
  166, 168
  attractions
    Allerton Garden ((808) 742-2623 *154*
    Poipu Beach *36, 166*
    Spouting Horn *154*
  general information
    Margo Oberg's School of Surfing
      ((808) 742-8019 *58, 166*
    Outfitters Kauai
      ((808) 742-9667 ⓣ ⓦ *166–167*
    Poipu Bay Resort Golf Course
      ((808) 742-8711 *44, 168*
    Snorkel Bob's ((808) 742-2206 *166*
  sports
    diving and snorkeling *166*
    golf *44, 168*
    surfing *36, 166*
Polihale State Park (Kauai) *29, 153, 157*
  attractions
    Polihale heiau *157*
Polipoli Springs State Park (Maui) *30*
  general information
    Park Information ((808) 984-8109 *30*
Pololu Valley (Big Island) *69*
  attractions
    Pololu Valley Lookout *69*
population *99, 112–113, 117, 154, 225, 241*
Port Allan (Kauai) *165*
Princeville (Kauai) *44, 68, 75, 152, 161–162, 168,*
  172, 174, 178
  accommodation
    Hanalei Bay Resort
      ((808) 826-6522 ⓣ ⓕ *174*
    Princeville Resort
      ((808) 826-9644 ⓣ ⓕ ⓦ *54, 68, 161–162,*
      168, 172
  festivals and special events *75*
  general information
    Makai Golf Course ((808) 826-3580 *44, 168*
    Prince Golf Course ((808) 826-2727 *44, 168*
    Princeville Airport *162*

  history *162*
  restaurants
    Bali Hai Restaurant ((808) 826-6522 *178*
    La Cascata ((808) 826-9644 *178*
  sports
    golf *44, 168*
Puako Petroglyph Archaeological Preserve
  (Big Island) *260*
Pukalani (Maui) *190, 212, 219*
  accommodation
    Hale Peno ((808) 572-1896 ⓣ ⓔ ⓦ *212*
  restaurants
    Upcountry Café ((808) 572-2395 *219*
Pukoo (Molokai) *227, 236*
  attractions
    Neighborhood Store *227*
  restaurants
    Neighborhood Store N' Counter
      ((808) 558-8498 *236*
Puna (Big Island) *254*
Punaluu Beach Park (Big Island) *69, 256*
Puohokamoa (Maui) *192*
Pupukea Marine Life Conserve (Oahu) *129*
Puu O Mahuka (Oahu) *129*
Puuhonua O Honaunau National Historic Park
  (Big Island) *257, 275*
  general information
    Park Information ((808) 328-2326 *257*
Puunene (Maui) *196, 199*
  general information
    Makena Coast Charters
      ((808) 874-1273 ⓣ ⓔ *199*
Puuwai (Niihau) *164*

Q **Queen's Beach (Oahu)** *35*

R radio *296*
Rainbow Park (Maui) *30*
  general information
    Maui County ((808) 243-7389 *30*
religion *11, 20, 109, 112, 225, 254*
restaurants
  general information *50, 55, 82–83, 117, 139, 174,*
    213, 294
  prices *295*
  restaurants with flair *55–56*

S **Sacred Falls State Park (Oahu)** *24*
  attractions
    Sacred Falls Pool *24*
    Sacred Falls Trail *24*
  sports
    hiking *24*
safety *See* security *297*
Sandy Beach (Oahu) *34, 73, 126*
  festivals and special events *73*
security *297*
Sharkfin Rock (Lanai) *38*
Shark's Cove (Oahu) *38*
  sports
    diving *38*
Sheraton Caverns (Kauai) *38*
  sports
    diving *38*
Shipwreck Beach (Kauai) *154*
  sports
    water sports *154*
Shipwreck Beach (Lanai) *243*
shopping
  general information *64–66*
  Honolulu and Waikiki *132, 134*
  what to buy *64–66*

Sleeping Giant (Kauai) *161*
snorkeling *38, 40*
South Point (Big Island) *256, 274, 281, 287*
  accommodation
    Becky's Bed and Breakfast
      ((808) 929-9690 Ⓣ Ⓕ Ⓔ *274*
    Macadamia Meadows Bed and Breakfast
      ((808) 929-8097 Ⓣ Ⓕ *274*
  attractions
    ancient canoe mooring site *256*
    Kalalea Heiau *256*
  restaurants
    Mark Twain Square ((808) 929-7550 *281*
    Shaka Restaurant ((808) 929-7404 *281*
Spreckelsville (Maui) *36*
Sunset Beach (Oahu) *35, 48, 67, 99, 129, 134, 138*
  accommodation
    Ke Iki Hale ((808) 638-8229 Ⓣ Ⓕ *138*
  attractions
    Banzai Pipeline *34, 48, 67, 99, 129, 134, 138*
  sports
    surfing *129, 134*
surfing *34, 36*

T **Tantalus (Oahu)** *26*
  attractions
    Job's Tears *26*
    Manoa Cliffs Trail and Puu Ohia Trail *26*
  sports
    hiking *26*
taxes *295*
telephone *296*
television *296*
time *295*
tipping *295*
tourist information *292*
tours
  adventure activities
    Activity Warehouse
      TOLL-FREE (800) 923-4004 *95*
  Big Island excursions
    Atlantis Kona TOLL-FREE (800) 548-6262 *268*
    Blue Hawaiian Helicopters
      ((808) 961-5600 Ⓣ Ⓦ *267*
    Body Glove Cruises
      ((808) 326-7122 Ⓣ Ⓦ *268*
    Captain Zodiac ((808) 329-3199 Ⓕ Ⓔ *268*
    Dolphin Discoveries
      ((808) 322-8000 Ⓔ Ⓦ *268*
    Eco-Adventures
      ((808) 329-7116 Ⓣ Ⓕ Ⓔ Ⓦ *268*
    Fair Wind ((808) 322-2788 Ⓣ Ⓔ Ⓦ *268*
    Hawaii Earth Guides
      ((808) 324-1717 Ⓕ Ⓔ Ⓦ *268*
    Hawaii Forest and Trail
      ((808) 322-8881 Ⓣ Ⓕ Ⓔ Ⓦ *268*
    Hawaii Pack and Paddle ((808) 328-8911 *269*
    Island Hoppers
      ((808) 969-2000 Ⓣ Ⓕ Ⓔ Ⓦ *267*
    Kailua Bay Charter Co.
      ((808) 324-1749 Ⓔ Ⓦ *268*
    Kilauea Volcano Yacht Cruises
      ((808) 935-5070 *269*
    King's Trail Rides ((808) 323-2388 Ⓔ Ⓦ *269*
    Kona Coast Cycling Tours
      ((808) 327-1133 Ⓕ Ⓔ Ⓦ *269*
    Kona Coast Express ((808) 331-1582 *267*
    Mauna Kea Summit Adventures
      ((808) 322-2366 *269*
    Ocean Safaris ((808) 326-4699 Ⓣ Ⓕ Ⓔ *268*

    Polynesian Adventure Tours
      ((808) 329-8088 Ⓣ Ⓕ *267*
    UFO Parasails ((808) 325-5836 Ⓔ Ⓦ *268*
    Waipio Rim Backroad Adventures
      ((808) 775-1122 *267*
    Waipio Valley Shuttle ((808) 775-7121 *267*
    Waipio Valley Wagon Tours
      ((808) 775-9518 *267*
  cruises *93*
    Navatek I ((808) 848-6360 Ⓣ Ⓦ *92*
  diving
    Eco-Adventures
      ((808) 329-7116 Ⓣ Ⓕ Ⓔ Ⓦ *92*
    Haleiwa Surf Center ((808) 637-5051 *93*
  diving and snorkeling
    Snorkel Bob's ((808) 823-9433, 742-2206 *93*
  fishing *93*
    Luckey Strike Charters ((808) 661-4606 Ⓦ *93*
  garden visits
    Pacific Adventures ((808) 324-1338 Ⓦ *90*
  glass-bottom boats
    Kailua Bay Charter Co.
      ((808) 324-1749 Ⓔ Ⓦ *94*
  helicopters
    Blue Hawaiian Helicopters
      ((808) 961-5600 Ⓣ Ⓦ *94*
    Island Helicopters ((808) 245-6258 *94*
    Ohana Helicopters ((808) 245-3996 *94*
  Kauai excursions *165*
    Bluewater Sailing ((808) 828-1142 *165*
    Captain Sundown's Catamaran
      ((808) 826-5585 *165*
    Island Helicopters ((808) 245-6258 *165*
    Jack Harter ((808) 245-3774 *165*
    Kauai Backroads ((808) 245-8809 *165*
    Ohana Helicopters ((808) 245-3996 *165*
  kayaking
    Ocean Safaris ((808) 326-4699 Ⓣ Ⓕ Ⓔ *94*
    Outfitters Kauai ((808) 742-9667 Ⓣ Ⓦ *93*
  Lanai excursions *244*
    Lanai EcoAdventure Service
      ((808) 565-7737 *244*
    Trilogy Ocean Sports
      ((808) 879-8811 Ⓣ Ⓦ *244*
  mainland tour operators *95*
    American Express
      TOLL-FREE (800) 952-8687 *95*
    American Hawaii Cruises
      TOLL-FREE (800) 944-8020 Ⓦ *95*
    Pleasant Holidays
      TOLL-FREE (800) 242-9244 Ⓦ *95*
    Sunquest TOLL-FREE (800) 357-2400 Ⓦ *95*
  Maui excursions *196*
    Adventures with the Gecko
      ((808) 843-4325 Ⓣ *196*
    AlexAir ((808) 871-0792 Ⓣ Ⓦ *194*
    Atlantis Submarine
      ((808) 973-9811 Ⓣ Ⓦ *196*
    Blue Hawaiian Helicopters
      ((808) 961-5600 Ⓣ Ⓦ *194*
    Flexible Flyer ((808) 244-6655 Ⓕ *196*
    Gemini Charters ((808) 661-2591 Ⓕ *196*
    Guy Aina ((808) 248-8087 *196*
    Kapalua Nature Society ((808) 669-0244 *196*
    Kiele V ((808) 667-4727 *196*
    Maui Cave Adventures
      ((808) 248-7308 Ⓦ *196*
    Maui Classic Charters
      ((808) 879-8188 Ⓣ Ⓦ *196*

Maui Princess ((808) 667-6165 ⓉⒻⓌ *196*
Pride of Maui ((808) 242-0955 *196*
Reefdancer ((808) 667-2133 *196*
SeaView Adventure ((808) 661-5550 *196*
Star Maui Limousine ((808) 875-6900 Ⓦ *194*
Star Party ((808) 281-0949 ⓉⒺⓌ *196*
Sunshine Helicopters
  ((808) 871-0722 ⓉⒻ *194*
Temptation Tours ((808) 877-8888 ⒻⓌ *196*
Volcano Air Tours ((808) 877-5500 *194*
West Maui Shopping Express
  ((808) 877-7308 *197*
Molokai excursions 231
Damien Molokai Tours ((808) 567-6171 *231*
Hawaiian Connection Tours
  ((808) 558-8396 *231*
Island Air TOLL-FREE (800) 652-6541 *231*
Molokai-Lanai Air Shuttle
  ((808) 567-6847 *231*
Waterfall Adventures ((808) 558-8464 *231*
multisport trips
Hawaii Pack and Paddle
  ((808) 328-8911 ⒺⓌ *92*
Oahu excursions 131–132
Atlantis Submarines
  ((808) 973-9811 ⓉⓌ *132*
Discovering Hidden Hawaii
  ((808) 946-0432 *131*
E Noa Tours ((808) 591-2561 Ⓦ *132*
Mauka Makai Excursions
  ((808) 593-3525 Ⓣ *132*
Navatek I ((808) 848-6360 ⓉⓌ *132*
Oahu Nature Tours ((808) 924-2473 *132*
Pleasant Holidays
  TOLL-FREE (800) 242-9244 Ⓦ *95*
Star of Honolulu ((808) 983-7827 *132*
Tommy's Tours ((808) 373-5060 *132*
planes
Island Hoppers
  ((808) 969-2000 ⓉⒻⒺⓌ *94*
Paragon Air TOLL-FREE (800) 428-1231 *94*
sailboarding and kayaking 93
sports and special holidays
Aloha Destinations ((808) 893-0388 ⒻⓌ *92*
underwater safaris
Atlantis Submarines ((808) 973-9811 ⓉⓌ *94*
Reefdancer ((808) 667-2133 *94*
SeaView Adventures ((808) 661-5550 *94*
whale watching
Body Glove ((808) 326-7122 ⓉⓌ *94*
Captain Zodiac ((808) 329-3199 ⒻⒺ *94*
Eco-Adventures
  ((808) 329-7116 ⓉⒻⒺⓌ *94*
Fairwind ((808) 322-2788 Ⓦ *94*
Hawaii Ocean Rafting
  ((808) 667-2191 ⓉⓌ *93*
Trilogy ((808) 879-8811 ⓉⓌ *93*
travel documents *291*
Tunnels (Kauai) *163, 166*
sports
diving and snorkeling *163, 166*
Turtle Bay (Oahu) *138*
accommodation 138

U **Ulupalakua (Maui)** *57, 191, 194*
attractions
Tedeschi Vineyard and Winery
  ((808) 878-6058 *191*
Ulupalakua Ranch *57, 191*

V **Valley of the Temples Memorial Park (Oahu)** *128*
attractions
Byodo-In Temple ((808) 239-5570 *128*
visa *291*
Volcano (Big Island) *52, 254, 274*
accommodation See Volcanoes National Park,
  accommodation 273
attractions
Akatsuka Orchid Gardens
  ((808) 967-8234 *254*
Volcano Winery ((808) 967-7479 Ⓦ *254*
restaurants 280
Volcanoes National Park (Big Island) *11, 13, 24,*
32, 34, 47, 50, 52, 68, 78, 99, 254, 256, 273–274,
280, 287
accommodation 52
Carson's Volcano Cottages
  ((808) 967-7683 ⓉⒻⒺ *273*
Chalet Kilauea
  ((808) 967-7786 ⓉⒻⒺⓌ *273*
Hale Ohia Cottages
  ((808) 967-7986 ⓉⒻⒺⓌ *274*
Hostelling International, Holo Holo Inn
  ((808) 967-7950 *274*
Kilauea Lodge
  ((808) 967-7366 ⒻⒺⓌ *68, 273*
Mauna Loa Cabin *34*
Mountain View Bed and Breakfast
  ((808) 968-6868 *273*
Namakani Paio cabins *34*
Pineapple Park ((808) 968-8170 ⓉⒺⓌ *52*
Red Hill Cabin *34*
Volcano Country Cottages
  ((808) 967-7960 *274*
Volcano House ((808) 967-7321 Ⓕ *32, 68, 273*
Volcano Inn ((808) 967-7293 ⓉⒻⒺⓌ *274*
attractions 32
Byron Ledge Trails *32*
Chain of Craters Road *11–12, 50, 254–255*
Crater Rim Road *254*
Crater Rim Trail *32*
Devastation Trail *32, 255*
Halape Trail Junction *33*
Halemaumau Trail *32, 255*
Hilina Pali Trail *32*
Kilauea Crater *11, 254*
Kilauea Iki Trail *12, 32*
Mauna Iki Trail *255*
Mauna Loa Trails *33*
Puu Loa Petroglyphs *255*
Puuo'o *254*
Steam Vents *255*
Sulfur Banks *254*
Thomas A. Jaggar Museum *255*
Thurston Lava Tube *255*
festivals and special events
Kilauea Marathon and Rim Runs
  ((808) 735-8733 *78*
general information
24-hour eruption report
  ((808) 967-7977 *12, 254*
Hawaiian Volcano Observatory Ⓦ *12*
National Park Service ((808) 967-7311 *34*
Visitor's Center ((808) 985-6000 *12, 254*
Volcano Golf and Country Club
  ((808) 967-7331 *47*

restaurants
Kilauea Lodge ((808) 967-7366   *56, 69, 280*
Lava Rock Café ((808) 967-8526   *281*
Steam Vent Café ((808) 985-8744   *281*
Surf's ((808) 967-8511   *281*
sports
golf   *47*
hiking and walking   *11, 32, 255*
W Wahiawa (Oahu)   *130, 149*
attractions
Birthing Stones   *130, 149*
Healing Stones   *130*
Waiakmoi Ridge (Maui)   *192*
Waialeale (Kauai)   *16, 24, 102, 149, 159, 165*
Waianae (Oahu)   *131, 150*
Waianae Coast (Oahu)   *131*
Waianae Mountains (Oahu)   *125*
Waianapanapa State Park (Maui)   *30, 193, 213*
accommodation
cabins ((808) 984-8109   *213*
Waikanaloa Cave (Kauai)   *164*
Waikapale Cave (Kauai)   *164*
Waikapu (Maui)   *186*
attractions
Tropical Plantation ((808) 244-7643   *186*
Waikele (Oahu)   *43*
general information
Waikele Golf Club ((808) 676-9000   *43*
sports
golf   *43*
Waikiki (Oahu)   *23–24, 35, 40–42, 48, 51, 72,*
75–76, 79, 99, 117, 119, 132, 143, 293
accommodation   *50–51, 137*
Banana Bungalow Waikiki Beach
((808) 924-5074 Ⓕ   *51*
Coral Reef Hotel ((808) 922-1262 Ⓕ   *137*
Halekulani Hotel
((808) 923-2311 Ⓣ Ⓕ Ⓦ   *53, 135*
Hawaii Prince Hotel
((808) 956-1111 Ⓣ Ⓕ Ⓦ   *136*
Hawaiian Regent Hotel
((808) 922-6611 Ⓣ Ⓕ Ⓔ Ⓦ   *136*
Hilton Hawaiian Village
((808) 949-4321 Ⓣ Ⓕ Ⓦ   *135*
Hyatt Regency Waikiki
((808) 923-1234 Ⓕ Ⓔ Ⓦ   *136*
Ilikai / Hotel Nikko
((808) 949-3811 Ⓣ Ⓕ Ⓦ   *136*
Outrigger Reef ((808) 923-3111 Ⓣ Ⓕ Ⓦ   *137*
Outrigger Surf ((808) 922-5777 Ⓣ Ⓕ Ⓦ   *137*
Royal Hawaiian
((808) 923-7311 Ⓣ Ⓕ Ⓦ   *54, 135*
Sheraton Moana Surfrider
((808) 922-3111 Ⓣ Ⓕ Ⓦ   *54, 118–119, 135*
W Honolulu ((808) 922-1928 Ⓣ Ⓕ   *135*
Waikiki Beachcomber Hotel
((808) 922-4646 Ⓣ Ⓕ   *136*
Waikiki Hostel and Hotel
((808) 922-3993 Ⓕ Ⓔ Ⓦ   *51*
Waikiki Joy Hotel ((808) 923-4402 Ⓣ Ⓕ   *137*
Waikiki Parc Hotel
((808) 921-7272 Ⓣ Ⓕ Ⓦ   *136*
attractions
Ala Moana Park   *119*
Diamond Head and Diamond Head Trail   *24*
Honolulu Zoo ((808) 971-7171   *120*
Kalakaua Avenue   *119*
Kodak Hula Show ((808) 627-3379   *120*
Kuhio Beach   *120*

Sheraton Moana Surfrider
((808) 922-3111   *119*
Statue of Duke Kahanamoku   *120*
Waikiki Aquarium ((808) 923-9741   *120*
Waikiki Beach   *23–24, 35, 120*
Waikiki Shell   *75, 120*
Waikiki War Memorial Natatorium   *120*
Wizard Stones   *120*
children activities
Rainbow Express ((808) 949-4321 Ⓣ Ⓕ Ⓦ   *56*
festivals and special events   *75–76, 79*
Ala Wai Challenge (January)
((808) 923-1802   *72*
concerts of the Hawaii Symphony   *120*
Oahu Oceanfest (May) ((808) 521-4322   *76*
Outrigger Waikiki Kings Race, May   *76*
general information   *118*
Ala Wai Golf Course ((808) 296-2000   *42*
Aloha Beach Services
((808) 922-3111   *120, 134*
Atlantis Submarines   *40*
Hans Hedemann Surf School
((808) 924-7778   *134*
Waikiki Trolley
((808) 596-2199 Ⓣ   *118, 132, 293*
nightlife
Banyan Court ((808) 922-3111 Ⓣ Ⓕ Ⓦ   *144*
Don Ho Show ((808) 931-3009   *136, 144*
Duke's Canoe Club ((808) 922-2268   *144*
House without a Key
((808) 923-2311   *135, 144*
Magic of Polynesia Show
((808) 971-4321   *136, 144*
Mai Tai Bar ((808) 923-7311   *144*
Scruples Beach Club ((808) 923-9530   *144*
Society of Seven ((808) 923-4450   *144*
Wave Waikiki ((808) 941-0424   *144*
restaurants
Bali by the Sea ((808) 949-4321   *139*
Chez Michel ((808) 955-7866   *140*
Ciao Mein ((808) 923-2426   *140*
Duke's Canoe Club ((808) 922-2268   *140*
Eggs 'n Things ((808) 949-0820   *140*
Furasato Japanese Restaurant
((808) 955-6333   *140*
Golden Dragon ((808) 949-4321   *139*
Hanohano Room ((808) 922-4422   *140*
La Mer ((808) 923-2311   *55, 135, 139*
Nick's Fishmarket ((808) 955-6333   *139*
Ochids ((808) 923-2311   *139*
Parc Café ((808) 921-7272   *140*
Singha Thai Cuisine ((808) 941-2898   *140*
Sizzler ((808) 973-5685   *140*
Surf Room ((808) 923-7311   *135*
Swiss Inn ((808) 377-5447   *143*
Wailana Coffee House ((808) 955-1764   *140*
shopping   *65, 134*
Ala Moana Shopping Center
((808) 955-9517   *118, 132*
Ali'i Plaza   *132*
Avanti ((808) 924-1668   *134*
International Market Place   *132*
King Kalakaua Plaza ((808) 955-2878   *132*
Nohea Gallery ((808) 596-0074   *134*
Rainbow Bazaar   *132, 136*
Royal Hawaiian Shopping Center
((808) 922-0588   *132*
Ward Center ((808) 591-8411   *134*
Ward Warehouse ((808) 591-8411   *134*

sports
  golf 42
  hiking 24
  outrigger rides 134
  surfing 120, 134
Waikolu Bay (Molokai) 230
Wailea (Maui) 16, 54, 56–57, 72–73, 90, 184, 189,
  196, 198, 209–210, 217–219, 221
  accommodation 54, 90, 189, 209
    Four Seasons Maui Resort
      ((808) 874-8000 Ⓣ Ⓕ Ⓦ 54, 209
    Kea Lani ((808) 875-4100 Ⓣ Ⓕ Ⓦ 54, 209
    Maui Polo Beach Club
      ((808) 879-1595 Ⓣ Ⓕ Ⓦ 210
    Outrigger Wailea Resort
      ((808) 879-1922 Ⓣ Ⓕ 210
    Wailea Ekahi ((808) 879-3043 Ⓣ Ⓕ Ⓔ Ⓦ 210
    Wailea Villas ((808) 879-1595 Ⓣ Ⓕ Ⓔ Ⓦ 210
  attractions
    Coastal Nature Trail 189
    whale watching 16
  children activities 57
  festivals and special events
    Whale Week of Maui (February)
      ((808) 879-8860 73
    Whales Alive (January) ((808) 874-8000 72
  general information
    Maui Classic Charters
      ((808) 879-8188 Ⓣ Ⓦ 16
    Ocean Activities ((808) 875-1234 200
  nightlife
    Outrigger Wailea Resort ((808) 879-1922 221
    Wailea's Sunset Luau 221
  restaurants
    Caffe Ciao ((808) 875-4100 219
    Carelli's on the Beach ((808) 875-0001 218
    Humuhumunuknukuapuaa
      ((808) 875-1234 56, 218
    Joe's Bar and Grill ((808) 875-7767 219
    Nick's Fishmarket Maui ((808) 875-7224 218
    Polo Beach Grill and Bar ((808) 875-4100 219
    Seasons ((808) 874-8000 217
  shopping
    Coast Gallery ((808) 879-2301 Ⓕ 198
Wailua (Kauai) 38, 44, 150, 158–159, 165–166,
  168, 172
  attractions
    Fern Grotto 159, 161
    Lydgate Beach Park 159, 166, 172
    Opaekaa Falls 159, 161
    Wailua Falls 159
    Wailua River State Park 161
  general information
    Smith's Motor Boats ((808) 821-6892 161
    Waialeale Boat Tours ((808) 822-4908 161
    Wailua Municipal Course
      ((808) 241-6666 44, 168
  shopping
    Bambulei ((808) 823-8641 65, 165
  sports
    diving and snorkeling 166
    golf 44, 168
Wailua (Maui) 193
  attractions
    Wailua Valley Lookout 193
  environs and excursions
    Waikani Falls 193
Wailua Bay (Kauai) 158

Wailua River State Park (Kauai) 161
Wailuku (Maui) 52, 72, 75, 184–186, 197, 202, 208,
  213–214
  accommodation 202
    Banana Beach Bungalow
      TOLL-FREE (800) 846-7835 52, 203
    Hono Kai Resort ((808) 244-5627 Ⓣ Ⓕ 208
    Maui North Shore Inn
      ((808) 242-8999 Ⓣ Ⓕ Ⓦ 52, 203
  attractions
    Bailey House Museum ((808) 244-3326 186
    Circuit Courthouse 186
    Iao Valley State Park ((808) 984-8109 Ⓕ 186
    Kaahumanu Church 186
    No Ka Oi Associates (massage)
      ((808) 242-7111 186
    Old County Building 186
    Territorial Building 186
    Wailuku Public Library 186
    Wailuku Public School 186
  festivals and special events
    Barrio Festival (May) ((808) 243-7855 75
    Hula Bowl
      (January) TOLL-FREE (888) 716-4852 72
  general information
    Maui Visitors Bureau
      ((808) 244-3530 Ⓣ Ⓕ Ⓦ 184
  restaurants
    Mushroom ((808) 244-7117 214
    Simple Pleasures ((808) 249-0697 214
  shopping
    Aloha Poi Factory ((808) 244-3536 197
Waimanalo (Oahu) 27–28, 67, 127
Waimea
  restaurants
    Merriman's ((808) 885-6822 284
Waimea (Big Island) 63, 69, 73, 76, 78, 88, 263,
  284, 286–287
  accommodation
    Belle Vue Bed and Breakfast
      (/FAX (808) 885-7732 278
    Hale Ho'onanea
      (/FAX (808) 882-1653 Ⓣ Ⓔ Ⓦ 278
    Kamuela Inn ((808) 885-4243 Ⓕ 278
    Mauna Kea View Bed and Breakfast
      ((808) 885-8425 Ⓕ Ⓦ 278
    Waimea Country Lodge
      ((808) 885-4100 Ⓕ Ⓔ Ⓦ 278
    Waimea Gardens Cottage
      ((808) 885-4550 Ⓣ Ⓕ Ⓔ Ⓦ 278
  attractions
    Kamuela Museum ((808) 885-4724 263
    Paniolo Park ((808) 885-7655 76, 78, 263
    Parker Ranch 263
    Parker Ranch Museum
      ((808) 885-7655 63, 263
    Puupelu and Mana House 63, 263
    Waimea Church Row Park 73
  festivals and special events 73, 76
    Forage Field Day (June) ((808) 885-0018 76
    Parker Ranch Fourth of July Rodeo
      ((808) 885-7311 263
    Parker Ranch Scholarship Rodeo,
      September 78
  general information
    Parker Ranch Visitor Center
      ((808) 885-7655 63, 263
  history 263

restaurants
  Edelweiss ((808) 885-6800 *284*
  Maha's Café ((808) 885-0693 *286*
  Paniolo Country Inn ((808) 885-4377 *286*
  Parker Ranch Grill ((808) 887-2624 *286*
Waimea (Kauai) *17, 54, 73, 81, 104, 153, 156, 171, 176–177*
accommodation *54, 171*
attractions
  Menehune Ditch *157*
  Russian Fort Elizabeth State Historical
    Park *156*
festivals and special events *73, 81*
  Cook Carnival, February *156*
general information *16*
history *156*
restaurants
  Jo-Jo's ((808) 338-0056 *177*
  Waimea Brewing Company
    ((808) 338-9733 *176*
Waimea (Oahu) *129*
attractions
  Waimea Valley Adventure Park
    ((808) 638-8511 *129*
Waimea Bay (Oahu) *34–35, 67, 99, 129, 134, 138*
sports
  surfing *34, 99, 129, 134*
Waimea Bay Beach Park (Oahu) *129*
Waimea Canyon (Kauai) *16, 18, 24, 28–29, 48, 67–68, 152, 157, 165, 167, 171, 176*
attractions
  Alakai Swamp Trail
    and Awaawapuhi Trail *28*
  Berry Flat Trail and Puu Ka Ohelo Trail *28*
  Canyon Trail *18, 28*
  Cliff Trail *18, 28*
  Ditch Trail and Koaie Trail *28*
  Iliau Nature Loop *28*
  Kukui Trail Loop *28*
general information
  Kauai State Parks Office ((808) 274-3445 *18*
  Outfitters Kauai ((808) 742-9667 Ⓣ Ⓦ *167*
sports
  biking *167*
  hiking *17, 28, 167*
Waimea Stream (Kauai) *17, 157*
Waimea Stream (Oahu) *129*
Waimea Valley (Oahu) *91, 135*
attractions *91*
  Waimea Falls *91*
sports
  horseback riding *135*
Wainiha (Kauai) *163*
Waiohinu (Big Island) *256, 281*
Waioli Stream (Kauai) *163*
Waipahu (Oahu) *43*
Waipio Valley (Big Island) *34, 65, 69, 90, 99, 266–267, 271*

accommodation
  camping *34*
attractions
  Hiilawe Falls *266*
  Nenewe Falls *90*
  Waipio Garden Eco Retreat *90*
  Waipio Valley Lookout *34, 69, 266*
general information *33*
  Hawaiian Walkways
    ((808) 775-0372 Ⓣ Ⓔ Ⓦ *272*
  Waipio Naalapa Trail Rides
    ((808) 775-0419 Ⓔ *271*
  Waipio on Horseback ((808) 775-7291 *271*
shopping
  Waipio Valley Artworks
    ((808) 775-0958 Ⓣ *65, 270*
Waipouli (Kauai) *158, 161, 177–178*
restaurants
  Aloha Diner ((808) 822-3851 *178*
  Bull Shed ((808) 822-3791 *177*
  Buzz's Steak and Lobster
    ((808) 822-0041 *177*
Waipouli Beach (Kauai) *172*
web sites *24, 79, 298*
  Bishop Museum www.bishopmuseum.org *298*
  discount packages www.bestofhawaii.com,
    www.travelzoo.com *299*
  general information www.hshawaii.com,
    www.bestofhawaii.com *299*
  Hawaiian culture www.hookele.com *299*
  Hawaiian language www.geocities.com *299*
  Hawaiian Volcano Observatory
    www.hvo.wr.usgs.gov *12*
  Honolulu Marathon
    www.honolulumarathon.org *47, 81*
  leis www.leisofhawaii.com *298*
  Maui information www.maui.net *299*
  Oahu information
    www.HawaiiAttractions.com *299*
  surf reports www.surf-news.com *298*
  surfing history www.surfart.com *299*
  tourist information www.gohawaii.com *299*
  weather www.weather.com/weather/us/
    states/hawaii or www.cnn.com/WEATHER/
    cities/us.hawaii.html *299*
  wedding information www.gohawaii.com *92*
  yellow pages www.surfhi.com *299*
wedding *92*
general information
  Hawaii Visitors and
    Convention Bureau Ⓦ *92*
wedding packages *92*
  Bali Hai Weddings ((800) 776-4813 Ⓦ *92*
  Weddings on the Beach
    ((800) 625-2824 Ⓦ *92*
weights and measures *296*
White Sands Beach Park (Big Island) *34*
  general information *33*
windsurfing *36*